Cross-Cultural Management

We work with leading authors to develop the strongest
educational materials in Business and Management, bringing
cutting-edge thinking and best learning practice to a global market.

Under a range of well-known imprints, including
Financial Times Prentice Hall, we craft high-quality print
and electronic publications which help readers to understand
and apply their content, whether studying or at work.

To find out more about the complete range of our
publishing, please visit us on the World Wide Web at:
www.pearsoned.co.uk

Cross-Cultural Management

A Knowledge Management Perspective

NIGEL HOLDEN

Prentice Hall
FINANCIAL TIMES

An imprint of **Pearson Education**
Harlow, England • London • New York • Boston • San Francisco • Toronto • Sydney • Singapore • Hong Kong
Tokyo • Seoul • Taipei • New Delhi • Cape Town • Madrid • Mexico City • Amsterdam • Munich • Paris • Milan

The book is dedicated to my family in Denmark, England, Portugal and Japan.

'We are more influenced by stories (vignettes that are whole and make sense) than by data (which are, by definition, utterly abstract).'

Tom Peters and Robert Waterman, *In search of excellence* (1982)

PEARSON EDUCATION LIMITED

Edinburgh Gate
Harlow
Essex CM20 2JE

and Associated Companies throughout the world

Visit us on the World Wide Web at:
www.pearsoned.co.uk

First published 2002

ISBN-13: 978-0-273-64680-8

British Library Cataloguing-in-Publication Data
A catalogue record for this book is available from the British Library

10

Typeset in 10/13pt Palatino Roman by 35
Printed in Great Britain by Henry Ling Limited., at the Dorset Press, Dorchester, DT1 1HD

Contents

List of figures

List of tables

Preface

This book was originally conceived – indeed commissioned – as a textbook on cross-cultural management, but in the writing it quickly emerged that the dominant view of culture in the field of management studies was, paradoxically, a severe constraint on the book's development. This view of culture, which will be discussed at some length, derives substantially from traditional anthropology as developed in the nineteenth century in the service of colonial empires. It seemed to me that, unless I were going to repeat the standard line, a substantial portion of the book would be taken up with the routine material on culture with the *de rigueur* regurgitations of the work of Hofstede, Adler and Trompenaars, the three most influential writers on the impact of culture on international business. I was almost bowing to the inevitability of not being able to strike out in a new direction when, luckily, enlightenment came.

I had begun to reason that cross-cultural management can no longer be seen as the management of cultural differences in popular interpretation. It must be related to managerial activity in the new geo-economy with its emphasis on global networking, organizational learning and knowledge management. The result of the enlightenment is, I hasten to add, not an earth-shattering reformulation of culture, but an attempt to examine the impact of cultural factors in international business from a fresh perspective: from the standpoint of knowledge management in the globalizing rather than globalized economy. The concept of knowledge management and its associated practices will be discussed in chapter 4. For readers unfamiliar with this relatively new field (or fad), it can be taken to refer to the management of procedures to facilitate inter-organizational sharing of know-how and experience. These days knowledge is seen as a company's most valuable resource for sustaining competitive advantage.

My further background reading of knowledge management confirmed that the issue of leveraging of cultural – or cross-cultural – knowledge worldwide is acknowledged by writers in this field to be a complex issue, but little work has been done beyond this recognition. But these authors nevertheless gave me a valuable insight: the possibility of treating culture as an object of knowledge management and, by extension, as an organizational knowledge resource. Traditional writing on culture and management in the context of international business does not view culture in this way. In this literature we find that culture is about fundamental differences, which hang like swords of Damocles over international companies, poised to undermine their negotiations and pervert their strategies. The solution to the putative problems created by these differences in the business world is, not surprisingly, more knowledge about cultural differences and the way in which cultural specialists classify and sub-classify those differences. This is a naive conception which is going to come in for heavy criticism in this book.

Thus, the two communities of learning and endeavour – the knowledge management fraternity and the culturalists – are in a kind of paradigmatic stand-off: the one group not quite knowing how to cope with culture as a knowledge resource; the other, as noted, not recognizing that culture in the world of goal-seeking organizations is precisely that. In the meantime, corporations operating internationally are daily handling this kind of knowledge directly and indirectly in an attempt to systematize it formally and informally to ensure survival and attain competitive advantage. That companies *do* operate in this way will be corroborated by four detailed company case studies, whose cross-cultural activities are investigated and analyzed from a knowledge management perspective.

Now to a confession: by the time the information was gathered on two of the four informant companies, the idea of exploring and interpreting their cross-cultural interactions from a knowledge management perspective had not taken shape in my mind. When the realization came, it was clear that I would have to modify my ideas about presenting the company experiences in the form of case studies. I decided that the unravelling of cultural impacts on companies and managers from a knowledge management perspective would need a different kind of presentation. The material and approach would require a more experimental technique, in which there would be scope for the capturing what case studies specialize in not capturing: *the idiosyncratic.*

The recorded experiences are based to a large extent on managers' utterances, spoken and written, about their company and their professional activities for it and with it. The documentary outcome is better seen as a sense-making story than a formal tract of *ex post facto* management wisdom. Bearing in mind that the company experiences will be interpreted from a knowledge management perspective and take account of the companies' evolution, a more appropriate name for these accounts would be *corporate knowledge histories*, a term which will be discussed more fully in the main text. Suffice it to say for now that the case studies are an expression of social constructionism: in other words, they are in a major way managers' own mental representations, mediated through language, out of which they make sense of, and share with others, their professional and organizational reality. But they are also informed by the interpretations of myself as 'the domain expert', adding an unavoidable subjective dimension to the sense-making. The approach is experimental and readers can judge for themselves whether it works.

As sense-making documents, the case studies are not written as bedrock for making narrow cross-cultural points, which would end up, almost inevitably, as lists of dos and don'ts, perpetuating stereotypes and ethnocentrism. They are a kind of knowledge management archive, a store of potential insight. Interestingly, knowledge management specialists are acknowledging the values of case studies and narratives for capturing culturally embedded knowledge. Burton-Jones (1999), for example, advocates the use of 'case-based systems, which provide a richer array of contextual information'. Davenport and Prusak (1998) report that 'research shows that knowledge is communicated most effectively through a convincing narrative', adding that 'Companies are beginning to use . . . technologies to record the narratives and nuances that carry so much of the real value of knowledge.' The case studies in this book should be a useful contribution to this aspect of knowledge management.

The four informant companies are: Novo Nordisk, the Danish pharmaceutical and biotechnology firm; Matsushita Electric Industrial Company, the major Japanese electrical and consumer electronics concern, alias Panasonic; LEGO, the Danish manufacturer of educational games; the Swiss-based Sulzer Infra, which supplies various forms of technological expertise to the construction industry. It was the case study about the Matsushita corporation which created the biggest challenge once I was committed to this new approach. This is the most detailed of the accounts, and it is also fully referenced, reflecting the fact that the contemporary globalization of this extraordinary company can only be explained against its evolution in the Japanese context since its foundation in 1917. This case study has every right to be termed a corporate knowledge history.

The point is worth making that, regardless of the new conceptual approach, this book is one of the very few on cross-cultural management that focuses on managers as managers with real tasks and responsibilities in the modern business world. The heartland of cross-cultural management is viewed in terms of knowledge management, organizational learning, and networking at local and global levels of interaction. This book says a good deal about culture, but it is not explicitly about culture. It is much more concerned with putting *management* back into the expression cross-cultural management. In line with this, there will also be no conflation of cross-cultural management with cross-cultural *communication*, a distinction that those in what has been facetiously termed 'the culture shock prevention industry' – the worldwide community of cross-cultural trainers, educators and consultants – have tended to disregard.

Although we shall be much concerned with managers, it is the firm – specifically the transnational corporation (TNC) as the driving force behind 'the global economy' (sic.) – which is an equally important unit of analysis and pivot of interpretation. The actions of firms and the consequences of those will be the prism through which we shall explore cross-cultural management as a practice. This book adds to the corpus of writing on management in three areas: globalization, knowledge management, and a third field which can be broadly termed 'culture and management'. The terms 'globalization', 'knowledge', and 'culture' are all notoriously debated words describing vast domains of learning, action and behaviour, around each of which has grown what I can only describe as a definitional quagmire.

I am bound to offend anyone who is in the mainstream as well as on the periphery of those subject areas, given that I am making, calculatedly, purely personal judgements about each to best serve the purposes of this book. Colin Cherry (1980), the author of a fine book on human communication, noted that: 'Language makes a hard mistress and we are all her slaves. Anyone who would consort with her, to study and understand her, lays himself open to a severe discipline and much disappointment.' That quotation, which applies with equal vigour to the study of culture, has never been far from my mind in the planning and writing of this book.

At all events, I hope that the book as a whole will appeal to a wide range of students of cross-cultural management and international business as well as to practitioners; that it may help them to make sense of the complex world in which they do business. I hope too that this book will be an encouragement for management scholars who, like me, are all too conscious that the treatment of culture in the general management literature has got into a rut. Although no longer the textbook of its first incarnation, this book should be a useful text to support the teaching of international management subjects in the widest sense. I should perhaps emphasize that this book does not claim to debunk the classic anthropological concept of culture or dismiss unduly the much revered, ubiquitously quoted work of Hofstede; but it does attempt to open new vistas for understanding and researching the complexities of human interaction in cross-cultural organizational contexts in the modern networked business world with its new 'knowledge intensification of economic activities' (Burton-Jones, 1999).

The book is in three parts. Part I, provocatively titled 'Anthropology's awkward legacy to the manager's world', consists of five chapters. Chapter 1 sets the tone of the book by contending that the concept of culture that has permeated management education and research over many decades is no longer serviceable in the modern global economy. To emphasize the point, five mini case studies on contemporary business situations are presented. It is shown that the 'non-cultural' information, that is information that is distinct from products of 'cultural awareness', is essential for explaining or analyzing the reported cross-cultural issue or behaviour at the heart of each case.

The second chapter sets the scene with a general critique of the way in which culture has been regarded in the general international management literature; and it is argued that this particular concept of culture has been a hindrance in the development of cross-cultural management as an intellectual domain. The chapter concludes with the conviction that notions of cross-cultural management must be allied to the nature of the new geo-economy with all that goes with it: instantaneous worldwide electronic communication coupled with the vision that in future firms will become 'knowledge-based', learning entities.

Chapter 3 takes the argument further, showing how culture-based notions of cross-cultural management are limited in their analytical scope and explanatory power. It is consequently argued that cross-cultural management is best conceived as an element of knowledge management, whereby culture – or rather knowledge of culture – becomes an organizational resource. The first three chapters have been written in a slightly polemic style: a lot of assumptions are being deliberately, but not unreasonably, challenged. It is time, it seems to me, to blow the cobwebs off cross-cultural management.

Chapter 4 introduces the concept and practice of knowledge management proper. Knowledge is introduced as a management concept, noting key terms such as 'tacit' and 'explicit' knowledge. Various models and typologies of knowledge are introduced. The three main aspects of knowledge work are discussed: namely, generation, codification and transfer. It is shown that the international (i.e. cross-cultural) aspects of knowledge management have been little researched, but it is noted that there are two prominent areas of international business activity where there has been significant underperformance in the transfer and sharing of knowledge: first, cross-border acquisitions in Europe by UK firms; and, second, in the imparting of Western management knowledge to Russia and former socialist countries.

Chapter 5 is devoted to issues of methodology, involving an introduction to the key research issues associated with the four informant companies, whose experiences are written up in case study form. It is explained that the four case studies (chapters 6–9) will be presented as sense-making documents. It is explained why an alternative name for these accounts might be corporate knowledge histories. The chapter concludes with a brief excursion into systems theory, which serendipitously provides a knowledge-oriented definition of culture.

The case studies (or corporate knowledge histories) forming chapters 6–9 constitute Part II. Each case has one or two big themes, but there are plenty of sub-plots which merit attention. The first case study is about the ethically conscious Danish pharmaceutical firm, Novo Nordisk, and the focus of interest is this company's novel way of activating compliance with its guiding precepts among its worldwide workforce. The next corporate knowledge history (chapter 7) concerns the Matsushita corporation of Japan, which is in the throes of adjusting its inviolate business principles, fashioned some 70 years ago, to the demands of globalization. The treatment of this huge corporation necessitates a journey through the life of the company's charismatic founder, Konosuke Matsushita, who was born in 1894 and died in 1989.

In chapter 8 we examine another Denmark-based TNC, LEGO, examining its policy and practices concerning the use of its company identity as the lynchpin for the diffusion of its international corporate culture. The company is a notable example of how a company, once it opens itself to knowledge from its subsidiaries abroad, can replenish its core values in striking ways. The next case study investigates the role of a newly established knowledge centre in disseminating experience and best practice throughout the Swiss-based Sulzer Infra (chapter 9). The case study is a snapshot of how a member company of a large industrial group is explicitly striving to become a knowledge-based organization in order to add value to its European business operations.

Part III devotes four chapters to analysis of the case studies and discusses various implications from academic and practitioner perspectives. The overall theme is the TNC as mediator of knowledge, values and experience, focusing on a very disparate set of challenges facing each company. Chapter 10 analyzes the four cases from a cross-cultural management approach, focusing on factors such as organizational learning and networking. This chapter introduces two new concepts for understanding the nature of cross-cultural communication in the business world: interactive translation and participative competence. These concepts provide links with international knowledge management, for these activities also involve acts of translation – both translation in the literal sense and in the sense of translating knowledge into action. Participative competence is the name of the competence needed for interactions on an equal footing in multicultural teams.

Chapter 11 considers implications of the analysis of the preceding chapter, probing the nature of translation and moving from there to a discussion of language, which is described, not without reason, as 'management's lost continent'. The chapter makes some unusual use of some rarely noted comments on language in Peters and Waterman's *In search of excellence*. Chapter 12 analyses the four companies' cross-cultural behaviour from a knowledge management perspective. The idea of looking at knowledge transfer as a form of translation will be further invoked. Looking at organizational processes as translation is not new, but I have avoided adopting the transcendental sociology-speak in which it is often discussed. This chapter contains various models, based on the case studies, about the transfer and transferability of cross-cultural know-how.

Chapter 13 brings everything together by presenting the case for reformulating the domain of cross-cultural management as an academic sub-discipline of international management and as a management practice. Appropriately, this chapter will, among other things, suggest that the cross-cultural manager is a form of knowledge worker and propose competencies associated with functions seen in this light. Following the Epilogue there is a glossary of the principal key terms that are associated with the notion of cross-cultural management which this book will advance.

Next, a word about my key term 'cross-cultural management'. I have decided to use this term rather than the related one 'intercultural management'. It is perfectly correct to say that authors do use the terms 'cross-cultural' and 'intercultural' interchangeably (Limaye and Victor, 1995), but a clear distinction can be made for strict intellectual purposes (though I wonder what practitioners would make of this distinction!). Pursuing Risager's (2001, forthcoming) line of argument, we may say that cross-cultural management focuses on comparative studies of management in different cultures, whilst the term 'intercultural' is more concerned with interactions between people representing different cultures. Usunier (1998) says much the same thing. According to him: 'The cross-cultural approach is a branch of comparative management which takes culture as its prominent explanatory variable, making it a distinct avenue in management research.' As for the intercultural approach, this 'is both an outlet for and a complement to the cross-cultural perspective: comparison across cultures helps to calibrate one's values against those of others, and finally to negotiate a common solution' (Usunier, 1998).

In the world of international business practice, managers plainly bring an intercultural and cross-cultural dimension to their thinking and behaviour, and drawing a sharp line between the two, even for theoretical purposes, may be counterproductive. In this book I have opted for cross-cultural as the preferred generalizing term for the following reasons. In the UK and USA there is no doubt that the term 'cross-cultural' prevails over 'intercultural' with respect to the international activities of managers. On the other hand, the term 'intercultural' has wide currency in several European languages, but it is clear that *interculturel* (French) and *interkulturel* (German) do not exclude the comparative dimension more strongly implied in the word 'cross-cultural'. A good example of this is to be found in Dupriez and Simons' book *La résistance culturelle* (2000). These Belgian scholars translate the term 'cross-cultural management' in Nancy Adler's well-known definition (which is cited in chapter 2 of this book) as *'le management interculturel'*! In the end, of course, the French language can only translate the term 'cross-cultural' as *'interculturel'*.

I have a further preference for the term 'cross-cultural'. As a fairly regular attender over the years of workshops and conferences in which the impact of culture on the world of business is a central or the main theme, I have come to the overwhelming conclusion that many of those from the academic community or the world of training who talk about intercultural management focus considerably on interpersonal communication across barriers of language and culture. Indeed, the emphasis on interpersonal communication is so strong *that the management dimension of interactions gets lost by the wayside.* I hope to get the balance right by focusing on the individual and groups in a set of intra- and inter-organizational relationships; not on the individual in single combat with cultural difference. I think that the term 'cross-cultural management', precisely because of its association with the intellectual sub-discipline of comparative management, has not lost this essential association. But I concede: there will be many occasions in this book when the words 'intercultural' and 'cross-cultural' may be considered to be synonymous for all practical purposes.

Finally, let me say a word about the style of writing. I have chosen to write with a certain pace where the arguments and topics permit. From this you may deduce that I belong to those who have never understood why serious books on management have to be so dry.

REFERENCES

Burton-Jones, A. (1999). *Knowledge capitalism: Business, work, and learning in the new economy.* Oxford: Oxford University Press.

Cherry, C. (1980). *On human comunication.* Cambridge, MA: MIT Press.

Davenport, T. H. and Prusak, L. (1998). *Working knowledge.* Boston, MA: Harvard Business School Press.

Dupriez, P. and Simons, S. (eds) (2000). *La résistance culturelle: Fondements, applications et implications du management interculturel.* Brussels: De Boeck & Larcier.

Limaye, M. R. and Victor, D. A. (1995). *Cross-cultural business communication: State of the art and hypotheses for the 1990s.* In: Jackson, T. (ed.) (1995). *Cross-cultural management.* Oxford: Butterworth Heinemann, pp. 217–37.

Risager, K. (2001, forthcoming). Cross- and intercultural communication. In: Ammon, U. (ed.), *Sociolinguistics: An international handbook of the science of language and society.* Berlin: Walter de Gruyter.

Usunier, J.-C. (1998). *International and cross-cultural management research.* London: Sage Publications.

The author can be contacted via his website at the following address: www.nigel-holden.com

Acknowledgements

This book could not have been written without the cooperation of the four informant companies. I wish to single out for warm thanks the following people for opening their doors to myself and my collaborators and for making arrangements for interviews at their headquarters and in subsidiary offices in various European countries, Japan, the USA and Australia: Henrik Gürtler and René Durup of Novo Nordisk; Takashi Ogawa, Yaoki Takahashi, Yasuo Kusumoto and Tim Watmuff of the Matsushita Electric Industrial Company; Kjeld Kirk Kristiansen, Poul Ploughman, Christian Majgaard of LEGO in Denmark and Mark Livingstone of LEGO Media in London; and Flooris van der Walt and Vesna Patjak of Sulzer Infra. I also record appreciation to the managers of the companies who were interviewed for the project – British, American, Danish, Japanese, Malaysian, German, Swiss, South African, Spanish, Australian and Dutch. They are the unsung heroes of the book.

I would also like to thank the following colleagues for assistance with interviewing and writing up the material for the case studies: Esben Karmark (LEGO); Mette Morsing and Mikkel Plannthin (Novo Nordisk). Several colleagues at Copenhagen Business School and Copenhagen University have been kind enough to read individual chapters and provide me very helpful feedback. I would like to thank Martine Gertsen, Karen Bjerre, Kasper Rasmussen, Jan Kristensen and, in particular, Anne-Marie-Søderberg. I would also like to acknowledge the advice of Marie-Thérèse Claes of the Institut Catholique des Hautes Études Commerciales (ICHEC), Brussels, and Gerhard Fink of the Vienna School of Economics. I am especially indebted to Roger Bell of ESADE in Barcelona for very useful comments on the final versions of the chapters making up Part I.

This book would not have been possible without a grant from the Copenhagen Business School Communication Initiative as well as supplementary funding from the CBS Department of Intercultural Communication and Management. The Consortium of European Management Schools (CEMS) also supported the enterprise. Without this support it would not have been possible for interviews to be conducted in several countries.

Grateful acknowledgement is made to all those sources which have granted permission to reproduce in this book material previously published elsewhere.

As for the great project of guiding this book from my manuscript to the end product, I would like to thank Geraldine Lyons and Paula Parish of Pearson Education, who provided valuable comments on how best to finalize the text for publication and promotion. I express considerable gratitude to Sarah Bury for her highly expert copy-editing.

Finally, I would also like to express considerable gratitude to the four reviewers who read and commented on drafts of the first eight chapters of this book. Their feedback was highly instructive and, to my profound relief, strongly supportive of the new direction I am trying to take in this book. One reviewer proposed an exceptionally ingenious restructuring of the chapters, but a combination of publisher's deadline and teaching commitments did not give me the option to take up this tantalizing challenge.

Nigel Holden
Copenhagen
March 2001

Publisher's acknowledgements

We are grateful to the following for permission to reproduce copyright material:

Figure 2.1 from *Organizational Culture and Leadership* by E. Schein (1985), Jossey-Bass Inc.: San Francisco. Reprinted by permission of Jossey-Bass Inc., a subsidiary of John Wiley & Son, Inc.; Figure 2.4 from *Culture's Consequences: Comparing values, behaviors, institutions and organizations across nations* (2nd edition) by G. Hofstede (2001), Sage Publications: London. Copyright © 2001 G. Hofstede, reprinted with permission; Tables 3.1 and 3.2 from *Managing Across Cultures: Issues and Perspectives* by P. Joynt and M. Warner (1996), International Thomson: London. Copyright © 1996 International Thomson; Table 4.1 from *Working Knowledge: How organizations manage what they know* by T. Davenport and L. Prusak (1998), Table 4.2 from *Common Knowledge: How companies thrive by sharing what they know* by N. Dixon (2000), reprinted by permission of *Harvard Business Review*. Copyright © 1998, 2000 by the Harvard Business School Publishing Corporation, all rights reserved; Figures 4.1 and 4.2 from *The Knowledge-Creating Company: How Japanese companies create the dynamics of innovation* by Ikujiro Nonaka and Hirotaka Takeuchi (1995), Oxford University Press: New York. Copyright © 1995 Oxford University Press, Inc.; Figure 13.2 from 'Intercultural Issues in Management and Business' in Cooper et al. (eds) (2000) *Wiley Handbook of Organizational Culture and Climate*. Copyright © 2000 John Wiley & Sons Limited.

Whilst every effort has been made to trace the owners of copyright material, in a few cases this has proved impossible and we take this opportunity to offer our apologies to any copyright holders whose rights we may have unwittingly infringed.

Part I

Anthropology's awkward legacy to the manager's world

'One's own way of life is simply human; it is other people who are ethnic, idiosyncratic, culturally peculiar.'

Terry Eagleton, *The idea of culture* (Oxford: Blackwell, 2000)

'National differences and antagonisms between peoples are daily more and more vanishing, owing to the development of the bourgeoisie, to freedom of commerce, to the world market, to uniformity in the mode of production and the conditions of life corresponding thereto.'

Karl Marx and Friedrich Engels, *The communist manifesto*
(Harmondsworth: Penguin, 1848/1985)

1 Culture: the specious scapegoat

'The frequence and sclerotic force of clichés, of unexamined similes.'

George Steiner, *After Babel* (1975)

'It seems a common human failing to prefer the schematic authority of a text to the disorientations of direct encounters with the human.'

Edward Said, *Orientalism* (1995)

OBJECTIVES

■ Criticizes the over-dramatic treatment of the alleged disruptive impact of culture on firms' international operations.

■ Highlights, in mini case studies, awkward cross-cultural management situations which cultural factors alone cannot explain.

■ Suggests that the time is ripe to rethink cross-cultural management.

QUAGMIRES, EARTHQUAKES AND TERMINAL DISEASE

No internationally operating firm, no manager however experienced in international business, can, it seems, ever escape from the possibility of misjudgement, misperception and mistakes in handling relationships with customers, suppliers and the full array of stakeholders. The general international management literature is replete with foreboding, representing cultural differences and even culture, plain and simple, as fiendish causes of this corporate undoing. For example, Hall (1995) claims that 'cultural differences are important enough to *ruin* a partnership that otherwise makes perfect economic sense' (added emphasis). But at least this is more restrained than web-based material of an American cross-cultural training consultancy propounding the ominous notion that cultural differences even *kill* business relationships.

In series of articles in *Harvard Business Review* ten years ago on the boundaries of business, one article was published under the iconic title 'the cross-cultural quagmire' (Hampden-Turner, 1991). Elsewhere, Frost (2000) has compared culture clash to an earthquake: 'Similar to the plates that cause earthquakes, which can exist alongside each other without an effect until they move together, different culture groups can work alongside each other in harmony until a change causes a clash' – a clash, note – 'This kind of clash can have severe repercussions for the organisation.' American writers H. N. Seelye and A. Seelye-James (1995) are equally emphatic. In their words: 'Culture clash happens when people from two different cultures come into contact. Sometimes the clash begins before anyone has a chance to introduce you properly, before you even open your mouth. Culture clash can lead to world-class fatigue or even clinical shock or depression. . . . What are the dastardly symptoms of culture clash? Is it contagious? Is it terminal?' The conviction that 'culture' can create havoc in international business is, of course, not new: for some 40 years management writers have been noting this (see Sackman et al., 1997). It is, however, novel – and disturbing – to find authors like Seelye and Seelye-James discussing culture clash with such pathological starkness.[1]

Yet there is nevertheless substance in these admonitions. The problem with them is the outrageous hyperbole. But, when Hoecklin (1995) warns that cultural differences, if not properly handled, can lead to 'management frustration, costly misunderstandings, and even business failures', she is right. The impact of culture, as popularly understood, *is* complex and wide-ranging in its variegated manifestations, according to languages and value systems in interplay, to the intersection of personalities, and the educational and social background of those personalities and professional experience and vocational affiliations; not to mention influences such as the general business environment, the industry sector, and the impact of technology.

But the problem with the utterances of the scare-mongering variety is that they are becoming increasingly out of touch with the temper and techniques of modern international business. Specifically they reflect a concept of culture that may not be the most useful for understanding and analyzing the impact of cultural factors on the new geo-economy which is challenging 'our industrial era notions of business organization, business ownership, work arrangements, business strategy, and the links between education, learning, and work' (Burton-Jones, 1999).

In chapters 2 and 3 I will examine the contention that there is a problem about the concept of culture that permeates management writing. In brief this concept characterizes culture both as an exclusive defining essence and as difference, whereby one cultural group is distinctive from other ones in terms of language, values, social mores, and so forth. This concept gives rise to forms of cross-cultural analysis which tend to focus overwhelmingly on cultural issues to the exclusion of other explanatory factors. In order to demonstrate the point, I will present five mini case studies in the form of short accounts of recent cross-cultural interactions of a topical nature. All are rich in cross-cultural components, but, as will be seen, cultural factors alone are insufficient to explain both the dynamics and underlying realities of the described situations.

The situations highlighted by the mini case studies relate to: seemingly unforeseen or at least underestimated post-merger frictions between the German and US managers in DaimlerChrysler; a serious case of mismanagement of technology transfer from Japan by the US carmaker General Motors; negative perceptions in Russia of Western management consultants; the localization policy of ABB, the Swedish–Swiss electrical engineering concern, in Poland; and the new face of *guanxi* (relationships and connections) in China.

FIVE MINI CASES

A way of testing the value of culture-as-essence and culture-as-difference as an explanatory toolkit is to examine attested situations in which there is an appreciable cross-cultural management component and to apply it. The method is to use five mini case studies which record cross-cultural misperceptions and clashes (there is also a case of clash avoidance) and establish the extent to which culture-fixated assumptions *significantly* facilitate explanation or analysis or otherwise. By culture-fixated assumptions I mean assumptions of the sort that isolate a priori cultural factors as the principal causes of misperception, friction or even breakdown of a business relationship.

The management literature in the widest sense of the word is full of stories and cases of how cultural difference between firms and markets, between persons making up multicultural project teams, between firms involved in mergers or alliances can create rifts among protagonists, damage reputations, or even undo a complete strategy. The impact of cultural difference can derive from so many different causes and may be so variable according to industry sectors and management styles in operation, according to cultural and organization values in contention, according to personalities, locations, business objectives, experience and expectations, according to the quality of interlingual communication that the very quest to make culture apprehensible as a concept and as a fact of life almost seems doomed from the outset. Indeed, many so-called 'culture clashes' have causes that are subtle and consequences that are downright insidious. Yet it is also debatable whether so-called cross-cultural awareness as the all-purpose panacea for coping with cultural diversity, ethnocentrism and culture shock can help managers to foresee the problems, let alone solve them when they manifest themselves. It is the very embeddedness of cross-culturally relevant knowledge in specific situations that firms need, but misjudge, simply miss, or generally lack access to. By way of example, therefore, consider the following five mini case studies which feature a brief outline of an issue highlighting some kind of cross-cultural clash or misperception and a commentary which will support the conviction that cultural awareness alone cannot explain the *context* of the described situations. It is the context which gives clarity of understanding (Burton-Jones, 1999), but which problematically can be most difficult to crystallize and shape as a knowledge resource.

Mini case 1: The limitations of 100 case histories of industrial mergers (DaimlerChrysler)

In May 1998 the German concern, Daimler, merged with Chrysler, America's third biggest automobile manufacturer. In September 1999, *The Economist*[2] reported on the state of the marriage. Noting that the deal was 'hailed as an inspiration, because of the neat fit of the firms' products and markets' and that the logic behind the merger was 'as impeccable as ever', the newspaper highlighted some post-merger setbacks, including:

• The defection of 'a stream of talented designers and managers' to Ford and General Motors 'down the road in Detroit'

• The issue of selecting one location for corporate headquarters; sooner or later the company will have to choose between Stuttgart and Detroit

• Clashes of management style at board level; German managers preferred reading 50-page documents before key meetings, whereas their American counterparts did more talking and wanted less documentation before the meetings (it appears that the American style has prevailed)

• Different styles at lower levels of management about the presentation of reports (German managers are inclined to accept the reports researched by subordinates, whereas the American style is 'look at' them later)

• No involvement for American designers in Mercedes cars

It is, however, remarkable to read that Daimler instigated a strategic analysis to ensure that the project was well planned and executed. This analysis reviewed 100 past mergers, noted that around 70% fail to achieve their goals, and concluded that the key to success lay less in price and more in strategic fit and post-merger integration. As *The Economist* reported: 'The result has been a post-merger plan devised with great attention to detail, a dozen teams of managers from the two sides focusing on every aspect of the merged team; a specially designed database to monitor daily progress; and an attempt to ensure the backing of the board at every stage.' In some respects the integration is running ahead of targets and in September 1999 it was anticipated that costs of around $1.4 billion would be saved by the end of the year. But, as *The Economist* said: 'Although merging the two companies was never going to be easy, nobody expected it to be this hard.'

The case raises some interesting questions. Did the company not expect the defections of key designers and managers? The answer must surely be 'yes'. That is par for the course with mergers, but *The Economist* seems to suggest that the leakage was worse than anticipated. Perhaps part of the problem was that in the post-merger fog of conflicting information the Chrysler personnel feared for their jobs or were miffed that they would not be given the chance to design Mercedes cars. And what about the wrangle over the location of the company headquarters? Surely the strategy managers had read up on the merger between the Swiss concern Brown Boveri and the Swedish group ASEA, which created the world's biggest engineering group, ABB? Surely they had read that the architect of the merger, the Swedish industrialist Percy Barnevik, with his almost pathological hatred of bureaucracy, had not permitted such a tussle to take place between groups in Sweden and Switzerland and so created the headquarters in Zürich (see Barham and Heimer, 1998)?

Then there was the issue of the frictions at board meetings, where the cerebral approach of the German managers jarred with their American counterparts who preferred succintness and focus. As noted, the American style prevailed, but that was not the only result of the cross-fertilization of the two corporate cultures. The Germans, it seems, are learning from their American colleagues how 'to use corporate resources in the most efficient way', whereas the Americans are benefiting from German 'self-discipline'.

But perhaps the most interesting issue to be raised is: why were the 100 case histories seemingly so limited in their relevance to the Daimler managers? Did those managers say 'nothing like that will happen to us', or were the case histories simply weak on cross-cultural hot-stops? It seems that the Daimler managers had not learnt that with mergers and acquisitions cross-cultural tensions tend to surface after the deal has been struck and these are generally not as well chronicled – and understood – as economic, financial and legal issues. In the meantime, the merger process has gone from bad to worse: a halving of net profit in the last fiscal year and impending lay-offs of 26,000 employees. As a later issue of *The Economist* (2001) noted: 'Only three years ago it seemed to be a marriage made in heaven', adding: 'It looks increasing as though Daimler-Benz picked the worst possible moment to buy Chrysler.' That suggests a fundamentally flawed business decision at the outset.

Our next example also concerns the auto industry, highlighting the reaction of General Motors to meet the onslaught of competition from Japanese carmakers. The information comes from a seminar paper written by a colleague, Charles Tackney, a labour relations expert at Copenhagen Business School, who specializes in life-time employment in Japan.

Mini case 2: The unforeseen consequences of not taking the tacit knowledge with the related explicit knowledge in technology transfer (General Motors)

'General Motors, in the face of increased Japanese exports and reduced market share, embraced JIT (just-in-time) and *kanban* production schemes throughout its complex motor vehicle manufacturing system. In June 1998, over a dispute involving threatened plant closure, failure to provide promised plant upgrades, and threats of "outsourcing", two plants were closed in strikes involving more than 9,200 workers. By the end of that ▶

Mini case 2 continued

month (a matter of mere weeks), almost the entire global GM manufacturing system ground to a halt. Over 125 factories were closed and more than 170,000 workers were out of work in five countries (USA, Canada, Mexico, Singapore, and Japan, where Isuzu workers were kept busy with other tasks). By the end of the third week of the strike, GM production loss was estimated at 106,000 vehicles per week. At that rate, direct and indirect effects of the strike to the US economy were estimated to cause a $2 billion drop in US GNP per week of lost production. And this obviously *underestimates* the global impact of this strike by 9,200 workers' (Tackney, 2000, original emphasis).

The point here is that GM, when it introduced the Japanese practices of just-in-time and *kanban*, merely took over the systems pertaining to technical processes. The company did not take account of the fact that these systems only work in Japan, not just because the Japanese worker is 'extremely loyal' to his or her company, but because in Japan (as in Germany) worker participation is encouraged and welcomed. Hence it might be said that worker participation is tacitly built into JIT and *kanban*; or, to put that another way, JIT and *kanban without* worker participation would be unthinkable. The fact that GM only took over the explicit aspects of the systems set the scene for tensions in the USA with repercussions for the carmaker in four other countries.

What on the surface might be taken as a complex US–Japanese cross-cultural misunderstanding is not just that. Admittedly GM failed to understand the human embeddedness of the systems in the society in which they evolved. But there is nothing to be blamed here on the mysteries of Japanese enterprise culture. All major carmakers in the USA and Europe have studied every aspect of the Japanese car industry since the end of the 1970s, and there is no single carmaker which has not been influenced by JIT and *kanban*. The mystery in this case is how on earth could GM not know about or discount the human element in these systems? Scores of books and articles have been written on the topic. GM has no excuse for ignoring what might be said to be common knowledge.

The third case concerns the uneasy relationship between Western management consultants and Russian clients. The example is based on material presented at a seminar in Moscow in 1996 which I attended and which sought to elucidate why the transfer of Western management know-how to Russia was so fraught with mutual recrimination and mistrust.

The prickly complexities of the relationship between Russia and the West, which the extracts highlight, beggars the imagination. These *pre-date* the Soviet period (1917–91); were not merely a facet of Soviet anti-Westernism, but also an influence on the character of the Cold War; and they have now resurfaced in the form of anti-Western swipes and postures which are a particular source of bafflement.

Mini case 3: The perception of Western arrogance in Russia

According to the Russian participants:

'Western consultants were perceived as ignorant, lacking "a Russia perspective", and inclined to find economic solutions to problems which Russians see as economic and social and cultural. They assumed too readily that privatised enterprises were now concerned to "increase shareholder value". Yet, that did not figure so much in Russian managerial thinking. Hence, Russian clients felt that the consultants were using economic criteria and rationales, which might be fine in a Western market economy, but which patently did not work in Russia especially now. This was seen as high-handedness and it went hand-in-hand with a Western reluctance to recognise that there had been industrial achievement during the Soviet period' (Holden et al., 1998).

Two other problems about Western consultants were highlighted:

'First, because they were often seen as incapable of assisting a Russian enterprise, they must have an ulterior motive. They were obviously spies paid for by foreign governments (foreign governments, note; not companies) to identify juicy take-over targets. Second, consultants had one tendency to make some things more complicated than they had to be, and another tendency to make Russians look stupid for not understanding simple things. In the first case everything was wrapped up in high-flown terminology; in the second, explanations would kept "at a basic level", as if Russians could not cope with anything more demanding. Western management catch-phrases, like KISS ("Keep It Simple, Stupid"), are guaranteed to go down like a lead balloon with Russian top managers who not only know that their own situation is anything but simple, but also expect that Western consultants will be bringing with them a complex and challenging intellectual toolkit' (Holden et al., 1998).

They hark back to Russia's 'ancestral suspicion of the West' (*Economist*, 1993). Russians look into their history and all too often see betrayal and abandonment by the West. For those with a knowledge of Russian history, much of this is uncomfortably redolent of Russia's deep-seated wariness of the West: the conviction that Western aid and investment, as well as Western-sponsored management training initiatives in Russia, are a ploy to weaken still further the Russian economy and keep Russia in a state of semi-colonial tutelage to the West.

The fact is that every person professionally involved with Russia needs to be fully aware of the vigour and occasional 'zaniness' – and sometimes the actual justice – of Russian perceptions about the motives of Western governments and companies. Today in Russia, then, there is more than a passing feeling that the West cannot be trusted. Nor is this mood restricted to politicians and bureaucrats. The following vignette, quoted by Wilson and Donaldson (1996), speaks volumes about prejudices just below the surface: 'The foreign boss of a growing company told a Russian sales representative that profit would go toward sorely needed equipment purchases, then later to salary hikes. "I know what you're doing," she protested. "I've read Marx. You're an exploiter."'

Every foreigner who seeks insights into developing relationships with Russian counterparts needs to be very clear on the potency of this ancestral suspicion. Solzhenitsyn (1991) captures the deep-seated Russian wariness, warning his fellow countrymen that Western firms 'must not be lured in on terms that are advantageous to it but humiliating to us, in come-and-rule-over-us style'. The general Western failure to understand the Russian context has cost Western corporations – and governments – dear in psychologically misconceived initiatives (such as business education based on market-economy practices which are beyond most Russians' experience) and misdirected development aid and other forms of financial investment.

The fourth case refers to ABB, the Swedish–Swiss electrical engineering giant, at the time of the collapse of the communist system throughout Eastern Europe. The source is Barham and Heimer's (1998) compendious study of the creation of ABB, the world's biggest – and fastest executed – industrial merger.

Mini case 4: The ability to trust insiders (ABB)

When the communists were swept from power in Poland in 1989, ABB had 4,000 workers involved in the company's joint ventures which had been signed with the communist authorities. Barham and Heimer take up the tale when David Hunter is appointed country manager for Poland in 1991 with a brief to implement the ABB policy of localization. Here is Hunter:

'"When I arrived in Poland, there had been a representation office of eight or nine people which had been selling products for some years. Now I was country manager, responsible for the market and customer relations. My task when I arrived was to create a local management team and acquire some new activities, and create the impression among the Polish government and community that ABB was a local organization. And, not least, with a lot of support from the business areas in carrying out improvements, I had to make the whole organization profitable."

'Hunter's first problem was image. ABB was seen as a company that had come in and stolen valuable State assets under the last Communist regime. A new privatization law was introduced in 1991, but ABB's first joint ventures had been agreed under the old joint venture law. There was a delay in convincing the new government that its intentions were honourable.

'Hunter remembers:

'"For the first year, we were engaged almost daily in defending ABB's presence from some heavy criticism. We had to get the message across. I consciously decided that our operations in Poland would be run by local management. The one lesson that is valuable to anyone trying to do business in emerging markets is that the risk of taking inexperienced local management into responsible jobs is less than taking an experienced expatriate who doesn't know the local situation"' (Barham and Heimer, 1998).

When the socialist countries collapsed under their own lethargy at the end of the 1980s, Western firms saw huge markets opening up before them. But, when they established offices, they showed an extreme reluctance to trust local people to work in managerial positions. ABB was one of the very few Western companies which, from the outset of the changes, had a policy of localization based on trust of local people. This does not mean that there were not cross-cultural spats, but local employees could feel confident that the company did not regard them as inherently inferior and generally not worth investing it. This is a lesson which Japanese companies have failed to learn; one of the hallmarks of their international management systems has been an endemic mistrust of foreign managers to take control of operations in their own countries (Kopp, 1999).

The point to emphasize is that trust is not a cultural trait; it is a behavioural one: 'a perceived notion regarding a partner's likely behaviour' (Sheth and Parvatiyar, 1992). Trust has 'intangible value' (Cauley de la Sierra, 1995): it signals variously a willingness to cooperate in a relationship by engaging in reciprocity and reducing uncertainty. As such, trust is a function of goodwill (Ring, 1998). It is a personal attribute, but can also be manifested as an institutional feature (as in the case of ABB above). Cross-cultural awareness is no substitute for trust; or rather, cross-cultural awareness *without* trust is of limited value in a wide range of cross-cultural business relationships.

In April 2000 *The Economist* ran a survey of China. A box titled 'tangled web' contrasted Chinese-style relationship-based business and the rules-based systems of advanced industrial economies (*Economist*, 2000b). The work of two Hong Kong academic economists, a Mr Li and a Mr Li, on *guanxi* – Chinese-style relationships and connections – awkwardly undermines foreign (i.e. Western) thinking about *guanxi* as 'some kind of spiritual ectoplasm'. After all, goes the argument, if you intend to do business in China, then you must know about *guanxi*.

Mini case 5: Why our view of *guanxi* may be getting outdated

Messrs Li explain that given the high cost of cultivating new relationships among the Chinese, 'it makes sense to do business first with close family, then neighbours from your home town, then former classmates, and only then, reluctantly with strangers' – and, exceptionally, strangers who are foreigners. The report continues: 'This is how the market reforms spread in China during the 1980s and 1990s. Instead of incurring the high fixed costs involved in setting up a rules-based system, the country took the cheaper route of relation-based development. That led to an explosion of markets, and to a rapid division of labour. That, in essence, is what the "Chinese miracle" is all about.'

Trickily, the Chinese government is trying to switch from a *guanxi*-based to rules-based system of economic governance, whilst pushing to enter the international economy. But 'the trouble is that in the absence of a rules-based economy, those splintered local markets cannot merge into regional, national or even international ones. Moreover, they create

▶

11

Mini case 5 continued

immense economic distortions through corruption and the misallocation of resources' owing to cosy relationships between banks and state customers as well as smuggling. The argument is that, as the relation-based systems of governance are bound to arise in a complex market economy and the cost of rules-based ones correspondingly fall, *guanxi* ought to be become redundant. But Messrs Li do not see it like that.

They argue that the transition from the first form of governance to the second is not as smooth as outsiders like to believe. They see the introduction of new rules that protect investment. Insiders see a state of flux created by changing relations among market participants. Outsiders see an opportunity to invest. Insiders see an opportunity to loot. This may explain, say Messrs Li, why you are finding it so tough to do business in China right now. This prompts this advice from the *Economist*: 'Beware, foreigner, beware.'

This is a revealing commentary on the impact of changes of economic structures on traditional ways of doing business in China. It shows very clearly how trust in business relationships is based on kinship ties, local ties, old acquaintances and, lastly, strangers, who may be divided into two categories: strangers who are Chinese and strangers who are foreign. Particularly untrustworthy are strangers from Western countries. But the nature of trust is not the same as in Western countries, for in China the closer the relationship through family, geographical ties, the greater the sense of obligation, in principle, not to let the other side down. Furthermore, the absence of a widely respected legal code in China means quite simply that (as they say) every-thing is negotiable, and the purpose of negotiation is not to get the best deal in a Western sense, but to secure the best possible advantages for oneself and one's group.

What foreigners tend to overlook is that negotiation with their nominal business partner may in reality involve other parties too who are connected through ties of interest and obligation to that partner (see Blackman, 1997). This partly explains why negotiations between Chinese and foreign business partners can become protracted and often break down. It is no easy matter for foreign business people, especially those from Western countries and accustomed to rationality, procedure and redress, to fathom out the workings of vertical and horizontal relationships, for which the Chinese have developed clear and well-understood rules for these linkages (Redding, 1993). It is a moot point indeed whether 'culture' can throw adequate light on the malleable nature of Chinese socio-economic networks without knowing *what is at stake* – financially or in terms of face lost or gained among those involved – and why.

GENERAL COMMENTARY ON THE FIVE MINI CASES

All of the five mini case studies are rich in cultural factors, but none of the five mini cases can be adequately understood purely in terms of cross-cultural analysis focusing solely or predominantly on cultural factors. Such an analysis would give a lop-sided view with cultural factors being deployed as specious scapegoats for unenlightened management behaviour and decisions. The case of General Motors could be presented as a grand US–Japanese cross-cultural clash of a very spectacular kind, but cultural difference was hardly a major cause of the $2 billion a week production losses. The Japanese were open with their know-how. The Americans, as was suggested above, did not do their homework well enough.

Much the same can be said of Daimler and its merger with Chrysler: the German managers failed to cover certain contingencies. The key issue is that a group of exceptionally intelligent Daimler analysts seemed not to grasp the scope of the knowledge requirement at the outset for handling a cross-cultural merger, and it seems that they depended heavily on the 100 case studies of other mergers, which they appear to have used as a kind of definitive or highly authoritative source of likely problems. Either the case studies were somehow defective or the analysts failed to draw pertinent conclusions for Daimler from the experiences of other international mergers. However tempting it might be to polarize the tensions into German and American cultural categories, these were almost inevitably an outcome of misunderstandings rather than a cause.

The example concerning Russia reveals anti-Western sentiment that goes back several centuries and cannot be understood purely as a complex post-communist reaction. In so far as culture is a factor in this case, it would be legitimate to talk about the undertow of an anti-Western xenophobia in Russian society.[3] The example with Poland emphasizes the necessity to trust, which is a not a cultural factor as such, but which can work to alleviate cross-cultural tensions. The example of China demonstrated that an incompatibility of business ethics may be behind cross-cultural frictions.

All of our five mini cases were characterized individually by factors, including cultural ones, which made up a specific context. Although all the cases are unique, it is straightforward to highlight various factors, some common to two or more cases, which created cross-cultural problems, that is inhibited the transfer of values, knowledge and experience from one cultural ambience to another. We may mention the following issues:

- The generation of uncertainty between interacting parties

- The critical role of trust

- The significance of historical factors and timing

- The complexity of cross-cultural knowledge embedded in particular situations

- Some components of cross-cultural knowledge (such as trust) are *not* cultural

- The limitations of 'normal' Western business logic to explain *rationally* what is normal business practice in non-Western countries

- The manifestation of xenophobia (not only in China and Russia; it may have been a subliminal factor influencing GM's inability or unwillingness to acquire the tacit knowledge behind Japanese production systems)

- Traditional thinking about a well-known phenomenon – in this case *guanxi* – may be out of date

- The history of organizations

In each of the five situations we could apply the well-known models and schemes of Hofstede, Trompenaars and E. T. Hall and so forth, whose contributions I examine in the next two chapters. Yes, there is ample evidence of the operation of Hofstede's differences relating to power distance, masculinity–femininity, uncertainty avoidance, individualism and collectivism. Yes, we can find plenty of examples of cultural differences and attitudes identified by Trompenaars. Yes, GM's unfortunate foray into Japan could be construed as a low-context/high-context cultural collision. Further probing of the situations would reveal how differences in education, social values, manners, language and so on all operate as disruptive influences of varying magnitude in the described situations. However, the evidence of the five cases suggests overwhelmingly that cross-cultural impacts on managers and organizations cannot be anticipated or meaningfully analyzed *solely* by the application of cultural categories such as values, language differences, or Hofstedian mental programmes *without* an appreciation of the peculiarities – even the idiosyncrasies – of contextual embedding.

OPERATION ZEBRA: THE NEED FOR A CHANGE OF VANTAGE POINT

Traditional cultural criteria appear to be insufficient to explain forms of cross-cultural mismanagement and miscommunication because they fail to capture, and therefore explain in a meaningful way, cultural and contextual factors which nonetheless have a bearing on the quality, progress and outcome of the interactions. This raises, then, a significant question. Is there an alternative methodology? The important thing, it seems, is to change our way of looking at cultural influences and develop ways of combining these influences with the business-contextual factors. This is by no means easy. It goes not just against accepted wisdom, but also against the way in which the standard view of culture has been wired into our brains. Let me use the zebra analogy. Europeans (or so I read recently) see zebras as white animals with black stripes, but African people see them as black animals with large areas of white. A zebra is still a zebra, however we see its stripes. So, by analogy, the challenge before us is to think of culture in a different way and see if new insights are generated.

This book is inviting no one to regard culture in a simplified way; it is *not* being proposed that values and differences count for nought; nor is it being suggested that cultural variables have *no* explanatory power. But it is being argued that the concept behind culture-as-essence and culture-as-difference does have limited explanatory power, as the commentary on the five mini cases surely established. This book proposes that change of vantage point can come about in two ways: first, by focusing on culture as an organizational resource and, second, by recasting cultural factors and influences as a set of internalizable objects of organizational knowledge. This means ceasing to regard them as sets of purely externalized phenomena which, to quote Bartholomew and Adler (1996), are 'no longer relevant . . . for the competitive environment of today's transnational firm'.

Once we begin to see culture and knowledge about culture as an organizational resource, then cross-cultural management focuses less on the management of cultural differences and more on the application of this resource, which is then a form of organizational knowledge, to resolve international management problems. From here it is a small step to the recognition that cross-cultural management is a form of knowledge management, which refers to 'the systematic and organised attempt to use knowledge within an organisation to improve performance' (KPMG, 1999). I will tackle knowledge management in chapter 4. Before then the immediate task, in chapters 2 and 3, is to consider the concept of culture which is most prevalent in management studies and research, and which is coming under increasing criticism from management scholars.

NOTES

1. I can extend the graphic images. In May 2000 I attended a seminar at the University of Århus in Denmark on international negotiation. A professor, a leading expert on the subject, referred scathingly of the way in which 'cultural enthusiasts' regard culture as 'a corrosive acid', crippling business endeavour.

2. A further article about the merger has been published by *The Economist* (*Economist*, 2000a).

3. Xenophobia appears to be a taboo word in cross-cultural writing. In the mainstream texts only Hofstede (1994) has an indexed reference to the term.

REFERENCES

Barham, K. and Heimer, C. (1998). *ABB – the dancing giant*. London: Financial Times Prentice Hall.

Bartholomew, S. and Adler, N. (1996). Building networks and crossing borders: the dynamics of knowledge generation in a transnational world. In: Joynt, P. and Warner, M. (eds). *Managing across cultures: Issues and perspectives*. London: International Thompson, pp. 7–32.

Blackman, C. (1997). *Negotiating China: Case studies and strategies*. St Leonards, NSW: Allen & Unwin.

Burton-Jones, A. (1999). *Knowledge capitalism: Business, work, and learning in the new economy*. Oxford: Oxford University Press.

Cauley de la Sierra, M. (1995). *Managing global alliances: Key steps for successful collaboration.* London: Economist Intelligence Unit/Addison Wesley.

Eagleton, Terry (2000). *The idea of culture.* Oxford: Blackwell.

Economist (1993). EC aid to the East. 10 April.

Economist (1999). DaimlerChrysler: Crunch time. 25 September, pp. 91–2.

Economist (2000a). Merger brief: The DaimlerChrysler emulsion. 29 July, pp. 69–70.

Economist (2000b). China survey. 8 April.

Economist (2001). Shrempp's last stand. 3 March.

Frost, A. R. (2000). Negotiating culture in a global environment. *Journal of management communication* 4(4): 369–77.

Hall, W. (1995). *Managing cultures: Making strategic relationships work.* Chichester, UK: John Wiley & Sons.

Hampden-Turner, C. (1991). The boundaries of business: The cross-cultural quagmire. *Harvard Business Review* September–October, pp. 94–6.

Hoecklin, L. (1995). *Managing cultural differences: Strategies for competitive advantage.* London: Economist Intelligence Unit/Addison Wesley.

Hofstede, G. (1994). *Culture and organizations: Intercultural cooperation and its importance for survival – software of the mind.* London: HarperCollins.

Holden, N. J., Cooper, C. L. and Carr, J. (1998). *Dealing with the new Russia: Management cultures in collision.* Chichester, UK: John Wiley & Sons.

Kopp, R. (1999). The rice-paper ceiling in Japanese multinationals. In: Beechler, S. and Bird, A. (eds). *Japanese multinationals abroad: Individual and organizational learning.* New York: Oxford University Press, pp. 107–28.

KPMG (1999). Knowledge management research report 2000. London: KPMG.

Marx, K. and Engels, F. (1848/1985). *The communist manifesto.* Taylor, A. J. P. (ed). Harmondsworth: Penguin Books.

Redding, S. G. (1993). *The spirit of Chinese capitalism.* Berlin: de Gruyter.

Ring, P. S. (1998). Trust. In: Cooper, C. L. and Argyris, C. (eds). *The concise Blackwell encyclopedia of management.* Oxford: Blackwell Publishers.

Sackman, S. A., Phillips, M. E., Kleinberg, M. J. and Boyacigiller, N. A. (1997). Single and multiple cultures in international cross-cultural management research. In: Sackman, S. A. (ed.). *Cultural complexities in organizations: Inherent contrasts and contradictions.* Thousand Oaks, CA: Sage Publications, pp. 14–48.

Said, E. W. (1995). *Orientalism: Western conceptions of the Orient.* London: Penguin Books.

Seelye, H. N. and Seelye-James, A. (1995). *Culture clash: Managing in a multicultural world.* Lincolnwood, IL: NTC Business Books.

Sheth, J. N. and Parvatiyar, A. (1992). Towards a theory of business alliance formation. *Scandinavian International Business Review* 1(3): 71–87. Also in: Ghauri, P. N. and Prasad, S. B. (eds) (1995). *International management: A reader.* London: Dryden Press.

Solzhenitsyn, A. (1991). *Rebuilding Russia: Reflections and tentative proposals.* London: HarperCollins.

Steiner, G. (1975). *After Babel: Aspects of language and translation.* Oxford: Oxford University Press.

Tackney, C. (2000). Organizational forms of the modern enterprise: A comparison of US, German, and Japanese employment (or legal) ecologies. Unpublished manuscript of seminar presentation held at Copenhagen Business School, 12 April 2000.

Wilson, D. and Donaldson, L. (1996). *Russian etiquette and ethics in business.* Lincoln, IL: NTC Business Books.

2 Culture: the anthropologist's legacy

'"Culture shock", a sense of being subverted by foreigners.'

Charles Hampden-Turner and Fons Trompenaars,
The seven cultures of capitalism (1993)

'We are indebted to anthropologists for most of our present understanding of "culture". Anthropologists have a rich tradition in studying non-industrial societies. . . . However, few anthropologists have concentrated on understanding the behavior of employees and managers in industrial societies.'

Richard Preston, Future directions in international comparative management research (1993)

OBJECTIVES

- Examines the current cross-cultural management literature, especially its dependence on a concept of culture deriving from nineteenth-century anthropology.

- Discusses this concept in terms of culture-as-essence and culture-as-difference.

- Argues that the fixation with culture shock is not productive for the development of cross-cultural management studies.

- Contends that Hofstede's great study is now out of date, belonging to a corporate – and political – world that no longer exists.

AN INITIAL FORAY INTO THE CROSS-CULTURAL MANAGEMENT LITERATURE

Chapter 1 opened with some desperate sounding assertions about culture as an insidious influence thwarting firms' international operations. But there are other voices arguing that the judicious handling of cultural differences can lead to competitive advantage (e.g. Dupriez and Simons, 2000; Harris and Moran, 1996; Hoecklin, 1995; Mead, 1994; Morosini, 1998; Schneider and Barsoux, 1997; Søderberg, 1999; Viney, 1997). According to Viney (1997), the way in which culture is handled 'is an important, possibly the most important element in the competition for business supremacy'. Schneider and Barsoux (1997), whose book is one of the best researched and most thought-provoking of the current cross-cultural management literature, make the point that the key thing about cross-cultural management is that its task is 'not to neutralise or contain cultural differences, but to build on them'. These authors recognize that building on them means fostering cross-cultural learning and participation. One of the aims of this book is to develop that productive line of thinking.

Belgian scholars Dupriez and Simons (2000) note that firms which are able to draw on the diverse experience of their multicultural workforce enjoy 'a wider and more open platform for addressing difficult problems in a critical spirit'. However, there is no empirical evidence to support this claim. It is, of course, easier to write about culture as a business problem rather than to describe it meaningfully and accurately as a source of organizational strength. Thus it is difficult to strike the balance between culture as 'a problem' and culture as a source of solutions to business problems. As Hoecklin (1995) notes: 'To think about cultural differences as a source of competitive advantage, there must be a shift in assumptions about the impact of cultural differences. . . . Culture should not simply be seen as an obstacle to doing business across cultures. It can provide tangible benefits and can be used competitively.'

Nevertheless all commentators seem agreed that culture is a problem area for management. Those who treat culture as a factor negatively impacting on firms' international operations will stress that its influence must be anticipated, controlled or limited. Those who see culture as a source of competitive advantage will emphasize the importance of releasing synergies from 'international and intranational diversity' (Tung, 1997). But, either way, culture and its consequences must be *managed*, and this, by general consent, is no easy task. Consider, incidentally, how many writers refer to the challenges of management and marketing *across* cultures, evoking images of the arduous assaults on Himalayas of confusion and dissonance. The titles speak for themselves:[1]

Managing across borders (Ghoshal and Bartlett, 1998)
Communicating across cultures (Guirdham, 1999)
Managing across cultures (Joynt and Warner, 1996)
Managing across cultures (Schneider and Barsoux, 1997)
Marketing across cultures (Usunier, 2000)[2]
International management: Managing across borders and cultures (Deresky, 2000)

Other titles invoke the sense of struggle or clash:

La résistance culturelle (Dupriez and Simons, 2000)
Culture clash (Seelye and Seelye-James, 1995)
The culture wars (Viney, 1997)
When cultures collide: Managing successfully across cultures (Lewis, 1996)

An idea to be developed in this book is that the essence of the task is not so much about operating across cultures as *through* them, by means of them. The view of culture as an instrument or agent rather than an obstacle is hardly new, but it does permit us to see culture as a potential for harmonizing collective efforts, releasing creativity, achieving tolerance, and widening intellectual horizons. But the key question is: can culture – or rather cultural difference – be *managed*? This is a hugely complicated question because how and what is managed depends not only upon the more obvious factors in cross-cultural equations, but upon one's view of culture, whether one is a researcher or a practitioner. This book should provide some insights, whilst throwing up no small number of further awkward questions.

The recognition that culture in the context of international business operations creates challenges and problems for firms and their management has given rise to a sub-discipline of international management studies called cross-cultural management. The current mainstream literature on cross-cultural management is reviewed both in this chapter and the next. The aim of this treatment in this chapter is to give a critique and review of the subject as a loosely defined discipline of the management sciences, yet nominally distinct domain of managerial activity. Both chapters continue the argument put forward in chapter 1 to the effect that the prevailing concept of culture in management studies, which is discussed below, is not equal to the task of elucidating fundamental issues at the heart of cross-cultural encounters in the context of modern business operations. The aim of chapters 2 and 3 is to begin the process of detaching cross-cultural management from the choking coils of culture as popularly conceived, and transpose it into the new heartland of business activity: the world of networks and knowledge management in the new geo-economy.

The literature on cross-cultural management issues is not easily specified. As surveys of this literature make clear, formal articles which directly treat cross-cultural management issues traverse in greater or lesser depth various disciplines of international management and international business as well as organizational theory, culture theory, and management communication (e.g. Bartholomew and Adler, 1996; Darlington, 1996; Roberts, 1977; Usunier, 1998). This eclectic coverage plainly suggests that the putative subject matter of cross-cultural management is diffuse, accessible from several management disciplines, and difficult to integrate – in a word, a real challenge to authors, researchers and readers. In this sense this literature merely continues the tradition of being 'a morass' (Roberts, 1977).

There are perhaps only three works on culture and management whose approaches to the understanding of culture and management in its international aspects have been very influential in the field: Adler's *International dimensions of organizational behavior* (1991); Hofstede's *Culture's consequences* (1980); and Trompenaars' *Riding the waves of culture* (1993). All three are pioneering in their own way: Adler for a study of the impact of culture on different organizational functions; Hofstede for his monumental worldwide study of work-related value orientations in more than 50 different countries; Trompenaars for the impact of cultural difference on doing business. They are arguably the principal creative sources on the thinking of many other writers on cross-cultural management issues. Hofstede, who is one of the world's most cited social scientists (Ulijn, 1998), has offered a much used – and abused – framework which has been internationally employed as an unerring paradigm 'where the questions and the dimensions are used as taken-for-granted assumptions' (Søndergaard, 1994).

The biggest influence on culture-and-management studies was unquestionably the publication of Hofstede's *Culture's consequences* in 1980, which is discussed further later in this chapter. All subsequent writing has paid due homage to this contribution, but there is discernible feeling among scholars of international management that the time has come for fresh ideas and approaches, for a new, post-Hofstedian view of the world. But would-be challengers face, among other things, the daunting prospect of conducting a multination study, built on solid theoretical foundations, with the explicit aim of creating a model of more or less universal validity which renders Hofstede's famous model invalid and obsolete.

Neither as a formal management discipline nor as a managerial function is cross-cultural management a clearly demarcated field. Yet to many scholars of management and indeed to practitioners in international business the term is plainly meaningful, suggesting a methodology for handling cultural differences which are predominantly seen as sources of conflict, friction or miscommunication. As such, cross-cultural management may be said to refer to procedures and policies which (a) moderate the impact of cultural differences on the execution of management tasks and (b) promote cross-cultural sensitivity, which may be taken to mean an empathetic ability to create 'culturally synergistic solutions' to international management problems (Harris and Moran, 1979).

The case studies in this book indicate that managers in international firms are, as a rule, more concerned about managing cross-cultural interactions (which is neutral and positive) than managing cross-cultural differences (which is potentially divisive and negative). This suggests that managers' conceptions of cross-cultural management are not isomorphic with the views of several of the authors already mentioned, for whom the differences are, as it were, sacrosanct. This highlights not only a certain gulf between management scholars and practitioners regarding cross-cultural management and international management studies generally (see, for example, Aaronson, 1996; Bartholomew and Adler, 1996; Locke, 1998; Søderberg and Holden, 2001; Wong-Rieger and Rieger, 1993), but is also symptomatic of the severe definitional vagueness surrounding the term 'cross-cultural management'. In this book the challenge will be, in effect, to reformulate the term and supply concepts that have intellectual bite for researchers *and* close the gap with the corporate world.

But this cannot be done until the concept of 'culture', as it is used in the management literature, has been reviewed: the very inverted commas hint at the terminological convolutions ahead. For, as we will soon discover, this most frustrating of terms tends, paradoxically, to confuse rather than clarify the nature of cross-cultural management. The following sections will introduce culture as derived from anthropology and assess its impact and some of the drawbacks. The initial case will then be made for forsaking this concept of culture, at least in its most difference-reinforcing manifestations, and for a corresponding reformulation of the field of cross-cultural management, whose starting point is emphatically not a concept of culture that informs anthropological investigation of life on Samoa or the Trobriand Islands, but the behaviour of globally operating firms in the modern economy.[3]

CULTURE: A BABEL OF DEFINITIONS

As Eagleton (2000) reminds us: 'We owe our modern notion of culture in large part to nationalism and colonialism, along with the growth of an anthropology in the service of imperial power.' This concept of culture, deriving from anthropology as it evolved in the nineteenth century, permeates international management writing. A good starting-point is Edward Burnett Tylor's (1871) definition:

> Culture . . . is that complex whole which includes knowledge, belief, art, morals, law, custom, and any other capabilities and habits acquired by man as a member of society. (*Encyclopædia Britannica*, 2000)

This definition makes it clear that culture 'is possessed by man alone' and is the product of behaviour and – this is often overlooked – is *not* behaviour itself. In keeping with Tylor's concept of culture is the famous definition of the American anthropologists, Kroeber and Kluckhohn (1952), which is still widely quoted by management authors today:

> Culture consists of patterns, explicit and implicit of and for behavior acquired and transmitted by symbols, constituting the distinctive achievements of human groups, including their embodiments in artifacts: the essential core of culture consists of traditional (i.e., historically derived and selected) ideas and especially their attached values; culture systems may, on the one hand, be considered as products of action; on the other, as conditioning elements of future action.

It may safely be said that Kroeber and Kluckhohn's concept of culture is a fair representation of culture as *essence*, whereby:

- The members of a culture system share a set of ideas, and especially, values

- These are transmitted (particularly from one generation to another) by symbols

- Culture is produced by the past actions of a group and its members

- Culture is learned

- Culture shapes behaviour and influences one's perception of the world (based on Adler, 1991; and Guirdham, 1999)

In this scheme language as the mediator of social intercourse becomes central to the idea of a given culture. Thus is created and perpetuated the tricky trinity of language, culture and *nation*, each component being dependent on, reinforcing, and enhancing the other two. And thus is created too an exclusive view of culture, which proves convenient for making comparisons of managers' educational background, decision-making style or modes of communication. But it is a view of culture which does not lend itself readily to the description and analysis of cross-cultural behaviour in today's business world. This issue will be further considered a little later in this chapter and chapter 3. In the meantime we should mention that culture can be used to represent an organizing principle at different levels of human endeavour: for example, the international, the national, the regional, the organizational, the professional, the personal. Hofstede (1994), for example, identifies six such broad levels of culture:

- A national level according to one's country (or countries for people who migrated during their lifetime)

- A regional and/or ethnic and/or religious level and/or linguistic affiliation level, as most nations are composed of culturally different groups and/or ethnic and/or religious and/or language groups

- A gender level, according to whether a person was born as a girl or boy

- A generation level, which separates grandparents from parents and children

- A social class level, associated with educational opportunities and with a person's occupation or profession

- For those who are employed, an organizational or corporate level, according to the way employees have been socialized by their work organization

Given these overlapping affiliations, Hofstede (1994) rightly points out: 'In research on cultural differences nationality – the passport one holds – should therefore be used with care.' Each of these levels may be seen as spheres of interaction, where the social production of meaning contributes to a concept of culture, according to which 'culture is . . . seen as a determining and not just a determined part of social activity, and therefore culture is a significant sphere for the reproduction of social power inequalities' (O'Sullivan et al., 1997). One might add that these inequalities do not just exist within societies, but also between them. One has only to think of globalization, which in some parts of the world – notably in the economically least developed countries – is synonymous with Americanization, westernization, neo-colonialism or godless capitalism.

In passing we should mention that the principal meanings of the generic term 'culture' are not entirely similar across European languages. For example, the German word *Kultur* and Finnish word *kulttuuri* strongly (but not exclusively) suggest 'the intellectual side of civilisation and society' (Koivisto, 1999), but without the negative connotations of snobbery that is typical of English society. (If a well-read German needs intellectual sustenance from his newspaper, he will turn to a section called *Kultur*; in Britain one turns to the coyly termed *Arts* section). The Russian word *kultura* likewise does not have a trace of inverted snobbery. Like the word 'culture' in other foreign languages, Russian also embraces the scientific meaning, referring to a milieu propagating micro-organisms (Grishina, 1993). But Russians, it seems, have problems extending the traditional meanings into organizational studies. Thus the term 'corporate culture' cannot be translated into Russian except by circumlocution (Holden et al., 1998).

The Japanese word for culture, *bunka*, focuses attention on literary or artistic production, implying the creation of a sophisticated object and even an improvement of an earlier version (shades, note, of the Japanese approach to quality management). Thus, when the Japanese (and the Chinese who created the Japanese word in the first place) use their word for culture, it refers to the skilled production of artifacts after a master of the craft. This is in contrast to the European languages which derive their word from Latin, where the basic meanings are associated with the cultivation of land and deities (hence *cult*).

But, within management studies, and especially international management studies, the classic anthropological concept of culture has tended to reinforce the conviction that culture can only be understood as a differentiating factor, separating one group of human beings from another – to focus on culture as an accumulation of general factors, which have subsequently been used as a yardstick for characterizing – and ultimately stereotyping – sociocultural systems such as national cultures or cultures associated with 'lesser', defined entities such as a company, a football team, the Freemasons, or a political party. Since culture is an expression of human products, both material and mental, which it is possible to observe and analyze at various degrees of abstraction and from all manner of ontological premises, the very word 'culture', as Schneider and Barsoux (1997) rightly observe, 'can be compared to exploring the ocean'.

The vastness and richness of this ocean is well captured in the following quotations of 'gurus' cited by Hoecklin (1995):

- *Tyler, E.* (1871). That complex whole which includes knowledge, belief, art, morals, law, custom, and any other capabilities and habits acquired by man as a member of society

- *Herskovits, M. J.* (1948). The man-made part of the human environment

- *Kroeber, A. L. and Kluckhohn, C.* (1952). Transmitted patterns of values, ideas and other symbolic systems that shape behaviour

- *Becker and Geer* (1970). Set of common understandings expressed in language

- *Van Maanen, J. and Schein, E. H.* (1979). Values, beliefs and expectations that members come to share

- *Schwartz, M. C. and Jordon, D. K.* (1980). Patterns of belief and expectations shared by members that produce norms shaping behaviour

- *Hofstede, G. H.* (1980). The collective programming of the mind which distinguishes the members of one human group from another

- *Louis, M. R.* (1983). Three aspects: (1) some content (meaning and interpretation) (2) peculiar to (3) a group

- *Hall, E. T. and Hall, M. R.* (1987). Primarily a system for creating, sending, storing and processing information

- *Harris, P. R. and Moran, R. T.* (1987). A distinctly human capacity for adapting to circumstances and transmitting this coping skill and knowledge to subsequent generations

Of the above authors, two – Edward Hall and especially Edgar Schein – make a key distinction about culture. They are concerned with *visible* culture and *invisible* culture. The significance of invisible culture has been emphasized by Hoecklin (1995), who argues that 'the essence of culture is not what is visible on the surface. It is the shared ways groups of people understand and interpret the world. These differing interpretations that cultures give to their environment are critical influences on interactions between people working and managing across cultures.' An aim of this book will be to develop not a different concept of culture, but a different *approach* to culture in line with Hoecklin's thinking.

In his publications, Hall, an anthropologist, whose famous notion of low-context (like the USA) and high-context (like Japan) cultures is briefly discussed in chapter 3, was primarily concerned with foreign cultures; Schein, a social psychologist, with organizational culture. It is Schein's typology that will be of use to us in the chapters ahead. He distinguishes three levels of culture, which reproduces his famous typology (see Figure 2.1). Artifacts are the visible face of culture, but they are not necessarily decipherable to, and may be seriously misunderstood by, outsiders. They can be associated with three kinds of manifestations: physical, behavioural, and verbal. At the invisible level Schein makes a distinction between assumptions which are associated with assumptions that are taken for granted by members of a particular group, and values which express themselves in the institutions of a society – such as family, religious faith, sport, political system, role of women, education and so forth.

But it should be noted for now that Schein's categories should not be seen as watertight. To take one of the most important of all cultural factors, namely language, we can without much difficulty see language as a physical manifestation:

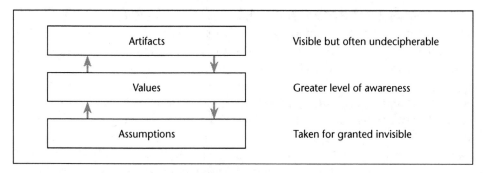

Fig. 2.1   Schein's model of organizational culture
Source: adapted from *Organizational Culture and Leadership* (1985) by E. Schein. © 1985 Harvard Business
School Publishing Corpn., all rights reserved.

in one form it bombards our eardrums; in another it assails our eyes. In another
sense language is a mental experience and as such is invisible. With it we can
decribe artifacts, values and assumptions. Furthermore, as the great American
linguist Edward Sapir (1956) noted: 'No two languages are ever sufficiently
similar to be considered as representing the same social reality. The worlds in
which different societies live are distinct worlds, not merely the same world with
different labels attached.'

In a similar vein Usunier (1998) has pointed out, 'language matters considerably,
both English as it is the worldwide language of business, and foreign languages
because they uniquely express culturally specific patterns in context-embedded
situations, such as consumption or work relationships.' Language – unique to the
human species yet so diverse in its structures, so variegated in its systems for
encoding and articulating meaning, and reflecting a distinctive world-view – will
inevitably prove to be a highly complex factor to handle in the different approach
to culture which will be advanced in this book.

CULTURE-AS-ESSENCE

General texts on international management and international organizational
behaviour which explicitly address cross-cultural issues devote a good deal of
space to a discussion of the word 'culture': perhaps too much! But, as surveys by
Roberts (1977), Adler and Bartholomew (1992), Darlington (1996), Cavusgil and
Das (1997) and Usunier (1998) make clear, this literature is very wide-ranging
in its approaches and in the dimensions used by researchers. It is, however, the
case that the international, cross-cultural management literature, in contrast to the
literature on organizational cultures, is not so much devoted to a discussion of,
and reflection on, the theoretical assumptions embedded in a certain concept of
'culture'.

In the general international management literature, culture is seen more as an area of interest, which is referring to something 'soft', human, unquantifiable, difficult to account for in rational terms and is provided with a label of convenience, namely 'culture'. Although, as will be noted below, there is a dissatisfaction among some management scholars about the limitations of the received culture concept, many who address the problems of methodology in cross-cultural management research (e.g. Cavusgil and Das, 1997; Darlington, 1996; Usunier, 1998) do not suggest that there is something restrictive about the fundamental concept of culture which informs research designs, methodologies and analyses. One scholar who has expressed unambiguous reservation is Schneider (1988):

> The construct of culture has caused much confusion. While there are multiple definitions, they tend to be vague and overly general. This confusion is added to by the multiple disciplines interested in this topic, which, while increasing richness, does not necessarily bring clarity. Anthropologists, psychologists, and others bring with them their specific paradigms and research methodologies. This creates difficulties in reaching consensus on construct definitions as well as their measurement or operationalization.

In 1952, when Kroeber and Kluckhohn registered 164 different definitions of culture, the word was mainly used in ethnographic studies and within different fields of the humanities. It would be a good two decades before cross-cultural management theory appropriated the word 'culture' as a major heuristic term, extending the traditional semantic boundaries to embrace both national and organizational values and behaviour. Today there is, not surprisingly, a lack of consensus in this academic field in general about the term 'culture'. But whereas scholars within organization studies have even been involved in 'culture wars' between functionalists referring to cultural systems as 'essential' and interpretivists understanding culture as a social construct (Alvesson 1993; Martin and Frost, 1997; Smircich 1983), the majority of cross-cultural management students have focused on culture as 'essence' and often used the term equivalently with nation-state.

The cultural dimensions of international management, including the interorganizational processes of international mergers and acquisitions, joint ventures and other strategic alliances, may be studied in different ways. However, the choice of culture concept strongly influences the overall theoretical framework and the research design. Most importantly, it also seems to have a bearing on results and implied recommendations to companies involved in cross-cultural cooperation. Unfortunately, as already mentioned above, the literature on international cross-cultural management has often not been very explicit and reflexive about the culture concept underlying the empirical studies and the recommendations for business practice.

The majority of the researchers, among them Hofstede and Trompenaars, seem to build upon the classic anthropological concept of culture, developed by Western anthropologists in the 1950s and 1960s. According to this essentialist understanding, culture is seen as a relatively stable, homogeneous, internally consistent system of assumptions, values and norms transmitted by socialization to the next generation. Moreover, it is seen as something that members of a cultural community, for example an organization or a nation, 'have' or 'belong to'. By virtue of the strong emphasis of sharedness, this view of culture also tends to 'entail blindness as regards social variation and diversity within a nation or an organization' (Risager, 2001, forthcoming). The term 'diversity' will be discussed later in this book.

Within this mainstream approach to the study of cross-cultural management issues, researchers tend to focus on cultural encounters between what they perceive as well-defined and homogeneous entities, for example a parent company and its subsidiaries in foreign countries. They tend to see organizational integration problems as being caused by objective cultural differences both at an organizational and a national level. Often they also share the ambition to find out which national and organizational cultures can coexist, for example in international mergers and acquisitions, and how they can benefit from the collaboration (see, for example, Søderberg, 1999 for a critique of the 'culture fit' approach). Their goal is largely normative – to advance general action instructions that may predict and thus minimize integration problems and promote more effective managerial action.

Yet it appears to be the case that the essentialist concept of culture referred to in this brief literature review does not seem to resonate with firms' and managers' experiences of cultural complexity in the business environment which is becoming globalized: globalized not only through the emergence of a consumer culture with converging tastes and demands, but through worldwide collaboration and competition supported by the borderless communication technologies. In a globalizing business world, cultural differences *are not* coalescing into a unitary business culture. Rather, cultural differences are manifesting themselves in new ways: for example, in the working environment of a multicultural project team collaborating across geographical and organizational boundaries or in e-mail-saturated cyberspace. This is where cross-cultural management *is waiting to be discovered*.

THE UNDUE INFLUENCE OF THE ESSENTIALIST CONCEPT OF CULTURE

Culture in the essentialist sense, to quote Gertsen and Søderberg (2000), 'is seen as an empirical category, a relatively stable, homogenous, internally consistent system of distinctive assumptions, values and norms, which can be objectively described . . . something that members of a group, an organization, or a nation have or bear collectively'. This essentialist or functionalist view can be valid if we want to understand the characteristics of a particular cultural system, such as a country or a company, but when, as in everyday international business practice, cultures clash and fuse with each other in myriad ways, the concept is unhelpful: it is virtually programmed to exaggerate the differences between cultures and to generate criteria to rank them competitively.

If that last point seems excessive, reflect on the huge literature in (American) English and, as it happens, in Japanese, in which the American (low-context) individualism is grossly counterpoised with Japanese (high-context) groupism, as if there was no such person as an 'individual' Japanese or an American who could act or think in collective terms. Alas, the American corporate brain, eager for cross-cultural simplifications, devoured the dichotomy as a sacred business truth in the early 1980s and so US firms have ever since made a rod for their own back when dealing with Japan. As John Nathan (1999), the chronicler of Sony, has observed, for American companies 'achieving *mutual understanding* with Tokyo has been a vexing challenge fraught with disappointment' (original emphasis). There seems to be no compatibility between the heavy plod of American feet and the smooth swish of Japanese sliding doors.

All in all, we are ensnared by a concept of culture, whose 'assumptions associated with the dominant paradigm (i.e. those of Hofstede) appear too generalizing and stereotyping' (Risager, 2001, forthcoming). Adler's (1991) widely used definition of cross-cultural management, with its emphasis on description, comparison and initiation into unknown cultural realms, is anthropologically motivated, heavily dependent as culture as difference:

> Cross-cultural management studies the behavior of people in organizations around the world and trains people to work in organizations with employee and client populations. It *describes* organizational behavior within countries and cultures; *compares* organizational behavior across cultures and countries: and perhaps, most importantly, seeks to understand and improve the *interaction* of co-workers, clients, suppliers, and alliance partners from different countries and cultures. Cross-cultural management thus expands the scope of domestic management to encompass the international and multicultural spheres.

Hofstede's (1980) celebrated definition of culture – so celebrated that it is hardly challenged – again stresses culture as difference. According to Hofstede, culture is:

> the collective programming of the mind which distinguishes the members of one human group from another . . . the interactive aggregate of common characteristics that influences a human group's response to its environment.[4]

The common reasoning is that it is possible, by surveying and systematizing the behaviour and stated attitudes of individual members, to penetrate and expose the core assumptions and values of any culture In this way it is possible to present cultures as objectively identifiable and well-defined entities which may be compared. And what, incidentally, would be the field of international management studies without its comparisons of national traits and performance? In this sense national competitiveness and essentialist culture go hand in hand. As long as the economic performance is judged as a facet of national behaviour, then essentialist views of culture will persist to explain that behaviour.

All in all, international cross-cultural management, as developed by writers over the last 40 years or so, is a somewhat murky area of management thinking. As is clear by now, the very term 'culture' is notorious. However, one can distinguish in management literature three primary uses of the term:

- Culture referring to an aspect of a national or ethnic grouping, including summations of characteristics with reference to distinctive (culture-specific) management style or negotiating style

- Culture referring to the special qualities an organization ('corporate culture')

- Culture referring to mental attributes, as in of Hofstede's (1980) famous formulation cited above

Beyond that, various writers use the word 'culture' very loosely so that it takes on acquired meanings. For example, John Viney (1997), author of the book *The culture wars*, argues that 'culture is an important, possibly the most important, element in the competition for business supremacy'. Here 'culture' does not mean culture at all. Viney's usage appears to mean something like: 'the advantage of cultural heritage', which is in keeping with the spirit of his book. McCrae (1995), in a discussion about barriers to internationalization, writes that 'culture will keep countries apart'. In this case the word 'culture' has moved from its standard semantic range into a related area, namely cultural difference. In fact, scrutiny of management texts reveals that many writers use 'culture' to mean this and not culture in a broad generic sense.

In their well-regarded *Managing across borders* (1998), authors Ghoshal and Bartlett *do not bother* to reference culture in the index, and their main discussion in the text is about culture in the sense of corporate culture. According to them, the only country which creates difficulties with respect to language and culture is – well, well – Japan; and 'the most enduring barriers to change in many of the companies we studied were *cultural*' (Ghoshal and Bartlett, 1998, added emphasis). All this bears out the conviction that 'the word "culture" brings up more problems than it solves' (Scollon and Scollon, 1995). Worse, perhaps, is that there is a tendency to discuss culture 'as it were a "thing" hovering over a society and influencing behaviour in a direct and uniform way' (Hoecklin, 1995). Your author has already in this chapter put a noose of inverted commas around the word 'culture' – to indicate that you and I know that culture is a severely problematical term, but without any assumption that your concept coincides with mine.

THE FIXATION WITH CULTURE SHOCK

We can safely say that in the broad cross-cultural management literature cultural difference is held automatically to give rise to cross-cultural misunderstandings and clashes. Resultant unpleasant experiences are sometimes classed as 'culture shock', a term which will be discussed in a moment. The royal road to alleviating misunderstanding, clash and shock is, it seems, always more knowledge about culture and the manifold ways in which this particular hydra rears itself. This is why books and articles about cross-cultural management say far more about culture than management. At all events, the argument seems to go, more knowledge about culture can allegedly lead to '(cross-)cultural sensitivity', or '(cross-)cultural awareness', which is the foundation for 'true' cross-cultural or intercultural competence. This book will take that way of thinking to task.

Taking the academic contributions to international cross-cultural management as a whole, it is clear that the literature reveals a preoccupation with three manifestly dominant core problem areas which have challenged international businesses since the 1950s and 1960s: the ethnocentrism, which binds and blinds; the maddening cultural diversity – Steiner's (1975) 'crazy quilt' of cultures and languages; and the disorientating effects of culture shock – the reeling against the inexplicable, the confounding press of Adler's (1991) 'uninterpretable clues'. These core problems and core solutions are presented in a thematic model (Figure 2.2).

Culture shock,[5] as experienced by the individual, has been described as the state of mind:

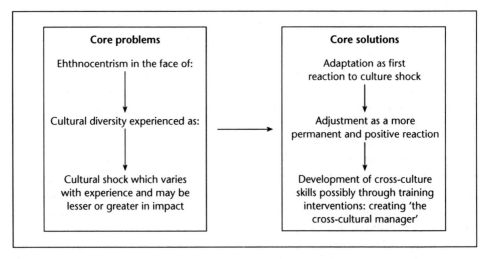

Fig. 2.2   Thematic model of core problems and core solutions in the cross-cultural management literature

precipitated by the anxiety that results from losing all our familiar signs and symbols of social intercourse. These signs or cues include the thousand and one ways in which we orient ourselves to the situations of daily life: how to give orders, how to make purchases, when and when not to respond. Now these cues, which may be words, gestures, facial expressions, customs, or norms, are acquired by all of us in the course of growing up and are as much a part of our culture as the language we speak or the beliefs we accept. All of us depend for our peace of mind on hundreds of these cues, most of which we are not consciously aware. (Oberg, 1960)

Ferraro (1994) argues that culture shock is a 'psychologically disorienting experience'; and his remedy is 'a general understanding of the concept of culture [which] can provide a fuller appreciation of other cultures, regardless of where one might be doing business'. It is in fact highly debatable whether any concept of culture which focuses *on itself* can soften the blows of culture shock, let alone lead to any kind of cross-cultural break through in the business world. Hickson and Pugh (1995) regard the cross-cultural manager as someone who can cope with culture shock and for whom the learning experience in one culture helps with entry and effectiveness in another one. This sounds reasonable enough until, incidentally, you reflect that there is no such person as the cross-cultural manager in any functional sense, that is holding that as a job title and performing tasks which make the company more efficient in its understanding and handling of cross-cultural influences on its international policy, strategy and operations. He or she is a mere idealization. This matter will come in for more scrutiny in the final chapter.

In so far as cross-cultural management is a *management* function at all, it appears to be primarily associated with international human resource management, itself an operational field forming an awkward fit with the formal domain of management studies (Tung and Punnett, 1993). At all events IHRM emerges as the main mediator and developer of cross-cultural management competencies in companies across a whole range of international management and marketing functions which plainly call for cross-cultural awareness and related management competencies. But, as this book will argue, it is possible, indeed necessary, to consider cross-cultural management from new, thought-provoking perspectives.

Major circumstances have altered the nature of cross-cultural management and thus call for a reformulation of the entire subject area spanning international management and cultural studies. There is plainly more to cross-cultural management than coping with culture shock, possessing above-average 'cultural awareness', and knowing how to manage (sic.) cultural differences. On the one hand, there are trends in global business and major shifts in the nature of management work and perceived competencies. On the other hand, there is among management scholars a growing scepticism when it comes to the usefulness of the prevailing essentialist culture concept. These developments have extended research agendas dramatically. Both sets of issues will be considered in due course. In the meantime, for culture shock enthusiasts, I reproduce Craig's (1979) representation of the condition with expatriates in mind (Figure 2.3).

31

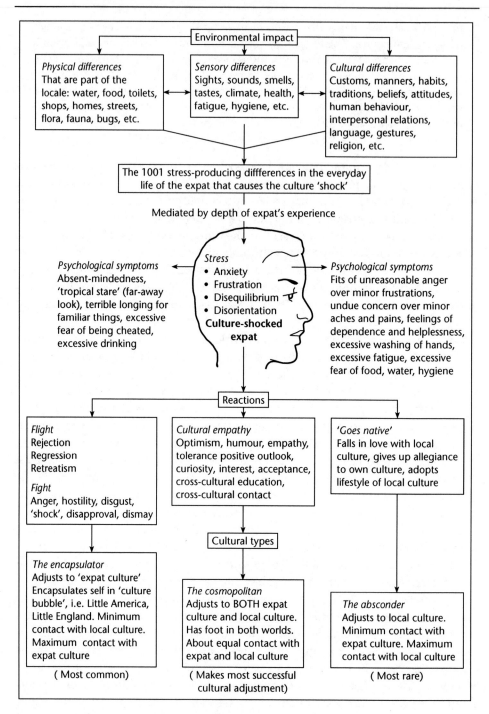

Fig. 2.3 The culture-shocked expat

Source: *Culture shock* (1979) by J. Craig, Times Books International, Singapore.

Sight of the model alone is enough to induce culture shock.

THE CROSS-CULTURAL MANAGEMENT LITERATURE: A MORASS AND ELEPHANT

The literary scholar, Terry Eagleton (2000), has pointed out that 'we are at the moment between disablingly wide and discomfortingly rigid notions of culture . . . between an empty universalism and blind particularism.' This phraseology reflects rather aptly the nature of models, schemata and classification systems relating to the impact of culture on management worldwide which we find in the general management literature. There is, after all, a multiplicity of such schemes to choose from.

In an article first published in 1970, Karlene H. Roberts of the University of California carried out a survey of 526 publications 'that might aid researchers initiating cross-cultural behavioral investigations relevant to organizations' (Roberts, 1977). A mere 4.2% of the surveyed articles 'focused on organizational behavior issues from a cross-cultural or international perspective'. She described the literature as 'a morass' and likened the task of evaluation of this kind of research as 'a little like the exercise of looking at an elephant – what one sees depends on one's vantage point'. She went on:

> Students of organizations come from many disciplines. It is virtually impossible to think simultaneously about the multitude of problems and research strategies addressed by anthropologists, economists, educators, psychologists, political scientists, and students of business. . . . The author's biases determine the kinds of questions covered and the methodological strategies discussed.

Her conclusion was damning:

> This review of cross-cultural research related to organizational behavior reveals a predominance of discussions and studies concerned with individual behavior in organizations. Most of the studies are based on surveys which are not well thought out. Empirical work concerned with more macro organizational variables is meagre. It is not well guided by theoretical underpinnings, data are often weak, and conclusions are difficult to comprehend.

When Roberts wrote that piece of damnation in 1970, cross-cultural management research was embryonic. Nearly 20 years later Usunier (1998) declared the field of enquiry to be 'still in its infancy', which suggests rather slow development of Robert's problematical pachyderm. But since the 1970s two events have changed the face of cross-cultural management research. First, corporate America was hit by several severe cross-cultural jolts as of the mid-to-late 1970s. Nothing had greater impact than the thunder-bolt from Asia: the spectacular growth and internationalization of the Japanese economy. The consequent preoccupation, if not outright obsession, with Japan and its management systems, as of the mid-1970s, duly put cross-cultural issues more solidly on corporate agendas and business school curricula in the USA and Europe.

The second event was the publication of a book by a Dutch professor which gave practitioners and professors (as it were) something they never had before: a powerful, empirically developed framework for explaining cross-cultural differences. It outmanoeuvred in sophistication and explanatory power E. T. Hall's (1959) broad classification of cultures into high-context and low-context varieties, which will be discussed presently. 1980 then saw the publication of Hofstede's remarkable and influential book, *Culture's consequences*. At a stroke, as it now seems, economic determinism, which sees organizations and their managers as rational actors, was confronted by culturism: the conviction that (national) cultural background influences how people work and that 'there is a link between management practice and the culture of a given society' (Byrkjeflot and Halvorsen, 1996).

At last the world had a scaled multidimensional model which *mapped and cross-referenced* cultural traits across several countries. Hofstede's study focused on work-related values, and he clustered national differences around four broad factors relating to power distance, masculinity–femininity, uncertainty avoidance, individualism and collectivism. His contribution in effect created a new landscape for international management studies. His work has not only achieved canonical status. Its findings have been found to be 'largely validated', according to Darlington (1996), but they have been repeatedly misapplied. Furthermore, the sweeping acceptance of the Hofstede model has been intellectually numbing. It is persistently overlooked that 'more and more different dimensions of culture are discoverable through administration of different sets of questionnaire items than Hofstede's' (Limaye and Victor, 1995). Figure 2.4 reproduces a sample of the famous Hofstede model, indicating power distance and uncertainty avoidance scores.

As Hofstede himself wrote in *Cultures and organizations* (1994), which was first published in 1991: 'Many readers evidently only read part of the message. For example, I lost count of the number of people who cited the book claiming that I had studied the values of IBM (or 'Hermes') *managers*. The data I used were from IBM *employees* and that, as the book itself showed, makes quite a difference.' But Hofstede has created a virtually uncontested paradigm, in which, to quote Søndergaard (1994) again, 'the questions and the dimensions are used as taken-for-granted assumptions.' It appears too that his model has been also used by trainers specializing in international negotiation: hardly a central purpose for which they were devised. Table 2.1 is a summary of the Hofstede's key questions about the four culture-related values.

The fact that Hofstede's data were gathered some 30 years ago and apply to a world that no longer exists seems to be generally ignored. Since 1980, the year in which *Culture's consequences* was first published, the Cold War has disappeared, communism is a limping shadow of its former self, the Asian tigers are no longer mere cubs, China is furiously marketising itself. More complicated, perhaps, is the

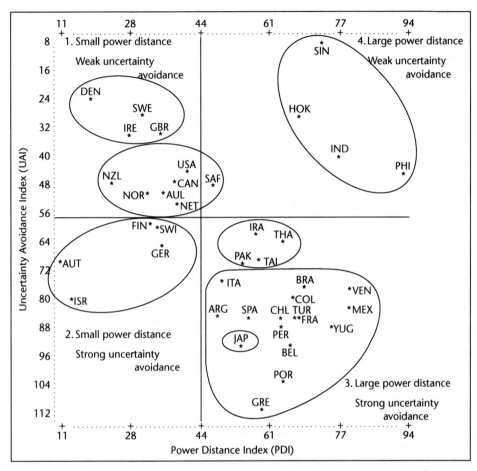

Fig. 2.4 Hofstede's model showing scores for power distance and uncertainty avoidance

Source: *Cultures Consequences* (2001) by G. Hofstede, Sage Publications, London.

fact that organizations worldwide are promoting and implementing *new* work values, many of which highlight cooperation and knowledge-sharing, and encourage empowerment and localization.

There is also a recognition that the emphasis on synergy, communication and relationship-building is in any case the hallmark of the most important group of people not to be in important managerial positions, namely, women (Claes, 1999). It seems hard to imagine that the work values of 1980 – or rather the late 1970s when the data were gathered – have not undergone significant shifts owing both to new pressures on individuals 'to deliver' and new possibilities for self-development. All this does not seem to deter the almost slavish homage to Hofstede's work, or rather to his models and the associated dimensions. Rarely do his many followers

Table 2.1 Summary of Hofstede's key questions about the four culture-related values

Value	Questionnaire item
Power distance	How frequently, in your experience, does the following problem occur: employees being afraid to express their disagreements with their managers?
Uncertainty avoidance	Company rules should not be broken, even if the employee thinks it is in the company's best interest.
	How long do you think you will continue working for this company?
Individualism	How important is it to you to have a job which leaves sufficient time for your personal or family life?
	How important is it to you to have considerable freedom to adapt your own approach to the job?
Femininity	How important is it to you to have a good working relationship with your manager?
	How important is it to you to work with people who cooperate well with one another?
Masculinity	How important is it to you to have an opportunity for high earnings?
	How important is it to you to get the recognition you deserve when you do a good job?

Source: Managing Cultural Differences by L. Hoecklin (1995).

discuss Hofstede's methodology, his approach to questionnaire design and translation, and his own views of the practical value of his survey.

Nevertheless, since 1980 cross-cultural management writing and research have, and in no small part thanks to Hofstede, been placed on a firmer footing, and this great achievement must be acknowledged. But the time has surely come to ease his grip on cross-cultural writing and thinking. Yet the fact is that despite Hofstede the general field of cross-cultural management lacks coherence; or, rather, to render that in a positive light, the field is so vast in its scope of nominal enquiry that it lacks an agreed central core for conceptual purposes and operational development. The notions of culture which have underpinned management studies for so long have failed to supply a sound and robust conceptual base for cross-cultural management, which has almost become a code-word for the management of cross-cultural differences.

Quite apart from that, researchers have been continually beset with 'contentious issues of ethnocentrism, functional and conceptual equivalence in comparative research' (Cavusgil and Das, 1997). Taking our cue from Roberts' elephant analogy, we may say that since the 1970s the beast has grown much larger and there are even more vantage points from which to examine it: not least, incidentally, because of the enormous output of publications relating to cross-cultural management in the broadest sense in languages other than English. French,

German and Japanese are three languages which come to mind. One can add Russian too. Despite the surge of the subject area and the general recognition that 'culture' in the generally accepted sense of the term influences modern business development, Usunier (1998) is probably correct to point out that cross-cultural management research is 'a significant but minority track among international management researchers'. But it ought surely to be a majority track.

NOTES

1. The list of titles is by no means exhaustive. The library of Copenhagen Business School currently lists 41 books in the fields of management, marketing, social psychology, linguistics, advertising and mass media, in which the words 'across cultures' appear.

2. The original title in French was *Commerce entre cultures*.

3. Samoa and the Trobriand Islands in the Pacific Ocean are sites of famous anthropological studies by Margaret Mead (1901–78) and Bronislaw Malinowski (1884–1942).

4. One critic, the Canadian management scholar Henry Mintzberg (1993), has taken a swipe at management scholars for being obsessed with 'half-baked ideas about the programming of human cognition'. A rare instance of frontal attack on the guru.

5. Culture shock is never an *exciting* human experience in the management literature. For a brilliant, touching and occasionally hilarious account of culture shock experienced in Russia, read Fallowell's *One hot day in St Petersburg* (1994).

REFERENCES

Aaronson, S. (1996). Dinosaurs in the global economy? American graduate business schools in the 1980s and 1990s. In: Amdam, R. P. (ed.). *Management, education and competitiveness: Europe, Japan and the United States.* London: Routledge, pp. 212–26.

Adler, N. (1991). *International dimensions of organizational behavior.* Boston, MA: PWS-Kent Publishing Company.

Adler, N. and Bartholomew, S. (1992). Academic and professional communities of discourse: Generating knowledge on transnational human resource management. *Journal of International Business Studies* 23: 226–32.

Alvesson, M. (1993). *Cultural perspectives on organizations.* Cambridge: Cambridge University Press.

Bartholomew, S. and Adler, N. (1996). Building networks and crossing borders: The dynamics of knowledge generation in a transnational world. In: Joynt and Warner (1996), pp. 7–32.

Byrkjeflot, H. and Halvorsen, T. (1996). The institutionalisation of industrial administration in Norway 1950–90: Consequences for education in business administration of domination by engineering. In: Amdam, R. P. (ed.). *Management, education and competitiveness: Europe, Japan and the United States.* London: Routledge.

Cavusgil, T. and Das, A. (1997). Methodological issues in empirical cross-cultural research: A survey of the management literature and a framework. *Management International Review* 37(1): 71–96.

Claes, M.-T. (1999). Women, men and management styles. *International Labour Review* 138(4): 431–46.

Craig, J. (1979). *Culture shock.* Singapore: Times Books International. Cited in: Schneider and Barsoux (1997).

Darlington, G. (1996). Culture – a theoretical review. In: Joynt and Warner (1996), pp. 33–55.

Deresky, H. (2000). *International management: Management across borders and cultures*. Upper Saddle River, NJ: Prentice-Hall.

Dupriez, P. and Simons, S. (eds) (2000). *La résistance culturelle: Fondements, applications et implications du management interculturel*. Brussels: De Boeck & Larcier.

Eagleton, T. (2000). *The idea of culture*. Oxford: Blackwell.

Encyclopædia Britannica (2000). www.britannica.com

Fallowell, D. (1994). *One hot summer in St Petersburg*. London: Jonathan Cape.

Ferraro, G. P. (1994). *The international dimension of international business*. Englewood Cliffs, NJ: Prentice-Hall.

Gertsen, M. and Søderberg, A.-M. (2000). Cultural change processes in mergers: A social constructionist perspective. Unpublished manuscript. Copenhagen Business School.

Ghoshal, S. and Bartlett, C. (1998). *Managing across borders*. London: Random House.

Grishina, E. A. (1993). *Sovremenniy slovar inostrannykh slov* (*Contemporary dictionary of foreign words*). Moscow: Izdatelstvo 'Russkii yazyk'.

Guirdham, M. (1999). *Communication across cultures*. Basingstoke, UK: Macmillan.

Hall, E. T. (1959). *The silent language*. New York: Doubleday.

Hampden-Turner, C. and Trompenaars, F. (1993). *The seven cultures of capitalism: Value systems for creating wealth in the United States, Britain, Japan, Germany, France, Sweden and the Netherlands*. London: Judy Piatkus.

Harris, P. and Moran, R. (1979). *Managing cultural differences*. Houston, TX: Gulf Publishing.

Harris, P. and Moran, R. (1996). *Managing cultural differences: Leadership strategies for a new world of business*. Houston, TX: Gulf Publishing.

Hickson, D. and Pugh, D. (1995). *Management worldwide: The impact of societal culture on organizations across the globe*. London: Penguin Books.

Hoecklin, L. (1995). *Managing cultural differences: Strategies for competitive advantage*. London: Economist Intelligence Unit/Addison Wesley.

Hofstede, G. (1980). *Culture's consequences: International differences in work-related values*. Beverly Hills, CA: Sage Publications.

Hofstede, G. (1994). *Culture and organizations: Intercultural cooperation and its importance for survival – software of the mind*. London: HarperCollins.

Hofstede, G. (2001). *Culture's consequences: Comparing values, behaviors, institutions and organizations across nations* (second edition). Thousand Oaks, CA: Sage Publications.

Holden, N. J., Cooper C. L. and Carr, J. (1998). *Dealing with the new Russia: Management cultures in collision*. Chichester, UK: John Wiley & Sons.

Joynt, P. and Warner, M. (1996). *Managing across cultures: Issues and perspectives*. London: International Thompson.

Koivisto, J. (1999). *Cultural heritages and cross-cultural management: Cross-cultural synergy and friction in Finno-Japanese management*. PhD thesis. Helsinki School of Economics and Business Administration.

Kroeber, A. L. and Kluckhohn, C. (1952). *Culture: A critical review of concepts and definitions*. Cambridge, MA: Harvard University Press. Quoted in: *Encyclopædia Britannica* (2000).

Lewis, D. (1996). *When cultures collide: Managing successfully across cultures*. London: Nicholas Brealey.

Limaye, M. R. and Victor, D. A. (1995). Cross-cultural business communication: state of the art and hypotheses for the 1990s. In: Jackson, T. (ed.). *Cross-cultural management*. Oxford: Butterworth-Heinemann, pp. 217–37.

Locke, R. (1998). Mistaking a historical phenomenon for a functional one: Postwar management education reconsidered. In: Engwall, L. and Zamagnani, V. (eds). *Management education in historical perspective*. Oxford: Oxford University Press, pp. 145–56.

McRae, H. (1995). *The world in 2020*. London: HarperCollins.

Martin, J. and Frost, P. (1997). The organizational culture war games: A struggle for intellectual dominance. In: Clegg, S. R., Hardy, C. and Nord, W. R. (eds). *Handbook of organization studies*. London: Sage Publications, pp. 599–621.

Mead, R. (1994). *International management: Cross-cultural dimensions*. Oxford: Blackwell.

Mintzberg, H. (1993). 'Globalization: Seperating the fad from the fact'. In: Wong-Rieger and Rieger (1993), pp. 99–103.

Morosini, P. (1998). *Managing cultural differences. Effective strategy and execution across cultures in global corporate alliances*. Oxford: Pergamon.

Nathan, J. (1999). *Sony: The private life*. London: HarperCollins.

Oberg, K. (1960). Culture shock: adjustment to a new cultural environment. *Practical Anthropologist* 7: 177–82.

O'Sullivan, T., Hartley, J., Saunders, D., Montgomery, M. and Fiske, J. (1997). *Key concepts in communication and cultural studies*. London: Routledge.

Preston, R. (1993). Future directions in international comparative management research. In: Wong-Rieger and Reiger (1993), pp. 13–25.

Risager, K. (2001, forthcoming). Cross- and intercultural communication. In: Ammon, U. (ed.). *Sociolinguistics: An international handbook of the science of language and society*. Berlin: de Gruyter.

Roberts, K. H. (1977). On looking at an elephant: An evaluation of cross-cultural research related to organizations. In: Weinshall, T. (ed.). *Culture and management: Selected readings*. Harmondsworth, UK: Penguin, pp. 56–104. First published in: *Psychological Bulletin* 74(5) (1970): 327–50.

Sapir, E. (1956). *Culture, language and personality*. Berkeley, CA: University of California Press.

Schein, E. (1985). *Organizational culture and leadership*. San Francisco, CA: Jossey-Bass. Quoted in: Hatch, M. J. (1997). *Organization theory: Modern symbolic and postmodern perspectives*. Oxford: Oxford University Press.

Schneider, S. (1988). National v. corporate cultures: Implications for human resource management. *Human Resource Management* 27(2). Also in: Redding, G. (ed.) (1995). *International cultural differences*. Aldershot: Dartmouth Publishing, pp. 231–46.

Schneider, S. and Barsoux, J. L. (1997). *Managing across cultures*. London: Prentice Hall.

Scollon, R. and Scollon, S. W. (1995). *Intercultural communication: A discourse approach*. Cambridge, MA: Blackwell.

Seelye, H. N. and Seelye-James, A. (1995). *Culture clash: Managing in a multicultural world*. Lincolnwood, IL: NTC Business Books.

Smircich, L. (1983). Concepts of culture and organizational analysis. *Administrative Science Quarterly* 28: 339–58.

Søderberg, A.-M. (1999). Do national cultures always make such a difference? Theoretical considerations and empirical findings related to a series of case studies of foreign acquisitions of Danish companies. In: Vestergaard, T. (ed.). *Language, culture and identity*. Aalborg: Aalborg University Press, pp. 137–71.

Søderberg, A.-M. and Holden, N. J. (2001). Rethinking cross-cultural management in a globalising business world. Unpublished manuscript.

Søndergaard, M. (1994). Research note: Hofstede's consequences: A study of reviews, citations, and replications. *Organization Studies* 15(3): 447–56.

Steiner, G. (1975). *After Babel: Aspects of language and translation*. Oxford: Oxford University Press.

Trompenaars, F. (1993). *Riding the waves of culture: Understanding cultural diversity in business*. London: Economist Books.

Tung, R. (1997). International and intranational diversity. In: Granrose, C. S. and Oskamp, S. (eds). *Cross-cultural work groups*. Thousand Oaks, CA: Sage Publications, pp. 163–85.

Tung, R. and Punnett, B. J. (1993). 'Research and international human resource management'. In: Wong-Rieger and Rieger (1993), pp. 35–53.

Tyler, E. B. (1871). *Primitive culture*. Quoted in: *Encyclopædia Britannica* (2000).

Ulijn, J. (1998). Geert Hofstede, the founder of a culture science. Contribution to: *Dale Research Encyclopedia of Management*. No further particulars.

Usunier, J.-C. (1998). *International and cross-cultural management research*. London: Sage Publications.

Usunier, J.-C. (2000). *Marketing across cultures*. London: Prentice Hall.

Viney, J. (1997). *The culture wars: How American and Japanese businesses have outperformed Europe's and why the future will be different*. London: Capstone.

Wong-Rieger, D. and Rieger, F. (eds) (1993). *International management research: Looking to the future*. Berlin: de Gruyter.

3 Some consequences of *Culture's consequences*

'Also noch einmal unsere Frage: was ist Kultur? In einer etwas menschlicher gefasste Definition ist es *die Fähigkeit, mit kleinen Gesten grosse Aussagen zu vermitteln.*'[1]

Raymond Saner, *Verhandlungstechnik* (1997)

'The search for differences among cultures is futile as an explanatory device. Rather, the underlying functions which produce traits should interest us so that we can develop explanations of phenomena operating together and apart.'

Karlene H. Roberts, On looking at an elephant (1970)

OBJECTIVES

- Introduces the notion of culture's periodic tables.
- Finds that cross-cultural writers show virtually no interest in the three major preoccupations of internationally operating companies – networking, organizational learning and knowledge management – all of which require competence in cross-cultural management.
- Identifies the terrain of cross-cultural management in the global economy.
- Supplies a new guideline definition of cross-cultural management.
- Suggests that cross-cultural management can be conceived as a form of knowledge management.

INTRODUCTION

Cross-cultural management is a branch of international management as an academic discipline which emerged in the 1960s. In those days international management was virtually synonymous with management of the (American) multinational corporation. In the intervening 40 years the subject area has broadened considerably. This is in part due to several significant events and general developments such as the rise of Japan since the mid-1970s, the emergence of the integrated European market since the mid-1980s, and the collapse of the Soviet Union in 1991; advances in communication technology and the related extension of the world wide web; the emergence of the so-called global economy; and the creation of new concepts of management, including re-engineering, empowerment, the learning organization, the cult of 'excellence', the management of diversity, and so forth.

Throughout these 40 years international management *as an activity* has evolved into a form of work which is becoming increasingly premised on a capacity for interactive global networking, teamworking and organizational learning. In this new order of things managers are becoming knowledge workers: 'From being functional specialists, managers are becoming sophisticated generalists, able to manage a potpourri of projects, people, resources, and issues' (Crainer, 1996). This leads to the proposition that cross-cultural management is a form of knowledge work; but before that contention is pursued further, it is important to grasp the logic behind it, as this notion is central to the entire development of this book.

One of the twentieth century's most influential management thinkers, Peter Drucker (quoted in Crainer, 1996), has noted: 'The single greatest challenge facing managers in the developed countries is to raise the productivity of knowledge and service workers. This challenge, which will dominate the management agenda for the next several decades, will ultimately determine the competitive performance of companies. Even more importantly, it will determine the very fabric of society and the quality of life in every industrialized nation.' In a globalized economy Drucker's challenge means raising the productivity of knowledge and service workers who will be in multicultural teams and network globally with arrays of stakeholders. Managing such workers will be one of the main tasks of the cross-cultural management, which it might be more appropriate to envisage as *the management of multiple cultures*, where cultures are not just a national or ethnically determined manifestation, but reflect what Bauman calls 'habitats of meaning', which cut through and across organizations without much regard for 'clear, sharp, enduring edges' (cited in Hannerz, 1996).

This book claims that the traditional approach to international cross-cultural management, whereby culture has been frequently used to equate with nation-state, is largely out of step with these new demands on management. Therefore academics as well as practitioners must take into consideration the multiplicity of various cultural communities existing and coexisting within organizational settings of an international company. As Bell (personal communication) rightly observes, the important thing is 'to make it crystal clear that the nation-state is not the cultural identifier in many cases; people are culturally complex and everyone has an individual profile of cultural inputs'.

It is, however, important to appreciate that it is not just that a new multicultural business environment is taking shape. We are also witnessing the emergence of the knowledge economy, in which firms face the challenge of developing an internationally distributed work environment that fosters organizational learning. This environment requires the sharing of knowledge to be facilitated within the company and among 'webs of enterprise' (Dicken, 1999) and arrays of networks which link it up with its stakeholders (Burton-Jones, 1999; Dixon, 2000) for use *years ahead* (Barham and Heimer, 1998). In this sense networks are the antennae of organizational learning.

NETWORKING AND ORGANIZATIONAL LEARNING

A network may be seen as sets of pathways to key resources: human assets, special knowledge, rare competencies, sources of finance, forms of influence, and so forth. Accordingly, networking is the activity of creating pathways to re-sources, competencies and capabilities needed by an organization to sustain its viability and to manage the resulting information channels. In its international dimensions the associated 'flows of power and information may actually be more important than those of money and utilities' (Thorelli, 1990). Networking is in fact a cross-cultural knowledge-sharing activity and is, as such, also a form of cross-cultural negotiation, in which protagonists strive to agree on (a) who is going to share with whom which mutually held resources and (b) the degree of access to those resources *and* degree of compensation or form of consideration for the privilege of obtaining that access. This description of networking is central to the way in which this activity is to be understood in this book. The word will *not* be used as a vague synonym for contact-making. Networking is also a practice which facilitates organizational learning.

In the new business economy firms face a major challenge: how 'to learn from many environments to which they are exposed and to appropriate the benefits of such learning through their global operations in transnational innovations' (Clegg and Clarke, 1999). The company as a learning organization may be seen as characterized by socio-interactive communication networks supporting the organization's mission, goals and strategy. It is line with this thinking that Keegan (1999) characterizes 'the hall mark of a global company' as 'the capacity to formulate and implement global strategies that leverage worldwide learning, respond fully to local needs and wants, and draw on all the talent and energy of every member of the organization. This is a task requiring heroic vision.'

For the last 15 years or so it has been recognized that organizations, if they are to survive, need to learn (for overviews see Argyris, 1999; Johnson and Scholes, 1999; Senge, 1990). A learning organization has been defined as one which is 'skilled at creating, acquiring, and transferring knowledge, and at modifying its behavior to reflect new knowledge and insights' (Garvin, 1998). In practice this means acquiring and exploiting knowledge from any source, for knowledge is 'the one sure source of lasting competitive advantage' (Nonaka, 1991). In this scenario the learning organization also becomes the knowledge-creating organization, a new kind of communicating entity both at the inter-organizational as well as interpersonal levels of interaction. In a recent survey on knowledge management, the *Financial Times* (1999) noted that knowledge is 'elusive and the task of tying it down, encoding it and distributing it is tricky'. This task represents the very core of business communication in the global economy; and it requires new forms of cross-cultural communication know-how.

The worldwide acquisition and exploitation of knowledge create, and are created by, conditions which Barham and Heimer (1998), in their impressive study of the Swedish–Swiss industrial giant ABB, describe as 'global connectivity'. This is not just a reference to the exploitation of new information and communications technology; this is also 'a frame of mind that encourages people to take independent action yet feel part of and responsible to a bigger whole from which they derive important competitive benefits and to which, in return, they must add value' (Barham and Heimer, 1998). In their influential study of the transnational corporation, Harvard scholars Ghoshal and Bartlett (1998) have pointed out that there must be 'a new management mentality' in globally operating organizations as they reach out for 'global efficiency, national responsiveness, and world-wide leveraging of innovations and learning'.

Leading firms that have adopted the creed of globalization are beginning to show us what forms business communication is now taking. ABB, for example, actively encourages its 5,000 profit centres around the world to 'depend on each other for ideas, information and resources' (Barham and Heimer, 1998) as a key element in its globalization strategy. Nokia, the Finnish mobile telephone concern, realizes that a Finnocentric view of the future in their business sector can block the influx of knowledge and ideas. So this company makes use of knowledgeable outsiders to help it discern future trends, whilst making English its corporate language (*Economist*, 1999). The Danish pharmaceutical and healthcare company Novo Nordisk wants all its employees, of which 3,600 work outside Denmark, to identify with the company's long-term objective of setting the standards globally for social responsibility practice and reporting (Novo Nordisk, 1999). All of these business activities depend on communication practices, the core of which lies in relationship management among employees and external stakeholders, organizational learning, and networking based both on interpersonal interactions and on global connectivity mediated via information technology.

These three companies would have no disagreement with the words of Jack Welch, CEO of General Electric and arguably the USA's most admired industrial manager: 'The aim of a global business is to get the best ideas from anywhere' (Barham and Heimer, 1998). But getting the ideas is only the first step. The second step challenges firms to 'become adept at translating new knowledge into new ways of behaving' (Garvin, 1998). It appears that the corporate world has yet to draw the cross-cultural implications of all this. The global economy, with its emphasis on networking and the related 'facilitation of multiple learning processes' (Ghoshal and Bartlett, 1998), will, in the word's of the twentieth century's leading management thinker, Peter Drucker (1998), 'require greater self-discipline and even greater emphasis on individual responsibility for relationships and for communications'.

The anthropology-based foundations of cross-cultural management seem hard-pressed to analyze behaviour associated with the knowledge-based economy and the need to develop the new managerial outlooks and competencies which are called for under shibboleths like 'the global mindset' (Jeannet, 2000) or 'global literacy' (Rosen, 2000). Today's firms are in constant pursuit of new concepts 'linking environmental complexity, strategic demands, and organizational capability' (Ghoshal and Bartlett, 1998), whilst learning how to mediate corporate knowledge, values and experience *vis-à-vis* the totality of their increasingly networked shareholders in all parts of the globe. Globalization is creating the need for new ways of understanding, managing and *down-playing* cultural differences, whilst creating new kinds of cross-cultural formats such as multi-cultural project teams with fluctuating memberships, varying longevity and locales of activity, which are impermanent, shifting and increasingly electronically created.

In such a world it is no longer feasible to see culture as a kind of unchained dark force undermining internationally operating firms at every turn. Culture shock, as was argued before, is passé as a construct for explaining forms of arduousness in cross-cultural relationships. As Schneider and Barsoux (1997) correctly point out, the embracing of culture in all its diversity 'as a resource rather than a threat is essential for responding to the demands of a global market economy, for reaping the full benefit of cross-border alliances, and for enhancing organizational learning'. This cannot be said loudly enough.

A TOPSY-TURVEY REPRESENTATION OF LOW-CONTEXT AND HIGH-CONTEXT CULTURE

A noted constraint on the development of cross-cultural management as an academic discipline is the fact that 'quite often, existing theoretical frameworks that have been developed from a domestic context, generally the USA, are applied to other countries and contexts' (Usunier, 1998). This does not merely point up a general problem of ethnocentrism in cross-cultural management research, but highlights the problem of American universalism which wants 'the world – the entire world – to be uniform, generalizable, lawlike, and explainable' (Hampden-Turner and Trompenaars, 1993). So, it is almost natural for Americans to assume that domestic concepts and research findings 'have wide applicability to how organizations (and people) operate in other nations'. A telling example is E. T. Hall's distinction between high-context cultures and low-context cultures, which has had the effect – which surely Hall did not want – of polarizing countries unnecessarily.

This well-known notion was propounded in Hall's famous book, *The silent language*, published in 1959. According to him, each type of culture is typified by its own broad communication style. Thus 'a high-context communication or message is one in which most of the information is already in the person, while very little is in the coded, explicit part of the message. A low-context communication is just the opposite; i.e. the mass of information is vested in the explicit code.' Quite apart from the practical objections to assigning the world's cultures into one group or the other (Claes, 2001), the USA has become the exemplar of low-context culture and Japan an icon for high-context culture.

Such an American self-view permits Americans to see themselves, at least in business, as rational and transparent, though that may not fit with how their foreign business partners see them. But the act of 'elevating' the Japanese to high-context status not only gratifies a deep-seated Japanese aspiration to be different from the rest of humankind, but also precludes the possibility of seeing them as otherwise. But let aficionados of Japanese ultra-high-context otherness and uniqueness meditate on Buruma's (1988) acute observation about something we rarely hear about: namely, the intellectual accessibility of Japan. As he has noted: 'The more formal a society, the more obvious the roles people play. In this respect the Japanese are quite scrutable.'

This suggests that some aspects of Japanese formal behaviour, which are very much on parade in interactions with foreigners, are low-context, if you grasp the underlying logic! Not a small condition, I admit, but bear in mind that grasping Japanese logic tends to mean clearing the brain of some interfering aspects of one's own (Western) logic. Intellectually and perhaps emotionally the latter task is unquestionably the harder one (Littlewood, 1996). But the final damnation of the USA–Japan low-high context square-dance is to be presented in glowing form in John Nathan's study of Sony (1999). The generally low-context style of Sony's business operations in the USA is no match for the high-context machinations of some of their American associates in the epic battle for Columbia Pictures: a fine example of role reversal, as it were.

Cross-cultural management research of course concerns itself with explanations of the impact of cultural variables on managers' behaviour and performance. This vast territory is a tapestry of writing covering comparisons of national cultures, including comparisons of managerial cultures associated with particular countries; negotiating styles; cultural impacts on specific business functions and operations, especially marketing, HRM, and mergers and acquisitions (M&A); contrastive characterizations of societal cultures and even markets based on cultural factors (such as values, ethics, education, role of women, consumer behaviour and so forth). Darlington (1996) produces two tables, reproduced below, which show, researchers' contrasting approaches to the study of national culture (Table 3.1), and comparisons of cultural dimensions (Table 3.2).

Table 3.1 Comparison of national culture studies (After Darlington, 1996)

Researchers	Perspective	Methodology	Implications
Hofstede (1982, 1991, 1991a)	Differences in behaviour	Work-related value survey	Distinct national cultures
Trompenaars (1984) Hampden-Turner and Trompenaars (1993)	Differences in behaviour	Value orientations Dilemmatics	Distinct national cultures, e.g. Seven Cultures of Capitalism – different sustainability
Lessem and Neubauer (1994)	Multiple levels of difference based on philosophies	Comparative surveys of art, religion, literature, philosophy and societal constructs	Four diverse management systems form a basis for European unity
Bonthous (1994)	Types of intelligence system	Comparative analysis of preferred styles	Need to develop a balance of all styles to avoid an organizational learning disability
Said (1991, 1994)	National literature	Comparative analysis of textual style and content	Appreciate the differences and recognize we make culture as part of self-organization process
Tayeb (1988, 1994)	National and corporate	Literature, cultural and work attitude surveys	Proposed causal model of culture
Maznevski (1994)	Differences in value orientation	Value orientations Training intervention with performance assessment	Proposed model of synergistic integration
Di Stefano and Lane (1992)	Differences in value orientation	Case studies Literature review	Profile of effective global executives
Adler (1991)	Trends in OB/HRM publishing	Literature review	Shift to cross-cultural interaction Recognition of culture's importance Leadership of academic/professional community of discourse
Heller and Wilpert (1981)	Participation in decision-making	Questionnaire	Five methods of decision-making and power displacement effect
Laurent (1983)	Managers' implicit theories on management	Questionnaire survey	Country clusters of implicit theory, e.g. organizations as authority systems

Source: *Managing Across Cultures* (1996) by P. Joynt & M. Warner.

Table 3.2 Comparison of cultural dimensions (After Darlington, 1996)

	Kluckhohn and Strodtbeck (1961)	Hall (1960, 1966, 1973) Hall and Hall (1987)	Hofstede (1980... 1991)	Trompenaars (1984... 1993)	Trompenaars and Hampden-Turner (1994)	Maznevski (1994)
Human Nature	Good, Evil, Neutral, Mixed: Changeable, unchangeable	Agreements	Uncertainty Avoidance index	Universalism: Particularism	Universalism: Particularism	Good/evil: changeable
Relation to Nature	Subjugation, Harmony, Mastery		Uncertainty Avoidance index	Internal: External Orientation	Inner: Outer Directed	Subjugation, Mastery, Harmony
Activity Orientation	Doing, Being, Being-in-becoming	Monochronic, Polychronic (interacts with individualism)	Masculinity index	Achievement: Ascription	Achievement: Ascription, Analysing: Integrating	Doing, Being, Containing and Controlling (Thinking)
Human Relationships	Individual, Collective, Hierarchical	Amount of space, Possessions, Friendship, Communication	Power Distance index, Individualism index	Equality: Hierarchy Individualism: Collectivism Affective: Neutral	Equality: Hierarchy Individualism: Communitarianism	Individual, Collective, Hierarchical
Relation to Time	Past, Present, Future	Past, Future	Long-term Orientation	Sequential: Synchronic Past, Present, Future	Sequential: Synchronic	
Space Orientation	Public, Private, Mixed	Public, Private				

Source: *Managing Across Cultures* (1996) by P. Joynt & M. Warner.

CULTURE'S PERIODIC TABLES

From Tables 3.1 and 3.2 it is clear that researchers' are overwhelmingly preoccupied with difference and comparison and only indirectly with the nature of interactions. This proceeds logically from their concept of culture, which has a seldom noted property: its amenability for generating lists and rankings. In the literature there are lists of cultural characteristics, of cultural and societal factors that impact on companies and managers, comparative cultural variations; lists of ideal attributes of global managers (not to mention, international managers, multinational and transnational managers, regional managers and Euro-managers), and corresponding lists of associated mindsets; check lists for creating synergy in multicultural teams, for assessing potential expatriate managers' needs, and negotiating with various nationalities; rankings of cultural constraints; and clustering of countries according to educational opportunity, propensity to change job as well as cultural similarities and differences, and so forth. The nature of the listings draws an analogy from the world of chemistry.

There are branches of chemistry which concern themselves with the description of the properties of individual chemical elements. There are other branches of the subject which concern themselves with the properties of substances, which are the products of chemical reactions. It is of course well-known that when, under given conditions, two chemicals combine, the resulting substance may have properties which are not associated with the constituent elements. A simple example is common salt (NaCl), a compound of a metallic element sodium (Na), which in its natural state reacts violently with air and produces very stable compounds, and chlorine (Cl), which is a greenish-yellow toxic and pungent gas. Now to the analogy. It seems to me that the discourse of writers and teachers of cross-cultural management is more preoccupied, as it were, with the properties of individual elements than with the product of their combinations. They tend to assume that a combination of elements must result in something unpleasant, unwanted or uncontrollable. At risk of exaggeration to make the point, this notion can be expressed formulaically as follows:

$C_1 + C_2$ = culture shock, friction, misunderstanding

In this equation C_1 and C_2 represent any given (national) cultures except each other. This view of the world is clearly conditional on seeing the world as made up of a huge number of clearly defined elements, but ignores the empirical fact that these elements occur in fused combinations in which the chemical and physical properties of the constituent elements have been transmuted to form a 'new' substance – this is the equivalent to the creation of a third culture (see Beechler and Bird, 1999, on the fusion of Japanese and American cultures to create a *third* one). In this case the equation can be expressed thus:

$C_1 + C_2 = C_3$, where C_3 is a new cultural hybrid

The study of C_1 and C_2 is comparative management. But cross-cultural management is much more concerned with C_3, a new cultural hybrid. The cross-cultural chemist, as it were, is interested, for example, in how to keep the new formation stable and in ensuring that its properties have utility, that is sustain a form of cooperation in contexts as diverse as international negotiation or complex as the creation of a strategic alliance.

The operational world of cross-cultural management is not readily definable or representable purely or even largely in terms of culture's equivalent of the chemist's periodic table. It will be helpful to explain the analogy for readers who are not familiar with chemistry. In chemistry, the periodic table is an arrangement of elements in rows in order of increasing atomic number or the number of protons in the nucleus. In the 1860s chemists noticed that certain groups of elements behaved in similar ways and tried to set the groups out clearly in the table. Nine distinct groups are recognized (*Dorling Kindersley science encyclopedia*, 1996). Hofstede's models, by the way, constitute an especially ingenious and elaborate form of culture's periodic table.

As cross-cultural management is or should be especially interested in C_3, the challenge is to understand and explain the world of cross-cultural fusions and fumblings within and among organizations. For this we need a new approach to understanding 'the chemical elements' of culture. The proper study of cross-cultural management is cross-cultural interactions, for which familiarization with the 'cultural periodic tables' is of course extremely useful, provided that it is recognized that the tables have severely in-built limitations. I will keep with the analogy for a little longer, but it should not be pressed too far. In chemistry an entire science is based on the periodic table; culture's periodic tables and its listings spawn a diffuse sub-field of management studies, namely cross-cultural management, that lacks paradigmatic coherence.

CROSS-CULTURAL MANAGEMENT: WEDDED TO THE PAST

One striking feature of many frequently cited schemes is that they are time-worn; they should be passé, but are reproduced as if they are valid for today's business world. E. T. Hall's promulgation of low-context and high-context cultures, which is still extensively quoted, is more than 40 years old (Hall, 1959). Hofstede's *Culture's consequences* was first published in 1980 and the data were gathered during 1968 and 1972.[2] Deresky (2000) reproduces a model of country clusters first published in 1985. Tyler's 130-year-old definition of culture, which was cited in chapter 2, is still quoted in management texts. Here are more examples.

Authors still cite an American professor, John Graham, and various collaborators on international negotiation, referring to research first published nearly 20 years ago (e.g. Graham and Herberger, 1983), whilst Usunier (2000) cites an article about negotiations with the Japanese published in 1970, as if the Japanese have not learnt a trick or two in the following three decades (Van Zandt, 1970). Laurent's well-known work on differences in managerial style, published in 1983 (when Mrs Thatcher was 'hand-bagging' Europe) is still quoted by current authors (Mead, 1994; Schneider and Barsoux, 1997). Likewise, the famous 1952 Krober and Kluckhohn definition of culture, which was quoted in chapter 2, is ubiquitously cited. In their co-edited book, Belgian authors Dupriez and Simons (2000) devote three pages to the work of the eminent, but long-departed anthropologists, Ruth Benedict (1887–1948) and Bronislaw Malinowski (1884–1942). Staggeringly, Harris and Moran (1996) compare 'typical' US and Japanese organizations based on work published more than a quarter of a century ago (Ouchi and Jaeger, 1974).

In an article in the *Harvard Business Review*, published in 1991, Hampden-Turner observed that 'the most important boundaries in the world today [are] the often subtle but all-pervasive differences in cultural perspective that shape how managers from different societies conceive their role and their work'. If we accept the truth of that, it is surely remarkable that the corresponding putative field of expertise – cross-cultural management – is regularly making use of models, concepts and human data that are *decades* old. How many people have ever thought that many of Hofstede's informants of three decades ago are now dead? Do their children and grandchildren really have the same values? That, logically, is what advocates of Hofstede appear to believe. Besides, was working for IBM in the 1960s, then one of the most prestigious American companies, the same as working for it nearly 40 years later? Are the work values so transferable across time as Hofstedians appear uncritically to believe? Can there be, I wonder, a field in the entire spectrum of the management sciences that is so regressive as cross-cultural management? Table 3.3 uses some historical data to emphasize the backward-lookingness of some cross-cultural management authors.

THE LITERATURE'S GRAND LACUNAE

Before passing further comment on the above schemes, classifications and representations, we can usefully turn to Bartholomew and Adler's (1996) survey of cross-cultural management topics in the mainstream international management

Table 3.3 Cross-cultural management: wedded to the past

Cited author and year of cited publication	Cited in current authors	Notable world events
Benedict (1934)	Dupriez and Simons (2000)	Hitler proclaims the Third Reich
Malinowski (1944/1989)	Dupriez and Simons (2000)	World War II: Bretton Woods Conference
Kroeber and Kluckhohn (1952)	Widely quoted	Eisenhower elected US President
Hall (1959)	Widely quoted	Castro proclaims Cuban revolution
Hofstede (data collection, 1968–72)	Hofstede (1980)	Vietnam War (1965–75); Cultural Revolution in China (1966–69)
Van Zandt (1970)	Usunier (2000)	The jumbo jet goes into service
Ouchi and Jaeger (1974)	Harris and Moran (1996)	Watergate
Hofstede, *Culture's consequences* (1980)	Widely quoted	Emergence of Solidarity in Poland
Graham and Herberger (1983)	Harris and Moran (1996)	The CD is first marketed
Laurent (1983)	Schneider and Barsoux (1997)	
Ronen and Shenkar (1985)	Deresky (2000)	Gorbachev becomes Soviet leader

literature. These scholars surveyed no fewer than 28,707 articles in 73 academic and professional management journals covering a five-year period from October 1985 to September 1990. They found that 661 articles (9.3%) on organizational behaviour and HRM had international scope, inclusion of culture, and culture's impact.

Three publishing trends were discerned in the period of the survey. First, Bartholomew and Adler note that there is 'the shift from single country studies and comparative articles to publications focusing on cross-cultural interaction'. Second, they find that the literature generally accepts that 'culture's impact on managerial behaviour has become well recognized . . . culture makes a difference to . . . organizational behaviour and human resource management'. But they note that research into the impact of cultural differences on (a) technological innovation and (b) the transnational firm is wanting. In their words: 'To date, the academic community, by itself, has remained primarily dedicated to single culture and comparative research which, while still necessary, *is no longer sufficient – and therefore no longer relevant – for the competitive environment of today's transnational firm'* (Bartholomew and Adler, 1996, added emphasis). But worse is to come.

The concept of cross-cultural management driving this book was a conviction that the field embraces collaborative learning, knowledge-sharing and networking. These are all activities which draw internationally operating companies into cross-cultural interaction on a major scale. What does the current cross-cultural literature have to say on these specific topics? The answer, extraordinarily enough, appears to be: not much. A search of the ABI/Inform and MCB Emerald databases, which cover articles in 1,000 mainstream management and related journals from 1998 to the present and 130 MCB journals across a broad spectrum of management topics from 1967 to 2000 respectively, using 'cross-cultural' and 'intercultural' in the key words produced the following results (Table 3.4):

Table 3.4 Selective literature search for items on cross-/intercultural learning, networking and knowledge-sharing

ABI/Inform	Total	MBC Emerald	Total
Cross-/intercultural learning	1	Cross-/intercultural learning	0
Cross-/intercultural networking	0	Cross-/intercultural networking	0
Cross-/intercultural knowledge-sharing	0	Cross-/intercultural knowledge-sharing	0

In addition, a search of books and other productions on cross-cultural management at Copenhagen Business School identified two articles with relevant titles: 'The cross-cultural transfer of management practices' (Gill and Wong, 1998) and 'An examination of cross-cultural quality management' (Yavas and Marcoulides, 1996). There can be no doubt that a more thorough search of databases and conference proceedings might pick up a few more references, but just a few would be the result of the trawl.[3] It is hard not to conclude that 'the cross-cultural knowledge industry' is not much enamoured of the world of organizations, being mainly content to conceive solutions in various forms of cross-cultural awareness. Culture in cross-cultural management studies, under the influence of the essentialist wing, looks incredibly variegated and maddeningly complex. Furthermore two cross-cultural management scenarios can never be the same, and the possibilities for cultural interpretations so rich. And therein lies the deception. Nobody seems to realize – or care – that culture conceived as essence and difference is simply a massive wheel reinventing itself.

There is some limited coverage of cross-cultural learning, knowledge-sharing and networking in the mainstream literature (e.g. Deresky, 2000; Harris and Moran, 1996; Schneider and Barsoux, 1997). Hampden-Turner (1991), writing in the influential *Harvard Business Review*, makes an explicit distinction between the more self-seeking American styles of learning knowledge-sharing and the Asian and continental European cultures, whose practices are more group-based. Writing in an anthology of writing on cross-cultural management, Hughes-Wiener (1995) is predominantly concerned with 'learning how to learn about other cultures'. His focus is the 'sojourner', which does not get us very far. But it is surely extraordinary that no author has, it seems, written a book on cross-cultural management from the three perspectives of learning, knowledge-sharing and networks as their point of departure. Evidently one does not write books on cross-cultural management that take a nominally non-cultural perspective. So when Bartholomew and Adler (1996) make a plea for a conceptual shift in cross-cultural management studies, they are truly a voice in the wilderness.

If we attempt to account for this perturbing situation, the following reasons suggest themselves. First, there can be little doubt that the dominance of essentialist culture makes it hard to develop new approaches, so there are no new conceptual frameworks which have been widely adopted. The result is a massive reliance on Hofstede and even Hall, who produced his low-context/high-context distinction some 20 years before the Dutch titan.[4] Second, it appears too that cross-cultural management writers generally prefer to regard actors in broadly definable cultural terms and not against the concrete background of organizational functions, real industries and real problems. Managers or other actors in cross-cultural situations are seldom seen as being involved in inter- or intra-organizational processes (such as learning, networking and knowledge-sharing), in which culture-as-difference and culture-as-essence become *awkwardly commingled with other factors*.

These other factors include information about organizations' policy and strategy, their decision-making structures, their vision as well as information on their products and services and relative status in their business sector or sectors. Rather than consider cultural phenomena as having *impacts*, which regrettably suggests the making of a damaging and enduring impression on structures and processes, the challenge is to research and understand how those phenomena weave themselves and do not weave themselves into organizations and organizational thinking. *That* is a challenge of a high intellectual order.

All in all it is not surprising that the only area of cross-cultural interaction that is covered in the general cross-cultural management literature is negotiation, which has, of course, the exciting ingredients of different communication styles and languages in contention. Cross-cultural negotiation is seldom seen as a collaborative mutual learning experience; it is rather presented as resolving *conflict*.

As if this were not bad enough, even the most detailed studies of the cultural dimensions of international mergers and acquisitions are produced by people who do not regard themselves as belonging intellectually to cross-cultural management studies (see Gertsen and other contributors in Gertsen et al., 1998). This point is worthy of more attention even though a small digression is necessitated. In these vastly intricate inter-organizational fusions the management of cultural difference combines high expectations, massive commitment of financial resources, the redeployment of hundreds or thousands of people, the relocation of a proportion of those staff in specialist management functions with new colleagues from the 'other' organization. There is a statistically high rate of underperformance, if not out and out failure. The much cited M&A underperformance is, from a behavioural point of view, connected to two factors, namely partner selection and lack of (inter-organizational) cultural fit, that is 'the way in which the integration or acculturation process is (mis)managed and the negative response of employees to widescale organizational change' (Cartwright, 1998).

The essentialist concept of culture is arguably incapable of equipping researchers with adequate conceptual tools for investigating and understanding these immensely complicated processes. That itself may explain why 'cultural clashes in *international* M&A still remain largely under-investigated, in spite of the interesting fact that they are cross-cultural not only at the organizational level but also at the societal level' (Larsson and Risberg, 1998). Besides, as a recent feature in the *Economist* (2000) on the DaimlerChrysler merger noted, 'the cross-border angle' – differences in language and culture – 'come to the fore only when other things are already going wrong'. Which suggests that 'culture' is not a cause, more a subsequent exacerbator of cross-cultural tensions.

Either way, the mainstream cross-cultural literature has remarkably little to say about M&A, which have some claim to be called cross-cultural management's grand theatre. This is the kind of intellectual indifference which is keeping the academic community permanently time-lagged behind the culture-vaulting operations of TNCs. In the entire field of international business, nowhere is the issue of culture more problematical *and* arguably more difficult to research than in

M&A activity. Yet 'the cross-cultural knowledge industry' (Segalla et al., 2000) keeps a safe distance. In one of the few contributions Olie (1995) makes a very important statement:

> Culture is not to be viewed as a simple variable that societies or organizations possess. It must be simultaneously understood as an active, living phenomenon through which people create and recreate the worlds in which they live. Culture is a lens through which we perceive the world surrounding us; it is sensemaking process, a frame of reference that guides our thoughts and actions. In acquisitions . . . *it has to be recreated.* (added emphasis)

These criticisms simply acknowledge the fact that the manifestation of culture in the everyday life of organizations and managers is overwhelmingly complex. But the real problem with these schemes is, as noted, that they are dependent on a restrictive concept of culture. One not immediately obvious consequence of this is a gulf between practitioners and management researchers with respect to culture in international business operations. It is worth quoting Bartholomew and Adler (1996), who are keenly aware of the need for new concepts and frameworks:

> Structurally, the academic community works on 'slow-cycle time'; significant time-lags occur between changes in firms' competitive environment and changes in scholars' conceptualizations.[5] Even longer time-lags occur between research design and ultimate research publication. . . . The academic community . . . continues to lack the rigorous conceptual and analytical frameworks needed to understand the impact of such [environmental] changes on organizational behaviour.

'The cross-cultural knowledge industry' seems to feel uncomfortable with that kind of notion. It prefers culture to be static, stable and replete with its periodic tables. Yet modern business life, with its emphasis on multicultural teamworking and resultant inter- and intra-organizational knowledge-sharing, is a permanent state of cultural recreation. This is the most demonstrably obvious point about culture in today's business world. For cultural purists this may be bad news, but that is the reality.

TOWARDS CROSS-CULTURAL MANAGEMENT'S NEW HORIZON

The schemes and representations cited in this and previous chapters have practical or academic relevance, but their explanatory power from the cross-cultural management perspective being advanced in this book is variable. The representations are too often confirmatory: that is they confirm, or least maintain, that in a given culture the attitudes and behaviour at the national level tend to be manifested like this rather than like that. They do not necessarily help to make sense of what happens and why in cross-cultural management situations when placed in the wider intra- or inter-organizational contexts, as the mini cases presented in chapter 1 attempted to demonstrate.

Adler's definition of cross-cultural management, which was quoted in chapter 2, may be held up as the representative definition of the field, but this definition and the thinking which still takes the nation-state as point of departure do not fully resonate with the interactions of transnational corporations and organizations in an increasingly globally networked economy. As Adler and a colleague noted in 1993: 'Discussions concerning the influence of culture on strategic efficacy remain time-lagged and disconnected from other corporate realities' (Adler and Ghadar, 1993). It would be a very bold person who would argue that these time-lags and the disconnections have been reduced in the intervening years.

There is more to this than a traditional reluctance on the part of management educators to 'get [their] hands dirty' (Aaronson, 1996) with research and training involvements with the corporate world. As a recent *Financial Times* supplement on business education noted, there is a new factor in the equation: 'Even the best business schools now realise that they have neither the global presence nor the wealth of knowledgeable faculty to satisfy the requirements of their largest international customers' (Bradshaw, 2000). It seems that those engaged in cross-cultural management and teaching are being perpetually outpaced by the changes in the world economy and in the nature of management work.

Hence, Segalla, Fischer and Sandner (2000) have chosen to criticize 'the cross-cultural knowledge industry for its slowness to develop new, business-specific information useful to the current problems that European firms face . . . cross-border integration problems associated with international mergers, acquisitions, joint ventures and alliances'. The unduly powerful Hofstedian grip on cross-cultural writing and thinking may be one reason for this 'slowness'. Another reason, paradoxically, concerns the growing reservations of cross-cultural management scholars about concepts of culture and methodologies for researching culture in international contexts. All this supports the argument for reformulation of the scientific domain of cross-cultural management.

The classic, essentialist concept of culture which has dominated the literature of international, cross-cultural management has been increasingly abandoned within the field of anthropology in which it originated (Søderberg and Holden, 2001). Anthropologists, as well as media and organizational analysts, are beginning to regard culture as based on shared or partly shared patterns of meaning and interpretation as opposed to sharing broadly consistent, though complex, patterns of behaviour and modes of existence. These patterns of meaning are produced, reproduced, and continually changed by the people identifying with them and *negotiating* with them in the course of social interaction. Thus, people's identifications with, and affiliation to, a multiplicity of different cultures, e.g. national, organizational, professional, gender and generational cultures, are subject to change, and boundaries between cultural communities become fluid and contingent (Hannerz, 1996).[6]

Under this approach, culture is conceived as being made up of relations, rather than as stable systems of form and substance (Haastrup, 1996). This implies that national cultures, corporate cultures or professional cultures, for example, are seen as symbolic practices that only come into existence in relation to, and in contrast with, other cultural communities. People's cultural identity constructions and their social organizations of meaning are, in other words, contextual (Fog Olwig and Haastrup, 1997). This relational approach to culture and the idea of cultural complexity suggest that every individual embodies a unique combination of personal, cultural and social experiences, and thus that ultimately any communication and negotiation is intercultural.

This social constructionist approach to culture implies that so-called cultural 'data' are in fact 'social constructs' made on the basis of the practitioners' and the researchers' own cultural thought patterns and the concepts and categories to which they are socialized. This approach to understanding and explaining culture will be developed in the course of the book. But an implication of social constructionism is that outcomes of cross-cultural collaboration and integration processes between organizations cannot be predicted with any certainty.

Unlike most research in the international business field, the constructionist approach is neither normative nor prognostic (see Kleppestø, 1998; Søderberg, 1999). Its most prominent scientific contributions to the study of cultural complexity in the management field are contextually sensitive, qualitative case studies focusing on the organizational actors' interpretations, identity-constructions and sense-making processes (Weick, 1995). The approach has been applied to investigations of cross-border mergers and acquisitions (Gertsen and Søderberg, 2000). Even so, as Bell points out, 'the categories used by observers are themselves culturally determined'; and he adds: 'It is of course a trap for any social scientist, but *worse for the cultural researcher*' (personal communication, added emphasis). With that important caveat, this book will make use of social constructionist perspectives both in the treatment of the case studies (chapters 5–8) and in developing the notion that cross-cultural management is a form of negotiation, whereby persons in interactions acquire *participative competence* for working in a multicultural team or mediating knowledge transnationally by means of in-company seminars.

We have already noted the reservations of Bartholomew and Adler (1996) about the development of cross-cultural management education and research. For their part, Cavusgil and Das (1997), in a study of 'problems of comparative research design, sampling, instrumentation, and data collection and analysis', conclude that many problems, after 30 years of discussion, 'still remain largely intractable or often ignored'. For their part, scholars Osland and Bird (2000) 'feel increasingly frustrated with the accepted conceptualisations of culture', adding that one consequence is that 'business schools tend to teach culture in simple-minded terms, glossing over nuances and ignoring complexities'.

'The cross-cultural knowledge industry' is, it seems, under some pressure to reformulate its guiding notions. A starting point is the recognition by Bartholomew and Adler of a need for 'a conceptual shift: from a hierarchical perspective of cultural influence, compromise and adaptation, to one of collaborative cross-cultural learning'. These scholars have also focused on the links between cross-cultural management and (a) technological innovation, (b) the management of transnational enterprises, and (c) strategic networks and social networks (Bartholomew and Adler, 1996).

The repositioning of cross-cultural management into the domains of what Burton-Jones (1999) envisages as the fusion of 'learning networks and business networks' would appear to be plainly part of the desired conceptual shift. Once this shift has been made (i.e. once it has been accepted by researchers), the quest will be on for new concepts of cultural complexity with greater explanatory power. This has been recognized by Belgian scholars Dupriez and Simons (2000), who, though wedded to a mainly essentialist concept of culture, define cross-cultural management (*le management interculturel*) 'as a form of management which, recognising the existence of local cultures, attempts to integrate the values upon which these cultures rest in different organisational functions and, at the same time, tries its best [*s'efforce*] to coordinate these functions in the heart of the company policy'.

This observation recognizes that cross-cultural management has something to do with transposing values from one cultural ambience to another. But that does not go far enough, partly because values are still signifiers of cultural difference. The task facing scholars of cross-cultural management is to make precisely the conceptual shift advocated above by Adler and Bartholomew (1992). As the forthcoming case studies will reveal, major companies have already made this shift in their operations. The purpose of this book is to stimulate new concepts to characterize this shift.

THE NEED TO REFORMULATE THE CONCEPTUAL FOUNDATION OF CROSS-CULTURAL MANAGEMENT

The scene is being set, then, for a concept of cross-cultural management as the management of multiple cultures within and among organizations, involving processes of knowledge transfer and organizational learning. These activities facilitate the functioning of networks which are composed of an inconceivably large number of overlapping social and information networks linking people and organizations worldwide. The classic concept of culture, which depends strongly on culture-as-essence and culture-as-difference, sits akwardly with such complex assemblages and comminglings of culture. This is where Bartholomew and Adler's enormously important notion of 'collaborative cross-cultural learning' comes in. It is, as we shall eventually see, one of the key factors in the reconstitution of cross-cultural management as a distinct sub-discipline of international management.

The identified terrain of the management of multiple, networked cultures is awesome, complicated, subject to change, and massively overlaid with technology. This is the new heartland of cross-cultural management, both as an operating domain and as a conceptual field for which the practitioners need new competencies and the academics need to develop more conceptual tools. This is the heartland which I will attempt to map out. Having concluded this short, sharp review of cross-cultural management as it is discussed and understood in the current literature, we can now move on cross-cultural management's new terrain. It will be helpful to introduce at this juncture a new definition of this conceptually problematical subject area, which both combats the restrictive, anthropologically derived culture concepts *and* acknowledges the shaping forces and influences on management thinking, attitudes and behaviour in the globally connected economy. From now on cross-cultural management will be conceived in these terms:

> The core task of cross-cultural management is to facilitate and direct synergistic action and learning at interfaces where knowledge, values and experience are transferred into multicultural domains of implementation.

The point has come at which to abandon culture for the time being. As cross-cultural management is being conceived as a form of knowledge management, then we need to know more about this activity, the assumptions which underpin it, and the particular challenges associated with the management of knowledge as an international organizational resource.

NOTES

1. 'Once more to our question then: what is culture? In definition framed in somewhat human terms it is *the ability to convey great thoughts* (lit. statements) *with small gestures*' (translation: N. J. Holden).

2. As this book was going to press, the second edition of Hofstede's *Culture's consequences: Comparing values, behaviors, institutions and organizations across nations* was published. According to the author, the book 'has been completely rewritten, as testified by a new subtitle that stresses its interdisciplinary aspirations' (Hofstede, 2001). Although it has been substantially updated, the basic material for analysis remains that which Hofstede used in the first edition of *Culture's consequences* (1980).

3. Cross-cultural learning is mentioned by Bartholomew and Adler (1996); cross-cultural knowledge transfer by Hu and Warner (1996); and cross-cultural networking by Bartholomew and Adler (1996) and by Hampden-Turner and Trompenaars (1996).

4. I do not wish to give the impression that Hall was solely well-known for the low-context/ high-context dichotomy. He also concentrated on the 'microcultural analysis' of culture: tone of voice, gestures, time and space (see Claes, 2001).

5. This is an insoluble problem. This book, which is trying to be innovative in some respects, will be basing concepts around company experiences which inform the case studies, for which the research began in 1998.

6. This paragraph drew the following comment from Roger Bell (personal communication), which is worth quoting: 'Ethnocentric unreconstructed national assumptions inform the way people deal in reality with contacts with the rest of the world. Holden's world of shifting cultural frontiers and moving habitats is not the world into which people are born or grow up in and they still need to be educated by the much maligned "so called cross cultural knowledge industry".'

REFERENCES

Aaronson, S. (1996). Dinosaurs in the global economy? American graduate business schools in the 1980s and 1990s. In: Amdam, R. P. (ed.). *Management, education and competitiveness.* London: Routledge, pp. 212–26.

Adler, N. (1991). *International dimensions of organizational behavior.* Boston, MA: PWS-Kent Publishing Company.

Adler, N. and Bartholomew, S. (1992). Academic and professional communities of discourse: Generating knowledge on transnational human resource management. *Journal of International Business Studies* 23: 226–32.

Adler, N. and Ghadar, F. (1993). A strategic phase approach to international human resources management. In: Wong-Rieger, D. and Rieger, F. (eds). *International management research: Looking to the future.* Berlin: de Gruyter, pp. 55–77.

Argyris, C. (1999). *On organizational learning.* Oxford: Blackwell.

Barham, K. and Heimer, C. (1998). *ABB – the dancing giant.* London: Financial Times Prentice Hall.

Bartholomew, S. and Adler, N. (1996). Building networks and crossing borders: the dynamics of knowledge generation in a transnational world. In: Joynt and Wasner (1996), pp. 7–32.

Beechler, S. and Bird, A. (eds) (1999). *Japanese multinationals abroad: Individual and organizational learning.* New York: Oxford University Press.

Benedict, R. (1934). *Patterns of culture.* Boston, MA: Houghton Mifflin. Cited in: Dupriez and Simons (2000).

Bonthous, J. M. (1994). Culture – the missing intelligence variable. *The Strategic Planning Society News,* March.

Bradshaw, D. (2000). Market place gets more crowded. *Financial Times: Survey of Business Education.* 23 May.

Burton-Jones, A. (1999). *Knowledge capitalism: Business, work, and learning in the new economy.* Oxford: Oxford University Press.

Buruma, I. (1988). *A Japanese mirror: Heroes and villains of Japanese culture.* London: Penguin Books.

Cartwright, S. (1998). International mergers and acquisitions: The issues and challenges. In: Gertsen et al. (1998).

Cavusgil, T. and Das, A. (1997). Methodological issues in empirical cross-cultural research: A survey of the management literature and a framework. *Management International Review* 37(1): 71–96.

Claes, M.-T. (2001). Direct/indirect and formal/informal communication: A reassessment. In: Cooper, C. L., Cartwright, S. and Earley, R. C. (eds). *The international handbook of organizational culture and climate.* Chichester, UK: John Wiley & Sons.

Clegg, S. and Clarke, T. (1999). The organizational impact of globalisation. A lecture delivered at Copenhagen Business School and based on Clegg, S. and Clarke, T. (1998). *Changing paradigms: The transformation of management knowledge in the 21st century.* London: HarperCollins.

Crainer, S. (1996). *Key management ideas: Thinkers that changed the management world.* London: Financial Times/Pitman.

Darlington, G. (1996). Culture, A theoretical review. In: Joynt and Wasner (1996), pp. 33–55.

Deresky, H. (2000). *International management: Management across borders and cultures.* Upper Saddle River, NJ: Prentice Hall.

Di Stefano, J. J. and Lane, H. W. (1992). *International management behaviour.* Boston, MA: PWS Kent.

Dicken, P. (1999). *Global shift: Transforming the world economy.* London: Paul Chapman Publishing.

Dixon, N. M. (2000). *Common knowledge: How companies thrive by sharing what they know.* Boston, MA: Harvard Business School Press.

Dorling Kindersley science encyclopedia (1996) (ed. S. McKeever). London: Dorling Kindersley.

Drucker, P. (1998). The coming of the new organization. In: *Harvard Business Review on knowledge management.* Boston, MA: Harvard Business School Publishing, pp. 1–19. (First published in *Harvard Business Review.* January–February 1988.)

Dupriez, P. and Simons, S. (eds) (2000). *La résistance culturelle: Fondements, applications et implications du management interculturel.* Brussels: De Boeck & Larcier.

Economist (1999). Survey of mobile telecommunications. 9 October.

Economist (2000). Merger brief: The DaimlerChrysler emulsion. 29 July: 69–70.

Financial Times (1999). Survey: Knowledge management. 10 November.

Fog Olwig, K. and Haastrup, K. (1997). *Siting Culture. The shifting anthropological object.* London and New York: Routledge.

Garvin, D. A. (1998). Building a learning organization. *Harvard Business Review on management knowledge.* Boston, MA: Harvard Business School Press, pp. 47–80.

Gertsen, M. and Søderberg, A.-M. (2000). Cultural change processes in mergers: A social constructionist perspective. Unpublished manuscript. Copenhagen Business School.

Gertsen, M. G., Søderberg, A.-M. and Torp, J. E. (eds) (1998). *Cultural dimensions of international mergers and acquisitions.* Berlin: de Gruyter.

Ghoshal, S. and Bartlett, C. (1998). *Managing across borders.* London: Random House.

Gill, R. and Wong, A. (1998). The cross-cultural transfer of management practices: The case of Japanese human resource management practices in Singapore. *International Journal of Human Resource Management* 9(1): 116–35.

Graham, J. and Herberger, R. (1983). Negotiating abroad – don't shoot from the hip. *Harvard Business Review.* July–August. Also cited in: Harris and Moran (1996).

Haastrup, K. (1996). *A passage to anthropology: Between experience and theory.* London and New York: Routledge.

Hall, E. T. (1959/1973). *The silent language.* New York: Doubleday. Also cited in: Usunier (2000).

Hall, E. T. (1960). The silent language in overseas business. *Harvard Business Review.* May–June: 87–96.

Hall, E. T. (1966). *The hidden dimension.* Garden City, NY: Doubleday.

Hall, E. T. and Hall, M. R. (1987). *Hidden differences: Doing business with the Japanese.* Garden City, NY: Doubleday.

Hampden-Turner, C. (1991). The boundaries of business: The cross-cultural quagmire. *Harvard Business Review.* September–October: 94–6.

Hampden-Turner, C. and Trompenaars, F. (1993). *The seven cultures of capitalism: Value systems for creating wealth in the United States, Britain, Japan, Germany, France, Sweden and the Netherlands.* London: Judy Piatkus.

Hampden-Turner, C. and Trompenaars, F. (1994). *The seven cultures of capitalism: Value systems for creating wealth in the United States, Britain, Japan, Germany, France, Sweden and the Netherlands.* London: July Piatkus.

Hampden-Turner, C. and Trompenaars, F. (1996). A world turned upside down: doing business in Asia. In Joynt and Warner (1996), pp. 275–305.

Hannerz, U. (1996). *Transnational connections: Culture, people, places.* London: Routledge.

Harris, P. and Moran, R. (1996). *Managing cultural differences: Leadership strategies for a new world of business.* Houston, TX: Gulf Publishing.

Heller, F. A. and Wilpert, B. (1981). *Competence and power in managerial decision-making.* Chichester, UK: John Wiley & Sons.

Hofstede, G. (1980/1991). *Culture's consequences: International differences in work-related values.* Beverly Hills, CA: Sage Publications.

Hofstede, G. (1982). Intercultural cooperation in organizations. *Management Decision* 20: 53–67.

Hofstede, G. (1991a). *Culture and organizations: Intercultural cooperation and its importance for survival – software of the mind.* London: McGraw-Hill.

Hofstede, G. (2001). *Culture's consequences: Comparing values, behaviors, institutions and organizations across nations* (second edition). Thousand Oaks, CA: Sage Publications.

Hu, Y. and Warner, M. (1996). Cross-cultural factors in competitive advantage at home and abroad. In Joynt and Warner (1996), pp. 376–97.

Hughes-Wiener, G. (1995). The 'learning how to learn' approach to cross-cultural orientation. In: Jackson (1995), pp. 380–99.

Jackson, T. (ed.) (1995). *Cross-cultural management.* Oxford: Butterworth-Heinemann.

Jeannet, J.-P. (2000) *Managing with a global mindset.* London: Financial Times/Prentice Hall.

Johnson, G. and Scholes, K. (1999). *Exploring corporate strategy.* London: Prentice Hall Europe.

Joynt, P. and Warner, M. (1996). *Managing across cultures: Issues and perspectives.* London: International Thompson.

Keegan, W. J. (1999). *Global marketing management.* Upper Saddle River, NJ: Prentice Hall.

Kleppestø, S. (1998). The quest for social identity – the pragmatics of communication in mergers and acquisitions. In: Gertsen et al. (1998), pp. 147–65.

Kluckhohn, F. and Strodtbeck, F. L. (1961). *Variations in value organizations.* Westport, CT: Greenwood Press.

Kroeber, A. L. and Kluckhohn, C. (1952). *Culture: A critical review of concepts and definitions.* Cambridge, MA: Harvard University Press.

Larsson, R. and Risberg, A. (1998). Cultural awareness and national versus corporate barriers to acculturation. In: Gertsen et al. (1998).

Laurent, A. (1983). The cultural diversity of Western conceptions of management. *International Studies of Management and Organization* 8(1): 75–96.

Lessem, R. and Neubauer, F. (1994). *European management systems: Towards unity out of cultural diversity.* London: McGraw-Hill.

Littlewood, I. (1996). *The idea of Japan: Western images, Western myths.* London: Secker & Warburg.

Malinowski, B. (1944/1989). *Les argonautes du Pacifique occidental.* Paris: Gallimard. Also cited in: Dupriez and Simons (2000).

Maznevski, M. (1994). Synergy and performance in multi-cultural teams. PhD thesis, University of Western Ontario.

Mead, R. (1994). *International management: Cross-cultural dimensions.* Oxford: Blackwell.

Nathan, J. (1999). *Sony: The private life.* London: HarperCollins.

Nonaka, I. (1991). The knowledge-creating company. *Harvard Business Review.* November–December: 96–104.

Novo Nordisk (1999) *Environmental and Social Report.* Copenhagen: Novo Nordisk A/S.

Olie, R. (1995). Cultural exchange in mergers and acquisitions. In: Jackson (1995), pp. 308–25.

Osland, J. S. and Bird, A. (2000). Beyond sophisticated stereotyping: Cultural sense-making in context. *Academy of Management Executive* 14(1): 65–79.

Ouchi, W. and Jaeger, A. M. (1974). Made in America under Japanese management. *Harvard Business Review* 52(5): 61–9. Also cited in: Harris and Moran (1996).

Roberts, K. H. (1970). On looking at an elephant: An evaluation of cross-cultural research related to organizations. *Psychological Bulletin* 74(5): 327–50.

Ronen, S. and Shenkar, O. (1985). Clustering countries on attitudinal dimensions: A review and synthesis. *Academy of Management Review*. September. Also cited in: Deresky (2000).

Rosen, R. (2000). *Global literacies: Lessons on business leaderships and national cultures.* New York: Simon & Schuster.

Said, E. W. (1991). *Orientalism.* London: Penguin Books.

Said, E. W. (1994). *Culture and imperialism.* London: Vintage.

Saner, R. (1997). *Verhandlungstechnik: Strategie, Taktik, Motivation, Verhalten, Delegationsführung.* Bern: Verlag Paul Haupt.

Schneider, S. and Barsoux, J.-L. (1997). *Managing across cultures.* London: Prentice Hall.

Segalla, M., Fischer, L. and Sandner, K. (2000). Making cross-cultural research relevant to European corporate integration: Old problem – new approach. *European Management Journal* 18(1): 38–51.

Senge, P. (1990). *The fifth discipline: The art and practice of the learning organization.* New York: Doubleday.

Søderberg, A.-M. (1999). Do national cultures always make such a difference? Theoretical considerations and empirical findings related to a series of case studies of foreign acquisitions of Danish companies. In: Vestergaard, T. (ed.). *Language, culture and identity.* Aalborg: Aalborg University Press, pp. 137–71.

Søderberg, A.-M. and Holden, N. J. (2001). Rethinking cross-cultural management in a globalising business world. Unpublished manuscript.

Tayeb, M. (1988). *Organisations and national culture.* London: Sage Publications.

Tayeb, M. (1994). Organisations and national culture: Methodology considered. *Organisation Studies* 15: 429–46.

Thorelli, H. (1990). Networks: Between markets and hierarchies. In: Ford, D. (ed.). *Understanding business markets: Interaction, relationships, networks.* London: Academic Books, pp. 443–58. First published in *Strategic Management Journal* 7 (1986): 37–51.

Trompenaars, F. (1984). The organisation of meaning and the meaning of organisation – a comparative study on the conceptions and organisational structure in different cultures. PhD thesis, University of Pennsylvania.

Trompenaars, F. (1993). *Riding the waves of culture: Understanding cultural diversity in business.* London: Economist Books.

Usunier, J.-C. (1998). *International and cross-cultural management research.* London: Sage Publications.

Usunier, J.-C. (2000). *Marketing across cultures.* London: Prentice Hall.

Van Zandt, H. R. (1970). How to negotiate with the Japanese. *Harvard Business Review.* November–December. Also cited in: Usunier (2000).

Weick, K. (1995). *Sensemaking in organizations.* Thousand Oaks, CA: Sage Publications.

Yavas, B. F. and Marcoulides, G. A. (1996). An examination of cross-cultural management practices in American and Asian firms. *Advances in International Comparative Management* 11: 51–68.

4 Navigating knowledge management

'When analysing "knowledge work", so-called, I am struck by an eerie sense of *déjà vu*.'

David Collins, *Management fads and buzzwords* (2000)

'The realization that knowledge is the new competitive resource has hit the West like lightning.'

Ikujiro Nonaka and Hirotaka Takeuchi,
The knowledge-creating company (1995)

OBJECTIVES

- **Introduces knowledge as a management concept.**
- **Discusses the broad principles of knowledge management and the nature of knowledge work.**
- **Finds that writers on knowledge management in its international dimensions tend to treat culture in a benighted way.**

INTRODUCTION

The purpose of this and the next chapter is to provide part of the conceptual background to the case studies, explaining why a knowledge management perspective will be used to frame the approach to the writing of them and to analyze their content. The task in this chapter is to explain what is meant by the expression 'knowledge management perspective'; but that, of course, requires first the clarification of another definitionally complex word – 'knowledge'. It will be emphasized that in the management context 'knowledge' means organizational knowledge rather than the contents of encyclopædias or reference books. After the ensuing discussion about knowledge management, attention will turn to cross-cultural management issues. By the end of the chapter it should be clearer how challenging the notion of knowledge as an organizational resource in the context of cross-cultural interactions of organizations is.

KNOWLEDGE AS A MANAGEMENT CONCEPT

It has already been noted that knowledge work is being viewed as a key activity in the new economy. We now need to understand what knowledge is in general and then what organizational knowledge is. If, to quote Eagleton (2000) again, the word culture is 'one of the two or three most complex words in the English language', then almost certainly, after words like 'God', 'nature', 'mind', and 'soul', the word 'knowledge' would be in the top ten. The question of what we know and, by inference, take to be true – or rather, in the words of Plato, accept as 'justified true belief' (Nonaka and Takeuchi, 1995) – has exercised some of the finest intellects of the human race. The quest for the understanding of the nature of knowledge, beginning with Plato and his student Aristotle, over the centuries has given rise to the two principal Western traditions of epistemology, which is the critical study of the theory of knowledge with reference to its methods, validation, and scope.

The first of these traditions is rationalism, associated with the continental European tradition. Rationalism is the belief that reason alone, without any reliance on experience, can reveal the nature of reality. The second is empiricism, which is most strongly associated with British philosophy and the two great empiricists, John Locke (1632–1704) and David Hume (1711–76). Empiricism holds that all knowledge is based on experience and that the human mind is not equipped with a set of concepts in advance of experience. In the nineteenth century attempts were made to reconcile these two philosophical streams, the leading protagonists being Immanuel Kant, Georg Hegel and Karl Marx. Their beliefs laid the foundations for philosophical discussion about the relationship between the self and the outside world, of which one manifestation is society, which is variously a theatre of action and a domain of signifying influences, both material and immaterial.

Nonaka and Takeuchi (1995) are correct to state that Western philosophical thinking is still largely dominated by a strong dualism or the 'Cartesian Split': the intellectual separation of subject and object, mind and body, or mind and matter. They contrast this with the Japanese philosophical tradition which has itself been strongly influenced by Chinese thinking, notably Confucianism, and Indian systems, notably Buddhism. At the root of Japanese philosophical thinking is the quest for oneness, harmony and complementarity. It becomes apparent therefore that there can be no objective, universal standard for knowledge: at best we can say it is the sum of what we know or think we know *and* our own particular standpoint. Whilst knowledge may elude formal definition to suit everyone, there can be less doubt as to the properties of knowledge:

- Knowledge is, in a strict sense, only created by individuals

- It is perpetually expandable – even an interpretation of an inviolate text which is in the spirit of that text is an addition to knowledge

- It can be stored in human heads and in what we might call 'technical repositories' such as books, other documents, databases, data files and so forth

- It can be stored in a systematic way (for example, according to subject arranged in alphabetical order in encyclopædias) to make it more accessible intellectually or retrievable from technical repositories

- It is often in the form of summary and part of the summarization process may include codification

- It can be shared: in principle, universally

- It can be forgotten and not used

In short, knowledge is generated; it is codified and coordinated; it is transferred; it is, then, in principle used. The purpose of these knowledge-generating processes is to serve the generator (for example, the scholar, who becomes more knowledgeable), the encoder or coordinator of knowledge (for example, an encyclopædia), and the user (the person who consults the encyclopædia) to extend or re-evaluate his or her existing knowledge. The idea of knowledge in the expression 'knowledge management' implies knowledge that is not scientific, that is, knowledge which 'is contained in and transmitted by scientific texts' and which is associated with a 'paradigmatic mode of thinking and knowing [which] is constituted by the traditional scientific logic for description and explanation' (Nymark, 2000). Knowledge management is concerned with organizational knowledge. As Nymark (2000) points out, there are two kinds of organizational knowledge. The first is the paradigmatic mode in organizational science, which:

> is ascribed to the kind of research that has been called functionalistic in organizational analysis. It has a positivistic origin and it is inspired by a natural science research methodology. It is primarily concerned with uncovering general, universally true laws and aims at context-free causal relationships. It is an approach that is appropriate for instance when examining the results gathered through large-scale questionnaires. However, it has little significance when it comes to analyzing the outcomes of single case studies.

The alternative approach is the narrative mode which:

> can be ascribed to a tradition which is commonly referred to as the interpretive paradigm in organization theory under which social constructivism is also found. In the narrative mode research is oriented towards comprehensiveness and it is highly contextual. . . . It is based on human action and intentionality. Thus the narrative mode of knowledge-creation is in focus when the concern is . . . with regard to uncovering values in the organizational culture for the individual employee, and the transference of the organizational culture to new employees. (Nymark, 2000)

It will clear that it is the narrative mode rather than the paradigmatic mode that lends itself better to the examination of cultural aspects of organizations' behaviour and interactions. As we shall see, the big preoccupation in organizations is with highly contextual types of knowledge, which represent sustainable forms of competitive advantage. This kind of organizational knowledge 'includes among other things patents, processes, management capabilities, technologies, practical experience and information about customers and suppliers' (Venzin, 1998). The fact that such knowledge is 'narrative', that is in human recountable form, has, as we shall see in the next chapter, important implications for the way in which the four informant companies' cross-cultural behaviour will be investigated and analyzed. Suffice it to say for now that defining 'knowledge' as in 'knowledge management' is no straightforward task. Here, for example, is the hardly eloquent, organizationally slanted definition of 'knowledge' supplied by Davenport and Prusak (1998):

> Knowledge is a fluid mix of framed experience, values, contextual information, and expert insight that provides a framework for evaluating and incorporating new experiences and information. It originates and is applied in the minds of knowers. In organizations, it often becomes embedded not only in documents or repositories but also in organizational routines, processes, practices, and norms.

Davenport and Prusak (1998) concede that 'this definition makes clear . . . that knowledge is not neat or simple'. In the following section on knowledge management in organizational contexts, we shall discuss the nature of what is called 'knowledge work': it is easier to understand organizational knowledge through the activities associated with its generation, transfer and exploitation than by a definition which will inevitably be epistemologically inadequate.

It is possible to make some major distinctions about the nature of knowledge. The most important distinction is that which is made between knowledge which is *tacit* and knowledge which is *explicit*. Tacit knowledge is 'personal, context-specific, and therefore hard to formalize and communicate'; explicit knowledge is that 'which can be articulated in formal language including grammatical statements, mathematical expressions, specifications, manuals and so forth [and] thus can be transmitted across individuals formally and easily' (Nonaka and Takeuchi, 1995). For the sake of argument, let us not quibble with the word 'easily' in that statement. Bresman et al. (1999) refer to tacit knowledge as 'know-how' and the 'more articulable dimensions of knowledge' as 'know-what'.

Burton-Jones (1999) expresses the distinction as follows:

> The critical difference between these two aspects of knowledge relates to how easy or difficult it is to codify or express the knowledge in terms which enable it to be *understood* by a broad audience. If knowledge can be *codified* in this way, it can be made explicit and thus readily transferable. Conversely, if it cannot be made explicit, it must remain tacit (literally 'silent'), thus difficult, if not impossible to transfer. As Michael Polanyi [1966] put it in his seminal work 'The tacit dimension', 'we can know more than we can tell'. (original emphasis)

Nonaka and Takeuchi (1995) segment tacit knowledge into two dimensions:

> The first is the technical dimension, which encompasses the kind of informal and hard-to-pin-down skills or crafts captured in the term 'know-how'. A master craftsman, for example, develops a wealth of expertise 'at his fingertips' after years of experience. But he is often unable to articulate the scientific or technical principles behind what he knows.
>
> At the same time, tacit knowledge contains an important cognitive dimension. It consists of schemata, mental models, beliefs, and perceptions so ingrained that we take them for granted. The cognitive dimension of tacit knowledge reflects our image of reality (what is) and our vision for the future (what ought to be). Though they cannot be articulated very easily, these implicit models shape the way we perceive the world around us.

They argue that the success of Japanese firms has been due to their ability to create explicit knowledge out of tacit knowledge through sharing processes and through various iterations to make this explicit knowledge tacit as a corporate resource. In this sense, Japanese firms are merely doing what has been expressed in another form by Percy Barnevik, the former chief executive of ABB and one of the greatest industrial managers of the twentieth century. Barnevik observed that, if you build a global industrial company in which you rotate managers and technologists around the world to share expertise and solve problems *and* develop deep local roots everywhere, then the organization has 'a business advantage, that is damn difficult to copy' (quoted in Taylor, 1991). Tacit knowledge is precisely that: damn difficult to copy; and leading Japanese companies may not necessarily be notably more adept of converting explicit knowledge into tacit knowledge than their Western counterparts. But overall 'there remains a great deal to be work to be done ... to describe the distinct and synergistic roles of explicit and tacit knowledge in sustaining competence-based advantage' (McEvily et al., 2000).

The distinction between tacit and explicit knowledge and the two dimensions of tacit knowledge will be of importance to us when we apply a knowledge management approach to the analysis of the case studies. However, this division of knowledge is not unimpeachable and has been cogently criticized by Maula (2000). Among her reservations are that the distinction between explicit and tacit knowledge as objective and subjective respectively are not clear-cut because 'our personal knowledge – and the firm's knowledge as well – is more or less influenced by our senses and earlier experiences and knowledge'. The assumption too that explicit knowledge 'is created through the rational functioning of the mind' is likewise questionable. We need to bear these reservations in mind, for, as we shall see later, the distinction between tacit and explicit knowledge is especially problematically when knowledge is transferred cross-culturally.

In passing we should mention other two properties of knowledge which we will refer to. Burton-Jones (1999) draws our attention to 'stickiness' and 'absorptive capacity':

Stickiness refers to the difficulty associated with codifying knowledge, i.e. turning it into explicit transmittable information. Readers will doubtless have encountered the problem of stickiness on occasion, when trying to get 'a thought down on paper'. In the firm, internal stickiness often hinders effective transfer of knowledge between individuals and departments.

Whereas stickiness slows down the export of knowledge, absorptive capacity affects how easily the recipient can understand it. Prior knowledge of a particular 'knowledge domain' or subject . . . tends to make it easier to understand new information that is related to that knowledge domain. The converse is also true, as many firms and individuals have found to their cost, when venturing into new knowledge domains.

For the sake of completion we should mention some other typologies of knowledge. Machlup (1980) made a distinction between five types of knowledge based on what he called 'areas of concern', which are associated with these statements:

- Knowing that something is so, and not otherwise

- Knowing how something looks

- Knowing how something happened

- Knowing how to perform a certain task

- Knowing how something (a cause or antecedent) is connected with . . .

- . . . Something else (a subsequent effect)

Fleck (cited by Brown and Woodland, 1999) identified ten components of management knowledge, one of which is meta-knowledge. Writers who are more concerned with 'knowledge in action' use more pragmatic typologies. Burton-Jones (1999) characterizes knowledge in relation to the firm using three criteria: knowledge within the firm; the specificity of knowledge to the firm; and its value to the firm. Davenport and Prusak (1998), making use of the experience of British Petroleum in introducing a company-wide knowledge management/organizational learning system (see below), classify knowledge management on the basis of principles which should underpin good practice. Their list is worth reproducing for its coverage (Table 4.1), as a number of their principles will be used to help analyze the case studies, but not as the prime conceptual tool.

However, to date, the most sophisticated list of types of knowledge has been developed by the American scholar, Nancy Dixon, an expert on organizational learning. She spent two years studying knowledge-sharing practices in a cross-section of organizations, including General Motors, Ernst & Young, Chevron, British Petroleum, Ford, the US Army, and the World Bank. Dixon (2000) bases her typology on three considerations:

- The intended receiver of the knowledge in terms of similarity of task and context

- The nature of the task in terms of how routine and frequent it is

- The type of knowledge that is being transferred

Table 4.1   Knowledge management principles

Knowledge management principles

- Knowledge originates and resides in people's minds
- Knowledge-sharing requires trust
- Technology enables new knowledge behaviours
- Knowledge-sharing must be encouraged and rewarded
- Management support and resources are essential
- Knowledge initiatives should begin with a pilot programme
- Quantitative and qualitative measurements are needed to evaluate the initiative
- Knowledge is creative and should be encouraged to develop in unexpected ways

Source: Reprinted by permission of *Harvard Business Review. Working Knowledge* (1998) by T. Davenport & L. Prusak. Copyright © 1998 by the Harvard Business School Publishing Corpn.; all rights reserved.

She then creates five categories of knowledge, not in terms of its content, but in terms of transfer characteristics (see Table 4.2 for a summary).

Dixon shows how the kind of transfer, the nature of the task, and the type of knowledge influence what she calls the design guidelines, which refer to the format of exchanges (i.e. face-to-face meetings and/or electronic forums, participation of senior managers, the role of knowledge specialists, the transferability of knowledge by electronic means, and so forth). The fact that Dixon's work is based on empirical studies makes her contribution to the practice of knowledge management particularly useful. We will make use of her conceptualizations in the next chapter and eventually in the analysis of the case studies.

KNOWLEDGE MANAGEMENT

'Knowledge management' is a fashionable term, indeed 'one of the hottest buzzwords in the corporate world', according to a contributor in a *Financial Times* survey of knowledge management published in November 1999 (Nairn, 1999). As a concept, knowledge management springs from the recognition that 'the dimensions of competition have . . . dramatically changed from the dependence on natural resources to . . . competition for intellectual resources' (Rasmussen, 2000). Knowledge management has been defined as 'the systematic management of the knowledge processes by which knowledge is identified, gathered, shared and applied' (Newing, 1999). Management consultants KPMG (1999) define it as 'the systematic and organised attempt to use knowledge within an organization to improve performance'. *Attempt* is the operative word, for, as we shall see, the implementation of knowledge management systems is not only organizationally demanding, it frequently encounters resistance.

Table 4.2   Five types of knowledge transfer

Serial knowledge
Definition: The knowledge that a team has gained from doing one task in one setting is transferred
    to the next time that team does the task in a different setting
Nature of the task: Frequent and non-routine
Type of knowledge: Tacit and explicit

Near transfer
Definition: Explicit knowledge a team has gained from doing a frequent and repeated task is reused
    by other teams doing very similar work
Nature of the task: Frequent and routine
Type of knowledge: Explicit

Far transfer
Definition: Tacit knowledge that a team has gained from doing a non-routine task is made available
    to other teams doing similar work in another part of the organization
Nature of the task: Frequent and non-routine
Type of knowledge: Tacit

Strategic transfer
Definition: The collective knowledge of the organization is needed to accomplish a strategic task
    that occurs infrequently but which is critical to the whole organization
Nature of the task: Infrequent and non-routine
Type of knowledge: Tacit and explicit

Expert transfer
Definition: A team facing a technical question beyond the scope of its own knowledge seeks the
    expertise of others in the organization
Nature of the task: Infrequent and routine
Type of knowledge: Explicit

But as a concept, knowledge management is, for all the hype, 'as vague as it is widespread' (Roberts, 2000). As we noted in the introduction, knowledge management is coming to prominence as it is becoming recognized that 'knowledge itself remains the paramount resource and thus the key economic progress' (Burton-Jones, 1999). Bresman et al. (1999), focusing on knowledge transfer in international acquisitions, account for this recognition as follows:

> In many industries, the importance of developing abilities to better utilize the knowledge contained in the firm's network has become apparent to managers. Many of the management fads of recent years have assisted in this process of recognition. Benchmarking has demonstrated the potentially great benefits of best practices transfer. Instances of failure of downsizing, on the other hand, have revealed the costs of losing knowledge. Empowerment and globalization have created local

knowledge with potential for utilization elsewhere, and information technology has given individuals increasingly differentiated knowledge, unknown to head office. One of the most cited reasons for the importance of knowledge management is the increasing speed of competition. . . . Reinventing the wheel, it is argued, is a serious waste of time when the requisite knowledge is already contained in other parts of the organization.

The linkage between knowledge management and competitiveness is a key theme. As Spender (1996, cited by Ramussen, 2000) has well put it: 'Since the origin of all tangible resources lies outside the firm, it follows that competitive advantage is more likely to arise from the intangible firm-specific knowledge which enables it to add value to the incoming factors of production in a relatively unique manner.' Writers may criticize the faddishness of knowledge management, concede that the concept is in its infancy, struggle with criteria, and cite both technical and human forms of resistance which undermine efforts to become knowledge-based organizations. As Dixon (2000) has observed: 'The term "knowledge management" has unwanted implications. The "management" part implies that this is something Management is in charge of, when what is wanted is that everyone in the organization be involved in the exchange as well as generation of knowledge.'

But writers are generally united in the conviction that one of the primary tasks of firms today lies in 'the protection and integration of special knowledge' (Burton-Jones, 1999). Davenport and Prusak (1998) supply the reason: 'Knowledge is the most sought-after remedy to uncertainty.' This entails the recognition that the key element in knowledge management is the continuous learning from experience; or, as more perceptively expressed by Collins, 'the continuous learning from experienceS' (added emphasis). In practical terms, the aim of knowledge management is to 'keep track of valuable capabilities used in one place that could be applied elsewhere' (Birkinshaw, 2000).

With reference to Japanese firms, Nonaka and Takeuchi (1995) are concerned with knowledge creation as a combination of tacit and explicit knowledge, made possible by socialization processes. They provide a neat model of four modes of knowledge conversion, showing the relationship between knowledge generated from within a company and that which enters it from external sources and the relationship between tacit and explicit knowledge (Figure 4.1).

As Nonaka and Takeuchi explain: 'Knowledge that is accumulated from the outside is shared widely within the organization, stored as part of the company's knowledge base, and utilized by those engaged in developing new technologies and products. A conversion of some sort takes place; it is this conversion process – from outside to inside and back outside again in the form of new products, services, or systems – that is the key to continuous innovation in Japanese companies.' Continuous innovation, in turn, leads to competitive advantage, as shown in Figure 4.2.

	Tacit knowledge	To	Explicit knowledge
Tacit knowledge	(Socialization) **Sympathized knowledge**		(Externalization) **Conceptual knowledge**
From Explicit knowledge	(Internalization) **Operational knowledge**		(Combination) **Systemic knowledge**

Fig. 4.1 Four modes of knowledge conversion

Source: *The Knowledge-Creating Company* (1995) by I. Nonaka & H. Takeuchi. © Oxford University Press, Inc.

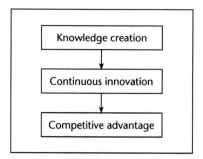

Fig. 4.2 Knowledge creation and competitive advantage

Source: *The Knowledge-Creating Company* (1995) by I. Nonaka & H. Takeuchi. © Oxford University Press, Inc.

Consistent with Nonaka and Takeuchi, Burton-Jones (1999) argues that 'only *tacit* knowledge, whether alone or in conjunction with explicit knowledge, can give a firm a sustainable competitive advantage.' Accordingly, firms need to acquire, create and protect tacit knowledge: the knowledge which is in the heads of their employees and embedded in the general organizational context of their work. Tacit knowledge, once acquired, can be developed as a company resource which is very difficult for rivals to copy; and therein lies true competitive advantage. Nonaka and Takeuchi (1995) place great emphasis on socialization as being central to the success of the knowledge conversion process, suggesting that the Japanese are particularly adept at socialization for this purpose. They certainly are when the socialization involves other Japanese. But when knowledge creation involves the Japanese and non-Japanese, then problems arise. A study comparing Japanese teamworking in the subsidiaries in the UK and China found that the Japanese-style consensus culture had proved 'highly problematical' in the UK case and that Anglo-Japanese teamworking relationships had been so beset for five years (Morita, 2000). The Chinese employees of the Japanese company were seen to be motivated, but had problems understanding how the Japanese used incentives (Morita, 2000). The Chinese in the study also lacked 'intellectual skills' for Japanese-style teamworking (Morita, 2000).[1]

A study of knowledge-sharing in 13 Japanese–Italian joint ventures, which happened to make use of the Nonaka/Takeuchi concepts found that 'the dialogues between the Japanese managers and the Italian managers were fraught with difficulty as each party atempted to learn about the verbal and nonverbal exchanges that constitute their conversations' (Kidd, 1999). The point I am making is that those who quote and propound the Nonaka/Takeuchi approach may overlook the fact that Japanese-style socialization is a highly embedded form of culture-specific communication behaviour. The transfer may be presented as impressively smooth among Japanese only, but when knowledge is to be shared among Japanese and non-Japanese even in the same company, the techniques of socialization can break down: common ground becomes elusive and the most complex language barrier in the industrialized world – that which separates Japan from the rest of the world – sows insidious confusion and bafflement. Our case study about the Matsushita corporation, which is featured in chapter 7, is a case in point.

But what, in a practical sense, does knowledge management actually entail? In essence, the task of knowledge management acknowledges that managers must continually update their knowledge without reinventing the wheel. As Dixon (2000) points out, this engages organizations in two kinds of knowledge activity. First they must find effective ways to translate their ongoing experience into usable knowledge. This is the act of creating what she calls 'common knowledge'. Second, they have to transfer that knowledge across organizational borders. This is the act of leveraging common knowledge 'across time and space'. The concept of common knowledge is going to serve us in a significant way in the next chapter, when we consider the question of using knowledge management concepts to handle cross-cultural know-how. Dixon (2000) describes common knowledge as the knowledge that 'employees learn from doing the organization's tasks . . . to differentiate it from book knowledge or from lists of regulations or databases of customer information'. She cites these examples of common knowledge: 'what an organization has learned about how to introduce a new drug into the diabetes market, how to increase refinery reliability, how to reduce materials cost on capital projects, and how to control the amount of pitch in wood pulp' (Dixon, 2000).

All these examples involve knowledge management: the generation of knowledge through external acquisition or internal creation, its codification, and transfer. The aim of knowledge management is to secure 'insights, judgements and understanding' (Davenport and Prusak, 1998) in order to develop company-specific knowledge, which can be converted into tacit knowledge, which both adds value to company activities in the widest sense and is difficult for rivals to copy. In other words, the task is to create and leverage common knowledge for organizational advantage. Adding value can be understood in terms of networking performance, providing improved solutions to customers' problems, and developing 'capabilities or competencies likely to be valuable in the future as well as the present' (Burton-Jones, 1999). Of course, knowledge management is an activity which is heavily dependent on information technology but, as we shall see, IT is, in principle, fine with explicit knowledge. Developing IT systems for handling the all-important tacit knowledge is more problematical: it is not only hard to capture, pin down and codify, but there must be knowledgeable human experts at the disposal of the company to attest to its relevance and potential value.

This may be relatively easy in the case of new knowledge developed in an R&D laboratory about high-temperature superconductivity, but in the case of knowledge about a new surgical technique, for example, this may need an appreciation of operating theatre practice and conventions which may be highly unusual for various circumstances: the possibly 'unique' concentration of surgical expertise and other factors such as those particular surgeons, that particular surgical team, that particular operation and patient. But suppose that particular hospital is in Russia, where the habitual shortage of basic medical supplies – one day, catheters, the next day, syringes – means that the operation is being performed in an environment that is highly accustomed to the *improvisation* of procedures. Such improvisation is crucial for an understanding of the conduct, *taken for granted* by the internal actors, that is surgeons, medical teams, managers of medical stores, chiefs of sterilization units, etc., and *utterly unsuspected* by foreign surgical experts not familiar with all that embedded knowledge. How do you transfer that kind of knowledge in which that operation is embedded?

Without finding an answer to that question, let us now briefly consider knowledge management, as an IT-supported activity, against the three main elements of practice: acquisition, codification and transfer of knowledge.

KNOWLEDGE WORK

Although knowledge work can be seen in terms of generation, codification and transfer of knowledge, these should not be seen as operationally discrete categories. All of them involve and overlap with (a) the use of a personal knowledge base, (b) the acquisition of new information, (d) the combination, processing, production and communication of information, and (d) the 'continuous learning from experiences' (Collins, 1998). Furthermore, the totality of knowledge work activities variously involve the knowledge worker in the consolidation, extension and attenuation of personal networks which, as Burton-Jones (1999) says of knowledge itself, transcend firm, industry and national boundaries.

Generation of knowledge: Acquisition and creation

The first thing to note about knowledge acquisition is that firms require a constant supply of knowledge inputs. Key issues include: (a) the selection and management of knowledge resources, (b) balancing knowledge supply and demand, and (c) acquiring the knowledge of other firms (Burton-Jones, 2000). Acquisition starts a variety of internal and external sources: printed and other documentary resources, computer databases, and personal interaction with other persons who are 'knowledgeable'. Creation is the act of combining these sources into new knowledge configurations. As we noted earlier, competitive advantage is linked to the acquisition of tacit knowledge which is not only in 'knowledgeable' people's heads, but embedded in their specific context. This contextual knowledge – the know-how associated with Japanese just-in-time manufacturing systems or the scenario surrounding our hypothetical hospital – is often rich and 'unique'. It is the kind of knowledge that a firm needs when it wants to acquire or merge with another one and finds that it disappears when they think they have it: as when Chrysler designers and engineers, not liking the shape of the newly formed DaimlerChrysler auto giant, went 'down the road' with their knowledge to Ford and General Motors.

Codification of knowledge

It is worth quoting Davenport and Prusak (1998) at some length on codification. They say:

> The aim of codification is to put organizational knowledge into a form that makes it accessible to those who need it. It literally turns knowledge into code (though not necessarily a computer code) to make it organized, explicit, portable, and as easy to understand as possible. . . . Knowledge managers and users can categorize knowledge, describe it, map and model it, simulate it, and embed it in rules and recipes. Each of these approaches has its own set of values and limitations, and they can be applied singly or in combination. Obviously, new technologies play an important role in the knowledge codification and make the prospects for those activities increasingly promising.

Codification is a problem, but not always a technical one. A critical factor, one that can only be made by a domain expert, is to decide what knowledge is relevant from the point of view of company goals and therefore worth codifying, but provided it can be, given that tacit knowledge is 'almost impossible to reproduce in document or database' (Davenport and Prusak, 1998). One method is to produce a knowledge map, which is a guide to knowledge sources that might be useful. Another might involve the creation of a model. As Davenport and Prusak perceptively observe: 'The greatest value of modelling knowledge processes lies not in reaching an exact understanding of knowledge input, output and flow rates but in identifying the variables in the model that can be affected by management action.'

One of the values of the forthcoming case studies will be to highlight kinds of tacit knowledge and, across all five, see to what extent tacit knowledge can de dimensioned.

Transfer of knowledge

As Collins (1998) points out, knowledge workers use a variety of information technologies to manipulate information: 'Technologies such as electronic mail, groupware, and information networks enable knowledge workers to share information with both individuals and groups. Portable computers equipped with fax/modems, supported by worldwide networks, allow knowledge workers to compute anytime, anywhere and to keep in constant contact with their office and colleagues.' Davenport and Prusak (1998) are emphatic that the most productive form of knowledge transfer is through face-to-face interactions, which take place not only at meetings and seminars that companies might arrange, but also in more casual encounters in company corridors. This point of view is endorsed by Dixon (2000) in her study: 'All of the knowledge management systems I studied that were initially designed as technology systems have evolved toward being a combination of technology and face-to-face meetings.'

Even so, knowledge management is still overwhelmingly preoccupied with technology: data repositories, intranet, communities of practice, corporate yellow pages, whilst 'skipping over' changes in attitudes, behaviours and beliefs (Klaila, 2000). If that were not bad enough, the challenges of the transfer knowledge between departments in the same firm are 'far from trivial' and 'the problems associated with transfer will increase with geographical and cultural difference' (Bresman et al., 1999). By its nature, as discussed above, participation in the global economy requires, in principle, the leveraging of knowledge from any source regardless of location, but it seems that the most valuable knowledge for TNCs – the knowledge that gives the chance of sustained competitive advantage – is that which resides in the brains of people worldwide: the all-important tacit knowledge, which is not only personal and hard to formalize, but also exceptionally difficult to manage even in a unitary cultural ambience (Burton-Jones, 1999; Nonaka and Takeuchi, 1995), let alone in contexts where the management of cross-cultural flows is the key to the leveraging of knowledge.

The issue over whether human interaction or man–machine interfacing is in the end the superior vehicle for transferring knowledge, especially of the tacit sort, is a moot question. The global chief knowledge officer of consultants Ernst & Young is quoted as saying: 'Technology is very important and I don't think that you can set up knowledge management without cracking the technology. It gives you the speed and the connectivity that you need to capture and distribute knowledge' (quoted in Manchester, 1999). Even though knowledge management systems are far more suited to handle technical information, the transfer of technical know-how can be still inhibited for context-specific reasons. This is well illustrated in this statement of an R&D manager working in the Danish subsidiary of a French MNC:

> When we have developed a new product, a new way of solving a problem, in principle we should transfer all the knowledge to other MNC units, but it is not possible. We can demonstrate the new solution in practice, provide the other units with technical descriptions and all the knowledge we codify. We can transfer the knowledge on the final solution in a codified form, but we cannot transfer the knowledge we gained by all the successful solutions to the problem. So, in a way we are only transferring the solution to a specific problem and not the underlying competence. (Quoted in Holm and Pedersen, 2000)

A company that has embraced information technology on a massive scale is British Petroleum. An article by Microsoft writers in *Oil and Gas Journal* summarized the BP achievement (Microsoft, 1999; see also Davenport and Prusak, 1998). The company set up a project team to design an IT-based global knowledge management system, which allowed every individual in the company to have the basic capability to communicate, and share information routinely, without the underlying infrastructure acting as a barrier to the flow of information. The project team decided to build the core system on a Microsoft Windows 95 platform. These included complex design activities for global services, such as Microsoft Exchange, Windows NT Server, desktop services, telecommunications, intranet and real-time collaboration, which includes the virtual teamwork desktop video conferencing system. These tools have created what BP calls its Common Operating Environment. The article concludes:

> The standardised environment gives users a much richer and more uniform environment. Customer satisfaction surveys have exceeded 98% and internal measures about service availability have exceeded 99%. 'Since rolling out this new system, I have been able to work in almost any location around the world with my laptop,' commented one user. (Microsoft, 1999)

Another employee said in an newspaper interview in April 2000 that BP was seeing 'real value coming through – whether it was a few million dollars in maintaining a refinery or learning to build petrol stations 20% faster' (*Sunday Times*, 2000). A more dramatic example of the success of the BP system concerning the companies operations in Venezuela is catalogued by Dixon (2000).

A manager was given the task of reducing BP's operation there from $70 million to $40 million *in seven weeks* using a team of eight. The task involved creating a design for a new operation, developing a plan for staff selection, determining how it meets financial goals, designing the human resources packages, and devising a communication and implementation plan for each element. Dixon shows how BP used its knowledge management systems to achieve the objective within the seemingly impossible-looking time frame. This episode suggests, among other things, that BP has gone a long way towards developing structures which 'handle the seemingly contradictory demands of reaping global benefits of scale and utilizing dispersed knowledge to be locally responsive' (Bresman et al., 1999).

The idea behind the Common Operating Environment approach is to make BP 'an integrated world-class global agile learning organization'. Indeed, the BP experience suggests that the company has gone a long way to realizing globally an operable system that recognizes that 'shared learning is inextricably linked to social interaction in teams' (Laursen and Mahnke, 2000). Note the emphasis on global learning rather than global creation and transfer of knowledge. A feature of the BP approach is the permutations of interactive systems and the creation of specific IT tools to unlock knowledge informally through 'virtual networking'. Davenport and Prusak (1998) quote this example:

> BP has also instituted what it calls Virtual Teamwork Business Networking Centres, which are used once a week for virtual coffee breaks. Up to twenty people at separate locations have joined in video conversations with no set agenda. . . . They discuss current work and describe problems they've been struggling with or ideas they've come across.

Clearly, an immense number of factors militate against the smooth and timely transfer of knowledge, and BP appears to have managed to control the limitations and frustrations to a large extent by (a) ensuring that the technology is not the servant of the users, and (b) creating a motivating global corporate culture. A report from the USA cited a survey of 4,500 scientists, engineers and managers in ten multinationals across North America, Europe and Asia, in which nine out of ten respondents said that 'they did not have access to lessons learnt by their firms (*Sunday Times*, 2000). In a similar vein the British Institute of Management found that 80% of a sample of 470 members said their firms lacked a knowledge policy (*Sunday Times*, 2000). Davenport and Prusak (1998) list various inhibitors which retard, erode or prevent knowledge transfer:

- Lack of trust
- Different cultures, vocabularies, frames of reference
- Lack of time and meeting places
- Status and rewards go to knowledge owners
- Lack of absorptive capacity in recipients
- Belief that knowledge is prerogative of particular groups, not-invented-here syndrome
- Intolerance for mistakes or need for help

The KPMG *Knowledge Management Report 2000*, which surveyed 423 organizations about their attitudes towards, and experiences of, knowledge management, found that the most committed companies had problems as follows:

- Lack of time to share knowledge (62%)

- Failure to use knowledge effectively (57%)

- Difficulty of capturing tacit knowledge (50%)

Other problems cited by KPMG included: lack of user uptake owing to insufficient communication; failure to integrate knowledge management into everyday working practices; lack of time to learn how to use the system or a sense that the system was too complicated; a lack of training; and a sense that there was little personal benefit in it for the user (KPMG, 1999).

CROSS-CULTURAL ISSUES

One of the problems in the knowledge management literature is that authors give the impression that knowledge management operates in a kind of unitary vacuum, in which diversity in terms of language, cultural and ethnic background, gender and professional affiliation are compressed into one giant independent variable, which is in any case pushed to the side. This approach may be convenient for conceptualizing, but is very limited for practical purposes in the modern international business world with its complex forms of cross-cultural learning, interactive networking, and knowledge acquisition and sharing. As Bertels and Savage (1999) have correctly observed, we are now in the 'Knowledge Era' in which 'cross-organizational and cross-cultural teaming' is central to the practice of knowledge management in international scope. As a consequence, knowledge management will become increasingly the management of the transfer of knowledge generated by cross-cultural teams. That presents one kind of managerial challenge. Another concerns the problem of acquisition of potentially high-grade knowledge from unfamiliar environments. A third problem has been highlighted by Doz and Santos (1997), who comment that the real challenge facing TNCs 'involves the management of knowledge in a single administrative system, but residing in a dispersed and differentiated locations'. The forthcoming case studies will shed light on all three issues.

When we specifically consider the international or global transfer of knowledge, then, as Bresman et al. (1999) have noted with respect to international acquisitions, the lack of personal relationships, the absence of trust, and 'cultural distance' all conspire to create resistance, frictions, and misunderstandings. This observation is consistent with the conviction that 'a significant source of dissatisfaction in organizations today is the poor structures and networks for mediating and diffusing knowledge, values and experience within the organizational environment' (Claes, 1999). The literature on mergers and acquisitions points in the same direction. In a study of 121 acquisitions in other EU countries by UK firms, Schoenberg (1999) demonstrates that 'firms' ability to successfully transfer functional knowledge consistently falls short of their expectations'. For example, in the key function of marketing he found that 'while 79% of acquirers who sought "some or more" knowledge transfer from the acquired firm, only 63% attained this level.'

This reinforces the conviction that cross-border – hence cross-cultural – knowledge transfer can founder, among other things, on what Szulanski (1996) calls 'the arduous relationship' between the source of the knowledge and the recipient. All this suggests that knowledge measurement, which aims to place a value on knowledge management work from one or more perspectives, may be especially difficult in cross-cultural settings because, as Venzin (1998) has noted, knowledge is 'generated in different language systems, (organizational) cultures, and (work) groups. If the context changes (e.g. culture), knowledge also changes.' This is an important point, which we will address later in the book.

But an interesting suggestion is made by the Swedish researcher Kleppestø (1998), who argues that what most other researchers describe as cultural clashes in cross-border mergers are actually quests for social identity. For researchers like Kleppestø, who take a social constructionist approach to understanding companies and the way, as it were, they really work, the tendency is to suggest that protagonists in mergers and acquisitions have to adjust to the new conditions by negotiating meanings with each other. The creation of meanings in this way is termed 'sense-making', a term that we will come back to in chapter 6 when we discuss the research methodology behind the corporate narratives. But the intriguing inference about Kleppestø's observation is that social identity in corporate settings may have a very great deal to do with the kind of knowledge that protagonists have access to, share, and *get recognition for handling.*

Davenport and Prusak (1998) are at pains to point out that 'knowledge sharing must be encouraged and rewarded', whilst Harvard Business School's Rosabeth Moss Kanter (quoted in *Executive Excellence*, 2000) emphasizes that knowledge work requires 'a new style of management that is more magnanimous'. Management, she says, 'has turned into coaching and encouraging, rather than ordering and directing'. And that forces 'managers and leaders . . . to be open to being taught things by their employees'. For people interested in extending those issues from parochial settings to inter-organizational cross-cultural interactions on the grand scale – that is, after all, what a cross-border merger or acquisition is – the scene is being set for new cross-cultural behaviours. Of course, the cross-cultural transfer of knowledge is nothing new. As a practice it goes back centuries. What is new is the study of the cross-cultural transfer of knowledge from a knowledge management perspective. Current writing about knowledge management in international contexts is dominated by TNCs and the way in which knowledge is transferred among organizational units. As Gupta and Govindarajan (2000) note:

knowledge flows within such enterprises occur not only along multiple directions but also across multiple dimensions, e.g., the flow of information pertaining to the Brazilian subsidiaries' financial peformance over the last quarter to corporate headquarters, the transfer of packaging technology from a Swedish factory to one in India, or the transfer of customer service skills from a Japanese subsidiary to one in the U.S.

With specific reference to the challenges of knowledge management in international business, Gupta and Govindarajan (2000) argue that 'conceptual work in this area is still in the early stages and empirical work is almost literally at the stage of infancy'. Consistent with that, Schoenberg (1999), in his study of cross-border acquisitions in the EU by UK firms, has concluded that 'we still know little regarding the relative ease of implementation of different types of knowledge transfer and resource sharing.' But these observations are not entirely true. There is one area of the cross-cultural transfer of know-how which has received a considerable amount of attention in the form of academic research publications, project reports and journalistic articles. This concerns the transfer of Western management know-how to Russia and other former socialist countries and republics of the USSR.

This mammoth crusade of enlightenment, costing Western governments, funding agencies and foundations millions of dollars since the collapse of the Berlin Wall in 1989, has almost been a spot lesson in how *not* to transfer knowledge.[2] A number of authors have noted that the misconceptions of educators about local learning styles and expectations as to the value of the know-how in particular circumstances have been non-productive and therefore a substantial waste of money (*Economist*, 1993; Hibbert, 1990; Holden and Cooper, 1994; Holden et al., 1998; Jankowicz, 1994; Lee et al., 1996). Signficantly, we now find authors who are writing about these processes from a knowledge management perspective (e.g. Hollinshead and Michailova, 2000; Husted and Michailova, 2000). Hollinshead and Michailova (2000), in a study of the transfer of management know-how to Bulgaria, note that both educators and trainees need to undergo a process of learning and *un*learning 'if "a bridge" is to be created between East and West'. This is an important insight, an insight of the kind that is not likely to emerge without direct experience in training processes and a sympathy towards local socio-cultural conditions. Creating a knowledge transfer system (such as a managemement training course) that uses that insight would be intellectually very demanding; but using a knowledge transfer system *without* it would not be likely to convince local people 'of the long-term benefits of the Western market-economy system or of the absolute desirability, let alone superiority of the Western way of life' (Holden, 2001). For knowledge management researchers who want evidence of how arduous relationships between the source of the knowledge and the recipient negatively affect knowledge transfer, let them take the next plane to Moscow, Kiev or Bucharest.

My purpose in discussing knowledge management is such detail is to make its concepts clear for one of the main tasks of this book: to use a knowledge management perspective as a means of analyzing cross-cultural management behaviour, having seen that 'culture' itself is highly limited as an explanatory tool for this purpose. In the next chapter I will introduce a concept of culture from a knowledge perspective. As far as I am aware, there is in the mainstream management literature no previous attempt to describe and analyze the cross-cultural interactions of TNCs from a knowledge management perspective. Dixon (2000), who writes illuminating on international knowledge transfer involving real situations, devotes only limited space to cultural issues. The word 'culture' does not appear in her index, but the term 'cultural *differences*' does.

The test-bed for the knowledge management approach will be the four corporate narratives which follow in Part II. The immediate task is to create a conceptual framework, making use of knowledge management concepts which serve two main purposes: to shed light on the context of the described cross-cultural interactions, noting special features of embedded knowledge; and to meet a crucial requirement for *sense-making*, a term which we will encounter again in chapter 5, to enable understanding of how protagonists' involvements in specific situations have 'either practical or symbolic relevance' (Gertsen et al., 2000) for their assumptions, actions and decisions.

Before we press ahead with the discussion of the research methodology in the next chapter, I ask readers to reflect a moment. In all the above discussion, knowledge management has been presented as if it is a completely new phenomenon, bound up with globalization, international networking and organizational learning. To put that point in perspective, I have added the following few paragraphs, by way of a coda, which will make it clear that knowledge management is as old as recorded history and no doubt older than that.

CODA: THERE IS NOTHING NEW UNDER THE SUN

Let be it said that what we term 'knowledge management' for organizational growth and survival is in a fundamental way not new at all. What previous eras lacked was knowledge that had not yet been discovered; nor, of course, could knowledge be 'electronically time-shifted' (Burton-Jones, 1999) and made, in principle, available instantaneously everywhere. The evolution of the human race may be seen as a progression towards 'the Knowledge Age', which is retrospectively linked to the Industrial Era, the Age of the Enlightenment, the Dark Ages, the Ancient World, and so on back to the Bronze Age, Iron Age and Stone Age. The ancient civilizations reveal the management of knowledge and organizational learning on a prodigious scale: one has only to think of the building of the pyramids in Egypt and in South America, the Great Wall of China, Stonehenge or the ziggurats of Babylon. But there were other kinds of knowledge too: the knowledge that created the vital and astonishing art forms, mathematics, astronomy, religious beliefs, and systems of divination.

Hannibal used knowledge of Alexander the Great's strategy and tactics to inflict crippling defeats on republican Rome; Scipio used knowledge of the strategy and tactics of Alexander and Hannibal to defeat the latter. Around 200 BC Indian and Arab traders used 'knowledge of the monsoons that blew across the Indian Ocean far to the south of the states bordering the Gulf and Arabian Sea'. According to maritime historian Lionel Casson, both Indians and Arabs co-operated in 'keeping what they knew about the behavior of these winds strictly to themselves' since 'neither was minded to divulge trade secrets to possible competitors' (Moore and Lewis, 1999). In the early modern era, Russia under Peter the Great (1672–1725) and Catherine the Great (1729–96) and the Japan of the Emperor Meiji (1868–1912), with its slogan 'Western knowledge – Japan spirit', represent examples of countries which actively sought foreign know-how to modernize themselves (for a treatment of Russia, see Hosking, 1997; concerning Japan, see Sansom, 1977). And, in the eighteenth and nineteenth centuries, the monarchs of Europe were desperate to learn – that means copy – Chinese and later Japanese techniques for making porcelain. This particular quest for knowledge involved 'unimaginable treachery and greed [and] cut-throat industrial espionage' (Gleeson, 1999).

Interestingly, these 'pre-modern' forms of knowledge transfer were pursued across barriers of language, culture and geography. Today's knowledge workers and corporate strategists could do well to study intercultural transfer of knowledge management in eras before we were dominated by the information technologies. Why should they think that the experience of the pre-modern world is totally irrelevant? It could be an unexpected source of insights and solutions: unvarnished human ingenuity and foibles clear as daylight, completely untrammelled by IT.

NOTES

1. In a meeting with Dr Morita in September 2000, when he gave me his paper, he confirmed that the Japanese company he investigated in China was, by coincidence, the same one which is featured in chapter 9 of this book.

2. It should not be assumed that before the collapse of the socialist countries those countries were completely ignorant of Western management techniques and theories. See Hollinshead and Michailova (2000) concerning Bulgaria; regarding the USSR, refer to *Business Week* (1990), *Financial Times* (1988), Hibbert (1990), Holden et al. (1998).

REFERENCES

Bertels, T. and Savage, C. M. (1999). A research agenda for the knowledge era: The tough questions. *Knowledge and Process Management* 6(4): 205–12.

Birkinshaw, J. (2000). *Entrepreneurship in the global firm.* London: Sage Publications.

Bresman, H., Birkinshaw, J. and Nobel, R. (1999). Knowledge transfer in international acquisitions. *Journal of International Business Studies* 30(3): 439–62.

Brown, R. B. and Woodland, M. J. (1999). Managing knowledge wisely: A case study in organisational behaviour. *Journal of Applied Management Studies* 8(2): 175–98.

Burton-Jones, A. (1999). *Knowledge capitalism: Business, work, and learning in the new economy.* Oxford: Oxford University Press.

Burton-Jones, A. (2000). http://www.burton-jones.com/knowledge.asp

Business Week (1990). From Red Square to Harvard Square: The making of a Soviet MBA. 28 May.

Claes, M.-T. (1999). Women, men and management styles. *International Labour Review* 138(4): pp. 431–446.

Collins, D. (2000). *Management fads and buzzwords.* London: Routledge.

Collins, R. (1998). Knowledge work. In: Cooper, C. L. and Argyris, C. (eds). *The concise Blackwell encyclopedia of management.* Oxford: Blackwell.

Davenport, T. H. and Prusak, L. (1998). *Working knowledge: How organizations manage what they know.* Boston, MA: Harvard Business School Press.

Dixon, N. M. (2000). *Common knowledge: How companies thrive by sharing what they know.* Boston, MA: Harvard Business School Press.

Doz, Y. and Santos, J. P. F. (1997). On the management of knowledge: From the transparency of collocation and co-setting to the quandry of dispersion and differentiation. *INSEAD Working Papers.* No.119–SM. Fountainebleau. Also cited in: Rasmussen (2000).

Eagleton, T. (2000). *The idea of culture.* Oxford: Blackwell.

Economist (1993). EC Aid to the East. 10 April.

Executive Excellence (2000). Knowledge workers. 17(1): 15–16 (anonymous).

Financial Times (1988). First Soviet business schools open. 30 July

Financial Times (1999). *Survey: Knowledge management.* 10 November.

Gertsen, M., Søderberg, A.-M., and Vaara, E. (2000). Cultural change processes in mergers: A social constructionist perspective. Unpublished manuscript under review. Copenhagen Business School.

Gleeson, J. (1999). *The arcanum: The extraordinary true story of the invention of European porcelain.* London: Bantam Books.

Gupta, A. K. and Govindarajan, V. (2000). Knowledge flows within multinational corporations. *Strategic Management Journal* 21(4): 473–96.

Hibbert, N. (1990). Training Soviet managers. *Industry and Higher Education* 4(4): 231–7.

Holden, N. J. (2001). Foreword. In: Sears, W. and Tamulionyte-Lentz, A. *Doing business behind the curtain: Working in Central and Eastern Europe.* Oxford: Butterworth-Heinemann.

Holden, N. J. and Cooper, C. L. (1994). Russian managers as learners: Implications for theories of management learning. *Management Learning* 25(4): 503–22.

Holden, N. J., Cooper, C. L. and Carr, J. (1998). *Dealing with the new Russia: Management cultures in Collision.* Chichester, UK: John Wiley & Sons.

Hollinshead, G. and Michailova, S. (2000). Blockbusters or bridge-builders? The role of Western trainers in delivering new entrepreneurialism in Eastern Europe. Unpublished manuscript. University of the West of England/Copenhagen Business School.

Holm, U. and Pedersen, T. (2000). The dilemma of centres of excellence: Contextual creation of knowledge versus global transfer of knowledge. Unpublished manuscript. Copenhagen Business School, Department of International Economics and Management.

Hosking, G. (1997). *Russia: People and empire 1552–1917.* London: HarperCollins

Husted, K. and Michailova, S. (2000). Knowledge sharing in Russian companies with foreign participation. Unpublished manuscript. Copenhagen Business School.

Jankowicz, A. D. (1994). The new journey to Jerusalem: Mission and meaning in the managerial crusade to Eastern Europe. *Organization Studies* 30(3): 281–99.

Kidd, J. (1999). Working together, but how? The need for intercultural awareness. In: Beechler, S. and Bird, A. (eds). *Japanese multinationals abroad: Individual and organizational learning*. New York: Oxford University Press, pp. 211–34.

Klaila, D. (2000). Knowledge management. *Executive Excellence* 17(3): 13–14.

Kleppestø; S. (1998). A quest for social identity – the pragmatics of communication in mergers and acquisitions. In: Gertsen, M. G., Søderberg, A.-M. and Torp, J. E. (eds). *Cultural dimensions of international mergers and acquisitions*. Berlin: de Gruyter, pp. 147–66.

KPMG (1999). *Knowledge Management Research Report 2000*. London: KPMG.

Laursen, K. and Mahnke, V. (2000). Knowledge strategies, firm types, and complementarity in human-resource practices. Manuscript of a paper presented at INSEAD, May 2000. Copenhagen Business School, Department of Industrial Economics and Strategy.

Lee, M., Letche, H., Crawshaw, R. and Thomas, M. (eds) (1996). *Management education in the new Europe*. London: International Thompson.

McEvily, S. K., Das, S. and McCabe, K. (2000). Avoiding competence substitution through knowledge sharing. *The Academy of Management Review* 25(2): 294–311.

Machlup, F. (1980). *Knowledge and knowledge production*. Princeton, NJ: Princeton University Press.

Manchester, P. (1999). A marriage of culture and technology. In: *Financial Times* (1999), p. I.

Maula, M. (2000). Three parallel knowledge processes. *Knowledge and Process Management* 7(1): 55–9.

Microsoft Energy Industry Solutions Case Staff (1999). Creating an agile learning organization. *Oil and Gas Journal*. Spring.

Moore, K. and Lewis, D. (1999). *Birth of the multinational: 2000 years of ancient business history from Ashur to Augustus*. Copenhagen: Copenhagen Business School.

Morita, M. (2000). Have the Japanese seeds matured into teamworking abroad? Paper presented at the 4th International Workshop on Teamworking, Nijmegen, Netherlands, 4–5 September.

Nairn, G. (1999). Benchmarking. In: *Financial Times* (1999), p. III.

Newing, R. (1999). The role of information technology. In: *Financial Times* (1999), p. II.

Nonaka, I. and Takeuchi, H. (1995). *The knowledge-creating company*. New York: Oxford University Press.

Nymark, S. R. (2000). *Organizational storytelling: Creating enduring values in a high-tech company*. Hinnerup, Denmark: Forlaget Ankerhus.

Polanyi, M. (1966). *The tacit dimension*. London: Routledge & Kegan Paul.

Rasmussen, K. (2000). Knowledge management in multinational companies: The use of shared space in cross-cultural settings. Unpublished working paper. Copenhagen Business School.

Roberts, B. (2000). Pick employees' brains. *HR Magazine* 45(2): 115–20.

Sansom, G. (1977). *The Western world and Japan*. Tokyo: Charles E. Tuttle.

Schoenberg, R. (1999). Knowledge transfer and resource sharing as value creation mechanisms in inbound continental European acquisitions. A paper presented at the 19th Annual International Conference of the Strategic Management Society, Berlin, October.

Spender, J.-C. (1996). Making knowledge the basis of a dynamic theory of the firm. *Strategic Management Journal* 17 (Special winter issue): 45–62. Also cited in: Rasmussen (2000).

Sunday Times (2000). Sharing knowledge boosts efficiency. Appointments section, 30 April: 16. Author: M. Coles.

Szulanski, G. (1996). Exploring internal stickiness: Impediments to the transfer of best practice within the firm. *Strategic Management Journal* 17 (Special winter issue): 27–43. Also cited in: Schoenberg (1999).

Taylor, W. (1991). The logic of global business: an interview with ABB's Percy Barnevik. *Harvard Business Review*. March–April.

Venzin, M. (1998). Knowledge management. *CEMS Business Review* 2(3): 205–10.

5 Towards culture as an object of knowledge management

'Not everything is culture-based.'

Jean-Claude Usunier, *International and cross-cultural management research* (1998)

'A database is like a black hole. It gives nothing back – no thank you, no smile, no sigh of relief, no enthusiasm on the other end of the line.'

Nancy Dixon, *Common knowledge: How companies thrive by sharing what they know* (2000)

OBJECTIVES

■ **Introduces the four informant companies whose experiences are written up as cases studies constituting chapters 6–9.**

■ **Discusses the notion of corporate case studies as sense-making documents.**

■ **Highlights the problem of contextual knowledge.**

■ **Proposes a knowledge-oriented definition of culture.**

INTRODUCTION

This is the final chapter of Part I of this book. Part II is devoted to the four detailed case studies which will provide the material for applying a knowledge management approach to cross-cultural management issues. These are not case studies of a conventional kind. They are to some extent histories of the four companies and can be read from a cross-cultural *and* a knowledge management perspective. I am using the expression 'case study' as a term of convenience, but the term *'corporate knowledge history'*, which will be explained in due course, may be a better description. The first task of this chapter will be to explain the overall case study approach. The second task will be to review the problem of contextual knowledge, as this is the particular kind of knowledge which the case studies will seek to identify and elucidate. The chapter concludes with a definition of culture which will be used to underpin the relationship between culture and knowledge in the case studies.

THE CONCEPT OF CORPORATE KNOWLEDGE HISTORIES

The four case studies are each an exploration of the respective companies' experiences of a cross-cultural management issue in accordance with the notion of cross-cultural management developed in this book. Each case study will in effect be a sense-making distillation of several informants' experiences regarding complex problems concerning the cross-cultural transfer and mediation of knowledge, values and experience. But there is a goal beyond sense-making. A key challenge is to create from those experiences concepts and possibly models for (a) defining cultural inputs as cross-cultural management knowledge and (b) reflecting cross-cultural knowledge transfer processes.

It is important to stress precisely why this approach is being adopted. As the five mini cases in chapter 1 made clear, the generation of knowledge about specific cross-cultural situations requires a lot of contextual information and the interpretation by an expert. It is being recognized that this kind of contextual knowledge is very valuable, but often very dense and detailed, so knowledge management specialists are calling for case-based systems. Here is an explanation from Burton-Jones (1999):

> Firms are nowadays beginning to address the *explicit to tacit* dimension through case-based systems which provide a richer array of contextual information. By studying the details of previous corporate experience in a situation analogous to one in which they find themselves, end users are often able to derive more value than by simply reading a set of prescribed rules or procedures. The net result (hopefully) is that they will better absorb the lessons that can be learned from the past and, in so doing, increase their level of tacit knowledge. The *tacit to tacit* dimension may also be partially assisted by a more context-specific approach to providing information. The lessons of experience tend to be encapsulated in a story rather than spelt out explicitly. (original emphasis)

'Hopefully' is indeed the operative word. The mini case study in chapter 1 involving Daimler revealed very clearly how a major corporation, determined to avoid pitfalls in a major international merger, can still come to grief even after poring over 'the details of previous corporate experience', enshrined in 100 case studies. Davenport and Prusak (1998) argue that some kinds of complex situation need a case-based reasoning approach, when 'applications require someone to input a series of "cases", which represent knowledge about a particular domain expressed as a series of problem characteristics and solutions.' They add that case-based reasoning 'works best when you have one or a few of the experts construct the cases and maintain them over time. There must also be a domain expert, someone knowledgeable about the area supported by the system, when an old case has become obsolete, and whether a new submitted case is actually correct.' Davenport and Prusak (1998) refer to firms that are applying case-based systems, but the focus is mainly on complex technical areas. However, cross-cultural know-how is precisely the kind that needs domain experts; and our case studies will give clear indications of what kind of expertise is most valuable.

As noted above, the following four case studies are not case studies in the conventional sense. In the world of management education and research the purpose of a case study is often to make generalizations on the basis of analysis of an organization. This kind of approach is unsatisfactory if the focus of a case study is cultural factors in the broadest sense of the expression. An important reason for opting for a different mode is that the traditional case study approach would almost certainly involve the treatment of culture in its essentialist garb. This could easily lead to a generalization of cultural factors which might reinforce prejudice, compound ethnocentrism, and perpetuate stereotypes. So we need an approach that can unlock cross-cultural management knowledge in such a way that the mind is opened to new ideas.

In this book, in order to unearth valuable insights into the production and application of cross-cultural management knowledge, the methodology makes use of a sense-making approach, an interview-based methodology which invites *several* informants in respondent companies to talk about specific experiences in narratives which can take the form of 'stories, excuses, myths, reasons for doing and not doing' (Søderberg and Gertsen, 2000). A sufficient number of accounts around one theme or sets of related themes from a number of informants from the same organization can help the researcher glimpse a picture of the organization as experienced and perceived by those informants. But the approach adopted here is not rigidly narratological, which, strictly speaking, means that the story delivered is that provided by informants without embellishment. In any case the researcher who gathers the narratives will structure them, so the process always involves some kind of subjective selection.

In the following case studies the domain expert – your author – will not be completely suppressing points of clarification and considered opinion. This is partly due to the fact that it is easier and more convenient for writer and readers to have an explanation in the main text of the case study rather than to confront a large number in the form of end-notes for subsequent clarification. At all events, even if the case studies are not narratives, a narratological approach has been adopted to enhance sense-making.

As Søderberg and Gertsen (2000) wisely note, and this is a most relevant insight for the handling of accounts about experiences involving other cultures: 'Narratives should not be seen as representing reality, but rather as constituting the narrator's reality.' In short, the narrative is a major aspect of the social construction of the professional domain of informants. The narrative articulates the informant's experiences, views and even emotional state *vis-à-vis* his or her organizational world. It tells us about (a) his or her understanding of social identities (including his or her own) and social relationships, which may or may not involve him or her directly, and (b) his or her knowledge and beliefs

(Fairclough, 1995). Importantly, as Søderberg and Gertsen (2000) remind us, these various forms of social construction are not exclusively personal. In organizational settings, narratives may be influenced by those of colleagues; indeed, narratives may be seen as the outcome of a negotiation process between the narrator and various interlocutors.

At first glance, the narratological approach looks insecure, but there are strong grounds for using it in organizational situations. It 'gives voice to a wide range of organisational actors' and 'shows in which ways their interpretations of organisational reality may correspond and differ' (Søderberg and Gertsen, 2000). This approach also gives due weight to people's emotions, which colour their impressions and reactions. This is particularly relevant when people are discussing cross-cultural experiences and processes which they may not be able to articulate in normal 'objective' language.

Thus the usefulness of the method depends on the researcher being a catalyst for generating productive responses and on his or her capacity to interpret those responses. Significantly, Søderberg, Gertsen and other researchers (Gertsen et al., 1998) have applied the narratological approach to the study of international mergers and acquisitions in order to assess the influence of cross-cultural factors on complex cross-border activities which are characterized as involving very high levels of financial investment and producing disappointing outcomes (Cartwright, 1998). Furthermore, as we shall discover presently, the narratological approach is *not* by any means unheard of in knowledge management practice.

Interestingly, one researcher in the field of social construction downplays, but does not minimize, culture clashes in strained M&A situations; he finds the emphasis on cultural difference as a cause simplistic, and argues that the so-called clashes are manifestations of the need of unsettled organizational actors to create new social identities in the new entity, in which so many of the familiar ways of doing things have disappeared or been modified (Kleppestø, 1998). This is the kind of perceptiveness that an essentialist cultural perspective may not have picked up. Not only that; it also supplies a really valuable insight into companies contemplating a merger or takeover. What is more, organization designers can actually do something with this kind of knowledge.

Sense-making is an important consideration both in the preparation and the analysis of the case studies, especially in cases where informants come from several countries and discuss highly subjectively their experiences and impressions of a multiplicity of contrasting cross-cultural interactions. It can throw retrospective light on organizational actors' quest for the clarification of the processes which create the meaning to which multiple cultures contribute. This activity is usually held to be a collective experience, in which to some extent participants – say, the members of a company – engage in social interaction to find common ground for thought and action. This social interaction may involve not just discussion, but *negotiation*, whereby participants attempt to stabilize 'the transfer of cultural understanding in organisations' (Nymark, 2000) – and, quite possibility, secure their own positions or functions as, for example, in a merger. This form of sense-making may help to reduce feelings of ambiguity and cognitive dissonance. As Gertsen and Søderberg (2000) explain:

> Sense-making is . . . a social process taking place within a community that is viewed as a network of intersubjectively shared meanings sustained through the development and use of a common language and everyday social interaction. Thus, studies of actors' cultural sense-making should focus on collective negotiations and discussions. Such an approach would highlight features of the very processes in which cultural interpretations are created, legitimized, and institutionalized.

Before we introduce the four companies acting as informants for the case studies, we have to consider two issues. The first recalls a comment I made in the preface: namely, that it was not until two of the four case studies had been prepared in draft form that I was aware of the significance of a knowledge management perspective for their presentation and analysis. In other words, the data were collected for analysis by other techniques. This, of course, is intellectually shocking. However, I justify the switch on the grounds of academic *force majeure*. Besides, I dare to think that a better book will emerge: not least because culture is a black box as far as knowledge management experts are concerned and because writers on culture and management, whether from a cross-cultural or intercultural perspective (to invoke the clear distinction for once), appear not to have seen what to me is now a rather obvious linkage of culture and knowledge. Despite the inelegance, the first two case studies have been redesigned to accommodate the new approach.

The second issue is highly problematical. The case studies are long: perhaps not for professors, students of business and actual or would-be domain experts, but certainly for some classes of enquirer and practitioner who tend to like information in the most compressed form possible. Not only that, but the case studies are also repositories of company history. Concerning length first, each of the four case studies is a very rich and detailed account of the core issues of relevance. Without richness and detail there is nothing to analyze, nothing in which to ground a knowledge management approach to cross-cultural phenomena, and nothing out of which to create concepts and models.

As for the historical dimension, it is useful to describe a technique developed at the Massachussets Institute of Technology called 'the learning history', which aims to 'capture knowledge about how an organization learns' (Dixon, 2000). The learning history is a narrative document (Dixon uses the word 'narrative'), composed by experts called 'learning historians', which may be between 20 and 100 pages long. Using a two-column format, the knowledge historians write up the event of an organization's history juxtaposed with quotations from actors about situations in which they were personally involved. As Dixon explains (2000):

The whole narrative is divided into sections or stories, each of which has a provocative title and begins with a prologue which sets the context for the quotes that follow. The learning historians who select the quotes that are used to tell the story and who comment on what is happening in the narrative are a small team composed of outsiders, often academics and consultants, and insiders, often HR personnel, all of whom have been trained in the learning history technique. This team conducts and record interviews during the period of the event, rather than retrospectively.

The described learning histories have been devised to facilitate learning processes in companies in order to stimulate innovation and promote change. The technique appears to have led to innovations in both the car industry and in the oil refining business in the USA. The following case studies do not follow the MIT format, but they are all in their own way learning histories, which are also concerned with the sense-making of the present through the prism of the past. Consistent with that, their purpose is to help make sense of complex cross-cultural exchanges of knowledge, values and experience, acknowledging that the all-important context is historically embedded. This point of view is consistent with the conviction of Nonaka and Takeuchi (1995), who stress the importance to knowledge workers of 'an understanding of the past': how the past influences present thinking.[1] The case study about the Matsushita Corporation (chapter 9) is truly a learning history, for it focuses very heavily on the past or rather on the way in which the company's past projects into the present.

It will have been noted that Burton-Jones, the expert of knowledge management, and Søderberg and Gertsen, the researchers interested in social construction through narrative, both use the word 'story'. For Burton-Jones (1999), key experience can be 'encapsulated in a story'. For Søderberg and Gertsen, a story *is* the narrative. The forthcoming case studies are both stories and histories about companies' cross-cultural experiences of knowledge transfer both internally and among their stakeholders in several countries. There is then a case for calling the following case studies corporate knowledge histories. A working definition is as follows:

A corporate knowledge history is a recorded version of events, experienced directly, indirectly or vicariously, by company actors ('narrators'); this version being an interpretation or elaboration of those events from a knowledge management perspective. Its purpose is *not* to provide *ex post facto* management wisdom, but to create a specific source of knowledge which, if judiciously analyzed, can provide insights into the tacit aspects of a corporation's behaviour. It is above all else a sense-making document.

Having read the four case studies, readers may judge whether the accounts conform to this delineation.

THE PROBLEM OF CONTEXTUAL KNOWLEDGE

It is important to emphasize that the case studies will encompass vast amounts of contextual knowledge. The challenge is to create useful knowledge categories from it and avoid something unwieldy – what Dixon (2000) calls an 'unstructured knowledge repository'. The intention will be to capture cultural knowledge and treat it as a resource. I now turn to the knowledge types and knowledge categories which will guide us from now on.

The contextual knowledge that our four corporations generate will be *thick*: that is to say, it is very rich, very wide-ranging, and is arcane, that is 'requires secret knowledge to be understood' (Hanks, 1986). The opposite kind of knowledge is *thin*, which I will describe as the minimum assumed by a knowledge user to be necessary for a specific objective, that is to support a decision. The account about the Matsushita Corporation is a good example of thick knowledge: not merely because it is knowledge about a Japanese company, which is therefore 'automatically different', *but because it has features which distinguish it from other Japanese corporations in highly significant ways.* The knowledge management perspective necessitates either the structuring of the case studies around specific knowledge categories or to compress the main points into those categories according to whether the user's need is for thick or thin knowledge. The designations thick and thin refer to knowledge types, and these are distinct from knowledge categories which are directly related to the specific subject matter of the case study in question.

The first knowledge type implies an academic approach; the second approach reflects the practitioners' need for high-value knowledge to come in concentrated forms, that is *thin knowledge masquerading as thick knowledge.* In a book like this there is no need to justify the former approach, as this is first and foremost an academic book. It goes without saying, of course, that thick and thin knowledge do not correspond at all to the tacit/explicit dichotomization of knowledge, though it will still be useful to make use of this distinction. Perhaps the best example in the entire management literature of the contrast between thin and thick knowledge is the work of Hofstede. His famous book *Culture's consequences* (1980) constitutes thick knowledge; his equally famous models are huge compressions of thick knowledge into thin representation.

For all its outward academic appearances, this book has pretensions to be useful to practitioners and consultants, for whom concentrated knowledge is preferable. So I have set myself the challenge of probing contextual knowledge which is the most difficult to capture and to analyze from a cross-cultural perspective and a knowledge management perspective. This will lead to a synthesis: a logical and straightforward step because culture is being viewed as knowledge. A challenge relates to the possibility of creating from all four cases some knowledge categories which apply generally to cross-cultural management as conceived in this book. Practitioners may not be very interested in the analytical procedures, but they should be interested in the resulting models, as the totality of material will be evaluated against Burton-Jones' (1999) three factors for characterizing the knowledge management perspective:

- Decision support

- Organizational learning

- Knowledge-sharing

In chapter 3 there was a discussion about the importance of networks and networking in the global economy. In our analysis of the case studies we will also note the way in which the informant companies use their networks to facilitate organizational learning and knowledge transfer and sharing on an international basis. There is a possibility of breaking new ground here. As Salk and Brannen (2000) note in a study of the role of national origins on the networking behaviour of German–Japanese joint-venture management team: 'Many network studies have been conducted in single organizations in uninational settings; it is therefore not surprising that the role of historical context and cultural origins has not received much attention.' The case study approach to be developed in this book is not based on any network approach, but it may help to address a lacuna in the current literature on networks in multicultural work environments.

THE INFORMANT COMPANIES AND METHODOLOGY

It is now time to describe the methodology for gathering the empirical data from the four informant companies. The approach to each company was facilitated through a personal connection: either an intermediary or a known member contact. A suitably senior manager was identified and he or she was provided with a short description of the broad research aims. There was great dependence on this person, as he or she might have to argue the case for participating in the project at a higher level within the company. The research was presented as an investigation into the international and cross-cultural transfer of knowledge, experience and values on the basis of extensive interviews. In all four cases this led to a discussion in the company with the researcher (or researchers) as a result of which a research topic was identified and general arrangements for interviews agreed. These 'pre-research' discussions were extremely important, as they often involved the people who would take part in the interviews. These initial meetings not only served to secure the cooperation and goodwill of the company, but also to communicate the researchers' own competence and credibility.

The four companies which agreed to take part in the project were Novo Nordisk (Denmark), Matsushita Electric Industrial Company (Japan), LEGO (Denmark), and Sulzer Infra (Switzerland). Interviews were held with managers, who were encouraged to talk freely and openly and perhaps unguardedly on the identified research topic. There was no standardized format for the interviews, but a question schedule was developed for each company. The questions depended heavily on the research topic and the responses on the status, experience and affability – and time availability – of the persons being interviewed. The research interviews were conducted at the headquarters of the Matsushita Corporation in Osaka and at several affiliated companies in the UK, Denmark, Spain, Germany and the USA. Novo Nordisk managers were interviewed in Denmark. One interview took place in Japan and a telephone interview was conducted with a manager based in the USA. LEGO personnel were interviewed at corporate headquarters in Billund in Denmark and at LEGO Media in London. Personal interviews with Sulzer Infra were conducted at the company headquarters in Zürich and at an affiliate company in the UK. Telephone interviews were conducted with Sulzer personnel in the Netherlands. The interviews were conducted over a two-year period from 1998 to 2000. Table 5.1 shows the topic associated with each of the informant companies.

One chapter is devoted to each case study. Taking a cue from the MIT learning historians, each account will begin with a prologue, which will focus on the overall theme in context and signal some of the key points from a knowledge management perspective. The following section provides the background to the company. Then come the principal sections describing the focal topic of the research as mediated by the informants and supported by various forms of company documentation. The subsequent sections of analysis and the conclusion are developed from both a cross-cultural management and knowledge management perspective.

However, the subject matter may require deviations from this scheme of presentation. It is usual with case studies that they contain relatively few

Table 5.1 Informant companies and principal research themes

Company and business	Principal topic
Novo Nordisk (pharmaceuticals; biotechnology)	Function of an internally appointed multinational team for facilitating conformity with company values and transfer of best practices
Matsushita Electric (consumer electrical and electronic products)	Quest for global corporate citizenship
LEGO (toys)	Cross-border transfer of identity
Sulzer Infra (construction expertise)	Creation of a knowledge-based company through cross-cultural organizational learning

references. But the exception is the Matsushita Corporation. The narrative theme – Matsushita's quest for global corporate citizenship – cannot be appreciated without an understanding of the development of the company since its foundation in 1917. For many students of business – students in the widest sense of the word – that year may sound almost prehistoric, but read it armed with Winston Churchill's dictum that if you wish to see far into the future, you must look deep into the past. As noted earlier, the material on the Matsushita Corporation will be presented as a learning history.

Table 5.1 makes it plain that we shall be concerned with a very wide range of phenomena and experiences in each of the four informant companies, which are each in different business sectors. But it is invaluable to have diversity, variety and complexity of subject matter with the cultural factors heavily embedded in organizational procedures, company philosophies and ways of doing business. Although the case studies focus on the mediation of knowledge, values and experience, the companies reveal strikingly different experiences: not least because the abundance of informants provided multiple voices and multiple vantage points. The case studies occupy the next four chapters, which form Part II of this book. The findings will generate four chapters of analysis and comment, concepts, models, and – something valuable and never imagined when the book was born – a new vocabulary for cross-cultural management.

TOWARDS A KNOWLEDGE-ORIENTED CONCEPT OF CULTURE

It is important to underline that the word 'variety' was used above as it is understood in systems theory, that is as requisite variety, 'the variety of anything' being defined as 'its number of distinguishable elements' (Beer, 1966). In brief, 'an organization's internal diversity must match the variety and complexity of the environment in order to deal with the complexities of the environment' (Nonaka and Takeuchi, 1995). This means that an organization must, as it were, interact with the environment on equal terms: the differential for maintaining this harmony or balance is the flow of information converted into usable knowledge. Dixon (2000), too, acknowledges the importance of variety, citing Conan and Ashby (1970) and referring to strategic transfer in her terminology: 'The variety within a system must be at least as great as the environmental variety against which it is attempting to regulate itself.' Dixon then goes on: 'We can assume that the Strategic Transfer will have to maintain variety within the inputs. The challenge, then, is how to *make sense* of the knowledge gained from complex experiences without losing the voices from multiple examples' (Dixon, 2000, original emphasis). The case studies have been prepared explicitly to make sense of culture in precisely this way, not as a manifestation of difference and otherness, but as a variety of distinguishable elements, and recognizing that this variety is the essence of culture as a resource.

When this book was in its infancy, a colleague, noting that I was attacking the essentialist (or functionalist) concept of culture, which has been so dominant in management studies, advised me that I must introduce my own concept of culture. That challenge was delivered to me before I realized the potential of the knowledge management perspective. Some months later, another colleague, an anthropologist, told me of one of the leaders in his field who 'as a point of honour' *never* defined culture in his writings. For some time I thought that I would not attempt a guiding definition: mine would be, literally, one among hundreds. And besides there was always a cop-out. Even if I had reservations about the concept of culture in its anthropologically derived package, I was certainly not denying culture as a fact of human existence, nor the influence of culture in its myriad manifestations on organizations, managers, their behaviour and decisions.

But, as I began to read the knowledge management literature, I was sensing the need for a guiding definition which was knowledge-oriented. Then, in that serendipitous way in which science sometimes progresses, I came across Dixon's book *Common knowledge*, which I have already quoted a good deal. I had already been using the word 'variety', mindful of its significance in systems theory, in an earlier draft of this chapter, when I discovered that Dixon referred to the famous 1970 Conan and Ashby paper. Suddenly I had my guiding definition of culture for the preparation and subsequent analysis of the case studies from a knowledge perspective:

Culture is varieties of common knowledge.

I humbly add it to the ever-lengthening list. Suffice it to say that I do *not* mean common knowledge in the flippant formulation of Collins (2000), who notes: 'The world of management is, by any definition of the term, a crazy place; where pools of common knowledge have a tendency to evaporate. During the 1960s and 1970s, for example, "common knowledge" advised managers that success, size and efficiency went hand-in-hand.' No, I do mean common knowledge in that sense: not common to *everyone*, but common to, and mainly fixed in, its place of origination, where it may lie darkly embedded behind a language barrier, behind a veil of strange customs, behind a closed door.

NOTE

1. In the Japanese version of the Nonaka and Takeuchi book, the word translated as 'past' is in fact the general Japanese word for 'history'.

REFERENCES

Beer, S. (1966). *Decision and control: The meaning of operational research and management cybernetics*. Chichester, UK: John Wiley & Sons.

Burton-Jones, A. (1999). *Knowledge capitalism: Business, work, and learning in the new economy.* Oxford: Oxford University Press.

Cartwright, S. (1998). International mergers and acquisitions: The issues and challenges. In: Gertsen et al. (1998).

Collins, D. (2000). *Management fads and buzzwords.* London: Routledge.

Conan R. C. and Ashby, R. W. (1970). Every good regulator of a system must be a model of that system. *International Journal of Systems Science* 1(1): 89–97. Also cited in: Dixon (2000).

Davenport, T. H. and Prusak, L. (1998). *Working knowledge: How organizations manage what they know.* Boston, MA: Harvard Business School Press.

Dixon, N. M. (2000). *Common knowledge: How companies thrive by sharing what they know.* Boston, MA: Harvard Business School Press.

Fairclough, N. (1995). *Discourse and social change.* Cambridge: Polity Press.

Gertsen, M. and Søderberg, A.-M. (2000). Cultural change processes in mergers: A social constructionist perspective. Unpublished manuscript. Copenhagen Business School.

Gertsen, M. G., Søderberg, A.-M. and Torp, J. E. (1998). *Cultural dimensions of international mergers and acquisitions.* Berlin: de Gruyter.

Hanks, P. (ed.) (1986). *Collins dictionary of the English language.* Glasgow: William Collins and Sons.

Hofstede, G. (1980). *Culture's consequences: International differences in work-related values.* Beverly Hills, CA: Sage Publications.

Kleppestø, S. (1998). A quest for social identity: The pragmatics of communication in mergers and acquisitions. In: Gertsen et al. (1998).

Nonaka, I. and Takeuchi, H. (1995). *The knowledge-creating company.* New York: Oxford University Press.

Nymark, S. R. (2000). *Organizational storytelling: Creating enduring values in a high-tech company.* Odense: Forlaget Ankerhus.

Salk, J. E. and Brannen, M. Y. (2000). National culture, networks, and individual influence in a multinational management team. *The Academy of Management Journal* 43(2): 191–202.

Søderberg, A.-M. and Gertsen, M. C. (2000). Tales of trial and triumph: A narratological perspective on international acquisition. Working paper no. 36. Copenhagen Business School: Department of Intercultural Communication and Management.

Usunier, J.-C. (1998). *International and cross-cultural management research.* London: Sage Publications.

Part II

Case studies: making sense of culture from a knowledge management perspective

'"Write that down," said the King to the jury, and the jury eagerly wrote down three dates on their slates, and then added them up, and reduced the answer to shillings and pence.'

Lewis Carroll, *Alice's adventures in Wonderland* (1865)

6 Case study 1
Novo Nordisk: cross-cultural management as facilitation

PROLOGUE

One of the biggest management challenges facing TNCs in the global economy concerns the transfer of company values from the corporate headquarters to local affiliates in such a way that:

(a) these values do not appear to be imposed from on high

(b) these values are not at variance with local work values

(c) local affiliates not only identify with the values, but also respond positively to the way in which those values are communicated to them

Values do more than inform corporate culture; they are also a statement about a TNC's total approach to business. Beyond that they represent an extremely important knowledge resource, reflecting what a corporation stands for and how it sees itself. No two TNCs have quite the same set of values; nor do they communicate them throughout the corporation in the same way. The company at the centre of this case study is the Danish biotechnology and pharmaceutical concern, Novo Nordisk. The key knowledge themes in this case study are:

- The role of a special taskforce, called Facilitators, to promote the transfer of company values and better practices worldwide

- The Facilitators as cross-cultural change-agents *par excellence*

- Facilitation as a form of cross-cultural knowledge management

The structure of this case study is:

- The company background

- Methodology

- Vision 21 and the Novo Nordisk Way of Management

- The Facilitator concept

- The objectives and general operations of facilitation

- Pre-facilitation

- The facilitation proper

- Post-facilitation

- Facilitation: an interim review

- Facilitation as cross-cultural management

- Self-management as a multicultural, multilingual team

- Interactions with units

- Facilitation as knowledge management

- How imitable is Novo Nordisk-style facilitation?

- Afterword: the Facilitators three years on

THE COMPANY BACKGROUND

Novo Nordisk A/S was established in 1989 as the result of a merger of two Danish pharmaceutical companies, Nordisk Gentofte[1] and Novo Industri A/S, which had previously been in fierce competition with each other. The two companies were founded in the 1920s and both were leading world suppliers of insulin before the merger. Today Novo Nordisk, whose headquarters are located just to the north of Copenhagen, is one of the world's biggest biotechnology companies, being the world's second largest producer of insulin, which is used in the treatment of diabetes, and the world's largest producer of industrial enzymes, which are used in the food industry as well as for the production of detergents. Its other pharmaceutical products include hormone preparations for gynaecological use, human growth hormone, and a preparation for the treatment of haemophilia. For the foreseeable future Novo Nordisk's corporate strategy is strongly shaped by its aim to remain a leading supplier of insulin and insulin delivery systems. The pharmaceutical business accounts for more than 75% of Novo Nordisk's total sales. The company turnover is in the region of 20,000 million Danish krone, which is $1,800 million.[2]

Novo Nordisk is one of the largest companies in Denmark, but by world standards it is small for a pharmaceutical company. Worldwide the company employs some 15,000 people and it is represented by wholly owned operations in 68 countries. It has manufacturing facilities in seven countries. As such, Novo Nordisk is one of Denmark's most internationalized companies. It is no exaggeration to describe the company as a knowledge-based organization. Seeing that no fewer than 3,000 of its staff are engaged in R&D and around 16% of its sales revenue is invested into these activities, the company motto might also be 'science is our business'.

Being in the pharmaceutical business, Novo Nordisk is an ethically conscious company. In Denmark, Novo Nordisk is perceived as a solid, if somewhat traditionally minded company, but it would be mistaken to regard it as conservative. The chief executive, Mads Øvlisen, is one of Denmark's most respected business leaders, and the company has no problem attracting the best students in Denmark from a variety of science, business and other disciplines. As a small player in an industry almost notorious for large-scale mergers, and failed mergers on a equally large scale, the Danish concern knows that it must be nimble and innovative if it is to rebut the unwelcome attention of one of the big corporations. Novo Nordisk's corporate culture is based on a strong value system, which reflects its wish to be known as science-based, ethical and international in outlook. The company is known to be wary of management fads, which are seen as short-term enthusiasms which can deflect its key staff from major tasks such as maintaining good relationships with its highly diverse international network of stakeholders, who include an occasionally hostile press and pressure groups who are concerned about the company's use of laboratory animals and gene technology.

As is the case of all mergers, the coming together of the two rival companies in 1989 created tensions and frictions, but sound management prevailed and the new company found favour with most employees regardless of their previous affiliations. But, as we shall discover, in the early-to-mid-1990s the company began to suffer from a creeping paralysis. It was becoming top-heavy and over-administered. As a consequence, its corporate management was perceived as being out of touch with employees even in Denmark, and it was recognized that many of the company's employees in other countries felt equally detached. This triggered a number of initiatives to reduce the sense of remoteness and improve both vertical and horizontal communication. For example, it developed the concept of the Novo Nordisk Way of Management and other ideals to encourage better practice throughout the company at every level, at every location. One initiative, focusing on an identified need to make the international subsidiaries feel more involved and valued within the company, is the subject of this case study.

It would, however, be wrong to talk of disaffection and at no point in the company's history can it be said that corporate management was seriously misjudging the situation or reluctant to introduce innovation when necessary. One indicator of the fundamental soundness of Novo Nordisk's management is the fact that the company has been in the Fortune list of the top 100 best-run corporations. Hence the Novo Nordisk approach to management is something of a model for other internationally operating concerns in Denmark, even if they are in quite different business sectors.

The initiative to improve communication and the transfer of values throughout the company worldwide resulted in the creation of a special 14-strong taskforce called Facilitators. As the name implies, they are change agents acting more as catalysts than enforcers. Before we examine the provenance of the Facilitator concept and study it in action, we need to know about the Novo Nordisk Way of Management and the other ideals because part of the Facilitators' task is to promote conformity – and, if necessary, enforce compliance – with these precepts. 'Compliance' is a strong word, but it should not be forgotten that, as a biotechnology company producing health-care products, its staff must always be aware that a shortcut here or a condoned malpractice there can easily bring the company into disrepute, expose it to press scrutiny worldwide, or even land it in a court of law.

METHODOLOGY

The information on the Facilitator concept was gathered by three researchers from Copenhagen Business School in summer and autumn 1998. They interviewed all but one of the 14 Facilitators personally. The fourteenth, based in the USA, was interviewed by telephone. There was a prior discussion with Henrik Gürtler, the senior manager responsible for the Facilitators, and a subsequent one with him upon completion of all the Facilitator interviews. The administrative head of the Facilitators and a senior corporate communications manager were also interviewed. The researchers devised an interview guide (or rather an initial one and a modified version after conducting seven interviews) and normally interviewed in pairs. The average interview time was 80 minutes. The researchers were not permitted to attend a facilitation session. The information in this case study on the Facilitators springs from interviews with the Facilitators themselves and Gürtler. A valuable documentary source was the highly commended MSc dissertation produced by one of the researchers, Mikkel Plannthin (1998). Information on Novo Nordisk itself is mainly from company sources. A further discussion was held with Henrik Gürtler and a senior administrator responsible for the Facilitators in June 2000. This provided an update and forms the final section of this case study.

VISION 21 AND THE NOVO NORDISK WAY OF MANAGEMENT

The merger in 1989 of Nordisk Gentofte and Novo Industri necessitated a new strategic platform for the new corporate entity. In the early 1990s the elements of this platform fell into place as Vision 21, which was a combination of mission statement and set of precepts for guiding the business thinking of Novo Nordisk as a global concern, as well as an ethical code for all its managers and employees, regardless of status and location. Vision 21 is summarized below under three elements: our purpose, our mission, and our way:

Vision 21: Our purpose

Our business is to discover and market products which satisfy real needs – improving the way people live and work

We find better ways to fight the burdens of disease and to provide sustainable biological solutions to industrial problems

Vision 21: Our mission

- We shall be the best in our business and a challenging place to work
- We shall grow as an independent company, making all important business, people, and policy decisions ourselves
- We shall pursue innovation in all our activities and aggressively build leadership positions in our markets
- We shall make Novo Nordisk our customers' preferred partner
- We shall deliver a competitive financial performance

Vision 21: Our way

Accountable	Each of us will be accountable – to our company, our colleagues and ourselves – for the quality of our efforts, for contributing to our goals, and for developing our culture and set values
Ambitious	We shall set the highest standards in everything we do and reach challenging goals
Open and honest	Our business practices shall be open and honest to protect the integrity of the company and each employee
Close to our customers	We shall seek simplicity in all our business processes, share information, and push initiative as close to our customers as possible to release personal energy and to constantly improve performance
Ready for change	We must foresee change and use it to our advantage. An ongoing dialogue between management and employees shall ensure that personal training and development activities strengthen our company and secure the employability of our employees, preferably within Novo Nordisk
Responsible neighbour	We shall all over the world conduct our business as socially and environmentally responsible neighbours, and contribute to the enrichment of our communities

Vision 21: our purpose, our mission, our way (Source: Novo Nordisk, 1997)

In 1994 a focused business strategy was formulated to guide the individual business areas, and in the following year the business areas were restructured accordingly. This led in 1996 to an alignment and restructuring of headquarter functions.[3] Along with this development came the recognition that Novo Nordisk needed a new management strategy that would make the task of management more straightforward and the company a more agreeable place in which to work. Seven years after the merger it was clear that attempts to standardize management procedures and routines had resulted in systems becoming centralized to the extent that individual employees and managers had little scope for independent action. One consequence of this situation in practice was that there arose a mismatch between the huge amounts of information being demanded by management and the ensuing feedback from management (Plannthin, 1998).

To counter this unsatisfactory situation, the company introduced on 1 January 1997 a new management concept which was called the Novo Nordisk Way of Management. Central to this management concept are the ten so-called Fundamentals, which are displayed below:

1. Each unit must share and use better practices.

2. Each unit must have a clear definition of where accountabilities and decision powers reside.

3. Each unit must have an action plan to ensure improvement of its business and performance and working climate.

4. Every team and employee must have updated business and competency targets and receive timely feedback on performance against these targets.

5. Each unit must have an action plan to ensure the development of teams and individuals based on business requirements and employee input.

6. Every manager must establish and maintain procedures in the unit for living up to relevant laws, regulations, and Novo Nordisk policies.

7. Each unit and employee must know how they create value for their customers.

8. Every manager requiring reporting from others must explain the actual use of the report and the added value.

9. Every manager must continuously make it easier for the employees to liberate energy for customer-related issues.

10. Every manager and unit must actively support cross-unit projects and working relationships of relevance to the business.

The ten Fundamentals of the Novo Nordisk Way of Management
(Source: Novo Nordisk, 1997b)

In a letter to all employees in January 1997 Mads Øvlisen, the CEO of Novo Nordisk, expressed the idea behind the new management tool: 'The Novo Nordisk Way of Management is a comprehensive and easy-to-use guide which should allow you to use your insight and judgment in complying also with the "local" management and quality system derived from this corporate basis for use in functions and departments throughout Novo Nordisk.' Today the Novo Nordisk Way of Management consists of the four elements: the Vision 21, the Ten Fundamentals, a Quality Manual, and set of Policies which cover 13 operational areas. These constitute the building bricks which make up 'the jigsaw puzzle' (Plannthin, 1998) of the management practices and ideals in every company location and in every aspect of company business. Behind the Novo Nordisk Way of Management is the recognition that the company operates in a highly competitive business sector, but that it is also in the health-care industry, where the company's products and services necessitate high ethical standards of performance, application of high quality levels, and permanent stakeholder goodwill.

Regarding quality, the policy enshrined in the Quality Manual is summarized below:

Novo Nordisk will develop and market high quality products and services that satisfy real needs and improve the way people live and work.

This will be accomplished by setting ambitious goals with a commitment to quality, and by continuously improving products, processes and services.

The commitment to quality and the follow-up on the quality objectives and performance extends to all functions, levels and employees of the organisation.

Quality systems will be based on the philosophy of the ISO 9000 standards, Novo Nordisk Fundamentals, and pertinent regulatory requirements.

Quality will be achieved by prevention of problems rather than by detection and correction.

Actual performance will be evaluated by recurring measurement and review.

Novo Nordisk quality policy (Source: Novo Nordisk, 1997b)

As noted above, the statement of Policies, which constitutes one of the key building bricks of the Novo Nordisk Way of Management, cover 13 operational areas. These are: communication, engineering, environment, finance, health and safety, human resources, information technology, legal requirements, patents, purchasing, quality, regulations, and risk management. As this case study will be much concerned with the communication of company policy throughout its worldwide locations, it is appropriate to present the Novo Nordisk view of communication in terms of policy and requirements:

Communication policy

Novo Nordisk will communicate openly, honestly and timely with each of its stakeholder groups.

Novo Nordisk will communicate with one voice as one company with one vision and shared values.

Novo Nordisk will plan and co-ordinate its communication efforts to ensure that the corporate messages are reflected in our key communications.

Communication requirements

- The unit must communicate timely and well prepared with relevant audiences.

- The unit must ensure that relevant internal stakeholders are informed in advance about a planned public statement.

- The unit must always communicate to staff at the same time or before any other audience is addressed.

- The unit must ensure that Novo Nordisk's quality and design standards are met in all Novo Nordisk's communications.

- The unit must ensure that all communications comply with relevant legal and governmental requirements as well as Novo Nordisk's business strategies.

- The unit must ensure that the Communications & Design Center signs off on all communications activities that have a company-wide scope or might influence the company's image.

Novo Nordisk communication policy and communication requirements
(Source: Novo Nordisk, 1997b)

The Novo Nordisk Way of Management was developed explicitly to meet the needs of local units and individual employees to enjoy more scope for initiative and decision-making, whilst meeting corporate management's aspiration for direction and control of the company. Like all such corporate creeds, the Novo Nordisk philosophy, as reflected in the Way of Management, is a mixture of pragmatism, ideals, business policy, and a set of guidelines for securing high levels of employee commitment. It tells all employees, wherever they work in the organization in terms of hierarchy or geographical location, *what* shall be done and achieved, but it is silent on *how*, because that is for local management to decide. The Novo Nordisk Way of Management was by no means the first company-wide initiative of its kind, but it was by far the most sophisticated.

But the various programmes aimed at improving business conduct, development procedures, cooperation, management effectiveness, communication, and so on, had a habit of attracting initial interest, but little more than that. In the words of one manager: 'We generally liked the ideas behind the programmes. We could comply with the ideas. But they always meant a lot of extra hours of work, and the problem was that you never got any feedback to all the changes you had made. Corporate management never commented upon it. And further, there were no sanctions at all to those who did nothing to change things according to the latest programme. It was highly demotivating.' Significantly, according to a senior corporate manager, past experience of these initiatives and programmes 'had little effect across borders. They were encapsulated and never seemed to make much difference outside a small enclave in corporate headquarters.'

The manager who made that comment was the person responsible for re-structuring the corporate headquarters in the mid-1990s. He would soon have the job of ensuring that Novo Nordisk Way of Management would become second nature to everyone working in the company and in overseas affiliates. Over the years a communication gap had become entrenched between corporate head-quarters in Denmark and local units. There was a plenitude of formal procedures, reporting systems and evaluation tools emanating from headquarters, whilst exchange of knowledge and information among local managers was minimal. If the Novo Nordisk Way of Management was seen as just another headquarters' enthusiasm, which after a while would be quietly discarded, then the new gleam-ing philosophy would be a sham. A way had to be found to create a new *esprit de corps* which made everyone feel part of the same team.

In the meantime corporate management was having to face some awkward ques-tions. Who at corporate headquarters knew exactly how Vision 21 was understood and interpreted by local personnel in Novo Nordisk worldwide? Who knew the degree of compliance to the Fundamentals in Brazil? Why was a particular local manager turning a blind eye to human resources policy? What would be done about it? Who knew what the local staff really thought about the company? How could they contribute to it beyond their immediate function and remit? How, literally and metaphorically, could the Fundamentals be translated into Chinese or Korean? In a complex transitional economy like Russia, how could they be certain that the Moscow personnel grasped why the company was so preoccupied with that mysterious brotherhood called *stakeholders*? How could they gain the trust of personnel so that they would open up and say whether they thought the company was doing the right thing and also the wrong thing? Why was the company only looking upon all these people as local employees and not as a global corporate resource as well? How, in a word, was the company to manage diversity? Henrik Gürtler, senior production manager turned high-profile trouble-shooter, vowed to change all this. There was too much at stake, too much to lose.

THE FACILITATOR CONCEPT

On 21 May 1996, with the approval of corporate management, Henrik Gürtler sent out an e-mail to 1,000 general and senior managers throughout Novo Nordisk.

111

The company needed 14 capable people 'spread over the globe in local units operating in many different countries' for headquarters' positions which he described as 'rather unusual in nature'. The positions, which were to do with a new Corporate Auditor and Facilitator team, were to be filled by 1 January 1997. Gürtler went on:

> All being part of one company, the ever recurring dilemma has been what should be determined or standardized by Corporate HQ or Business Units in DK and what should be determined or standardized according to local needs in each separate unit. One way or the other, systems, procedures, work instructions and records must of course be in place and in control in each local operating unit in order to run the local business. The question is just to which [sic] extent standardization of approach is applied at the local level, the regional level, the business unit level or the corporate level. And, in an other [sic] dimension, to which [sic] extent this standardization of approach is done out of Denmark.
>
> Presently we find ourselves in a situation where a variety of systems, procedures and follow-up mechanisms have been, or are in the process of being standardized by HQ DK. Follow-up is to a large extent focused on whether or not these systems and procedures are used.
>
> The consequence has been little room to maneuver and to apply own judgment re: choice of methods or tools locally and also a significant increase in the upward directed data-flow and central control – however as yet without a similar increase in consolidated data-flow, and feedback the other way.
>
> The general perception by people at large in the company in DK and elsewhere is that it has become unnecessarily difficult to work and manage at Novo Nordisk. Too many activities point 'upwards' and too few point 'downwards'. The hierarchy is perceived as using more time and effort on data-collection, control and explanations than on consolidated data – dissemination, feed-back and help to the operating units. Not to mention outward directed activities with a true customer focus.

The task of the Corporate Auditors and Facilitators – hereafter just Facilitators, the name by which they are known throughout the company – was to assist corporate management in transferring the values associated with the Novo Nordisk Way of Management to all units throughout the world. But there was more to it than that. Gürtler realized that, if all units complied with the company philosophy and precepts and conscientiously lived up to the goals and values, that would make communication amongst units smoother and faster. That, in turn, could reduce barriers to the sharing of knowledge and stimulate more innovation and cooperation among units. He also believed that the synergy would contribute to the same standards of ethical conduct wherever Novo Nordisk did business: customers could always be sure of obtaining the same kind of service and quality when dealing with Novo Nordisk, no what matter unit they were dealing with. The Facilitators would be change agents of a highly unusual kind.

Gürtler saw the jobs of the Facilitators as high profile and high impact. As a reflection of their responsibility and importance, the Facilitators would be appointed at upper director level. The appointments would be for three to five years. Current positions were not a barrier. The company would appoint the best team it could, provided that the manager of a local unit did not stand in the way. As for track-record, potential Facilitators had to fulfil certain prerequisites. They would need to demonstrate:

- a basic understanding of how Novo Nordisk (NN) operates, including the structure, the logistics, the values, the internal networks, the markets and the customers

- an analytical, fact-based, systematic approach and good planning skills

- a proven capacity to work effectively with and deal with people from other cultures

- excellent communication and listening skills

- good problem identification skills and a demonstrated flexibility in problem resolution

- good presentation skills

- an ability to work independently for extended periods of time

- an ability and willingness to be mobile, as the job may require travelling in excess of 100 days a year, depending upon the location (home base) of the Facilitator

Those appointed as Facilitators without a qualification as lead auditors in compliance with the ISO 9000 Standard certification would be required to take and pass an approved course. There was another important consideration. Gürtler was building a team, so he was also after diversity as expressed in factors such as age, sex, educational and professional background, national and ethnic affiliation, language skills, managerial experience and general personality. Diversity would mean a blending of different knowledge and experience which could be channelled into creative synergy, new ideas and fresh solutions to old problems. But the diversity available would, of course, be related to the number of applicants for the positions and individuals' own background. In the event, within a week, Gürtler received 120 applications from all around the world. Selecting the pioneer group of 14 proved a difficult process. In some cases local general managers were prevailed upon to release a genuinely valuable member of his staff. But by September the team was in place. Table 6.1 summarizes the background of the first group of Facilitators. In the column about language ability, the key is as

Table 6.1 Summary of the backgrounds of the first group of Facilitators

Initials, age and location	Nationality (gender)	Education	Years with the company and previous appointment(s)	Language ability
JDA (38) Denmark	Danish (m)	MSc (business)	12 yrs; Sales and Marketing Director NN Farmaka; previously commercial positions in Denmark, Canada and Austria	D, E, G
AB (46) Denmark	Danish (m)	MSc (mechanical & production engineering)	17 yrs; began his career in pharmaceutical packaging and has had positions in production and logistics	D, E
JAC (62) France	British (m)	BSc (biochemistry)	19 yrs after a career in the food industry; previously General Manager for NN enzymes in the UK and General Manager for NN Bioindustri in France	E, F
KD Denmark	Danish (f)	PhD (pharmacology)	13 yrs; from 1992 Director of diabetes research	D, E
GE (44) Denmark	Danish (m)	MSc (anthropology) PhD (psychology)	6 yrs; previously a university lecturer in management and organizational development	D, E, G
YCG Singapore	Malaysian (m)	BSc (pharmacy)	13 yrs; various sales and marketing functions in SE Asia; previously General Manager in Taiwan	E, M, Ch
PG (43) USA	Danish (m)	BSc (chemical engineering) MSc (economics)	9 yrs; process engineering before joining NN; Regional Manager for Health-care in Latin America	D, E, Sp
SG (40) Spain	Spanish (m)	BSc (business)	9 yrs; financial controller before joining NN; Finance and Admin. Director for NN Spain	E, Sp
PFH (40) Denmark	British (m)	Law degree	3 yrs; IT consultant with PriceWaterhouseCoopers before joining NN; previously IT manager in internal audit	E, D
EK (57) Denmark	US citizen (m)	MBA (marketing and organization)	23 yrs; previous NN managerial positions in biochemical business and quality management	E, D, Sw
CK (62) South Africa	South African (m)	BSc (pharmacology)	20 yrs; NN General Manager/Director in South Africa, UK, Germany	E, G
KO (48) Denmark	Danish (f)	MSc (microbiology)	18 yrs; previously scientific positions and finally leader of enzyme research	D, E
JS (50) USA	US citizen (f)	BSc (business)	13 yrs; previously Director of Business and Employee Services for NN USA	E, Sp
MY (61) Japan	Japanese (m)	BSc (agricultural chemistry)	14 yrs; positions in technology management before joining NN; General Manager for Japan	E, J

follows: Ch = Chinese; D = Danish; E = English; F = French; G = German; J = Japanese; M = Malay; Sp = Spanish; Sw = Swedish.

By September 1996 the 14 Facilitators had been selected. The requirement for 14 such specialists was not coincidental. It was estimated that having one Facilitator per 1,000 employees would enable all units in the company to be facilitated in a three-year period; and that proved to be accurate. At the stage of shortlisting and final selection there were delicate exchanges between Henrik Gürtler, who would be overseeing the implementation of the Facilitator concept, and general managers of sundry units around the world, who were being asked to release a vitally effective person for the greater good of the company. Gürtler got his way. The Facilitators all had the diversity he was hoping for. The selected 14, some of whom already knew each other, met for the first time as the senior taskforce in Copenhagen. Then on 16 October 1996 they were literally unveiled by Gürtler to a conference of some 450 senior managers from Novo Nordisk worldwide. On this occasion 75 units from different parts of the world volunteered to undergo a facilitation.

According to one Facilitator, the units had three motivations to volunteer themselves: to show off; to get it over with quickly, 'while the concept was not fully developed; or to get feedback on their performance – 'a real wish for facilitation'. The Facilitators then spent a week taking a course which qualified them as lead auditors in accordance with the ISO 9000 Standard, receiving their certification from the International Register of Certified Auditors. But still they did not exactly know what they were supposed to do; or rather, it was, in principle, clear what they were expected to do, but everything depended on how they, as a team, working under the general guidance of Gürtler, would *create* the job among themselves. No other corporation on this planet had anything quite like it.

Our interviews with the Facilitators took place about a year or so after the project came into operation. By then they had, among themselves, established their own routines and procedures. An intense bonding process had drawn them very tightly together as a group. They developed their own professional discourse, a subset of Novo Nordisk language specific to the task they called facilitation. This word soon came to connote their total operational domain as Facilitators as well as to a specific interaction with a unit. To help with the distinction, the word 'facilitation' will refer to the operational domain; an interaction with a unit will be termed a (or *the*) facilitation. To keep the account lucid, it will be as well to describe first the task of the Facilitators as it evolved in that first highly experimental year and a half. With that as the backdrop, attention will be directed to various issues, beginning with the objectives and general operations of facilitation, leading to a review of the entire facilitation, and concluding with observations on facilitation from the perspectives of cross-cultural management and knowledge management respectively.

THE OBJECTIVES AND GENERAL OPERATIONS OF FACILITATION

In this section I will outline first the objectives and operations of facilitation in general terms, then examine the process in three phases: pre-facilitation, the actual facilitation, and post-facilitation. As a rule of thumb, a facilitation, beginning with the pre-facilitation encounter with the unit manager *in situ* and concluding with the agreed final report and action plan, takes roughly one working week. According to company guidelines, a facilitation is described as 'a structured, planned assessment of the status of implementation of the Novo Nordisk Way of Management with a unit or within a project or process with the aim of developing agreed actions for improvement'. In line with this, the process of facilitation is focused on two main objectives:

1. Assessment of the status and application of the Novo Nordisk Way of Management.

2. Ensuring a balance between business objectives and targets and the methods by which these business objectives are met.

When it comes to the facilitation of a unit, all arrangements, including its scope and fact-finding methods (i.e. interviews, observation, verification), will be made with the unit manager. The owner of a facilitation is the unit manager *not* the Facilitators. The unit manager ensures that the Facilitators obtain sufficient background, interview a representative number of staff, and agree follow-up action with the Facilitators.

As we shall see, one of the striking features about the Facilitators' *modus operandi* has been the way in which they have described their work and then codified it, thus creating, quite independently, procedures and even their own rules of professional practice. Thus they characterized facilitation work as comprising three main components, using the key words: assess, assist, facilitate.

1. Through on-site auditing/facilitating of departments, factories, affiliates, to *assess* whether or not the company-wide minimum standard requirements or 'ground rules' as specified in the Novo Nordisk Way of Management were met.

2. Through on-site advice and help, to *assist* the unit in question in correcting identified non-conformity with these requirements.

3. Through on-site identification of 'best practices' applied, to *facilitate* communication and sharing of these best practices across the organization.

Facilitators always operate in pairs, which they refer to as duos. Membership of the duos is perpetually changing so that wherever possible a given pair embodies the best combination of professional competences, language ability or cultural knowledge for facilitating a particular unit. Not all Facilitators believe that it was essential to get the best matched duo for given situations, though several conceded that facilitations in Asia went better with an Asian colleague. First, this was not always possible for practical reasons. Second, professionalism and integrity could outweigh specific limitations in domain knowledge. The precise composition of duos is, however, decided by Gürtler's administrative staff, who make the necessary logistical arrangements to ensure the widest interaction among the Facilitators for their own professional development. It would in any case be against the spirit of the entire Facilitator concept if even a small number of them became type-cast for specific kinds of facilitation. Nevertheless, experience had shown that, if legal experts were being facilitated, it was helpful if one of the duo had a legal training. Facilitations with engineers and R&D staff were more productive if at least one of the duo had a technical or scientific background.

There are two main types of facilitation:

1. Facilitation of a Novo Nordisk unit.

2. Facilitation of a cross-organizational unit or project/process group.

In the beginning the first type of facilitation was by far the most common, but, as we shall see, the latter type is now more in demand by company units. However, more cross-organizational facilitations are anticipated in the future. As such facilitations may have important strategic and policy-making consequences, these are likely to be closely scrutinized by top management. This may have two outcomes for Facilitators. First, they may lose some independence. Second, cross-organizational facilitations may require new approaches and skills.

In summary, the Facilitators:

- Obtain objective evidence through a fact-finding process

- Provide objective, validated assessments and conclusions

- Include recommendations for improvements, where appropriate

- Agree on action plans with unit or process managers

- Follow-up on the implementation of the action plan

- Fulfil their responsibilities in a manner demonstrating integrity, objectivity and professional behaviour

The Facilitators are Novo Nordisk's international change agents, and they operate with the full backing of corporate management. Although the somewhat intimidatory word 'audit' has been dropped from the operational vocabulary, a major aspect of the Facilitators' job is precisely that. In the beginning of the scheme Facilitators were only too aware of being suspiciously regarded throughout the company – in their own words – as 'cultural watchdogs', even 'the KGB of corporate management'. However, all the evidence is that facilitation has proved to be a generally beneficial experience (for example, nobody has been summarily dismissed as a result of a facilitation). One of the key purposes of facilitation is to ensure compliance with the Novo Nordisk Way of Management. But things may not be quite so clear-cut. As one Novo Nordisk employee (not a Facilitator) told us: 'A social contract has been made between top and bottom in the organization: "if you (units and affiliates) comply with the ten fundamentals, we (corporate management) will not interfere with how you run things".'

Although the word 'compliance' is entirely unambiguous, some Facilitators use the word with a certain distaste. It smacks too much of enforcement, paralyzing the very empowerment that facilitation is supposed to encourage. On the other hand, it was found that in Japan, a country of vastly complicated checks and balances between those who govern and those who are governed, it was both desirable and expected that Facilitators represented the authority of the company. This, incidentally, represents a nice juxtaposition between Japan, *the* masculine country *par excellence* in the Hofstedian compass, and Denmark, one of the most feminine countries. Over many centuries, the Japanese have become accustomed to relentless exhortation from superiors and guardians of approved civic conduct; it is part of life. In Denmark it would be seen as abrasive intrusiveness.

With this as background we can proceed to look at Facilitator work in the three phases mentioned above: pre-facilitation, the actual facilitation, and post-facilitation. Then, in the concluding sections, we will examine the Facilitator work first from a cross-cultural management standpoint and then from a knowledge management perspective.

THE PRE-FACILITATION PROCESS

As with negotiation, the key to facilitation lies more with sound preparation than with any other factor. Compendious background information on a unit to be facilitated must be gathered and assimilated by the Facilitators. Documentary materials will include:

- Organizational diagrams

- Staffing lists by name, title and date of hire

- Results of previous organizational audits or reviews (a standardized process at Novo Nordisk)

- Climate survey results

- Unit mission and/or goals

- Unit business plan

The Facilitators also check among themselves and then with contacts in their personal company network for factual evidence about a unit, its performance, the quality of its management, personalities involved, and the nature of specific problems or opportunities confronting it. In the meantime, Home Base will try to pair the unit with the most appropriate duo of Facilitators. In the preparation phase the duo will make contact with the unit management and compile for them a pre-facilitation package, which can be accessed by the company's so-called Intraweb FACIT system. It is extremely important in this phase to involve the unit management so that they feel that they are the owners of the facilitation. This has not always proved easy. The terms 'facilitator' and 'facilitation' could not initially be straightforwardly translated into languages like Japanese, Chinese and Korean, and the concept needed careful, occasionally diplomatic, explanation. A unit in Hong Kong was convinced that facilitation was a waste of time until they had experienced it.

Psychologically it is seen as very important by the Facilitators to involve the unit manager and key staff as quickly as possible so that they are involved in planning meetings (where the Facilitators meet the unit manager to discuss all aspects of the facilitation) and information meetings (where the Facilitators meet the management team and entire staff who are to be facilitated and explain the background, objectives and process). At such pre-facilitation meetings (as well as in the main facilitation meetings themselves) Facilitators have learnt to behave with intelligence and tact.

According to company estimates, the Facilitators work approximately 40 weeks a year. This means in practice that they are involved in 60 on-site facilitation days. The on-site facilitation process usually takes one week, based on the following estimates: $1\frac{1}{2}$ days for preparation; $1\frac{1}{2}$ days for the facilitation itself; 1 day for the report; and 1 day for the follow-up. But, realistically, with preparation before the site visit and the various ways of following-up a standard facilitation, involving two Facilitators, the facilitation can be regarded as taking three weeks of company time. In some rare complicated cases the follow-up has extended over several months (calendar months, that is; not months of dedicated company time). The Facilitators could not support the follow-up without an effective back-up system, headed by Henrik Gürtler, at Home Base.

Finally, it must not be overlooked that one of the most crucial aims of the pre-facilitation phase is to make certain that the Facilitators and the unit manager agree on those aspects of the Novo Nordisk Way of Management which are least observed, least understood, least complied with. Remember that the Facilitator's *raison d'être* and his or her perceived integrity and professionalism are inextricably linked with the company's guiding principles and precepts. He or she has no authority to tackle issues from any other stand-point.

THE FACILITATION PROPER

As already noted, facilitations are conducted by a team of two Facilitators. Once the pre-facilitation phase has been concluded and all essential arrangements made, the two Facilitators travel to the unit. Normally, an opening meeting is held with the unit management to confirm agreements made during the planning process, including the purpose and scope of the facilitation, the process to be followed, and practical arrangements. For the sake of simplicity it is possible to regard a facilitation as comprising four aspects.

In Facilitator terminology the first aspect is called *fact-finding*, but this is not a strictly accurate designation in that, as we have seen, the Facilitators have already accumulated several facts about the unit. So this phase, which involves interviews, observation of procedures and possibly verification of results (technical, commercial or administrative), is more concerned with the corroboration of facts or otherwise. Generally, interviews are the most productive form of enquiry. There is no agreed format. Sometimes both Facilitators interview together, sometimes independently; there may be one interviewee, or there may be several. It depends on the circumstances and the wish of the unit manager. A second aspect of the process involves the *perusal of unit documentation*. Facilitators are within their rights to request units to supply information on job descriptions, development plans or performance evaluations, business plans, minutes of meetings. Although we learnt of cases where unit managers were being obstructive (especially when it came to forms of recommended action they did not approve of), we did not hear of an instance of refusal to make unit documents available. Although English is the corporate language of Novo Nordisk, some unit documentation is in the language of the country. If that language is Thai, Turkish or Czech, it is unlikely to be produced for inspection by Facilitators.

The third aspect of a facilitation is concerned with *identifying better practice*. When the Facilitator concept was being disseminated throughout Novo Nordisk, many who were sceptical about its chances of having real impact easily overlooked the fact that a major task of the Facilitators was to identify examples of better practice so that good ideas, new applications, new marketing ideas could be picked up and transferred to other parts of the company. The Facilitators make extensive use of the company Intraweb system and Home Base in order to make certain that examples of better practice have the best possible chance of reaching the units which can take advantage of them. The fact that Facilitators make it known that they are seeking examples of better practice can help a unit to feel that it has something to contribute to units in other countries and is therefore a useful local cog in a bigger global machine.

The fourth aspect of facilitation is described as *closing and reporting*. The Facilitators prepare a report listing action points which they discuss with the unit manager and possibly members of his staff. A final report, incorporating jointly agreed action points, is prepared and will be signed by the Facilitator and the unit manager. The parties also agree on how best to communicate the facilitation results to relevant unit members. Copies of the final report go to the unit manager's immediate superior and to Henrik Gürtler as the member of corporate management responsible for the Facilitators. Copies of the report do *not* go beyond Gürtler.

POST-FACILITATION

One of the Facilitators will be designated as responsible for the follow-up of the facilitation. It is the responsibility of this Facilitator to follow up with so-called action nominees of the given unit in order to verify that the agreed action plan is being implemented (or has been completed). If the unit has problems in comply-ing with a specific aspect of the action plan (for example, meeting a deadline), the manager is required to notify the appropriate Facilitator in good time with an explanation. This may require further discussion with the Facilitator team to agree a modified action item. In the event of complete compliance with the action points, the unit manager will be notified by the responsible Facilitator that there will be no further follow-up and that the facilitation is concluded.

If, for whatever reason, a unit fails to execute the agreed action points, then the Facilitator issues a note of non-conformity, which compels the Facilitator and unit management to reach consensus. In the event of these last-ditch attempts failing, the Facilitators are empowered to report the non-conformity to Henrik Gürtler, who both as the manager responsible for the Facilitators and as a member of corporate management, will take appropriate action. That could, in principle, mean the serving of notice on a member or members of a non-compliant unit. We only heard of one case of intransigence on the part of a unit manager. In the event the individual resigned by way of bowing to the inevitable.

FACILITATION: AN INTERIM REVIEW

The Facilitator concept is an experiment; it is a gamble and a massive investment in human capital. The background against which the concept took root was not propitious. It was seen as yet another scheme dreamt up by corporate manage-ment. Its detractors were many, sceptical, even hostile. The Facilitators themselves were placed in an invidious position at the outset, being seen as unnecessary, interfering enforcers of a corporate management that never understood life in humbler incarnations. Remarkably, the Facilitators proved their value within their first year. Word got around the company that facilitation was worthwhile after all and units started to apply voluntarily to participate in the programme. They were being seen a helpful, positively minded and effective internal consultants, who discussed rather than imposed. So it was that the Facilitators developed a *modus operandi* – 'management system' might be too strong a term for it – which one neatly characterized as 'diversity by design'.

Somewhat bizarrely, the Facilitators, who had been figures of suspicion, now began to acquire a certain mystique. This situation forced Gürtler and headquarters

121

corporate communications staff to prepare information materials on facilitation in order to demystify its purpose, its processes and the personalities associated with it. It is hard to account for the mystique, which was a reaction that the Facilitators themselves did not encourage, but it is probable that it was to do with the fact that employees were being treated in a wholly unusual way and exposed to an exceptional and impressive kind of knowledge about the company. It may not be an exaggeration to say that the Facilitators were held in some awe by some employees. Rightly or wrongly, the impression projected and indeed the impression experienced by the Facilitators themselves is that they were an isolated enclave. Despite the fact that the Facilitators were acquiring and acting upon vast quantities of company information, much of which was confidential and had to be handled with great sensitivity, they felt isolated from mainstream decision-making and information flows. This, as we shall see, was a key factor in creating the intense bonds of loyalty to each other, which was one of their defining features as a group.

Many of the Facilitators, even those who were resident in Denmark, were aware of being removed from their previous, familiar professional milieu within the company and of now feeling that they did not belong anywhere. This situation had a further convoluting dimension to it. Some of the Facilitators were conscious of a kind of divide between the Danish and non-Danish members of the team, but it would be utterly mistaken to talk of frictions and tensions. On the other hand, Gürtler and his staff recognized that this was an unwelcome factor in the group dynamics. Accordingly, there is discussion – nothing more at this stage – about the feasibility of setting up groups of Facilitators on the basis of some kind of geographical-cultural unity. But the Facilitators do not as yet approve, thinking that would eventually propagate centres of isolation, leading to retrenchment and parochialism.

Nevertheless, as noted above, there developed among the Facilitators a powerful sense of loyalty and commitment to each other. It was noticeable to the three of us who interviewed them that they were exceptionally self-protective. The famous motto of the Three Musketeers 'One for all and all for one' applied to them in full measure. There were many strands to the bonds: the deep commitment to the company and its ideals, and their respect for their own diversity in terms of educational background, professional competences, achievements within the company, not to mention their recognition that they were *special*. What is striking to the observer is the extent to which the Facilitators, as a cross-culturally diverse group in its own right, have become both self-educating and self-empowering. This is real synergy. The fact is the Facilitators have written their own script, but modify it so that the job of facilitation is continually creative and immensely intellectually and professionally satisfying to the Facilitators.

But all this would not be possible, were it not for the fact that they have been given exceptional independence and discretion. They are virtually self-managing.

Nevertheless, their relationship with Gürtler is crucial. They are the actors in his show. Like all good stage directors, he has planned everything thoroughly in advance, chosen the best people for the parts, but, even though the play appears to be enjoying a winning run, he is always present behind the scenes. He knows that in a year's time it will be a slightly different play: a few new actors, some new sub-plots, some new techniques of audience involvement. His style is to guide rather than direct. Somewhat to his own surprise, he is called upon by the Facilitators to help them resolve issues and conflicts. They seem to depend on him, but awkwardly. How is it, he has occasionally wondered, that this group of highly intelligent people seem incapable of resolving a seemingly straightforward issue or conflict? Is it a judgement they want or simple reassurance? Are the two the same? His relationship with them both tests and exhilarates him. In the way of Scandinavian managers he is reluctant to intervene in a heavy way, though this has happened. Although he is considerably respected by all the Facilitators, his style of management is seen as remote by those who, like the Americans, expect a hands-on approach or the Asians, for whom management should be visibly authoritarian and paternalistic leavened with benevolence.

The key questions concerning the Facilitators are, of course: has the investment been worth it? And, how, in any case, do you measure their contribution to the company? These are issues which were not of direct concern to the researchers, but the impression given by the Facilitators themselves and by Gürtler is that the benefits are outweighing the nominal costs. At the time of writing (June 2000) the experiment is continuing. But the future poses big challenges to the facilitation as a management tool. What sort of career paths can be open to Facilitators after three years in the job? How can Facilitators be developed to undertake inter-organizational facilitations? Should future groups of Facilitators be essentially self-managing or should they be under more control from corporate management. Should there be fewer Danes in the team? Is there such a thing as optimum diversity mix in terms of management experience, experience of Novo Nordisk, professional competences, linguistic abilities and cultural knowledge? Should there be new procedures for recruiting new Facilitators? Fortunately, there are some concrete answers to some of these questions and they are discussed in the final section of this case study, which is in the form of an update on the Facilitators since the original interviews in 1998.

FACILITATION AS CROSS-CULTURAL MANAGEMENT

The Facilitators constitute a complex multicultural taskforce, challenged to ensure that any unit of Novo Nordisk is complying with the company's business philosophy and management precepts and to make better practices, identified in any unit, available throughout the company. From a cross-cultural management perspective there are two key dimensions:

123

- Their self-management as a multicultural, multilingual team

- Their interactions with units they facilitate

We now consider each of these perspectives.

SELF-MANAGEMENT AS A MULTICULTURAL, MULTILINGUAL TEAM

The Facilitators consist of 14 people with some 200 years of collective experience of the company, and most of those years were connected with a variety of scientific, technical, commercial and personnel functions involving the exercise of considerable responsibility. Seven were educated to masters level and beyond. Their educational range covered law, anthropology, various branches of engineering, various sciences and business. Between them they had operated in key positions in several countries outside their country of origin. All spoke a language additional to their native one. They were six Danes, two Americans, two Britons, a South African, a Spaniard, a Malaysian and a Japanese. Three of the group were women, of whom two, incidentally, had previously held down exceptionally important jobs in R&D. And, finally, they all had two things in common, which Table 6.1 (see page 114) cannot convey. First, they had extensive international networks within the company. Second, each and everyone was completely committed to Novo Nordisk; all identified with the rationale for the Facilitator concept; and each one was determined to make an impact.

In their work with all other members of the team, as well as in their duos, the Facilitators were continually transferring knowledge and experience. Crucially, from the outset they respected each other's professionalism. Despite disparities in age and length of service with the company, the Facilitators readily espoused a culture of equality. As a result, there was no informal leader among them, no one person designated as a spokesperson for the group. They valued the diversity they represented. Danes were the most numerous nationality and although, as we noted, there was a slight sense of division between them and their non-Danish colleagues, they did not assert themselves as a national group. That would be an altogether unDanish thing to do, but could have happened with a preponderance of national groups with a well-known penchant for establishing individual dynamism (and to hell with what others think): the Germans, Americans, the British, the Japanese. To some extent, therefore, the management of the group was by osmosis, linked to a strong shared commitment to the Facilitator concept. When, as it occasionally did, osmosis failed, they turned to Henrik Gürtler.

It may be too strong to suggest that the Facilitators formed a completely distinctive sub-group within Novo Nordisk, but a notable feature of their unity as an entity was the evolution of their own discourse. They could speak of facilitation with a certain clinical detachment. Facilitation was a complex interweaving of processes which only they observed and influenced and in which they, unavoidably, participated. As one Danish Facilitator told us: 'Once I tried to explain to my mother what a Facilitator was, but she just could not understand.' They began to write their own materials, including a charter of standards, procedures and guidelines.

Unlike many multicultural teams, the Facilitators are, as far as we can tell, a permanent rather than transient team (even if personalities change), so they take a long-term view of facilitation and regard its outcomes – ideas, practices, insights into the Novo Nordisk Way of Management – as a resource which can be beneficially tapped by the company. These outcomes would in all probability not have been made available to the company without the Facilitators as a multicultural, multilingual professional team.

INTERACTIONS WITH UNITS

In all the phases of facilitation which bring them into direct involvement with units, the Facilitators are aware that their function requires not only exceptional communication skills and listening skills, but also a capacity to adapt behaviour – and dress – according to circumstances. Regarding language issues, the normal language of facilitation is English, but it is Danish if a Danish duo happens to be conducting a facilitation in Denmark. In some countries where the knowledge of English is relatively weak among members of a particular unit, the facilitation may require the services of an interpreter. A facilitation in Moscow, despite some language problems, proved to be one of the most productive interactions of its kind. This suggests that an approach based on listening and consultation may be a valuable way of developing collaborative learning with Russians, who have a well-known aversion to being treated by 'wise' Westerners as second-class citizens in their own country.

Regarding personal adaptations, the two Asian facilitators have found it difficult to adjust to the less formal, more relaxed style of things in Scandinavia. In Denmark these meetings can proceed with casual dress (non-Danish facilitators have bought casual business wear for facilitations in Scandinavia), but in more formal business cultures like Japan or Germany more formal attire is expected. The appropriate use of first names, surnames and titles has proved to be an intricate cross-cultural learning experience. The Facilitators might use the first name of their fairly Westernized Japanese colleague, but would not dream of using that name, even with the *de rigueur* 'san' after it, in front of Japanese staff his junior.

In India, it seemed, there had to be meticulous use of titles in front of 'lesser mortals'. For example, it was found fairly early on that facilitations in Asia (including India) proceeded better if one of the duo was either the Malaysian or Japanese facilitator. Duos consisting of Europeans and Americans came across as somewhat tutorial and assertive. For all the European and American Facilitators, the handling of interpersonal relationships in more hierarchically organized cultures, especially when junior people are present, has proved a difficult learning experience. The Danish Facilitators, brought up and educated in a country where informality is (generally) a way of life, found the adjustment to more formal cultures quite difficult. The relaxed Danish style *can* be interpreted as lack of professionalism in more assertive cultures.

FACILITATION AS KNOWLEDGE MANAGEMENT

One of the rationales behind the Facilitator concept was the perceived need to disseminate better practice throughout the company on a worldwide basis. Although the company had installed a sophisticated and expensive intranet communication system, it was found – not for the first time – that individuals prefer human interaction to electronically mediated exchanges with colleagues, even when they know each other well. Thus, a calculation behind the Facilitator concept was that it met the need for interfaces with direct human contact. As argued above, the Facilitators appear to have proved themselves to be highly adept at identifying valuable knowledge and examples of good practice. It would not be a misnomer to call them cross-cultural knowledge brokers (but we should not forget that they also act as mediators of company philosophy and management precepts as well as (*ad hoc*) consultants). They gain knowledge in four key ways: interviewing, observing, verifying and studying relevant documentation.

The quality of exchanges can be constrained if (a) unit representatives do not have a very good command of English; (b) interpreters are used who may be unfamiliar with the concepts and terminology associated with, and the rationale behind, facilitation; and (c) the language of the unit lacks conceptual or lexical resources for discussing facilitation. By extrapolation of the evidence provided by the Facilitators, we can identify two broad classes of language associated with these limitations. The first class comprises languages like Russian, languages which have not yet shed the veneer of socialist thought and not yet assimilated the terminology – and jargon – of the market economy. Thus we are referring to the languages of East and Central Europe as well as to 'imperial' Russian as the main professional language of non-Russians resident in the former USSR. The second class relates to languages which go under the vast rubric 'oriental': Korean, Japanese, Korean, Turkish. These are all non-Indo-European languages which are based on a non-Western world-view and which are spoken by peoples whose concepts of management are pragmatic and who are, as a rule, mystified as to the peculiar Western (especially American) tendency to over-systematize and jargon-ize the language of *merely* running a business.

Several commentators on knowledge management have noted a tendency of people to resist participation in knowledge-sharing activities. Their lack of absorptive capacity (to use the jargon) is put down to general human cussedness, a sense of threat or reluctance to change working style. In the above account we encountered two kinds of resistance. First, it will be recalled that the Facilitator concept was initially greeted with scepticism and suspicion in certain parts of the company. It was seen as yet another corporate management fad that would not take root. Behind this façade lies what might be called the darker picture. The Novo Nordisk experience suggests that it can prove difficult to introduce knowledge-sharing schemes when management has a credibility problem with its employees. One remarkable feature of the Novo Nordisk case is that within a year the Facilitators had managed to establish themselves and largely eradicate the negative sentiments towards them. In a sense they have directly helped to reinforce corporate management's reputation within the company.

Writers on knowledge management view organizational learning as an intimately related activity. In this case study we have every reason to believe (although we never explicitly investigated this) that better practices have been successfully transplanted from unit to unit around the world as a result of facilitation. This suggests that the Facilitators have taken tacit knowledge from one location and transferred it as explicit knowledge to other locations, where it may again become tacit knowledge with local inflections, as it were. But there can be little doubt that the most significant group of learners within Novo Nordisk is that of the Facilitators themselves. Through becoming Facilitators they have extended their professional knowledge base by:

- Absorbing and documenting 'new' knowledge about the company from the point of view of units, each with a different embedding in three interacting levels of culture: national, corporate and professional

- Adapting personal behaviour and communication styles to suit local conditions

- Sharing 'facilitation know-how' with other Facilitators

- Prioritizing acquired knowledge

- Converting knowledge into suitable formats for transfer to potential beneficiaries in the company

- Combining their existing professional knowledge with that of other Facilitators in duos or on a group basis

- Doing all these things cross-culturally through the application of intelligence and tact

The personal and organizational achievement behind the latter point cannot be emphasized enough.

HOW IMITABLE IS NOVO NORDISK-STYLE FACILITATION?

Novo Nordisk's Facilitators are cross-cultural change agents precisely in the spirit of cross-cultural management as it is advanced in this book. They operate in sets of multicultural domains; they transfer knowledge, values and experience from one domain to another to support managers there; and every facilitation is a synergistic experience which is nevertheless managed. This raises a key question. Could other companies develop a comparable system? In principle, yes, but the challenges are legion. First, the Novo Nordisk experience indicates that the Facilitators must be given real independence and powers of discretion. Top management has to trust its seasoned professionals. Second, it is the case that between them the Novo Nordisk Facilitators have a huge number of years' experience of the company – in different countries and in a variety of professional competences. Third, the Facilitators represent an extraordinary array of talent, (international) experience, linguistic ability, as well as diversity of educational and professional background. Fourth, when the Facilitator positions were announced, corporate management agreed that applicants' current positions should not be a hindrance. Fifth, they get total support from headquarters in the form of one of the most senior managers in the entire company.

But this is not all. Novo Nordisk is a Danish company. As such it is permeated with Danish and Scandinavian cultural values, which stress consensus, conciliation and egalitarianism, in which confrontation is not relished and hierarchy disdained, in which control over people is loose rather than tight, and in which human development is not be overridden by economic considerations (see the Further Reading section at the end of the chapter). That the Facilitators are the product of the Scandinavian management system can be no coincidence. It might perhaps be more difficult for the Facilitator concept to take root in the more muscular management cultures of the USA, the UK or Germany, not to mention the authoritarian, rigid, ethnocentric management cultures of Japan or Korea, for whom in any case cross-cultural communication is often a form of angst. But perhaps the true litmus test for any company that thinks it could emulate Novo Nordisk is to ask itself two questions. First, would it, like Novo Nordisk, think of facilitating cleaning personnel at corporate headquarters? Second, if it thought about it, would it, like Novo Nordisk, actually do it, listen to the outcome and act prudently on it?

AFTERWORD: THE FACILITATORS THREE YEARS ON

As noted earlier, the information on the Facilitator concept in this case study was gathered in 1999. Since that time, there have been some important developments. First of all, Novo Nordisk is creating a demerger of its two main businesses. There will be a new holding company called Novo A/S. The name Novo Nordisk will apply to the health-care business, and the enzyme business is called Novozymes A/S. The demerger will also spin off three other specialist companies. What will happen to the Facilitators? The three-year experiment commenced in 1997 and no fewer than 200 facilitations have taken place. The Facilitator concept been judged at all levels and in every quarter to have been a success.

As a result, the Facilitators will continue, but their personnel will change. Six were to be replaced by autumn 2000. Of the six who were leaving, one was retiring completely. Another was to combine retirement with part-time work as a Facilitator. The remaining four have all been offered jobs within or outside the company which represent significant promotions. For all the original group, facilitation has been an organizational learning experience of professional self-enrichment, for which it may be hard to find a parallel in any other company. There can be no doubt that they have earned their collective and personal promotion.

In the new structure facilitation will become a central service to which individual Novo companies subscribe. Between them they will pool some 25 million Danish krone (around £2m or $2.8m). In the new structure the Facilitators will work directly for the CEOs of the new Novo companies, who will have access to their reports. This means that the Facilitators have been promoted, but it is an important departure in another way. In the past their reports went to Henrik Gürtler, the senior manager responsible for the Facilitators, and did not go beyond him. It will be recalled that in the early days the Facilitators were regarded in some quarters as policemen, who would divulge to corporate management. In three years the Facilitators have shown that this never was their role, so they have achieved company-wide confidence; the units now know that the objective of facilitation is get everybody working better within the company guidelines, not going after 'wrong-doers'. Despite the new reporting procedure, the Facilitators will still enjoy professional independence.

How has Novo judged the success of the Facilitators? First of all, they have been subject to the company's own personnel quality system on the customary six-monthly basis. On the six occasions to date, the Facilitators have been judged to be 'suitable and effective'. Now that the Facilitators have been an operating group for three years it is possible to pinpoint precisely in what ways they have had a significant impact. First of all, the company has recognized that compliance simply does not happen by itself and the Facilitators have had considerable success worldwide not only in securing compliance, but pinpointing why it was difficult for particular units to adhere to company guidelines. Second, facilitation has helped the company identify where it lacks competencies for handling particular issues. Third, they have acted as a catalyst for setting up communication between various domains of the companies, which in the past may not have known that another entity in the company had grappled with a similar problem and found a solution. This has even resulted in the setting-up of cross-functional interest groups, which would otherwise never have come into existence. Thus the Facilitators are a pragmatic force for localization and empowerment. Fourth, the units had discovered that, if they entered into a frank and open dialogue with the Facilitators, the outcome was almost invariably constructive. Fifth, units that had been facilitated were contacting Facilitators asking them advice on other issues. Hence, they had become a very valuable resource of knowledge and experience, tapped not just in corporate headquarters, but throughout the Novo companies worldwide. All this is acknowledged by the CEO, Mads Øvlisen, who has proudly described them as 'the global messengers of the [Novo Nordisk] culture'.

How important are the Facilitators to the transfer of good practice? The Facilitators have become very knowledgeable about examples of good practice in virtually every corner of the company. It has been found that when a Facilitator says to a particular unit 'I have seen this instance of good practice', it has more impact than any other method that the company has devised. Indeed, the personal interaction has led, literally, to the dismantling of the internal IT support system for transferring good practice. As it became known that the Facilitators were seeking examples of good practice, it proved an incentive to units to make certain that they had something to offer other parts of the company.

The company can also thank the Facilitators for rooting out malpractices which affected the company worldwide. In a certain country a Facilitator duo was able to unearth a malpractice that was not only a serious breach of company rules, but also a punishable crime in that country. This particular breach was well-known to the company (and not unfamiliar other major pharmaceutical companies as well). For the first time the company was able to identity exactly how the malpractice was being perpetrated. Once this information was transmitted to headquarters, a meeting of *all* senior managers responsible for regional businesses was immediately called. As a result Novo was able for the first time to take corporate action to stamp out the scam.

In what ways has the task of facilitation evolved in the first three years of operation? There are two significant things to report. We have already noted that the Facilitators had to learn on the job, and to do this they brought an abundance of professional experience and know-how. But the units, too, had to learn about facilitation because we are, in the end, talking about a symbiotic process. Once the units became aware of the positive benefits of facilitation, they began to demand more of the Facilitators. As noted above, Facilitators are being increasingly used for independent advice by specific units. But of great significance is the fact that they have been asked to conduct cross-functional facilitations. At the time of writing about one in six facilitations is of a cross-functional nature. For example, they have facilitated value-chains and in a similar vein relationships between R&D staff and production personnel. They have also been called in, apparently to good effect, to get to the source of perceptual mismatches between senior management at Novo headquarters and their counterparts in the USA.

Finally, now that three years have passed, has it been decided to change the job specification? The answer is surprisingly little. The generic skills are virtually the same as those required by Henrik Gürtler in his memo of May 1996. But in a memo in April 2000, in which Gürtler advertises for six new Facilitators, specific professional backgrounds, specific cultural backgrounds, and specific language competencies are being sought (Table 6.2).

Table 6.2 Latest brief job description of the Facilitators

Specific professional backgrounds sought
- HC discovery/development
- HC international operations
- HC marketing
- EB marketing/sales
- EB production

Specific cultural backgrounds sought
- People from China/India/South East Asia
- People from Central/Eastern Europe
- People from North/South America
- People from Norway/Sweden/Finland

Specific language competencies sought
- Command of Chinese language(s)
- Command of French language
- Command of German language
- Command of Japanese language
- Command of Portuguese and/or Spanish language

And then we preferably need at least 3 of the 6 new Facilitators to be women.

NOTES

1. Nordisk Gentofte was founded by the Danish Nobel Prize winner, Professor August Krogh.
2. According to the 1999 annual report, Novo Nordisk's turnover in 1998 was 20,000 million Danish krone, a 16.8% increase over turnover for the previous financial year.
3. Known as the MAX project in the company, MAX denoting 'maximizing value'.

FURTHER READING

Readers interested in Danish management may find the following publications useful:
Fivelsdal, E. and Shramm-Nielsen, J. (1993). Egalitarianism at work: Management in Denmark. In: Hickson, D. (ed.). *Management in Western Europe*. Berlin: de Gruyter, pp. 27–45.
Hofstede, G. (1994). *Cultures and organizations: Software of the mind*. London: HarperCollins.

Schramm-Nielsen, J. and Lawrence, P. (1998). Scandinavian management: A cultural homogeneity beyond the nation state. *Entreprises et Histoire* 18: 71–91.

Schrøder, J. (1987). *The cultural basis of Danish management.* Knebel, Denmark: Office of Social Development. Originally published in Danish under the title: *Hvad har Grundtvig at sige den Danske leder?*

REFERENCES

Plannthin, M. (1998). In the shadow of the good facilitator: An analysis of culture control among the international Facilitators at Novo Nordisk A/S. MSc dissertation: Copenhagen Business School (in Danish).

The following Novo Nordisk publications have been consulted:

Max News (August and October 1996)
Novo Nordisk (1997). *Operationalizing Vision 21.*
Focus: Facilitating change (video) (1997a)
Novo Nordisk Way of Management: A short interpretation guide to the fundamentals (1997b)
Novo Nordisk Annual Report (1997c)
Novo Nordisk Annual Report (1999)
Novo Nordisk Environmental and Social Report (1999a)
The facilitation process: Charter of standards, procedures and guidelines (1998)

The following leaflets:

Charter for companies in the Novo Group (2000)
Facilitator: Conducting the follow-up within the Novo Group (2000)
Sustainability: Profiting from our principles (2000)
You have been facilitated: A corporate perspective (1998)

Novo Nordisk web site (2000)
Copies of sundry internal e-mails and memos (1997–2000)

7 Case study 2
Matsushita Electric: a learning history

PROLOGUE

This case study is in the form of a learning history (see chapter 5). At its core lie the philosophy, vision and institutional legacy of the founder of one of the world's largest and most powerful commercial organizations, the Matsushita Electric Industrial Company of Japan. At first glance this may not seem like a particularly prepossessing subject. But consider what we are talking about – the intertwining of three remarkable stories: the story of the founder, Konosuke Matsushita (1894–1989), who was by any standards one of the greatest industrialists of the twentieth century; the story of his company, which in the 1980s was an icon of Japanese management practices and which today is finding it difficult to adjust to the demands of globalization; and the story of Japan itself, a country whose impact on the twentieth century, in peace and war, has been both incalculable and controversial.

The Matsushita Electric Industrial Company (MEI), the supplier of electrical and consumer electronics products under the principal brand names of Panasonic and Technics, was ranked the world's twenty-sixth corporation and the third biggest electrical company in the Fortune Global 500 of 2000 (*Fortune*, 2000). Matsushita's business is divided into four main product groups: consumer electronic and electric appliances; information and communication equipment; electrical and electronic components; and video and audio equipment. The company, which in 1999 had revenues totalling $65 billion, employs some 290,000 people, of whom some 150,000 are non-Japanese employees working for the company in 218 overseas subsidiaries in 40 countries (*Fortune*, 2000; Panasonic, 2000a).

The aim of this case study (or learning history) is to bring the three stories together in order to produce a tableau of rich and complex contextual knowledge, which is essential for explicating (a) the company strategy of globalization and localization, (b) relationships between local affiliates and corporate headquarters, and (c) the impact of the past on contemporary thinking, behaviour, and even company structures.

It is very important to emphasize that among Japanese corporations Matsushita Electric is decidedly *sui generis*.[1] Thus the company-specific experiences reported in this case study should *not* be taken as typical of other Japanese corporations;

that would be a very serious missing of the point. Nevertheless, against that it can be said that the Matsushita case throws up various critical instances of the way in which domination by one national group in a corporate culture can be a constraint on the transfer of knowledge, values and experience throughout an immensely large organization. In contrast to the other three case studies, this is one is heavily referenced, as the kind of knowledge under consideration is in many respects specialist, and readers may wish to consult experts on specific topics. The main sources of information for this case study are various publications of the company and Konosuke's personal think tank, the PHP Institute; the biography of Konosuke Matsushita by Harvard professor, John Kotter (1997); and interviews with Japanese and non-Japanese managers (see also 'methodology' below).

The Matsushita case has many unusual features, the most striking of which is the centrality to the entire organization of a company philosophy that comprises a basic management objective, a company creed and a set of business principles. This philosophy took shape in the founder's mind in the 1920s and all the elements were articulated by 1933. This in many ways humanistic philosophy was created at a time when Japan was becoming a hotbed of ultra-nationalistic xenophobia. The same philosophy was used as a rallying call in the grim post-war years to re-unify the company and even restore national dignity; and its somewhat naive universalism was put into service in the cause of internationalization during the 1970s and 1980s and then again in the 1990s in the cause of globalization. A major cross-cultural issue concerning the philosophy, as we shall see, is that it can be said to permeate the professional lives and thinking of the company's *Japanese* employees, but for its non-Japanese employees throughout the world it can variously be a source of confusion, bemusement, Japanese self-mystification (something of a Japanese speciality, it must be said) and even irrelevance. This philosophy has huge implications for an understanding of the Matsushita Corporation. It is worthwhile reflecting on these characteristics as they occur in the following pages. The philosophy:

- was essentially formulated in the Japan of the 1920s and 1930s

- was derived out of experience; there appears to be no previous model

- was developed by a Japanese entrepreneur for Japanese people

- contained universalistic, humanistic (quasi-religious) elements

- creates powerful employee identification with the company

- contained elements which were decades ahead of their time and largely influenced by other countries

- was learnt by successive generations of Japanese employees

- distinguishes Matsushita from other Japanese companies

- endured after the retirement and the death of Konosuke Matsushita

- is being kept alive by the company and a dedicated publishing organization

- still serves as the basis for company thought and action, influencing decision-making and the style of business

METHODOLOGY

During 1998 and 1999 ten Japanese and nine non-Japanese managers and executives were interviewed about the company's attitudes and policies towards globalization. Interviews took place at the company headquarters in Osaka and at various company locations worldwide: Australia, Denmark, Germany, Spain, the UK and the USA. Japanese managers were interviewed in Japan, Denmark, the USA and the UK.

A standard interview schedule was used for non-Japanese interviewees. With Japanese informants the interviews were conducted more as guided conversations to allow them scope to provide wider, possibly more revealing answers. It has been the author's experience over many years that in interviews with Japanese company personnel questions should be posed with a *deliberate* vagueness so that the informant can make a dignified retreat from a particular 'unpleasant' question and certainly in a way that he – and occasionally she – might find inquisitorial. Interviews with Japanese informants lasted approximately one hour; with non-Japanese informants up to two hours. In several cases the non-Japanese managers supplied revealing, though unsolicited views on their experiences of Japanese management practices. In addition, in all but two of these locations, the contact with informants was resumed over dinners. This was especially the case in Japan, where business socialization provides an ideal opportunity to double-check earlier comments and touch on topics which throw useful peripheral light on the core questions.

Each informant was asked to give his or her views of the challenges of globalization facing the company at present. It is not possible to say with any certainty that non-Japanese informants were less open in their responses than their counterparts in the other countries, but it was noticeable that, whereas the non-Japanese managers felt able to criticize aspects of the company philosophy, *all* the Japanese informants without exception expressed the view that the company philosophy was a sound foundation for the company's operations as a global player.

The written data on MEI are based on three kinds of source: the general external documentary material about the company in English; company materials supplied to the author, including in-company newsletters, organization charts, in-company training manuals, as well as confidential materials on business strategy; and material, published by the PHP Institute in Tokyo, which supplies an abundance of material on the eponymous founder of Matsushita Electric Industrial Company and his business philosophy. The PHP material is both adulatory and bland so has been used with some caution.

Before proceeding to the case study proper, two important points need to be mentioned. First, the treatment of the topic will also require discussion of Japanese history in the twentieth century and, unavoidably, of Japanese cultural values. Second, large and famous Japanese corporations tend to be extremely sensitive about any kind of criticism. It may be regarded as disloyalty. I have therefore chosen to disguise the precise identity of some of the non-Japanese informants, as their comments were often outspoken and critical of the company. But, as we shall discover, the critical comments were often a *cri de cœur* – a plea for the company to shake off its conservatism.

THE KEY KNOWLEDGE MANAGEMENT THEMES AND ISSUES

Ever since the first Europeans alighted on the shores of Japan in the middle of the sixteenth century, its inventive, diligent and industrially talented people have shown a capacity for organization, assimilitation of foreign ideas and techniques, and implementation of large-scale projects that has caught the rest of the world by surprise, challenging and even defying assumptions. Mindful of that, the presentation of the Matsushita company in this case study will be appropriately unconventional in order to maximize its value as a learning history.

The knowledge themes in this case study are exceptionally diverse. Overall the knowledge is 'thick' (see chapter 5), providing the context for explicating the behaviour of a huge Japanese corporation. The focus on the life of the founder may appear to be excessive, but the company he founded and built up cannot be conceived without him, without what Ghoshal and Bartlett (1998) call 'the saga around the life and philosophy of Konosuke Matsushita'. Hence the need for an unconventional approach. The knowledge in this case study:

- is strongly contextual, being embedded in Japanese cultural traditions, social practices *and* specific events in the history of Japan in the twentieth century

- is of the kind that needs interpretation by a domain expert

- represents a source of insight into the Japanese corporate mind *without* invoking the 'uniqueness' of Japanese culture

- challenges conventional uninformed Western management thinking about Japan

STRUCTURE OF THIS CASE STUDY

The first six sections of this case study are devoted to the historical embedding of the Matsushita company, using a periodization built around the life of the founder. The first section is a scene-setter, which will immediately convey the importance of the presentation of the Matsushita experience as a learning history. The sections are as follows:

- A man of his times and ahead of his times

- 1894–1929: a hundred yen investment

- 1930–45: grand vision and interesting times (interesting as in the Chinese proverb)

- 1945–56: anguish, restoration of fortunes and a personal think tank

- 1956–61: towards retirement

- 1961–89: philanthropist and management philosopher

- Internationalization and globalization

- The discourse of globalization

- Cross-cultural management issues

- A knowledge management perspective

- Afterword

Note: to avoid confusion between the name of the company and the founder, Matsushita will henceforth refer to the company and KM (by which he is known throughout the company) to the great man.

A MAN OF HIS TIMES AND AHEAD OF HIS TIMES

In the fraught year of 1932 a Japanese businessman by the name of Konosuke Matsushita announced a management philosophy for the electrical goods company which he had established in 1918. KM described the year 1932 as 'a time of grave social and political tension in Japan'. It was. In that year:

> A group of young military officers calling themselves the Blood Brotherhood murdered Finance Minister Inoue and Baron Dan, the director of Mitsui, Japan's biggest industrial and financial conglomerate. Their declared motive was to save Japan from 'evil' influences. Then, on 15 May 1932 . . . 78-year old Prime Minister Inukai was slain by officers who disliked his resistance to army expansion in Manchuria and were angered by his efforts to make peace with China. . . . The same day, attempts were made to bomb Mitsubishi Bank and Tokyo police headquarters, and to kill Count Makino [a senior civilian advisor to the Emperor]. (Seagrave, 1999)

Japan was embarking on a period of government by assassination, which would culminate in war on the Asian mainland and in the Pacific, unleash the epic struggle with the USA, and lead to ignominious defeat and national humiliation.

In the 1930s KM devoted his energies to building up his company. In 1933 he introduced a key feature of the organizational design: his company would be divisionalized, the first in Japan to be so. KM was already a leading entrepreneur, he was an inventor of electrical appliances and had a flair for sales promotion and marketing. He also had a business philosophy which embraced not only his employees and the company's customers, but also appealed to other interest groups. In short, in the 1930s this businessman, whose education had been so rudimentary, was already concerned about stakeholder value, a good five decades before it became a fashionable management concept in the USA. His products had a good reputation for quality. Order books were full and the company expanded.

In December 1941 Japan, lusting after empire in Asia and glory throughout the world, was plunged into a war of shocking ferocity with the USA, Great Britain and other countries. Its armies swept through the Asian mainland and its navy took command of the Pacific Ocean, but Japan's empire was short-lived and the early glory of stunning victories on land and sea eventually gave way to catastrophic defeat. In August 1945 the war in the Pacific came to end with the devastating atom bomb attacks on the cities of Hiroshima and Nagasaki. After its defeat, Japan was a country utterly demoralized, its economy was in ruins, entire cities were wastelands of rubble and ruin. At least two million of its soldiers had perished. Tens of thousands, abandoned on the Asian mainland, were unaccounted for, and perhaps half a million citizens had succumbed in the horrific saturation bombing of the home islands (Baudot, 1980). For the first time in its 2,000-year history, Japan would be occupied by an alien military power, the victorious USA. On 22 August 1945, exactly one week after the Japanese surrender, KM sent out an extraordinary appeal to his workforce: 'Production is the basis of recovery. Let's reaffirm the traditional Matsushita spirit and commit ourselves to the restoration of the nation and the elevation of our culture.'

To put that remark in context, try to imagine a major German industrialist inspirationally declaring in 1945, three weeks after the death of Adolf Hitler and the collapse of Nazi power, that the employees of his company should draw on their *esprit de corps* to restore the dignity of Germany and its culture. In other words, try to imagine such a German industrialist with a transcendental vision of his company shouldering the pain and hopes of his shattered nation. It does take a great leap of imagination.

In 1946, a very bleak year for Japan, KM set up his own personal think-tank to study human nature and ways to combat poverty. This same man in the 1950s would become revered in Japan as the living god of management. His company, which narrowly avoided being closed down by the Americans after the Pacific War, grew and grew until, as we have seen, in 1999 it was the world's twenty-sixth biggest industrial company, employing 270,000 people worldwide (half outside Japan), and with earnings of $60 billion in that year. KM died in 1989. But the Matsushita philosophy, which was essentially formulated in Japan in the

1920s and 1930s, remains central to the company's way of doing business, to its self-perception, and to any understanding of the company as a global concern.

New Japanese employees of the company are imbued with the core company values through intensive processes of 'cultural and spiritual training' (Ghoshal and Bartlett, 1998), whilst for the benefit of all employees worldwide the PHP Institute produces biographies of the great man, anthologies of his sayings and writings, as well as reminiscences of colleagues: in Japanese, English, French, Spanish and German. When he died in 1989, his company was one of the biggest consumer electronics companies in the world; its management systems were famous in and outside Japan; and it was bequeathed a 'grand vision [which] top management has always been willing to translate into specific objectives and immediate priorities' (Ghoshal and Bartlett, 1998). But it was a company that was becoming increasingly rigid in its thinking and lacking innovative drive. Now to the beginnings of the story.

1894–1929: A HUNDRED YEN INVESTMENT

Konosuke Matsushita was born into a well-off family in 1894 in a small village in Wakayama prefecture. But, when he was four, his father's disastrous business activities reduced the family to destitution. The young Konosuke was sickly and his formal education came to an end when he left school at the age of nine. There were no social connections to ease his path to apprenticeship with an employer of standing in the community. These were severe disadvantages, but the boy was both conscientious and inventive. He was first apprenticed to a dealer in charcoal braziers in Osaka, the Birmingham and Pittsburgh of Japan. In the following year, 1905, he joined a company which sold bicycles imported from the USA and Britain: 'one of the latest inventions of modern civilization' (PHP Institute, 1994).

Then, in 1910 Konosuke joined the Osaka Electric Light Company, becoming so adept at wiring that in 1917 he was promoted to the prestigious position of inspector. That same year Konosuke developed a new kind of electrical socket. The Osaka Electric Light Company showed no interest. Thus was born one of the world's great entrepreneurs. Konosuke decided to found his own company with an investment of ¥100 which was about the price of an imported bicycle. His business premises were his own small tenement apartment. On 7 March 1918 he moved from there to bigger premises and founded on the same the Matsushita Electric Appliance Factory. The company manufactured insulator plates and KM's new invention, the two-way socket.

By 1914, at the outbreak of the First World War, Japan was by far the most rapidly industrializing nation in Asia. It had started to industrialize about the same time as Germany in the 1880s,[2] and by the early twentieth century the country was revelling in one of the great technical wonders of the time: electrical power. From the 1860s Japan, under the stirring slogan 'Western knowledge–Japanese spirit', acquired from America and the leading European countries knowledge and techniques covering everything from military know-how (and regalia) to ballrooms, from railroads to telegraph systems. In the annals of knowledge management there never was such as frenzy of learning from abroad: it was seen as a patriotic duty.

The interaction of Japan and the Western world in the latter half of the nineteenth century should be required reading for any (international) student of knowledge management (see Beasley, 1990; Sansom, 1977). The Japanese of the time were showing a remarkably absorptive capacity to use the relatively new language of knowledge management. By the turn of the century many companies, which by the 1970s would become world famous, though possibly under different names, were already notable industrial manufacturers: Mitsubishi in heavy engineering; NEC in telephone exchanges; Sumitomo in mining. Some of the firms set up trading and banking divisions, the new conglomerates becoming known in the 1920s as *zaibatsu*. At the time of the outbreak of war with America in 1941 the entire Japanese economy was dominated by just four *zaibatsu*.

In the First World War (1914–18) Japan had been a non-combatant, but had benefited economically. However, after that appalling conflict the country was plagued by financial crises, bankruptcies, and social unrest. Still, the Matsushita Electric Appliance Company fared well. Indeed, it would never experience really severe financial problems until the bleak years after the Second World War. By the end of 1918 KM was employing 20 people and had set up a company cultural and sports association called the Hoichi Kai, the one-step society. By keeping in step, Konosuke and his workers had a better chance of keeping the company together. This was the first of many bold and stunning initiatives for improving his employees' welfare and motivating them behind him. In 1920, and it is hard to capture the excitement of this, the company installed its first telephone: to the workers its presence symbolized the modernity of outlook and the growing reputation of the company. In those days a telephone call cost ¥1,000.

Throughout the 1920s the company prospered. In 1923 KM displayed his talents as an inventor once again by creating a new bicycle lamp. In those days in Japan bicycle lamps were candles or simple petroleum lamps, which the slightest breeze would extinguish. Battery lamps were coming on to the market, but their power lasted only two or three hours. Konosuke's innovation was a bullet-shaped lamp which could shine for between 30 and 40 hours. At first it was difficult to get bicycle dealers to stock the new lamps, so he introduced a successful promotional scheme nationwide to sign up more dealers. This strategy worked and boosted sales in Osaka and later throughout Japan. This was the basis of the exclusive dealership system for Matsushita products which operates to this day. In 1925 he adopted the English word 'National' as the brand name for his products. He had come across the word 'international' and learned that national related to an entire people. The use of the word symbolized what he wanted his products to be used and valued by the entire Japanese people.

In 1927 KM advertised his National bicycle lamps in national newspapers, using an unusual graphical technique for the time. It was the first time that advertisements had been placed in Japanese newspapers to promote factory products. The bicycle lamp was not his only successful product around this time. KM also invented his new electric iron, a product that was superior in performance to existing offerings and which he offered at 30% lower than the current market price. He banked, correctly, on economies of scale.

By 1929 the Matsushita Electric Appliance Company was employing 300 people and sales were in the region of ¥100,000 a month. In the same year KM renamed the company the Matsushita Electric Works. More significantly, he elaborated 'the basic management objectives' and the company creed. As such KM's basic management objectives and company creed predate by an entire decade the otherwise first generally accepted mission statement. With slight modifications, their wording is as follows:

The basic management objective

Recognizing our responsibilities as industrialists, we will devote ourselves to the progress and development of society and the well-being of people through our business activities, thereby enhancing the quality of life throughout the world.

The company creed

Progress and development can be realized only through the combined efforts and cooperation of each employee of our company. United in spirit, we pledge to perform our corporate duties with dedication, diligence and integrity.

The basic management objectives and company creed (PHP Institute, 1994)

Thus, before the Wall Street Crash of 1929, KM had shown that he was not just an entrepreneur, an inventor and a marketer, but also a compassionate manager with immensely advanced ideas for the time on managing and motivating people. With the benefit on hindsight we may safely say that there was only one other industrialist with whom he stands comparison: Henry Ford. But, of course, the pioneer of assembly-line mass production was never held to be a compassionate manager. At the end of 1929 the Matsushita company was in a precarious position. When company executives suggested that he must reduce his workforce by half, KM would not hear of it. He told them: 'Let's cut production by half, but do not dismiss even one employee. . . . We will continue to pay the same wages they are getting now, but there will be no holidays. All the workers should do their best to try to sell the backlog.' By February 1930 the excess stock had been sold and the company returned to full production.

1930–45: GRAND VISION AND INTERESTING TIMES (INTERESTING AS IN THE CHINESE PROVERB)

The first radio broadcasts in Japan began in 1925 and by 1930 the domestic production of radios was about 200,000 sets. Knowing that these radios – like bicycle lamps and electric irons – were unreliable, KM decided to manufacture a better model. After three months his technicians produced a radio which would be marketed under the National brand name. They also entered the model in a competition organized by Tokyo Central Broadcasting (nowadays NHK) for the best radio set. The Matsushita device won the competition, leading to a rapid expansion of sales. By 1942 MEI had become Japan's biggest supplier of radios, producing 30,000 units a month.

In 1932 KM underwent a religious experience through his involvement with the Tenrikyo sect, which propounds humanistic precepts in keeping with the Christian ideal of 'love thy neighbour'. On one occasion he witnessed a large number of adherents of the sect 'working cheerfully and energetically to construct a memorial hall to the founder' (PHP Institute, 1994), and they were working without being paid. KM pondered what he had seen and drew parallels between this spiritually-inspired labour and the purpose of his company. It occurred to him that the true purpose of his company was to help improve the human condition. And so it was that he began to evolve a company philosophy based on the conviction that the ultimate aim of manufacturing was to eliminate poverty and foster prosperity: this idea, of course, fitted perfectly with the rationale behind his basic management objectives and the company creed which he had articulated in 1929. Out of this vision for his company KM would develop an extraordinary set of corporate values which have since become central to company thinking and behaviour without dilution or modification.

On 5 May 1932 KM addressed all his office workers, presenting them with the mission for the company. He declared:

> Our primary purpose is to eliminate poverty and increase wealth. How? By producing goods in abundant supply. . . . Water, that is, tap water, is a resource that is processed and priced. . . . A traveller, thirsty from a long journey, who turns to a roadside water tap and drinks his fill will not be accused of wrong or punished for drinking the water itself. Why? Because the price of water is so very low. . . . This is what the entrepreneur aims at: to make all products as inexhaustible and as cheap as tap water.

KM revealed his grand vision, announcing a 250-year plan for the completion of the company mission, which called for nothing less than the eradication of poverty from the face of the earth. The 250 years were divided into ten phases, each phase consisting of period for 'construction' (10 years), 'application' (10 years) and 'fulfilment' (5 years). Thus KM was a pioneer of what is today called corporate social responsibility (Holden, 2000).

In his President's Message to the company employees in July 1933, KM set out his business principles, which supplement the basic management objectives and company creed. It is these three statements which form the basis of the Matsushita philosophy.

The business principles

1. *Service to the public:* To provide high-quality goods and services at reasonable prices, thereby contributing to the well-being and happiness of people throughout the world.

2. *Fairness and honesty:* To be fair and honest in all business dealings and personal conduct, always making balanced judgements free of preconceptions.

3. *Teamwork for the common cause:* To pool abilities and strength of resolution to accomplish shared objectives, in mutual trust and full recognition of individual autonomy.

4. *Untiring effort for improvement:* To strive constantly for improvement of corporate and personal performances, even in the worst of adversity, so as to fulfil the firm's mission to realize lasting peace and prosperity.

5. *Courtesy and humility:* To be always cordial and modest and respect rights and needs of others, thereby helping enrich the environment and maintain the social order.

Note: the basic propositions (in italics) were as articulated in Japanese by KM in 1933; the explanations with their modern feel were authorized by the company in 1993. Several English-language versions of the basic propositions have existed over the years. There are now versions in several languages, as the business principles are often on display in Matsushita offices worldwide.

The Matsushita business principles (Source: Kotter, 1997)

In 1933 KM introduced a major restructuring of Matsushita. Ahead of his time he introduced the division system. His was the first company in Japan to be so organized, but in fact the process began in 1927 when he set up an independent management system for the electrothermal appliances division. In 1933, KM organized the company into three divisions according to product line: Division One for radios; Division Two for light fixtures and batteries; and Division Three for wiring implements, synthetic resins and electrical heating appliances. Each division became a self-supporting entity with its own factories and offices, and each was responsible for controlling business operations: manufacturing, sales, research and development, accounts. According to the PHP Institute (1994), KM introduced this 'epochal organizational reform' for two reasons: to encourage independent and responsible management and to train personnel. Another reason was that KM never enjoyed the best of health. In

December 1935 he introduced another important change: the Matsushita Electric Works was incorporated as Matsushita Electric Industrial Co. Ltd, the full name which is still used today.

The idea of training or, to be more precise, the idea of his company fulfilling a kind of educational function, was never far from KM's mind. As far back as 1922 he had conceived the idea of a school which was both a manufacturing operation and a training centre. In 1934 he set up his Employee Training Institute, where recruits – in those days primary school-leavers – took a three-year course in basic engineering and commerce. In Japan at that time public courses took five years and were only available to school-leavers at secondary level. Upon completion of their course, the trainees were awarded a qualification enabling them to work as a clerk. The technical education was strengthened in 1936 with the establishment of an engineering school within the Institute. The young trainees were, of course, imbued with the company philosophy.

In 1935 the Matsushita company had about 3,500 employees and manufactured some 600 kinds of product in its three divisions. As ever the diligent, watchful manager, KM set out a set of basic rules 'to prevent sloppiness in management and arrogance among employees' as a result of the company's rise to prosperity. A key motivation behind the rules was the conviction that the entire company should be run on the basis of a single management philosophy. Article 15 of the basic rules states: 'No matter how successful Matsushita Industrial may grow, each employee shall treasure the spirit of the independent entrepreneur, and deal with customers with humility and honesty.' We note in passing how, some 60 years later, it has been fashionable to regard employees as entrepreneurs; and, ironically, not least in Japan, as it currently shifts from being an economy benefiting producers to one favouring consumers.

In the 1930s Japan moved inexorably to war. In 1937 its troops invaded China, which made conflict with the USA and Great Britain inevitable. In the following year the National Mobilization Law came into force, which in effect rationed raw materials to manufacturers, made them subservient to the military authorities, and compelled them to release young men among their employees for military service. By 1940 Japan's military leaders believed that Japan could establish an Asian empire, calculating that it could knock out the meddlesome USA in a lightning blow and count on Hitler to subdue Britain, which would, as a consequence, be unable to protect its possessions in Asia. The Matsushita company had very little choice but to comply with government legislation and military requirements, to the extent that it was obliged to open plants in several territories occupied by Japanese forces in the 1930s and 1940s: China, Korea, the Philippines and Indonesia. Not only that, as Japan's position became more and more desperate, the company, which was well-regarded for its manufacturing skills, was forced by the military authorities to build both ships and aircraft for the war effort.

1945–56: ANGUISH, RESTORATION OF FORTUNES AND A PERSONAL THINK TANK

In 1945 Japan was a psychologically and materially devastated country. As we saw above, KM made his extraordinary declaration in August of that year. But it would be many years before his injunction could be carried out. By October the company resumed production of electric irons and other appliances and put in place practices in accordance with the requirements of the American occupying authorities. But before there could be any sustained recovery, there was a bolt out of the blue. The American authorities regarded MEI as a company run by a *'zaibatsu* family'. As such MEI was investigated under the provisions of the Law for the Elimination of Excessive Concentrations of Economic Power, which came into force in February 1947. This put the very existence of the company into jeopardy and threatened KM with being purged.

In May 1947, after a vigorous campaign waged both by KM (he visited occupation headquarters in Tokyo 50 times) and his supporters, the Americans relented and dropped their charges. For the next three years KM struggled with legal restrictions on his business operations and massive debts. The company was on the point of collapse. In January 1949 he said in a management policy statement: 'If the result of our hard work is not black ink, and if it does not contribute to the prosperity of the country and society nor to the enhancement of standards of living of our employees, Matsushita has no reason to exist. If it has no reason for existence, we should dissolve Matsushita Electric.'

But it did not come to that. The Korean War, which broke out in June 1950, enabled Japan to be a major supplier to the UN forces' procurement programme. The demand was so massive that it kick-started the entire Japanese manufacturing economy. This, coupled with the fact that US-imposed restrictions were lifted, allowed MEI for the first time after the war to resume dividend payments. Business confidence returned to Japan and to MEI. In January 1951, KM and his leading managers began to evaluate the company in a global context, a task which KM likened to 'founding the company all over again'. In the same month he declared that he would visit the USA 'to acquaint himself with what were then the world's most advanced management philosophies and practices' (PHP Institute, 1994). It proved to be an awe-inspiring experience in two ways. First he became convinced that 'democracy is a way of achieving prosperity', and prosperity was the antidote to poverty. Second, he confirmed his belief that America's greatness – and part of that greatness lay in its defeat of Japan in war – was attributable to superior technology. KM visited American production plants and was duly impressed, purchasing state-of-the-art equipment for installation in his factories in Japan.

In the following year he visited the USA again and made his first trip to Europe. One of his most important destinations was Eindhoven, the home of

Philips, the Dutch electrical company, and upon returning to Japan he proposed a technological tie-up. At first the Philips managers demurred, but then accepted a deal whereby Matsushita paid a 4.5% technical guidance fee and Philips paid the Japanese firm a management fee of 3%. The Matsushita corporation was beginning to grow and, like many other Japanese companies, was beginning to produce annual growth rates exceeding 8%. In January 1956, KM declared that the company's post-war reconstruction was complete and that it was time to introduce ambitious development plans. Accordingly, he announced a five-year plan, whereby sales would increase from ¥22 billion in 1955 to ¥80 billion in 1960. The company's workforce would have to grow from 11,000 to 18,000, and the capital base expand from ¥3 billion to ¥10 billion. The plan was greeted by polite scepticism in the company, but there was no resistance. He justified his optimism with these slightly mystical words: 'This plan is certain to be fulfilled, because it is something desired by consumers.' And he added: 'In this sense, we have an "invisible contract" with consumers.' In fact the key figures were all achieved well ahead of target. In 1960 Matsushita sales stood at ¥105.4 billion; its capital base was ¥15 billion; and the company now employed 28,000 people throughout Japan. Little wonder that KM was known throughout the company and indeed throughout Japan as 'the living god of management'.

As we noted above, in the 1930s KM experienced a form of religious enlightenment through his association with the essentially pacific Tenrikyo sect, as a result of which he also began to see his company as a kind of spiritual entity with the sacred tasks of eliminating poverty by promoting prosperity and contributing to the good of society. But the Japan in the 1930s right through to the nation's defeat in 1945 was not receptive to other-worldly notions which could be construed as hostile to, or incompatible with, the land-grabbing visions of Japan's ultra-patriotic militarists, who dragged the Japanese people into catastrophic war. In the immediate post-war years the Japanese would eventually become more receptive to appeals to the humanistic, reflective element in their character. This is why in August 1945 KM could call on his workforce to 'reaffirm the traditional Matsushita spirit and commit ourselves to the restoration of the nation and the elevation of our culture'.

In November 1946, the month in which he was officially purged from his company, KM established an organization – though institute is a more accurate word for it – with the aim of studying human nature and helping keep Japan 'from ever again embarking on anything as suicidal as World War II' (Kotter, 1997). The organization was given the name PHP, standing for 'peace and happiness through prosperity'. The institute's first activities were public meetings in Osaka, in which KM would reflect on Japan's misery and argue the cause of prosperity and happiness. But his audiences were confused, as KM himself admitted: Life was hard. People were not so interested in idealism until grieving had passed and bellies were full.

The success of the PHP Institute in the post-war years is debatable and its only tangible result was the publication of a monthly magazine *PHP* from April 1947. Its other important consequence was that PHP was, for KM, as he himself admitted, his 'emotional mainstay' during the anxious, stressful post-war years. During this time he faced the very real possibility of the company disappearing and of his own exclusion from involvement in the reconstruction of the shattered Japanese economy. In 1961, when he retired as President of Matsushita, PHP activities became the major focus for KM: it would, as we shall see, become his personal think tank and publishing house for his wide-ranging writings. PHP would not be his last visionary venture.

1956–61: TOWARDS RETIREMENT

In KM's last years Matsushita, as we noted earlier, experienced spectacular growth, but it was essentially a domestic company. Exports were soaring. KM was all too aware that the company faced increasing competition in the home market and, if it were to internationalize, it would be facing powerful US and European corporations. In a meeting with divisional managers in October 1958 he announced that the way ahead for the company was to force down production and distribution costs, if possible by as much as 10%. It was a tall order, but without the resulting cost-cutting mentality *and* the rigorous application of statistical quality control and value engineering (and brain-storming), Matsushita may have lost the favour and orders for radios from another company poised for worldwide renown, Toyota.

At the same meeting KM stressed another factor that would enable Matsushita to do the impossible (at the time the company was working feverishly to meet the targets of his 1956–60 five-year plan). He urged the company to make use of 'collective wisdom'. In his words: 'We must learn to collect wisdom from others, including people from outside the company, in order to expand our perspective. Not only must we collect additional knowledge, we must also ask other corporations for support in helping us implement new ideas. If we only see problems from our own vantage point, our ability to overcome them will be extremely limited. Tapping into collective wisdom on the other hand will enable us to achieve our mission' (quoted in Kotter, 1997). KM, not for the first time in his career, was articulating practices that belonged to the future. In this case he was a good 25 years ahead of his time. To use today's jargon, he was advocating bench-marking and propounding the concepts of the learning organization and knowledge-based company.

His last great act as President of Matsushita was again in pioneering mode. In January 1961, the year of his retirement, KM announced that MEI would become the first prominent Japanese corporation to adopt the five-day week. He reasoned that in the USA they used the five-day week and had high productivity levels, and that the company's workers should be entitled to have more time to *enjoy* prosperity. He believed that the idea was good for the company, for its employees, and for Japan. Not for the first time KM met resistance. This time the concern was that the company, with its significantly lower wage rates than in the USA, would lose a vital element of competitive advantage. He was, after all, asking for a 17% reduction in the working week. Not allowing himself to be browbeaten by the company's management, nor its union (which initially liked the plan but later distanced itself from it), so it was that in April 1965 MEI became the first major firm in Japan to adopt the five-day working week. Everyone, except KM, was amazed when it emerged that productivity had risen significantly.

In January 1961 KM announced his retirement to the annual management meeting with these words: 'I have decided that at last the time has come for me to resign as president and, in the position of chairman, take a back seat, so to speak, in the company's management. ... My retirement will not disadvantage the company. In fact, I am convinced that it will be an important plus in its future development.' He devoted most of the rest of his life to PHP. But he was far more than in the back seat of the company. To paraphrase Ghoshal and Barlett (1998), the saga around the life and philosophy of Konosuke Matsushita was to become the strongest source of institutionalization of Matsushita's organizational systems. In any case, whilst KM remained as Chairman, his authority was never seriously challenged; in Japan, of course, the more venerable you are, the more your wisdom is respected.

1961–89: PHILANTHROPIST AND MANAGEMENT PHILOSOPHER

KM retired at the age of the age of 65 and he lived for a further 29 years. During these years he contemplated the nature of humanity and reflected on ways to achieve peace, happiness and prosperity. Supporting these endeavours, he made use of the PHP Institute as the principal outlet for his writings, which, as we shall see presently, were by no means confined to the subject he knew most about: business management. Establishing himself in an elegant house just east of Kyoto, in August 1961 he installed a dozen or so researchers to help him with his projects. They in fact did the writing, KM delivering the concepts and ideas.

One of his main preoccupations was the future of Japan. One scheme envisaged a mammoth infrastructure project, to be accomplished over many centuries, which would double the amount of useable land available to Japan. Another proposed the conversion of Japan into a tax-free state, and another argued for a radical reorganization of the Japanese education system, in which corporations provided learning for life. In the process, many universities would become redundant and close, so saving the Japanese exchequer billions of yen each year.

All in all he wrote, or rather co-wrote, over 40 books, including an autobiography and works on the various aspects of his 'way of thinking'. Between 1974 and 1976 no fewer than 11 books were published under his name. As Kotter (1997) has pointed out, KM's writings on business management were on the more obvious topics such as marketing or financial strategy. He discussed 'human nature, the role of profit, the customer, the power of belief, and the importance of self-reliance', stressing the 'human side of management, and leadership'. These writings represent essential guides to his business philosophy, and their contents are required reading for all MEI employees in Japan. In this way the Matsushita spirit is reinforced and transmitted. As the company internationalized, so PHP began to produce KM's writings first in English (in 1970) and then in other languages for the benefit of the company's foreign employees.

It was in 1964 that KM took a momentous decision as Chairman that is still shrouded with controversy in and outside the company: he stopped the company from developing main-frame computers (Kotter, 1997). Some observers saw this as proof that KM was not the all-seeing management guru imbued with what one admirer called 'collective wisdom and gut-level intuition' (Eguchi, 1997). The company was not to re-enter the computer business until 1977 and only then as a manufacturer of semiconductors. It is significant, though, that this step was taken in the very first year in office of the President, Toshihiko Yamashita. The popularizing editions of KM's life and writings appear to omit this episode.

In 1973 KM, who was by now approaching 80, announced that he was stepping down as Chairman and would retain his association with MEI in the capacity of Executive Advisor. In his declining years KM received many distinctions, including honorary doctorates from universities in Japan and the USA, awards from the governments of Belgium, Malaysia and Spain. He was also awarded various honours from the Japanese government, including the country's highest civilian award, the Imperial Order of the Paulownia Flowers shortly before his death in 1989. In addition to donating much of his considerable fortune – '$291 million out of his own pocket', according to Kotter (1997) – to a number of philanthropic causes, which included the installation of the prestigious Japan Prize for technological achievement, he founded a remarkable institution which had aimed at nurturing Japan's leaders for the twenty-first century.

Established in 1978, the Matsushita School of Government and Management has certainly attracted highly talented young people who spend two years studying human nature according to KM, engaging in various good causes, ranging from helping to build irrigation systems in Africa to working as labourers in steel plants. All this with the intention of developing character through humility. It is a very Matsushita-esque concept, typical of a man who, with a minimum of education, rose to be Japan's greatest philosopher–entrepreneur.

KM died of pneumonia on 27 April 1989 aged 94. The company which he had founded in 1918 with his wife and brother-in-law had become a corporate legend. Later that year Japan's so-called bubble economy burst. As a result, Japanese management, which had struck fear in the board-rooms of Europe and the USA, and which was probably symbolized by KM more than by any other industrialist, began to lose its mystique. KM's death and the dramatic semi-collapse of the Japanese economy were to have major consequences for the company in the 1990s and beyond. And there was another factor in the equation too: globalization. The issue we are concerned with now is this: to what extent is the globalization of MEI, to which the company is completely committed, compatible with the spiritual legacy that KM bequeathed. In order to tackle that issue, we need to become more familiar with the internationalization of MEI and the overall development of the company in the 1990s.

INTERNATIONALIZATION AND GLOBALIZATION

When KM developed his business philosophy in the late 1920s, his company was a small, struggling concern. He had never been abroad and had probably met few foreigners in his life other than Koreans and Chinese who had settled in Japan. He did business in Japan and had no ambitions to engage in exporting. When the company did expand overseas, it was in conjunction with Japan's imperial presence in Asia, supplying local Japanese business concerns and the Japanese army. As we noted above, the company did not begin an active policy of internationalization until the early 1950s, when the company fortunes had been restored after the Second World War. Wherever Matsushita executives did business in the world, the KM philosophy was used as the basis for interactions with employees, customers and suppliers. Serendipitously, that philosophy had universal dimensions which the company considered would make it attractive to business partners in Europe and the USA, where it saw the best potential for growth. Along with other Japanese corporations, Matsushita experienced very rapid growth rates and by the mid-1980s the company had established manufacturing facilities, branch offices and distribution centres in every continent.

Matsushita duly became a famous company, renowned for its management systems; its founder, whose face was featured on the front page of *Time* magazine in 1962, became a celebrity. In 1983 the company and its founder were the subject of Pascale and Athos's influential book *The art of Japanese management*. In their paean to the Japanese company these authors wrote:

> Matsushita has become a great corporation that makes more than money, and is likely to go on doing so, for it has become an organizational system that meets the needs of society, its customers, its executives, and its employees, and it is 'programmed' to adapt as may be necessary to changes that may come. (Pascale and Athos, 1983)

However, since that was written, observers of Matsushita (e.g. *Economist*, 1999; Ghoshal and Bartlett, 1988, 1998; Hoover, 1991; Kotter, 1997) have remarked on the conservatism of the company and its general inability both to innovate and break away from what Ghoshal and Bartlett (1998) call 'the saga around the life and philosophy of Konosuke Matsushita' and his 'profound and lasting influence on [the company's] administrative legacy'. Before we pick up those points, let us consider the company's philosophy of globalization.

Matsushita Electric has had no qualms about pressing into service the basic objectives and philosophy to suit its needs as a transnational corporation employing tens of thousands of employees all over the world. As the text of the current company web site states: '[KM's] conviction that a company remains indebted to society continues to be the foundation on which policies are built. Directed by these policies, we . . . are determined to improve the lives of people in the societies in which we do business, whilst providing the highest quality Panasonic products at reasonable prices to our customers' (Panasonic, 2000b). According to Yoshihobu Nakamura (1998), a senior HRM executive based at the company headquarters in Osaka, the philosophy 'is considered paramount in conducting business' and 'constitutes the basis of business administration and underlies all decision-making processes'. As for globalization, as Nakamura explains, the basic objective of the company is that:

> As indicated in the basic objective, we aspire toward global coexistence. Soon after the company's inception, our objective was clearly defined as bringing prosperity to the world and realizing social progress and happiness by endlessly developing business which is satisfactory to people and society.

The company philosophy of globalization has the following six tenets:

1. We will operate our business in such a way that we are welcomed by the host country and we will carry out our business activities honoring local customs.

2. We will promote business in accordance with the host country's policies. Also we will make continuous efforts to have the host country understand the management philosophy of our company.

3. We will manufacture products and provide services that are competitive in international markets in terms of quality, performance, and cost, so that we can provide customers with added value.

4. We will promote global transfer and exchange of technology under a world-wide research and development system.

5. We will practice autonomous and responsible management, build up a strong management structure and generate our own capital for the expansion of our business.

6. We will manage our overseas companies with local employees and develop the skills of local employees for their advancement.

This philosophy of globalization derives, of course, from the company's basic objective as fashioned in the late 1920s and early 1930s. Indeed, at a casual glance the key injunctions appear to be easily adaptable to the era of globalization. But scrutiny of the wording makes it clear that the tenets reflect the age of 1970s- and 1980s-style *internationalization*, when Japan was engrossed in nation-building through economic achievement, rather than the theoretically borderless globalization of the 1990s and beyond.

First, we should note that firms today which regard themselves as global do not bother with distinctions such as host countries, as this designation smacks of inequality, even neo-colonialism. Second, the emphasis on host countries both predicates and perpetuates a clear-cut distinction between Japanese and non-Japanese employees within the company itself. Third, the requirement that the host country must 'understand the management philosophy of our company' is rich in sub-textual connotations. Experts on Japanese culture will detect the implicit assumption that any other country *will have* difficulty understanding the company philosophy because that philosophy is Japanese and must perforce remain mysterious to non-Japanese employees and customers. Thus, far from being a charter for globalization, the Matsushita philosophy of globalization is an expression of what might be termed *ethnocentric globalism* – with all the contradictions that the term implies.

The above comments about the company discourse are reinforced through the findings of an international research project into the globalization of Matsushita which I conducted during 1998 and 1999. Both Japanese and non-Japanese managers served as informants. Research interviews with Japanese managers in Japan, the USA, Denmark, and the UK reveal no awareness of incompatibility between the basic company objectives and the philosophy of globalization. This is hardly surprising in the sense that these managers have been virtually indoctrinated with the Matsushita philosophy since their very first day as employees of the company (Holden, 1990). As for non-Japanese employees of the company, interviews during the same period conducted with managers in the USA, Germany, Spain, Australia and UK revealed a less clear-cut picture.

One non-Japanese manager interviewed for this case study bluntly described the company philosophy as 'meaningless'. Another suggested that the company deliberately wanted to retain a Japanese mystique over business operations. A third US manager, with several years experience of the company, expressed it thus: 'The message from Osaka [the company headquarters] is "you don't understand our way of doing business".' This is why, I was reliably informed, a company training centre in the USA waits *six months* before giving new executive recruits an induction programme on what working for a company like Matsushita Electric really entails. As the manager of the facility explained: 'They cannot grasp it until they have lived it for a few months, and then you have to explain what they have been experiencing and why.' A European manager declared that there was 'too much looking down from the top' and that the company culture was not suited to people who were now urgently needed: those 'with unorthodox talent'.

One senior European manager, who had been with the company for more than ten years, described it as 'old and tired'.

The lack of innovation in company practices, especially with respect to adapting organizational structures to suit the globalized economy, was a source of frustration among non-Japanese managers. 'We are too divisional', said a European manager. On three continents there was, to quote one non-Japanese HRM manager, 'tunnel vision about globalization': a serious indicator that the discourse of globalization is unequally diffused and unequally understood within the company subsidiaries. As for localization, one European informant said that the company had been discussing this for ten years, but there was always mistrust of non-Japanese managers. As evidence of that, in terms of handing over complete managerial control of local operations, of 58 operations in Europe there are only eight European managing directors. This suggests that either the company *fears* to implement point six of its philosophy of globalization or that European managers are held to be incapable of 'running the show' in their own region.

These frustrations confirm that in the countries in which the interviews were conducted non-Japanese executives have to cope with the so-called 'rice-paper ceiling': the amalgam of cultural and organizational issues that are not official but which may constitute a barrier to their advancement (see Kopp, 1999). This issue and implications for the nature – and analysis – of Japanese management outside Japan has been the subject of an enormous literature starting in the 1980s (for a general overview, see Beechler and Bird, 1999; Jackson, 1993; Kopp, 1999; Trevor et al., 1986; White and Trevor, 1983). It also has considerable significance as an influence on the character of the company discourse of globalization, to which we now turn.

THE DISCOURSE OF GLOBALIZATION

First of all, as noted, the globalization discourse derives from the basic management objective, which was formulated some 70 years ago, and is therefore an emanation of the Japanese side of the rice-paper ceiling. This discourse, first fashioned in the Japanese language, is predominantly, if not exclusively, a kind of creed for Japanese members of the company, which they will digest uncritically because the thinking behind them stems from the vision of the legendary KM. But for many non-Japanese managers in Europe and the USA, the same discourse, admittedly in translation, is evidently a source of confusion about the way in which the company is planning – or possibly not planning – its future.

Thus we may conclude that the discourse of globalization within the Matsushita corporation is not a unitary system equally embracing all employees. Rather it is a complex fusion of sacred, inviolate shibboleths for the Japanese employees to make them psychologically dependent on the company (*Economist*,

1999), and of locally received variants which, whilst facilitating localization to some degree, reflect and produce differing degrees of comprehension and mystification, and are sometimes even ignored. This state of affairs suggests that the company has in large measure failed, according to the findings of this case research, to make 'host countries' understand the management philosophy in the USA, Europe and Australia. A more disturbing conclusion is that the management philosophy and the derived philosophy of globalization do not represent a sufficiently robust platform for creating within the company a shared global mindset which adapts the Matsushita message to suit business conditions. Rather, that platform is used to interpret business conditions to suit the message (Holden and Salskov-Iversen, 2001).

But this is not to say that the company's top management is completely unaware of these issues. In June 2000 a new president took over with a mandate to make the company more aggressive and responsive to industry trends, making it more visible to customers worldwide. Kunio Nakamura, who was Chairman and CEO of Matsushita Electric's operations in the USA in the early 1990s, has set himself the task of changing the corporate management culture worldwide. His catch-phrase is the Five S's: speed, simplicity, strategy, sincerity and smile (TWICE, 2000). This is hardly traditional Matsushita language.

As we noted above, the Japanese discourse perpetuates the Japanese in-group and the non-Japanese out-group; the former speaking the 'natural' language of the company, the language of nearness to the company origins, whilst the latter must, it seems, make do with potted versions of the essential truths. Foreign employees are often confused or perplexed by the company philosophy; and they know that there can be no thrusting of the Matsushita ideals into twenty-first-century global thinking until younger managers, for whom KM's *presence* is less potent, assume positions of real responsibility.

The sancrosanct nature of the business philosophy, and the seeming impossibility of altering it, means that issues that are becoming important to other major companies as global corporate citizens are screened out of prominence. Thus, whereas other companies' mission statements and business principles reflect modern-day concerns such as sustainable development, human rights, diversity and equality of employment, and even invite independent verification of companies' handling of such issues, Matsushita Electric appears not to stick its neck out. There is one notable exception, however: since 1991 the company as pursued a policy called 'harmonious coexistence with the global environment', based on the Matsushita Environmental Charter initiated in that year (Matsushita Electric, 1998). It could of course be argued that all modern-day concerns of the kind referred to above are automatically subsumed in the original company mission and objectives.

Two issues of almost incalculable strategic importance for Matsushita can be highlighted:

- The problem of global strategy development by a single national group at the top of a company

- A general reluctance to grant empowerment to local managers, whilst ensuring that key positions in the majority of worldwide subsidiaries are retained by Japanese managers

CROSS-CULTURAL MANAGEMENT ISSUES

The rich and complex knowledge mediated in this case study emphasizes three problem area which have profoundly crippled knowledge-sharing:

- The problem of transferring ethical values from a core national culture to local affiliates, as these may be vitiated through mutual misperceptions of the nature and meaning of those values

- The failure sensitively to decompose ethical values and reconstruct them to suit local needs in order to minimize cynicism

- The persistence of a top management, mononational discourse which is not shared by employees of different nationalities working for the company in other countries

A KNOWLEDGE MANAGEMENT PERSPECTIVE

The deeply embedded knowledge, which has been the focus of this case study, is precisely the kind that is most inaccessible to varieties of outsiders (possibly including in this case hundreds, even thousands of foreign employees). It is also, incidentally, quite unlike the kind of sanitized information, generated at headquarters in Japan in the form of training manuals, for enlightening foreign staff about the company, its founder and his philosophy, and Japan itself.[3]

This case study was presented as a learning history. This kind of knowledge has various applications. It can serve as a basis in its own right to supplement existing knowledge on (a) Japan, (b) Konosuke Matsushita, and (c) the Matsushita corporation. The knowledge can, in principle, be used by the company itself for improving knowledge-sharing and driving forword *genuine* localization. It can be used to qualify the well-known case study of Nonaka and Takeuchi (1995) about the Matsushita daughter company which developed a new bread-making machine. These authors suggest that the development of this device was in no small way attributable to the company's ability to create and share knowledge. In contrast to that, this case study suggests that the entire corporation as a globalized entity has much to learn about knowledge management when its non-Japanese employees are involved. Owing to limited knowledge-sharing between the two classes of employees, the current style of knowledge management at Matsushita can be characterized as:

- Stimulating substantial redundancies in knowledge production

- Concentrating a disproportionate amount of knowledge for decision-making in Japanese hands

- Failing to exploit instances of best practice from outside Japan because best practice is held only to emanate from the place of origin of the Matsushita philosophy and value system, that is Japan

It seems that the first step in knowledge management is that Matsushita must learn to share the company with *all* its employees.

AFTERWORD

This chapter would never have been written if a young man, whose inventiveness was unceremoniously spurned by his employer, the Osaka Electric Light Company, had not, in 1917, invested ¥100 in a humble business with his wife and brother-in-law. It is appropriate to devote the last lines of this contribution to this great man.

By any standard, Konosuke Matsushita was one of the most remarkable industrialists of the twentieth century and he merits a worthy biography in English. The current hagiographical treatment of his life and work actually detracts from his greatness. A fitting starting-point of any reappraisal may be to bestow on him, rather than on the American writer Howard Bowen, the title 'the father of corporate social responsibility'. Finally, I refer to the vastly perceptive observation of an American informant, who said that 'the problem with the Japanese bosses is that they regard KM like an Old Testament patriarch. Actually he is a New Testament figure' – a brilliant insight, but immensely difficult to convey to those who inhabit the Matsushita corporate heartlands in Japan.

NOTES

1. Readers who may find it difficult to grasp in what ways the so-called homogeneous culture of the Japanese can produce markedly different corporate cultures may wish to contrast Kotter, *Matsushita leadership* (1997) with Nathan, *Sony: The private life* (1999). This becomes an even more interesting exercise given the strong antipathy these companies have towards each other. In fact, antipathy is a crafted understatement.

2. Parallels between Japan and Germany are not infrequent. Viney (1997) and Hampden-Turner and Trompenaars (1993) emphasize the historical similarities. Buruma (1995) contrasts how Japan and Germany coped with their participation in the Second World War.

3. In the USA Matsushita/Panasonic training managers make use of materials supplied from the Matsushita training headquarters near Osaka. The effectiveness of these materials is strongly influenced by the local training officers' depth of knowledge of Japan. Those with expert knowledge can provide essential glosses. Panasonic GmbH in Germany have produced their own explanatory booklet on the evolution of the company and its philosophy.

FURTHER READING

Matsushita, K. (1988). *The quest for prosperity: The life of a Japanese industrialist*. Tokyo: PHP Institute.

Matsushita, M. (1995). *The mind of management: Fifty years with Konosuke Matsushita*. Tokyo: PHP Institute.

PHP Institute (1997). *The Matsushita perspective: A business philosophy handbook*. Tokyo: PHP Institute.

REFERENCES

Baudot, M. (ed.) (1980). *The historical encyclopedia of World War II*. New York: Greenwich House.

Beasley, W. (1990). *The rise of modern Japan*. New York: St Martin's Press.

Beechler, S. and Bird, A. (eds) (1999). *Japanese multinationals abroad: Individual and organizational learning*. New York: Oxford University Press.

Buruma, I. (1995). *Wages of guilt: Memories of war in Germany and Japan*. London: Vintage.

Economist (1999). Putting the bounce back into Matsushita. 22 May: 67–8.

Eguchi, K. (1997). *Managing for success: Inspiring episodes from 22 years with Konosuke Matsushita, one of this century's most distinguished industrialists*. Tokyo: PHP Institute.

Fortune (2000). The Fortune global 500: The world's largest corporations. 24 July.

Ghoshal, S. and Bartlett, C. A. (1988). *Matsushita Electric Industrial (MEI) in 1987*. Harvard Business School: case study 9–388–144. Boston, MA: Harvard Business School Publishing Division.

Ghoshal, S. and Bartlett, C. A. (1998). *Managing across borders: The transnational solution*. London: Random House.

Hamden-Turner, C. and Trompenaars, F. (1993). *The seven cultures of capitalism: Value systems for creating wealth in the United States, Britain, Japan, Germany, France, Sweden and the Netherlands*. London: Judy Piatkus.

Holden, N. J. (1990). Preparing the ground for organisation learning: Graduate training programmes in major Japanese corporations. *Management Education and Development* 21(3): 241–61.

Holden, N. J. (2000). Matsushita Electric: Why global corporate citizenship is so elusive. Proceedings of the 4th International Conference on Corporate Reputation, Identity and Competitiveness. Copenhagen Business School, May.

Holden, N. J. and Salskov-Iversen, D. (2001). In: Cooper, C. L. and Cartwright, S. (eds). Management and globalisation: A constructivist approach. *Wiley handbook of organizational culture and climate*. Chichester, UK: John Wiley, pp. 429–48.

Hoover, D. (1991). Matsushita Electric Industrial Co. IMD case study GM 468. Lausanne: Institute for Management Development.

Jackson, T. (1993). *Turning Japanese: The fight for industrial control of the new Europe*. London: HarperCollins.

Kopp, R. (1999). The rice-paper ceiling in Japanese companies: Why it exists and persists. In: Beechler and Bird (1999).

Kotter, J. (1997). *Matsushita leadership: Lessons from the 20th century's most remarkable entrepreneur*. New York: Free Press.

Matsushita Electric (1998). *Annual Report*.

Nakamura, Y. (1998). International Human Resources Development by Matsushita Electric Industrial Co., Ltd. Asian Regional Conference on Industrial Relations. (No further particulars; manuscript supplied by Nakamura.)

Nathan, J. (1999). *Sony: The private life*. London: HarperCollins.

Nonaka, I. and Takeuchi, H. (1995). *The knowledge-creating company*. New York: Oxford University Press.

Panasonic (2000a). Information supplied by Mr Yaoki Takahashi, Personnel Department, Panasonic (UK) Ltd during 1998–2000.

Panasonic (2000b). http.//www.panasonic.com/host/company/profile/global.html

Pascale, R. T. and Athos, A. G. (1983) *The art of Japanese management*. Harmondsworth, UK: Penguin Books.

PHP Institute (1994). *Matsushita Konosuke (1894–1989): His life and his legacy*. Tokyo: PHP Institute.

Sansom, G. (1977). *The Western world and Japan*. Tokyo: Charles E. Tuttle.

Seagrave, S. (1999). *The Yamato dynasty: The secret history of Japan's imperial family*. London: Bantam Press.

Trevor, M., Schendel, J. and Wilpert, B. (1986). *The Japanese management system: Generalists and specialists in Japanese companies abroad*. London: Frances Pinter.

TWICE (This Week in Consumer Electronics) (2000). Nakamura outlines new Matsushita. (Author: S. Smith). 4 October: www.twice.com

Viney, J. (1997). *The culture wars: How American and Japanese businesses have outperformed Europe's and why the future will be different*. London: Capstone.

White, M. and Trevor, M. (1983). *Under Japanese management*. London: Heinemann.

8 Case study 3
LEGO: transferring identity knowledge

PROLOGUE

Almost everyone knows the LEGO brick, the plastic building block in the bright colours that provided many of us with endless possibilities for play as children. The genius of the LEGO brick lies in its simplicity in that it can be used by children in ways that are only limited by their own imagination. The simple ingenuity of the LEGO brick and its contribution to children's play and development the world over were recognized when *Fortune* magazine in the USA and the Association of British Retailers recently named LEGO the Toy of the Century over such other toy classics such as Barbie and the Teddy Bear. Established in 1932, the LEGO Group is today among the world's largest toy producers. To date it has sold some six billion construction elements in 140 countries, of which two billion are the famous bricks. Its largest market is the USA, which accounts for one-third of the company's sales. LEGO has production facilities in Denmark, where it is headquartered, the USA, Switzerland, the Czech Republic and Korea. In addition, there are marketing and product development centres in the USA, Germany, Italy and the UK. In 1999, the LEGO Group had a turnover of approximately $1 billion and the company employed approximately 7,800 people worldwide. Perhaps best known for its famous construction toys, LEGO has, since the 1990s, strategically diversified into three new business areas: LEGOLAND family parks, media products, and lifestyle-branded merchandise.

A striking feature of LEGO's international strategy is to play down, if not suppress, its Danish origins. If LEGO is in the USA or Germany, it wishes to be perceived as a German company or US company, and so on. Behind this ethos is a simple notion: that play is universal. So it was logical that the company should be a globalized company in terms both of market coverage and the mindset of the employees. Thus, for LEGO, a key challenge is to ensure that the company values and corporate identity, which may both be regarded as knowledge resources to employees, can provide guidelines for aligning behaviour and actions in the company itself and *vis-à-vis* the marketplace.

Although a company's identity is expressed through everything it does, it is recognized that identity is important both as a focal point of employees' own attitudes towards the company and as an intangible element of marketing programmes. Thus companies need a clear idea of their own identity in their orientation towards employees and customers. Accordingly, the *control* of identity is a critical issue, which becomes more complex when the values, (ideal) behaviour and attitudes associated with identity are to be equitably diffused through an internationally operating company. The case of LEGO is especially interesting in that its identity is constructed around, and is for, the future of the world – children.

The structure of this case study is as follows:

- The company background

- Methodology

- The global mission

- LEGO values and identity

- LEGO Media International

- The LEGO revolution in the USA

- Cross-cultural management issues

- A knowledge management perspective

- Managing identity as cross-cultural knowledge transfer

- Managing identity from a knowledge management perspective

- Afterword: a quintessentially Danish company nevertheless

THE COMPANY BACKGROUND

Humble beginnings

The LEGO Company traces its beginnings from 1932 when a Danish carpenter, Ole Kirk Christiansen, opened a small workshop for making wooden toys in the town of Billund in Jutland in the west of Denmark. It was set up as a family business and that is essentially how it has remained to the present day, and Billund has always remained the headquarters of the company.

It was in 1934 that Christiansen called his small company, which then employed six or seven people, LEGO, which stood for both his company and the toys it made. He can hardly have imagined that some 50 years later LEGO would be a household name for toys throughout the world. Christiansen was a perfectionist in the art of toy-making and he made certain that all the carpenters he employed shared his commitment to craftsmanship. Ahead of bigger and more prestigious Danish companies in those pre-war days, Christiansen put up a wooden sign in his workshop for both his craftsmen and customers to read: 'Only the best is good enough.' His slogan should not be taken at face value. What he really meant was 'only the best is good enough *for children*', for he believed that children deserved toys that were made with care and attention. And how lucky for him, incidentally, that the word LEGO goes smoothly into the phonetic systems of most of the world's languages without connoting anything obscene, derogatory or misleading. (In spoken Japanese it becomes REGO, but this is not a source of confusion as there is no remotely similar-sounding Japanese word.) The word LEGO, as it happens, is a combination of the first two letters of the Danish words LEg GOdt, which means 'play well'. LEGO clearly was a reflection of the founder's values, including his respect for children, which anticipate the modern company's emphasis on the manufacture of high-quality toys that stimulate childrens' creativity and imagination, whilst fostering their healthy development and learning through play. During the Second World War, when Denmark was under Nazi occupation from April 1940 to May 1945, the LEGO Company managed to keep going.

From wooden toys to plastic building bricks: first steps towards internationalization

In 1947, Ole Kirk Christiansen, with remarkable perspicacity, saw the potential of a new material, which had undergone rapid development during the war: plastics. In that year he purchased the company's first injection moulding machine, and the LEGO Company began to produce toys in both traditional wood and still highly novel plastics. As early as 1949 LEGO introduced to the Danish market the forerunner of LEGO building bricks, as we know them today. These were the revolutionary 'Automatic Binding Bricks', which were hollow on the inside and had four or eight studs on the top. Automatic Binding Bricks could only be used for making simple stacked structures. It would be some eight or nine years before LEGO devised its well-known coupling system.

By 1950 Ole Kirk Christiansen's workshop had been replaced by a little factory, the number of employees has risen to 140, and the company has developed a successful business selling LEGO toys to retailers all over Denmark. In that year his son, Godtfred Kirk Christiansen, became the company's assistant managing director. Part of the LEGO legend is that Ole Kirk Christiansen made his son Godtfred promise him that LEGO would never make war toys when he inherited the company one day. The legacy of this promise lives on in the modern LEGO where the thought of producing war toys would be considered heretical.

In 1954 there was a major development in the product concept. The Automatic Binding Bricks were called the 'LEGO System of Play', and the bricks began to be marketed as this concept in the following year. But the truly significant breakthrough occurred in 1958 with the invention of the new coupling system for the LEGO brick. Tubular protrusions were added inside the hollow brick, which not only meant greater structural stability but also made combination possibilities almost infinite. On the advice of the company lawyer, a worldwide patent on the new coupling system was taken out in the same year.

1958 was also the year which marked the death of Ole Kirk Christiansen. He was succeeded as Managing Director by his son, Godtfred Kirk Christiansen, who remained in this office until 1979 when he became Chairman of LEGO. In that year his son, Kjeld Kirk Kristiansen,[1] took over as Managing Director. By this time LEGO had long ceased to be just an operator on the Danish market. In fact its internationalization began in the 1950s when LEGO opened its first sales outlets abroad, in Norway and then in Sweden. Shortly after that LEGO was selling its products into Germany, whose economy was beginning to pick up following the catastrophe of the Second World War. According to company legend, Godtfred Kirk Christiansen stated that if the company could take on Germany, it could take on the world.

Under that conviction LEGO began to establish itself on markets in Western Europe on a country-by-country basis. For example, LEGO Vertrieb AG was established in Switzerland in 1957, and LEGO UK Ltd was established in the United Kingdom two years later. A sales and marketing subsidiary was set up in Australia in 1962. In a move to internationalize production and marketing operations, a new Swiss manufacturing subsidiary, LEGO AG, was established in 1974; then, in 1980, LEGO Systems Inc. in the USA, which had been established in 1973 as a sales and marketing company, was expanded into a manufacturing facility. Prior to these developments, all LEGO's international sales were based on exports from the LEGO production facilities in Billund in Denmark.

With production facilities on two continents and sales in most of the world, LEGO began, in the mid-1908s, to establish its identity as a global company. After he took over the company in 1979, Kjeld Kirk Kristiansen, as we shall see later, made some important contributions to the sophistication of LEGO values and identity for the era of globalization. In the meantime, international operations continued apace. Following the fall of the Berlin Wall in 1989, LEGO made a priority of establishing markets in Eastern Europe, setting up sales offices in Hungary in 1992 and in Russia in 1996. Meanwhile, in the early 1990s, the company recognized that it was in a crisis. It must give up its traditional go-it-alone thinking which was too closely bound up with the famous toy brick.[2] So it began to further internationalize itself by placing product development units outside Denmark. In 1996 LEGO established its first independent company outside Denmark, LEGO Media International and in 2000 it took over a leading American producer of smart toys.

METHODOLOGY

The material in this case study was gathered by Esben Karmark, a PhD candidate at the Copenhagen Business School, who studied the LEGO Company between 1997 and 2000. He interviewed key managers at the LEGO Company headquarters in Billund, Denmark, about the issue of the cross-cultural transfer of the

LEGO identity. All in all, 15 interviews were conducted. The informants included two members of the LEGO Company executive team, Kjeld Møller Pedersen and Christian Majgaard, managers in finance, marketing and the product development department, a member of the LEGO Global Brand Development Team, and the manager of the LEGO Idea House, an in-house resource centre for the development of the LEGO culture and identity.

LEGO Media International in London was studied between 1999 and 2000. Here, interviews were conducted with the general manager as well as other members of the management team. Furthermore, an interview was conducted with a LEGO media manager at LEGO Inc. in Enfield, Connecticut, in the USA. LEGO Media employees who had experience in working at both the LEGO headquarters and LEGO Media were also interviewed. All interviews lasted between 60 and 120 minutes.

THE GLOBAL MISSION

As was noted above, it was the aim of the LEGO Company in the 1950s to become (then) an international company; today it regards itself as a global one. It was and remains central to the philosophy of internationalization *pace* globalization that no country has advantages over other countries where LEGO has established its own companies. Nor is Denmark excluded from this formulation. Thus it is a deliberate business strategy for companies and production facilities in the LEGO Company outside Denmark to be run by country nationals. And this polycentric form of control is taken a stage further: the LEGO Company was conscious not to impose the company culture of the Danish headquarters on the companies outside Denmark. However, the company rigorously ensures that a common standard is applied to its products and marketing. This means in practice that the LEGO brand itself is one of the key elements of corporate culture; and in this respect the headquarters in Billund takes centralized control by issuing brand guidelines to all companies outside Denmark.

With the company's diversification into markets other than the toy market (or play materials market as the LEGO Company prefers to call it) and its dispersal across national borders, the LEGO Company has experienced a growing need to ensure that knowledge about its values and identity is shared by everyone in the company. As Executive Vice-President Christian Majgaard explains: 'When the brand only stood for one thing we were not so conscious of the LEGO values as we are now. We have seen the emergence of a strong consciousness of what the LEGO brand stands for throughout the 1990s.' It is the LEGO Company's strategic goal to be the world's strongest brand among families with children by the year 2005. (Coca-Cola, beware.) In order to realize this goal, LEGO decided to extend its product range from construction toys to include amusement parks, media products, and lifestyle products. The rationale here is to reach a greater number of what the company considers to be its core customers: children under the age of 16 and their parents. This diversification strategy was significantly influenced by the popularity of video games, which are absorbing demand away from the construction toy market. Thus, in order to maintain its position as one of the largest toy manufacturers in the world, LEGO has had to expand and elaborate the range of product it offers to customers. Underpinning the diversification plan, LEGO is focusing on three strategic priorities, namely the LEGO brand itself, the 'People and Culture' concept, and profitable growth. The first two priorities are inextricably bound up with the LEGO Company's values and identity, which are so central to its overall business strategy.

The implementation of the diversification strategy resulted in 1999 in a major restructuring of the company worldwide. Called the Fitness Program, this reorganization regrouped its 30 sales companies into seven regional companies across the world. The aim was to create what Kjeld Kirk Kristiansen called in a CNN interview in February 2000 a global brand organization. The Fitness Program, which was introduced shortly after LEGO, for the first time in its history, incurred a financial loss (1998), rapidly produced positive results. The company was able to announce that sales for the 1999 financial year stood at $1.25 billion, yielding a profit of $60 million. The concept of the global brand organization means ensuring that values, which are well-embedded and taken for granted at headquarters in Billund, are also understood and respected in subsidiaries that were previously operating with a high level of independence. As we shall see, the company set about achieving this aim through formulating clear identity guidelines for the products in the new businesses. This meant that the headquarters of the company was establishing a kind of identity quality control. In the meantime, to strengthen all these developments, LEGO has developed a new strategy of being open both for acquisitions and alliances.[3]

The values and identity of the LEGO Company together constitute guidelines as to what types of product should be developed and made, and how these should be presented to customers. In order to specify exactly LEGO's values and identity as they are today and how they, ideally, shall evolve in the future, the LEGO Company has set up a 'Culture Board' and a 'Brand Board', which are made up of members of top management. The Brand Board, for its part, is supported by a 'Global Brand Development Team', which is composed of managers from all of the LEGO businesses. We now explore in greater detail LEGO's values and identity.

LEGO VALUES AND IDENTITY

Since its foundation in 1932, the LEGO Company has maintained a concern for its identity. We see this in the etymology of the company name (i.e. LEGO = play well). We have also noted that the founder, Ole Kirk Christiansen, was much concerned with the quality of his toys: 'Only the best is good enough' ran a sign in his original workshop. The founder's son, Gotfred Kirk Christiansen, or GKC, as he is known in the company, added to the LEGO identity. He is personally credited with the invention of the studs-and-tubes system. It is this concept of the child's building brick that evolved into LEGO's core product since the early 1960s and has remained the symbol of the company ever since.

GKC also perceived that the toy bricks of his day lacked what he called 'system', by which he meant the possibilities for them to be combined to create structures more sophisticated than simple houses. So he formulated the principle of 'system in play' for all LEGO products. This meant that all LEGO bricks, regardless of shape and size, were designed to fit together. With their bright, 'official' primary colours (blue, red, yellow) plus black and white, the bricks *are* LEGO, being frequently used as a standard corporate symbol in all company publications and web pages. They are also used decoratively in LEGO offices around the world.

GKC was also responsible for formulating, in the 1970s, the 'ten LEGO characteristics' that LEGO products were meant to embody. These characteristics represent a set of guidelines for new product development and marketing policy:

- Unlimited play possibilities
- For girls, for boys
- Enthusiasm for all ages
- Play all year round
- Stimulating and absorbing play
- Endless hours of play
- Imagination, creativity, development
- Each new product multiplies the play value
- Always topical
- Leading safety and quality

The LEGO ten product characteristics

LEGO's top management considers these product characteristics to be as relevant for the company today as they were when they were written 30 years ago. But they are more than characteristics; they are also the foundation of the company value system. This means that LEGO is somewhat unusual as a company, as its value system derives from its products and is not based on a set of precepts which explicitly specify (ideal) employee attitudes and behaviour. Consequently, the company's identity is very strongly associated with the LEGO brand, which is considered to be the company's most valuable asset. Thus, the characteristics are an expression of values through which the company in turn expresses its own identity.

It is the responsibility of the LEGO Brand Board, mentioned above, to establish the permissible ways in which the values and identity are expressed – and enshrined in a key company document, the LEGO Brand Book, which is the LEGO manager's Bible, wherever he or she works on behalf of the company. The LEGO Brand Book describes how the LEGO brand values are closely related to both LEGO cultural values that have evolved throughout its history as well as top management's vision for the future, and states that the core essence of the LEGO brand lies in stimulating creativity. All in all, the LEGO brand should express both Ole Kirk Cristiansen's notion of good play, GKC's ten LEGO characteristics and Kjeld Kirk Kristiansen's vision for the LEGO Company. This LEGO Vision, as it has come to be known within the company, is plainly a direct evolution of the precepts guiding the company since the 1950s. In its *Brand Book* (LEGO Company, 1999) it states that the LEGO name shall become a universal concept associated with three notions: idea; exuberance, and values:

Idea	Exuberance	Values
• Creativity	• Enthusiasm	• Quality
• Imagination	• Spontaneity	• Caring
• Unlimited	• Self-expression	• Development
• Discovery	• Unrestrained	• Innovation
• Constructionism[4]		• Consistency

Components of the LEGO Vision

In yet further refinements, the LEGO Company expresses its values and identity through two corporate affirmations: its fundamental beliefs and its mission, which are presented in the boxes that follow.

LEGO fundamental beliefs

Children are our role models.

They are curious, creative and imaginative. They embrace discovery and wonder. They are natural learners. These are precious qualities that should be nurtured and stimulated throughout life. Lifelong creativity, imagination and learning are stimulated by playful activities that encourage hands-on and minds-on creation, fun togetherness and the sharing of ideas. People who are curious, creative and imaginative – who have a childlike urge to learn – are best equipped to thrive in a challenging world and be the builders of our common future.

LEGO fundamental beliefs

The LEGO mission

To nurture the child in each of us.

All LEGO products appeal to children's imagination and creativity by offering them unlimited possibilities.

The LEGO mission

It is a key concern for LEGO that the products today continue to live up to the characteristics of creativity and quality. Regarding quality, a recent publication, 'A Profile of the LEGO Group for the year 2000' (published by the LEGO Company on *www.lego.com*, 2001) noted three dimensions:

> In our largest business area, LEGO Play Materials, we associate quality with the following requirements:
> Technical quality: Our play materials must have such properties as durability, stability, consistent colors and product safety.
> Consumer quality: Our play materials must provide unlimited opportunities, permitting children to play with them in many different ways.
> Development quality: Our play materials must be attractive to children and retain their interest year after year. They must stimulate and develop children's senses, motor abilities, imagination, creativity and intelligence.

It is impossible to exaggerate the importance of children and their development within the LEGO Company. 'Children are our vital concern – as a dependable partner for parents, it is our mission to stimulate children's imagination and creativity, and to encourage them to explore, experience and express their own world – a world without limits.' It can all be summed up in the expression 'respect for children', the foundation value of the company. But the idea was never to produce toys for passive entertainment and diversion; LEGO was created to provide children with stimulating play materials, manufactured to very high-quality standards, which support their own development and self-expression. The company has coined a perversely unstimulating word to convey this idea: *edutainment*.

Another identity driver is the LEGO Company's status as a family-owned business. It is held that customers like to associate a family-run company with the manufacture of toys for children, whose own development is directly influenced by their families. In an interview on CNN's *Business Unusual* programme in February 2000, Kjeld Kirk Kristiansen emphasized that the fact the LEGO Company is family-owned has a significant impact on the way LEGO is run. He pointed out that family ownership means that the LEGO Company can engage in long-term strategies without having to glance at shareholders' demands for often unrealistic short-term results. In his words: 'It is easier to follow a long-term strategy and to stick to your values than if you had to follow the movements of the stock market.'

The identity of LEGO then can be seen to be composed on three main elements: the product, the brand itself, and the mission. But there are other factors too: the family-owned status of the company; the de-emphasis of the Danish origins of the company; and the corresponding emphasis on the localization of management. To these we may add another factor, which is certainly felt by LEGO employees. In the words of a London-based manager: 'LEGO is about a genuine set of values that have stood the test of time.' In other words, there is within the identity of LEGO a sense of stability which goes back to the values upon which the company was founded in 1932. As we noted above, identity places a very significant strategic role in LEGO. It is also a facet of a company over which central management can never have complete control.

Furthermore, the perception identity varies at different locations around the world: no two countries share identical values about the status of children in family life and in society in general, about the nature of play and education, about the role of educationally oriented toys in children's lives. So, how does LEGO, which calculatedly does not impose its (Danish) management values on its foreign affiliates, ensure that its managers throughout the world share more or less the same perception of the identity and carry out their company tasks with the 'right' attitude? And how is knowledge of the LEGO identity diffused throughout the company? To answer these questions, we shall examine the experience of a LEGO subsidiary company based in London, called LEGO Media International.

LEGO MEDIA INTERNATIONAL

The task of LEGO Media International is to develop interactive software and market it on a worldwide scale. In the early 1990s the company recognized the need to extend its product range into the expanding and highly lucrative market for educational software. A strategic business unit, called Darwin, was set up at the company headquarters in Denmark with the remit to move the company into this market. An off-shoot project was based in London, which was seen as the centre and leading-edge of the software industry in Europe. The Darwin project not only endorsed the necessity for LEGO to develop a software arm, but also recommended that a new LEGO company be formed and based in London. So it was that LEGO Media International came into being and was set up in London in 1996 as a highly experimental venture. The fact that there was already a LEGOLAND family park in Windsor in the vicinity of London was also a factor in the choice of location for the new company.

This move was a major departure from LEGO tradition. Although the company had encouraged independent product development in the USA, this was the first time that LEGO was going to permit a wholly owned subsidiary company to have global responsibility for the production and marketing of LEGO-branded goods – in this case media products. As such, it is the first and only company in the LEGO Group outside headquarters with such a wide product mandate. LEGO Media International also operates in a rapidly growing, innovative industry with highly compressed cycle times. The issue we will address is, of course, the challenge of ensuring that the people working for LEGO Media International fully understand the values embodied by the company identity and work with them accordingly.

By entering into a new business area such as media products for children, the LEGO Company has opened up the potential to build on the company image. LEGO already has a strong position among the world's leading brands, but to become the best-known brand by 2005 requires that the LEGO Company reaches a wider target audience than can be achieved by the toy-based categories alone. One factor behind LEGO's entry into this new business area was the awareness that 'kids are getting older younger'. This means that children today tend to stop playing with conventional toys at an earlier age than in the past in order to direct their attention towards other things such as computer games and other media products. LEGO, as one of the world's best-known suppliers of toys, had little option but to take up a key position in this market. But it does so with a very big advantage: the power of the LEGO brand to reach out to children who may have already enjoyed LEGO bricks. As the London Media PR manager explains: 'One positive benefit that we can bring as inspiration for LEGO to do things differently is that we can make LEGO into something for older kids. You know, if they see that something is available on Play Station they think it's cool – kids today want cross-media reference.'

When it opened in 1996, LEGO Media employed seven people. It has now grown into an organization of more than 100 staff, most of whom come from the software or the publishing industry. It has recruited ambitious young people, mainly British, with creative talent from a completely different business sector (i.e. software), many of whom offer technical competences with limited commercial backgrounds. But many of the key marketing and commercial positions are held by people from various European and non-European backgrounds. All the LEGO Media employees have something what Billund cannot offer: they bring pace to their activities and many have experience of the exceptionally fast-moving software industry, where sometimes the lead-time for developing a new software product can be as little as two months. All this contrasts dramatically with development times of up to several years for the company's traditional construction toys.

Apart from one manager and four people in product development, none of the current employees has a LEGO background. The average age is 23 and the British managing director is in his early thirties. Thus LEGO Media personnel have created a corporate culture which is quite different from the culture of the group headquarters in the quiet town of Billund in Denmark. But, as we shall see, the age profile is but one factor.

LEGO Media produces, but does not manufacture. LEGO Media in fact produces more than software titles. It also publishes a LEGO magazine and LEGO books and is now moving into the production of children's and family pro-grammes for television, film and the Internet. With expanding sales in the USA, LEGO Media has opened up an outlet in Connecticut and will strengthen its London-based film and Internet offerings with a production unit in Los Angeles.

In terms of employees, LEGO Media is a small company, but its sales are in the region of $160 million, making it a very significant contributor to the group at large. There is no doubt that the LEGO style of management, which is hands-off in the Danish way and strongly supportive of localization, has given the management team at LEGO Media freedom of operation, and this may be a major factor in account-ing for its success to date. But, the key question is: has this involved a compromise of the LEGO identity, the traditional child-centred glue of the company?

THE LEGO REVOLUTION IN THE USA

In spring 2000, LEGO made its first major purchase of another company by taking over a high-technology toy firm, Zowie Entertainment, in Mateo, which is about 30 kms from San Francisco. The move is partly a response to the Danish concern that the company can no longer hold on to the 'go-it-alone' philosophy of the founding father.

The US company specializes in innovative smart toys and had earned from *Newsweek* the accolade of producing 'the IT toy of the year'. The takeover suits both companies. The American business secures massive investment from its new parent company and was in any case looking for a partner in the form of a major Toyama. LEGO was easily the most interesting match for the Zowie's founder, John Lemoncheck, who liked the idea of the Danish company being unquoted on the stock exchange – one does not have to worry about grumbling financial analysts and shareholders. LEGO now owns a company which can enable it to be a world leader in computer toys. After the deal was struck a joint 60-strong Danish–US taskforce was set up to develop joint projects, but the number rapidly swelled to 200. As well as software designers and engineers, the taskforce also has child psychologists, whose task is to involve children, several thousand of whom already cooperate with Zowie Entertainment to help with the creation of new generations of the LEGO computer toys.

The first few months of the new arrangement have meant a considerable amount of transatlantic travel, frequent video-conferencing and intensive e-mailing. The nine-hour time difference between California and Jutland is forcing changes in work patterns in both locations. A striking feature of the takeover is its relative smoothness and there can be no doubt that both companies' commitment to children was a positive factor. There can be no doubt too that Zowie Entertainment saw no problem is merging with the LEGO identity. The fact that the new entity is called LEGO Lab San Mateo speaks volumes for a so far remarkable collaboration.

The LEGO identity in cross-border management

Consistent values and a strong product idea have always been used in LEGO to bind the company's business units into an integrated whole. But hitherto these concepts applied to physical objects: construction toys, media products for children, lifestyle products for children such as clothes and watches, and amusement parks. But software is, as it were, metaphysical. There is nothing tangible from which to derive anything about the company's identity except through company name and logo on packaging materials. As we saw above, the traditional identity of LEGO and its value system have been based directly (and lovingly) on one quintessential product, the famous toy brick. The nub of the challenge is reflected in this comment by Mark Livingstone, the General Manager of LEGO Media:

> LEGO Media spent considerable time discussing the concept of basing our products on the values of the LEGO Group rather than the physical play materials. Our objective is to demonstrate how lateral and innovative we can be in the virtual world. We feel liberated rather than constrained by the LEGO Group's traditional values and concepts, which we are now extending into media products for children aged between two and sixteen.

Behind Livingstone stands the central message from the company headquarters in the form of a guideline in the LEGO Brand Book: 'Products and services marketed under the LEGO brand can take many forms . . . As a creative software as long as that software is loyal to the values of the LEGO brand, allowing children to explore and express themselves.' As LEGO considers both children and their parents as their core consumers, the idea is that any LEGO product, including software materials, should provide both groups with valuable benefits. As far as adults are concerned, LEGO wants the consumer to experience the benefits of learning togetherness with their children; and, as far as children are concerned, LEGO wants them to experience play as self-expressive stimulation. The company's wish is that in their different ways children and their parents will find infinite opportunities for enjoying the brand. The challenge to LEGO Media is to develop and market its software products in a way that is consistent with those values. The challenge to the company headquarters is to make certain that this is what happens, without imposing any kind of 'cultural imperialism' on its novel London subsidiary.

LEGO Media has skilfully and sensitively taken over the core company values and adapted them not to suit its own culture, but to reflect the nature of software play materials. As we shall see presently, the company has modified the ten characteristics of traditional LEGO products for this purpose. But let us consider first the guidelines being evolved by LEGO Media in its own presentation materials. First, it identifies itself with the long-standing core values of LEGO:

> The central task of the LEGO Group is to stimulate children's imagination and creativity. By taking children's interests seriously, and by encouraging them to explore, experience and express their own world, the LEGO Group has achieved market dominance in Europe and a leading position among the world's top ten manufacturers. Now at LEGO Media International, we are extending this philosophy, stimulating in fresh ways with surprising new media products.

Then LEGO Media develops its own gloss on the traditional product philosophy:

> Unlike conventional ready-made toys, LEGO products are components which can be combined, altered and dismantled in an almost infinite variety of ways. This makes them inspiring, challenging, educational and fun for children all over the world. Children develop by testing their own limits and those who play with LEGO products derive growing pleasure as their skills improve. Similarly, parents come to regard the LEGO Group as a trusted partner whose products offer increasing value for money as they buy more. Our task at LEGO Media International is to inspire the same feelings of consumer confidence as we develop the concept of constructive play through innovative media.

Then LEGO Media explains its management philosophy, which is based on the LEGO Vision:

> The management team is backed by the LEGO Vision, a formal set of values that must be reflected in all new product design, packaging and marketing, as well as in the way we conduct our business and communicate with consumers.

LEGO Media General Manager Mark Livingstone explains: 'We took the LEGO Vision of idea, exuberance and values and then asked ourselves: what does that mean in a software context?'

The company was given considerable independence over the evolution of its own philosophy in order to develop its own corporate identity, but the process always had to unfold in consultation with senior managers at headquarters in Denmark. In fact, the creation of the modified identity for LEGO Media was achieved with relatively little intervention from headquarters. As a result, LEGO Media was able to achieve its objective of building on 'the natural fit' between LEGO play materials and media products. As stated in the LEGO Media's presentation material: 'By faithfully applying LEGO design elements and the concept of constructive play, we are ensuring that traditional and contemporary LEGO ranges feed off each other's success.'

One of the more remarkable instances of corporate headquarters not overriding its London subsidiary concerns the modification of its own mission as a new entity within the LEGO group of companies and the adaptation of GKC's ten product characteristics. LEGO Media recognizes that as a LEGO company it must 'unlock childrens' imaginations and satisfy parents' wishes'. Accordingly, the London affiliate's mission is to 'make children's play more constructive':

- By inspiring them to be creative

- By encouraging social play

- Through customized game play

- Through a mix of structured and open-ended play

- Through mental and physical challenge

Parents (or at least adult purchasers for children) can have reassurance about the quality and performance of LEGO Media products:

- In our rigorous attention to product testing

- In the helpful way we treat our customers

- In the clarity of our packaging and print

- In the consistency of our brand marketing

A notable feature of this case study about LEGO is that its managers outside Denmark find it easy to identify with the company and its traditional values. A London-based marketing manager told us: 'What I love about the brand, as a marketer, is that it stands above all for quality and an attention to detail.' LEGO Media's sales director for Europe and the Middle East commented: 'LEGO has high ethical standards. We don't put our name on just anything.' Again, in an expression of high regard for the company, the LEGO Media PR manager said: 'It is the only company that I have worked for where I really believe in the company story.'

Thus the brand and the values that the LEGO Group have ensured that people have come to expect of it through decades of consistent dedication to quality and wholesome play for children serves as a kind of beacon for LEGO Media employees when developing software products. Accordingly, LEGO Media takes great care to develop software for children that is creative and which can provide children with a genuine learning experience. That the LEGO brand is vital to LEGO Media is acknowledged by the London company: 'In the crowded children's software marketplace, LEGO values give us a unique point of difference. Parents feel reassured by the LEGO name – it is their guarantee of carefully tested products that combine fun with imaginative content.'

All in all, then, the LEGO heritage informs the LEGO Media identity, even though the latter has elaborated its own interpretation of the LEGO identity. This is acknowledged in the LEGO Media presentation brochure:

The character of our business is distinctive. LEGO Media International takes youthful flair and harnesses it to a framework of values that have proven their worth over many years. The result is an enterprise that's responsive yet responsible, inspired yet never impulsive.

Our task now is to explore the LEGO experience from a cross-cultural management point of view, making use of statements supplied by company managers in Denmark and the UK. Then we will attempt to interpret this experience from a knowledge management perspective.

Millennium meetings

In order to improve its global networking, LEGO has introduced the concept of 'Millennium meetings'. These take place periodically and involve executive board members from Denmark and senior managers working for LEGO in regions such as Europe and the Americas.

In 2000, some 90 members of the LEGO Americas management team participated in the first 'Americas' Millennium Meeting' which was held by the LEGO Executive Team (corporate board) and involved CEO Kjeld Kirk Kristiansen and three executive vice-presidents – Poul Ploughmann, Peter Eio and Christian Majgaard. The agenda included presentations by Kjeld, Christian and Poul who emphasized the importance of strategic planning, innovation, building brands and dreams. The pronouncements of the company's senior officers give an illuminating insight into how LEGO currently views itself.

Concerning strength of the brand, Majgaard stressed that, although the company operates a single-brand strategy based on the LEGO name and the LEGO logo, the challenge is continually to create new product ideas and business ideas which closely fit the core values. Such ideas would be measured by three criteria:

- The accumulated awareness of our values and image

- Status on children's wish lists

- Customer satisfaction

Behind this aspiration stood the business realities. Although the company's most valuable asset was its brand, described as 'fantastically strong' by Ploughmann, there was no room for complacency. The company was doing everything to ensure that all its stakeholders were aware of the LEGO values and how these were seen as the foundation for business growth and the corporate culture. Thus the company had set 2005 as the target year for LEGO to be most well-known brand among families with children. Ploughmann saw the future and the company's overall profitability in terms of a novel trinity composed of 'groundbreaking concepts, compelling stories and aggressiveness'. A ground-breaking concept was anything from LEGO which seized the consumer with a sharp sense of excitement and surprise.

Ploughmann stressed the importance of the worldwide LEGO culture and with the year 2005 firmly in mind he introduced his own vision, a concept he called 'the Dream'. The Dream had three core elements: strengthening the brand, attaining profitable growth and developing the corporate culture. Central to its realization was the conviction that working for LEGO meant that employees were in an exciting, creative and happy environment where things changed, had to change. This necessitated the development of managers who were entrepreneurial in temperament and capability and diverse in national, linguistic and professional backgrounds. Only managers such as these could create the key conditions for change and carry them through the company.

At the end of the Millennium meeting Kjeld Kristiansen summed up everything with these words: 'It seems that there is much agreement. It is good that we all share the same commitment and the same sense of what challenges we will have to take on in order to become a global brand-organization.'

CROSS-CULTURAL MANAGEMENT ISSUES

Since the early 1990s LEGO has ventured into three new and strategically important business areas: the LEGOLAND parks, lifestyle products and media products for children. In many cases these developments have entailed LEGO setting up a presence in countries outside Denmark. In each case the company has applied its philosophy of transferring its values, as symbolized in the philosophy associated with the famous toy brick. However, it would be mistaken to see the company policy of hands-off localization as a trustful detachment of headquarters. As Christian Majgaard, a member of the LEGO Company's executive management, explained, a factor in this policy is to stimulate cross-cultural learning:

> LEGO has pursued a core model in our business development throughout the 1990s. When establishing new companies we have mixed employees from the old LEGO culture with new employees. The employees from the old culture act as culture carriers, and when the old culture meets new ways of looking at things we achieve a fruitful crossing of old and new.

It is just as well that headquarters take this point of view, as LEGO Media considers diversity as one of its key strengths. Not only that: it regards the high concentration of one nationality – Danes – at headquarters as something of a deterrent to creativity.

When LEGO Media was established in London, a local employee with ten years' experience of working with LEGO, Conny Kalcher (now director of LEGO Media Film and TV production), was a member of LEGO Media's executive team with special responsibility for transferring knowledge of the LEGO values and identity to the London company:

It's interesting to see the development that has taken place. When we started this we were only a few people, and we had discussions about what sort of software we were going to make. The attitude then was a bit like, okay in the beginning we have to make something that's related to LEGO, and we will make two or three games, and then we have probably run out of ways to relate them to LEGO. . . . In the beginning it was a bit difficult because I was the only one from LEGO and the others were from the software business. And it was like they knew what this was about, and I did not really know what it was about. I might have known about LEGO, but I did not know anything about software. But as they learn to understand LEGO, that LEGO is more than plastic items you sell in a box; the deeper the understanding they got of LEGO, and the more I learned to understand their world, the more both parties could appreciate each other. My role was very much to bring these values to LEGO Media, and after a couple of months these values were internalized here.

In the early formative period of LEGO Media, considerable emphasis was placed on creating a mission statement that reflected traditional LEGO values without constraining the scope in the new company. Kalcher explains:

In the beginning we had a seminar with the aim of writing [the mission statement] up. That is, what was our purpose, and how should we take values that stood for LEGO; which of the old ones should we not include, and which new ones should we include to achieve what we wanted to achieve? . . . The vision with Idea, Exuberance and Values . . . we all know that we are low on exuberance – in what we are offering to the consumer from the toy category our exuberance is, perhaps not low but low in comparison to the two other dimensions. That is, it is a strong idea, and there are plenty of values but exuberance, that is about running around shouting WOW! and that is not our strongest side on the toy front. And exuberance is what sells computer games, it has to make a strong impression, it has to be fun, and there has to be plenty of action. That's why it was important for us to be 'hot' in that category. Overall we really have spent a lot of time on, and talk a lot about, what values LEGO stands for, and what we should measure us against.

This emphasis on fun is a good example of cross-cultural learning. The idea of fun as a core element in any LEGO product offering was wholly new. According to Carsten Wammen of the LEGO global development team, the company has recently modified its mission statement to express a stronger emphasis on fun. Behind this was a realization that the LEGO values and identity were beginning to be presented in increasingly cerebral ways; and there was a fear that the company might be losing its touch with children's way of thinking.

The cross-culturally interesting point is that fun is not central to Danish life (having a good time, yes, but a rib-tickling experience of pure mirth, no), whereas English life is virtually inconceivable without references to having fun. So, if LEGO had not chosen the UK as the base for its software operations, it is very likely that the Danish would have continued its unconscious, subliminal transfer of Danish seriousness. But the credit goes to headquarters for its willingness to adapt its mission statement. As a result there has taken place not only a re-formulation of company values, but also a reinterpretation of them. This small example reveals very clearly how cross-cultural learning can prove to be a force for revitalization in a family-owned company which, like LEGO, is all too conscious of the weight of tradition.

It seems overall that the LEGO Media employees accept the scope that they are offered, whilst conforming to company policy about developing what it regards as socially desirable products. Kalcher again:

> We might start out with a game, which then is made into a toy. What we cannot do, and what we should not do is to make something that does not fit our brand – that does not fit our value system. That means that we should not make 'shoot them up' games, we should not make anything that racist or sexist. We should make something which is deeper and more intellectual in relation to children, something that fits children's potential for development.

There is one final cross-cultural point to be made. This concerns the contrasting image that LEGO has in Europe and the USA respectively. It might first of all be thought that LEGO has a uniform image all over the world. But employees of LEGO Media do not entirely share this belief. In their experience, the LEGO image in the USA is significantly different from the image in Europe. LEGO, they suggest, is more of a lifestyle product in Europe, whereas the image in the USA is more closely connected to the traditional LEGO products of bricks and mini-figures. Perceptions of the company image are strongly associated with how employees in the company interpret the company's identity. The company may do well to investigate this contrasting image, as it suggests that consumers in Europe, on the one hand, and consumers in the USA, on the other, may be drawing on different aspects of the corporate identity. That has implications for not only how LEGO differentiates its appeal to consumers on both sides of the Atlantic, but also their stakeholders, among whom must be counted millions of children and their parents. Awareness of differences in a company's image can lead to valuable knowledge of how to differentiate the way in which a company's identity is expressed towards the consumers and other external stakeholders.

A KNOWLEDGE MANAGEMENT PERSPECTIVE

It is important to state at the outset of this section that the general lack of friction between LEGO headquarters and the London subsidiary is because English is the corporate language. Indeed, one could describe the English language as thoroughly domesticated within LEGO. This creates conditions for what Christian Majgaard calls 'shared mental space' between the two entities. Until and unless there is shared mental space, there can be no adequate transfer and sharing of knowledge. Shared mental space is the guarantor of what knowledge management experts call 'absorptive capacity', that is the presence of enough related knowledge to absorb new knowledge. A common language is a form of shared mental space; differences between languages can be a severe – occasionally almost total – constraint on achieving this condition.

As has already been noted, LEGO does not wish to impose its management style on its foreign subsidiaries, but does wish to transfer its notion of a children-oriented corporate culture and its emphasis on creativity and design. This otherwise 'unnatural' separation of powers, as it were, is made workable by the fact that LEGO has latched on to its identity, which is symbolized by the world-renowned toy brick, as the focal point of the company ethos and pivot of employee attitudes and behaviour. The identity therefore is a special kind of knowledge resource within the company. In LEGO Media, for example, knowledge about LEGO identity and associated values which back up the all-important brand has inspired and guided the development of new products and concepts, which might not have materialized at headquarters. All in all, messages about product design criteria, for example, are conveyed in the form of guidelines rather than directives. These guidelines are intended to stimulate and not hamper creative impulses.

As we noted in the discussion earlier about the value of fun, the lack of tight control over identity from Denmark permits new ideas and therefore new knowledge about the identity. Thus, as also noted, the capacity of the company to admit new interpretations of the identity from outside corporate headquarters permits revitalization. In this sense the transfer of identity knowledge within LEGO appears to be associated with openness, which makes cross-cultural synergy a possibility. As LEGO Media's PR director says:

> The brand promise is essential. LEGO Media is striving for continuous improvement – we are trying to do things better than anybody else. An analogy between the LEGO brick and software is that software is never finished – there is a similarity between designing LEGO toys and designing software. And it is important that we do not become McBrand.[5]

This is a very interesting form of transfer of technical knowledge resulting in cross-cultural synergy. It works because designers saw analogies and similarities despite the fact that designing software would appear to be very remote from designing construction toys. So it is that LEGO Media is able to cleave to old values, such as the emphasis on product quality, and introduce a competely new value, fun, without 'the old guard' at corporate headquarters feeling that there has been a compromise or deviation.

In so far as knowledge management, whether consciously or unconsciously practised, is supposed to add value to company performance, the LEGO experience demonstrates that in the case of LEGO Media employees feel good about working for the entire group, identifying with the values of the whole group and not focusing 'narrowly' on their own company. This is well expressed by one

London manager: 'What attracted me to LEGO was the reputation of the warmth of the company, and it is a fantastic brand.' In a similar vein, the marketing manager of LEGO Media stated: 'LEGO is very much about the brand, and to me the LEGO brand stands above all for quality, and what I love about the brand is the attention to detail.'

MANAGING IDENTITY AS CROSS-CULTURAL KNOWLEDGE TRANSFER

The concept of the LEGO identity can be directly traced back to the philosophy of the company's founder, Ole Kirk Christiansen, in 1932. Christiansen's emphasis on respect for children and the importance of making them toys of good quality to stimulate their creativity and overall development have always remained at the core of the company value system. Consequently, from its very origin, LEGO has linked together in the minds of its employees the concept of the brand more as a set of values than a complex of consumer benefits. The brand, the values and the company history have commingled to create a special identity, with which, it seems, employees readily identify (perhaps because the company can always appeal to the child in each of them).

This identity has been both carefully groomed and controlled by the corporate headquarters. The company has been astute enough to appreciate that the identity cannot be frozen in time. It is probable that the emergence of educational software in the early 1990s compelled the senior management to realize this. They realized that they would not be able to survive as a supplier of conventional toys unless they moved with the new media products. As we saw in the case of LEGO Media, the company in effect trusted their London subsidiary to reformulate the identity as long as it did not affect the power of the brand. As a result, a remarkable instance of cross-cultural learning took place: first, the software developers found inspiration in the LEGO's design practices for conventional toys; second, the UK team found it straightfoward to accept that socially undesirable software games were out of the question; and, third, the collaboration led to the introduction of a 'new' concept: fun.

The processes of transferring ideas and practices are not explicitly managed by the company as a cross-cultural activity, nor as an exercise in knowledge management. Yet both are key elements in these processes. From both perspectives it is noticeable that the knowledge exchanges between Denmark and the UK are characterized by relatively little resistance; the cross-cultural learning has plainly taken place in 'shared mental space'. It was suggested above that this was attributable to the fact that the Danish colleagues possess an exceptionally good command of English. But there may be another factor at work. The Danish way of management, which stresses consensus and lack of confrontation and dislikes highhandedness, may have been conducive to the creation of a cross-cultural learning atmosphere. If that is so, then the Danish – or at least LEGO – variation on the theme suggests that cross-cultural learning has a greater chance of succeeding when the nominally senior group in knowledge exchanges is not too concerned about imposing its values and thinking on others.

MANAGING IDENTITY FROM A KNOWLEDGE MANAGEMENT PERSPECTIVE

Since the days of Ole Kirk Cristiansen the LEGO values have traditionally been connected to more abstract values ('play well'). But it was the invention of the LEGO brick that caused the new values to become increasingly associated with, and symbolized by, the brick. For example, the brick gave birth to the value of 'constructionism' which in LEGO lore means that LEGO products are designed so that by building with the bricks the user can create something that is wholly original. The notion of constructionism leads to the related value of creativity, which encourages people to combine the bricks and colours in inventive ways. These values extend to LEGO product developers, who have created the LEGO watch, which has a studs-and-tubes-inspired design, comes in the LEGO colours, but allows the wearer to change its look and colours.

With diversification into software, however, the company has entered into a market in which the products are 'virtual' in nature. Accordingly, LEGO has had to re-evaluate its organizational identity to incorporate values that are not just associated with tangible products. The section above on LEGO Media International shows how LEGO's 'object-related' values have had to be reinterpreted by the London-based employees in LEGO Media to suit the presentation of media products to the children's market. This has been achieved in such a way that the fundamental, but also more abstract, values of good play, high quality and creativity are all part of LEGO's media products. This reinterpretation has signalled to all the employees of LEGO and its customers that the values, even in more abstract form, are just as powerful and distinctive as those associated with the LEGO bricks. One of the LEGO Media managers has suggested that the analogy between LEGO and software is that software is never finished. Software has 'constructionism' – you can always build on it in a creative way. However, the challenge for LEGO Media is to develop 'constructionist' software into a product that is distinctively LEGO.

The experiences traced in this case study show how the establishment of LEGO Media has expanded the scope of possible interpretations of the LEGO values (and it is likely that the same phenomenon will emerge from the LEGO Lab San Mateo in California). This process of reinterpretation is a form of knowledge management in the sense that each reinterpretation renews the company's knowledge of itself. An interesting concomitant of this process is that LEGO has expanded its portfolio of core competencies, which are much concerned with the communication of a consistent identity both within the LEGO group of companies and with its stakeholders, including children everywhere. It is in fact hard to over-estimate the value of the LEGO identity as a source of inspiration to employees.

Provided that they understand the immutable fundamental values of the companies, employees are empowered to apply them creatively and thus add to the company's core competencies, which may be seen as the collective learn-ing of the organization. The significant thing about the shift from a traditional form of management of identity to one that recognizes identity as a knowledge resource only took place after the company set up LEGO Media International in London in 1996. In other words, the willingness of the company to be genuinely open to foreign ideas has been a significant step in developing LEGO into a knowledge-based company. Thus, the LEGO Company provides a very clear example of how company identity can start life as a store of company values associated with the country of origin and then become a repository of expandable organizational self-knowledge through creative cross-cultural collaborations.

AFTERWORD: A QUINTESSENTIALLY DANISH COMPANY NEVERTHELESS

We learned that LEGO has a policy of playing down its national origins as a Danish company and that, correspondingly, it abhors 'cultural imperialism'. As we saw, it actively restrains itself from imposing its management style on local subsidiaries. But we cannot leave it at that. LEGO is in its own way one of the most quintessential of Danish companies. Its attitudes to children and the way in which the company wishes children to create their own world through its products draws striking parallels with the great Danish writer of fairytales, Hans Christian Andersen (1805–75). Andersen wrote fairytales which do not merely have a timeless quality, but do not always specify the location of the story. The Little Mermaid, the Tin Soldiers and Thumbellina may or may not be Danish. Nevertheless the writer was strongly influenced by Danish folklore. Children who read the stories enter a world of enchantment and use their imagination. So, whereas Andersen used words to enable children *anywhere* to create a fantasy world, LEGO makes products which appear not to be especially Danish and which serve children in an similar way. Has no one ever noticed before that LEGO is in the fairytale business and making a fortune out of it? Perhaps that it is why so many people, regardless of nationality, like working for LEGO.

NOTES

1. For some reason the founder's grandson preferred spelling his name with a K.
2. 'Crisis' is the word used in a leading Danish newspaper, *Politiken* (16 August 2000), in an article, 'Legomandens værksted', about LEGO's acquisition of an American firm.

3. *Politiken*, 'Legomandens værksted', 16 August 2000.

4. 'Constructionism' in LEGO language means that bricks are capable of being used in endless combinations. It is a property of the bricks. In that sense constructionism is different from creativity.

5. McBrand suggests an ominous combination of Toys Я Us in McDonald's format – or vice versa.

9 Case study 4
Sulzer Infra: creating *One Winning Team*

PROLOGUE

Modern international business requires teamwork: which means that the company must assemble teams within their globally spread companies to pool knowledge and experience. Difference in language and (national) cultural background can make it difficult to create international teams and ensure that all members cooperate and communicate straightforwardly, *unless they can all identify with the company and what its stands for*. This means that a successful multicultural team cannot merely focus on the project that has, as it were, created that particular team, but it must learn to cooperate within itself. But how does it learn this? And, if it has positive learning and knowledge-sharing experiences – and negative ones, come to that – how can these experiences be made available to other beneficiaries in the company? And what is the role of headquarters' management in ensuring that the groups are well-motivated, task-oriented, and inclined to knowledge-sharing.

Some answers to these questions are provided in this case study, which highlights the Swiss industrial concern, the Sulzer Corporation. Specifically, we will study a constituent company, Sulzer Infra, which provides infrastructure solutions to a range of industries. Sulzer Infra has a vision of being a knowledge-based company and it sees special-purpose teams drawn from several of its European subsidiaries as the catalysts for realizing the vision and consolidating the company's competitiveness. Accordingly, the key knowledge themes in this case study are:

- The assembly, motivation and work characteristics of international teams

- The role of headquarters in creating a team-based performance culture

- The (national) cultural and linguistic barriers to the sharing of knowledge and experience

The structure of this case study is as follows:

- The company background

- Methodology

- The concept of *One Winning Team*

- The Sulzer Infra Academy

- The seminar on Vision and Strategy 2002

- P-Teams and the Know-how Ring

- Sulzer Infra CBX: a newcomer's impression

- CBX participates in the seminars

- A Dutch perspective

- A cross-cultural perspective

- A knowledge management perspective

- Participants' feedback

- And what about the music?

THE COMPANY BACKGROUND

The Sulzer Corporation was founded in Switzerland in 1834 by the Sulzer brothers, who established it as a heavy engineering concern, its original products including steam engines and foundry equipment. Headquartered in Winterthur near Zürich, on the very site of the first factory, Sulzer Corporation today employs 21,000 people and has a turnover of nearly US$4 billion. The company was divisionalized according to specialities, but a general distinction is made between Sulzer Medica and Sulzer Industries. Sulzer Medica develops, manufactures and markets a range of implants and orthopaedic materials as well as products for use in cardiovascular treatment. Sulzer Industries comprise five principal business areas: pumps and compressors, monitoring equipment, process equipment, web machines and infrastructure solutions. At the time of writing the company is undergoing a significant restructuring of its divisional structure. In this case study we will be concerned with Sulzer Infra, the division which provides infrastructure solutions to the building industry. Approximately 40% of the revenue of the Sulzer Corporation comes from Europe. Approximately 25% of the company business is generated in the USA. The remainder of the revenue comes from Asia/Australia, Latin America and Africa.

Sulzer Infra employs just over 5,000 staff, making it the second largest divisional employer in the Sulzer Corporation and with a turnover of about $1 billion accounts for about 20% of the entire corporation's turnover. Unlike the other Sulzer businesses, Sulzer Infra provides specialized services; it does not manufacture. It has 13 subsidiaries in Germany, one in Brasil, two in the UK, one each in the Netherlands, Italy, Portugal and Hungary; two in Austria, and 11 in Switzerland. Sulzer Infra describes itself as 'an internationally active services provider, concentrating on specialised infrastructure solutions for work and production processes in buildings, and aiming at long-term partnering with customers.

... Our professional co-workers create economic solutions for customers' needs in the field of engineering contracting, building services, and communication technology.' Sulzer Infra provides the following services:

- *Building services*: design, installation and maintenance of technical building infrastructures, with expertise in heating, air conditioning, ventilation and energy optimization

- *Engineering contracting*: manufacturing processes, clean-room technology, refrigeration and thermic installations

- *Infrastructure services*: comprehensive management and operation of infrastructures for building

- *Consulting services*: product-neutral consultancy, offering concepts for optimal comfort, cost and eco-efficiency

- *Communication services*: design and realization of integrated communication infrastructures for the transmission of data, sound and images

The following selected list of recently completed projects will exemplify the scope and competence of Sulzer Infra:

- Installation of fire sprinkler and deluge systems at Munich Airport

- Installation of air-conditioning systems in restored fire-damaged rooms of the Hofburg Palace in Vienna

- Ventilation systems for the tobacco processing plant of Philip Morris at Neuchâtel in Switzerland

- Design and installation of an ice-rink for the Hanover Expo 2000

- Infrastructure solutions for Bugatti International's exhibition and demonstration centre in Alsace

- Modernization of production facilities in Brazil for the Roche pharmaceuticals concern

Other well-known clients include the Tate Modern and British Museum in London, the Bank of International Settlements in Basle, Bayer, Novartis, and Andersen Consulting.

Now to the background situation of Sulzer Infra. In the mid-1990s there was a major recession in the European construction industry. This affected the company, which was found not to have the flexibility to cope with severe business conditions. McKinsey, one of the world's leading management consultancy firms, was invited to diagnose the company and its problems. The result was the closure of small affiliated companies and a recognition that Sulzer Infra had been running its European operations in a decentralized manner which meant that branches in various European cities were too often competing with local companies and not exploiting the wider pan-European business opportunities in a coordinated fashion. This necessitated not just central coordination from headquarters, but also the setting-up of mechanisms for exchanging technical and commercial information among the European affiliate companies.

But there was no tradition in the company of cross-border exchange of experience and sharing of information. The well-established local companies, although belonging to the same group, were accustomed to working independently under the general support of headquarters in Winterthur, and for the most part they saw no need to learn from each other. As the head of management development for Sulzer Infra explained: 'The British had a problem being compared with the Germans, and the Germans found the British to be insular. The Swiss didn't like to be told things by the Germans.' Yet the business logic demanded a pan-European approach to projects and market opportunities. Such attitudes and the ingrained parochial practices which they engendered were not only incompatible with a pan-European business strategy, but they could also undermine it. Sulzer Infra had no alternative but to introduce initiatives to create a new mindset among its employees throughout Europe.

In 1997 therefore Sulzer Infra embarked on its scheme of central coordination, which was created on a vision which gave new concepts and was underpinned with strategic aims. A key aim of this vision-led coordination was to encourage the company to bid for big European contracts which smaller local companies would not be able to compete for.[1] The plan entailed reorganization, the cultivation of new values, and the recognition that the key to success lay in developing a new pan-European teamwork concept. The concept was supported by the motto *One Winning Team*, and it would be through teamwork that the company would realize its business objectives under a programme termed 'Vision and Strategy 2002'. In this case study we shall explore the concept of *One Winning Team*, learn how the company communicates Vision and Strategy 2002, and then focus attention on the P-Teams, the special cross-border taskforces which are becoming the key transmitters of knowledge, creators of focused networks, and a major element of organizational learning. Next a few words on methodology.

METHODOLOGY

The main informants for this case study are the Sulzer Infra Academy, the company's educational facility for promoting culture change through an emphasis on organizational learning and knowledge management. A key interview was conducted with Flooris van der Walt, the Head of the Academy, in July 2000. This was followed by interviews with Sulzer Infra personnel in a recently acquired UK subsidiary, which is still in the process of integrating its style and behaviour to the parent company. In the UK, three managers were interviewed in September 2000.

One was a director of consultancy services, another was a specialist in procurement, the third in technical bids. All of these informants had taken part in Academy seminars and were involved in the company's international activities, but were not involved in P-Teams or the Know-how Ring. Further interviews, conducted by telephone, were made with two representatives of Sulzer Infra Netherlands in October 2000. A final interview was held with van der Walt in November to finalize the content of the case study.

THE CONCEPT OF *ONE WINNING TEAM*

The ethos and culture of Sulzer Infra have been developed around a three-word motto *One Winning Team*, which aims at adding value at the level of every co-worker's internal and external contributions. This motto is fleshed out by a set of declarative principles termed *Our vision – Our contribution*:

Our vision

Is to continuously improve the working and living environment of people in buildings through innovative infrastructure solutions.

Our contribution

Is to provide and manage infrastructure solutions.

We enhance the competitiveness of our customers by

- Our passion to continuously learn and teach, and to anticipate future needs

- Our expertise across infrastructure life cycles and

- Our ability to serve specific customers on a truly global basis

We endeavour to achieve

- Quality

- Integrity

- Accountability

In all dealings with our business partners, our co-workers, the Sulzer Corporation and the public. Our success is based on the belief in *One Winning Team*.

Sulzer Infra's vision and contribution

The concept of *One Winning Team* is underpinned by an initiative directed to managers that goes under the acronym LEAP, which is associated with the keywords highlighted below.

L   Leadership: customers as partners; leadership as practised
E   Excellence: total quality; quality services; business integrity
A   Aspiration: innovative solutions; continuous renewal; individual and team success
P   Performance: constant benchmarking; culture and communication; prosperity

Keywords associated with LEAP

Sulzer Infra places considerable emphasis on teamwork, as exemplified in the company motto *One Winning Team*. A Sulzer Infra publication on leadership principles states that its division places 'more value on teamwork than on individual achievements and on hierarchies'. Against that there is much emphasis on 'entrepreneurial responsibility' through 'dialogue, honesty, trust and support'. In this case study our focus will be the understanding and implementation of teamwork in international management contexts. We shall presently study the concept of the team within Sulzer Infra, but first it will be useful to learn about the company's technique for inculcating into staff the concept of *One Winning Team*. The facility within the company responsible for this task is the Sulzer Infra Academy, whose role and *raison d'être* is described below. The main framework for its activities is Vision and Strategy 2002, the development platform which links team performance and corporate business goals. We consider first Sulzer Infra Academy and a seminar developed by the Academy to help realize Vision and Strategy 2002.

THE SULZER INFRA ACADEMY

Sulzer Infra Academy was established in 1998. Its purpose is to promote the company-wide exchange of experience and ideas for continuous renewal. The Academy is a catalyst for personal and organizational development geared at maintaining long-term competitive advantage. It runs a range of programmes, called seminars, which are concerned with the future-oriented development of competencies and attitudes, for staff at all levels. The Vision and Strategy 2002 seminars bring together 100 people from all the European companies and usually last two working days spread over three days. The Academy runs approximately 20 seminars with eight different topics a year. A key feature of all its educational programmes is that they are cross-company and cross-divisional and are designed to maximize the quality of interactions without permitting language barriers among participants to undermine the process. Here is the company's own description of the present and developing role of the Academy.

The Sulzer Infra Academy embodies the principle of Sulzer Infra as a teaching organisation. The Infra Academy has two completely interrelated parts:

1. As a centre for regeneration and for driving Infra

   - By challenging, provoking and questioning it will operate as a change catalyst promoting Entrepreneurial Excellence.

   - As a centre where leadership development can take place in a stimulating and challenging environment where external experiences can also be brought into the company and where management can work on topics crucial to the success of Infra Group.

   - As a regeneration centre where management teams can come together to work on team and business development issues and where they can avail themselves of other members of management and experts as facilitators.

   - It will be through the leaders trained and developed by the Academy that Infra will in the future be driven.

2. The **real** learning impact will involve all 5,000 employees of Infra.

   - The leadership culture developed, trained and generated by the Academy will determine the personality of our company through learning from and teaching each other and through the consequent living according to our beliefs and values.

   - All employees will be in daily contact with renewal through P-Teams, management meetings etc. with the Academy operating as a highway for bringing operational excellence and best practice to all employees.

It is envisaged that the Infra Academy will therefore contain four major elements:

1. Cultural
Through the challenging and stretching of existing and future managers the Academy will promote our values and culture throughout the organisation. '*The medium will be the message*' in that *how* we experience the learning and teaching process will be as important as the content itself. The process will therefore be highly interactive, stimulating and informative, it will be based on operational case studies and on learning from our own experiences and from the experiences of others in an environment of 'each one learning from the other'.

2. Management Development
Building up gradually as required, the programmes will consist of professional, living modules sourced internally or from corporate, or from external facilitators.
The majority of the modules will be based specifically on our business requirements and while the traditional learning and teaching of technical managerial skills (Finance, HR, Mktg., IT, etc.) will be included, the programmes will concentrate on management competencies, interpersonal skills and how we *use* our managerial skills in practice. The training will again be team based using personal experiences, practical case studies, observation, feedback and assessment from self, peers and senior management.

3. Management Briefings/Management Challenge

The objective here being to keep the management up-to-date and informed on best practice and new developments and to provide management with stimulation and to challenge to think outside of their usual mindsets.

The briefings/challenges could include corporate programmes, external or internal workshops condensing from the essence of the management development modules outlined above. The workshops would be concise, ranging from two hours to one day and could be provided to entire management teams on site in the subsidiary.

4. Knowledge Management

Given the methods we will be using within the Academy it is likely that we will build up over a period of time a databank of knowledge and experience from various sources such as case studies, individual experiences, course materials, reference books etc., which it is essential remains active within the company. In co-ordination with the Know-how Rings and best practices we need to consider how this information will be managed and made available (e.g. Intranet).

Description of the Sulzer Infra Academy (Sulzer Infra: The Infra Academy, 2000)

THE SEMINAR ON VISION AND STRATEGY 2002

In March, May, September, October and November 2000 the Sulzer Infra Academy ran a three-day seminar for about 100 managers at a time from all the European companies with the key aim of focusing their attention of achieving the ambitions and aspirations of Vision and Strategy 2002. This seminar, as we shall see, was a carefully planned event, structured so that it never lost sight of its key aims, which are held together by the company value system and enshrined in the four key words: Simplicity, Speed, Customer Orientation, Enthusiasm. The seminar involved: musical interludes; the formation of work groups which discussed, wrote, drew, and even painted their experiences; and a presentation by the company president who explained how his personal values were aligned with those of the firm. Within their various groups participants were encouraged to speak about their own ideals and values as facets of the way they identified with the company. For some individuals it was a difficult, but nevertheless enlightening experience.

They discussed with colleagues how they saw the company now, where they thought it might be in 2002, what would ensure that the company realized its aspirations and what might inhibit that. They learned about teamwork and in particular the key role of the P-Teams (see below), the new multifunctional, interdivisional and increasingly multicultural taskforces which were being developed as the critical mechanism for knowledge and experience change. At certain points in the proceedings participants wrote questions and comments on cards for senior managers forming a panel. There were two presentations contrasting individualism and teamwork. At one seminar a keynote address was made by the director of the Zürich Chamber Orchestra, Howard Griffiths, who had already been invited to select recorded music which would be played at various times in the seminar and which was produced on a CD for all participants.[2] At other seminars addresses were given by a famous round-the-world yachtsman (Jean-Claude Fehlmann), a mountaineer (Sir Chris Bonington), two explorers (Arvard Fuchs and Sir Ranulph Fiennes), even an astronaut.

Considerable attention was paid to the venue and its appointments. It was a hotel in Martigny in Switzerland, which had all the necessary facilities, including a huge auditorium and spacious anterooms where everybody could *see* everybody else. The hotel was outstanding in lighting and sound systems. For each day there was a set of objectives, as follows:

Objectives of Day 1

- Explain Infra's heritage and develop a common understanding of the seminar

- Create an understanding for the *One Winning Team*

- Offer an opportunity to communicate openly with the top management

Objectives of Day 2

- Using the Vision and Strategy 2002 for operational excellence

- Sharing personal reflections of values

- Dealing with leadership (LEAP)

- Raise topics which accelerate the transformation process

Objectives of Day 3

- Discuss/define my role and contribution

- Agree common responsibility for realizing *One Winning Team*

- Identify concrete topics for P-Team projects

- Identify personal actions for implementing the vision and strategy

Although the company language is English, it was known in advance that mastery of this language was by no means uniform across the participants. The company paid for professional interpreters to be on hand, who interpreted simultaneously into Dutch, German, French and Spanish. The interpreters were briefed beforehand, as they were not just static interlocutors, but were also required to move from group to group, discussion to discussion. Part of the plan was to ensure that on Day 2 participants were involved with colleagues they did not know previously and preferably from other countries to get a cross-section of perspectives and inputs on how to reach the ideal 2002. On the third day groups were mainly formed by people from the same company so that implementation of the ideas could be discussed in real workteams.

A striking feature of the seminar is that it continually involved energy and movement. Every single person had the opportunity to contribute. At one point participants were asked *as a team* to produce a painting that represented the results of their discussion, and their future plans to reach the optimal company in 2002. One group trod in the paints and left their footprints on the paper provided all pointing in the same direction. Whilst the painting was being done, music was being played. The idea was that the paintings, which would eventually be for all to see, would become a visual stimulus of the groups' discussions. There was further auditory reinforcement of the experience because each person was given a CD of the music being used at the seminar and at other significant occasions of group activity. The thinking of the Sulzer Infra Academy is that music and painting are forms of communication which cross language barriers.

The questions which will concern us in due course are: how do the participants react to the seminar as a way of realizing the concept of *One Winning Team*? Did the seminar help them to meet one of Infra's key aims – 'to unblock communication across the European companies'? Did it stimulate networking, promote organizational learning and knowledge exchange? And what role, if any, was played by differences in language, national culture and professional affiliation? Before we tackle these questions, it is important to understand the function and rationale behind the P-Teams, which are central to achieving company strategy.

P-TEAMS AND THE KNOW-HOW RING

According to Sulzer Infra's HR and organization development manager, the company has most of the knowledge, skills and abilities that it needs. The challenge is to learn how to access them and make them available where there are needed in the company in a timely way. The company calls its teams P-Teams, whose task in brief is to 'identify areas for improvement, find the solutions and instigate changes in our processes, our (market) profile and in key personnel matters'. The P of P-Teams is an amalgam of 'Personnel, Processes and Profile that form the basis of our performance culture'. The three key words represent the three Ps of operational excellence.

P-Teams operate throughout Sulzer Infra at various levels: group, divisional, subsidiary company and branch office. They are also composed of persons from differing cultural, linguistic and professional backgrounds. How these people interact is central to the success of the P-Team concept, which is now discussed. P-Teams are usually made of five to eight members 'drawn from levels below the management team'. According to an internal communication:

The P-Team members are selected on an interdepartmental basis and cross-hierarchical basis and are chosen for their ability to identify and analyse the need for change and to research, create and develop new ways of working.

Usually P-Teams will identify for themselves where their priorities lie and at other times they will work on pre-determined projects. These projects are openly communicated within the subsidiary company and the P-Teams are researching the opinions of their co-workers, soliciting and developing improved processes and new ideas.

In all cases the P-Teams have direct access to senior management: in a subsidiary company this means direct contact with the subsidiary manager. In each case P-Teams have a formal agreement with their subsidiary manager concerning their terms of working, which include a time-frame within which the subsidiary manager will respond to their recommendations.

Sulzer Infra has no fewer than 40 P-Teams in operation, and at the seminar just discussed the following were cited as important international topics: pan-European inter-divisional account management, e-commerce, job rotation, optimization of installation processes, and optimal use of the company infranet. Their importance is being seen as central to the overall development of Sulzer Infra. In the words of the company president: 'We have achieved the turn-around, but it is just the beginning. Now we have to transform ourselves, to realign our organisation and to focus on the three Ps of operational excellence, on sustainable profitability and on ensuring the continuing process of change and improvement.' The P-Teams cooperate with what the company calls the Know-how Ring.[3] We will discuss this concept presently. Suffice it to say that the P-Teams and the Know-how Ring between them have the responsibility for ensuring that 'knowledge and solutions that are best practices are communicated and multiplied throughout the entire organisation'. Their cooperation is decisive for developing Sulzer Infra into a learning organization 'in the sense of learning from and teaching each other'.

The company was quick to realize that the role of the P-Teams was not an easy one and that as catalysts of change they could encounter resistance. Accordingly, the company provides training on P-Team activity and has also developed employees at various levels as facilitators,[4] whose task is to coach the P-Teams to work constructively in difficult situations. All the facilitators have received training in English or German. The facilitators are involved with a group for several months and arrange workshops to diagnose issues and promote healthy feedback.

The Know-how Ring is another team, but its main task is to develop best practices, innovative ideas and initiate assignments for the P-Teams to implement. A Know-how Ring is formed of a steering group of four senior managers, six subsidiary managers (which includes the managing director of Sulzer Infra CBX) and nine specialists from defined areas who will be key in the future success of the company. A key function of the Know-how Ring is to identify examples of best practice. After agreement from the management team of the company these practices are introduced at the local company level. Working together, the P-Team facilitators and the Know-how Ring create communication and coordination structures for distributing new knowledge throughout the company at large. Being composed of senior key managers, the Know-how Ring is a major vehicle for the implementation of best practices and innovations.

SULZER INFRA CBX: A NEWCOMER'S IMPRESSIONS

At the end of 1998 Sulzer Infra took over a UK firm, CBX, which had been part of the Xerox Corporation until 1994 and then established itself through a management buy-out. The newly acquired company, now known as Sulzer Infra CBX, provides specialist technical and management services in the area of facilities management (FM). That is, CBX provides clients who are generally large institutional bodies, ranging from government departments to international corporations, with the full benefit of an integrated approach to the management, cleaning, catering, and building maintenance of premises and corporate infrastructure as a whole, covering the lifecycle of workplace provision, with every aspect integrated to optimize cost and quality. In FM there are two key factors which define business logic. First, clients are looking for a reduced number of interfaces as a result of 'IT proliferation'. Second, clients want suppliers to take over responsibility for finding FM solutions.

The Swiss-based company had been considering the possibilities of such an acquisition since early 1998 in order to increase expertise in the wider FM market in Europe, a business sector contiguous to Sulzer Infra's traditional operations, where it made sense to have a stronger footing. The take-over by the Swiss firm was not contentious and Sulzer Infra CBX (hereafter CBX) has generally gone about its business as in the past. Control from Switzerland is seen as relatively hands-off, but is part of the company's commitment to diversity.

CBX is being significantly integrated into collaborative projects with the European companies of Sulzer Infra. One current project is concerned with setting up 22 data centres in Europe for a major TNC. The company is also creating a 'competence centre', a launch-pad for developing a pan-European basis for FM operations. This knowledge development, which is an intranet with business and social dimensions, is now underway in Spain, Austria and Germany.

The UK company has been involved with P-Teams and the Know-how Ring, but as yet there is no direct mechanism whereby the noteworthy outcomes in CBX are disseminated throughout the wider company. However, as will be noted, their participation in the Sulzer Infra Academy seminars has proved valuable for informal exchanges of knowledge. P-Teams were seen by the UK managers as a method of avoiding 'reinventing the wheel', 'a drilling-down process' for untapping potentially useful knowledge. As CBX has more expertise in FM than the rest of Sulzer Infra, the UK firm finds that it gives more knowledge in this field than it receives, priding itself on its skills of managing long-term relationships with clients. But this is in fact a one-sided picture, as CBX has, through its absorption into Sulzer Infra, benefited considerably from a major broadening of its customer base in Europe. The upshot is that CBX has secured business for which it otherwise could not have bid. There have even been follow-up contracts, but the UK company seems reluctant to accept this.

CBX PARTICIPATES IN THE SEMINARS

All three of the managers we interviewed for this case study had attended the seminars arranged by the Sulzer Infra Academy, and there were divergent rather than conflicting views of the experience. One manager said that 'we all play the stereotypes'. The German colleagues were 'earnest'. The French colleagues refused to speak English, even if they could. Participants from the UK 'sat in the sun' and joined in the seminar when it was necessary to 'speak louder'. The Swiss were 'available' to keep things running smoothly.

There was complete agreement that the seminars were exceptionally well-organized and all three found it useful to meet new colleagues. One apparently very effective contribution had been the presentation by Karl Bochsler, President of Sulzer Infra, who convincingly related his life to the company values. One of the UK managers had developed a piece of business software in which a senior financial manager from the headquarters in Switzerland had shown immediate interest. The British man was 'delighted' to be able to share his know-how and discover that it might have application in other parts of the company. But their reservations are worth noting. The seminar was described as 'emotive – deliberately so', and did this really suit that kind of audience?

One of the UK managers stated that participants needed more background in concepts of business strategy to get maximum benefit from the seminars. He also noted that participants in the seminar likewise needed some kind of preparation for the event. In the case of CBX there had been no such preparation, *but there was supposed to have been*. Furthermore, the perceived need for a background in business strategy appears to be based on a misunderstanding. The organization and orientation of the seminars do not have that requirement. At all events the CBX managers had attended the seminar without an appropriate briefing, despite the best efforts of the Sulzer Infra Academy. This might explain why the three people seemed not to know beforehand exactly what the seminar was supposed to achieve. One of the three informants considered that the seminar was too long, but his colleague (whose business software idea had created unexpected interest) denied this. All three, however, agreed that 100 or so people were too many: 'There is a limit to how many people you can network with.' But this comment overlooked the fact that the key aim of the seminar was to enable people to identify with the strategy and policies of the company.

One of the UK managers considered that the seminar did not fully reflect the diversity in the company, suggesting that most participants strongly represented the engineering expertise of the company, and that it should encourage greater participation by younger employees. But this conviction does not seem to match the reality, as the Academy is very careful to ensure that each seminar contains a genuine reflection of company expertise and experience, as well as national background. It is perhaps not surprising that only one of the three managers had found the networking aspect of the seminar directly useful.

In terms of interpersonal communication at the seminars, all three admitted that their inability to speak another language was a weakness. One described it as an 'embarrassment'. They were all aware that as native speakers of English they had an apparent edge in interactions with colleagues for whom English was a second language, but they were equally aware of a tendency to take over. One recalled how he had been involved in a conversation with a colleague from France and one from Germany. For his sake both were speaking in English, but both were struggling with the language. The British man recognized that this intellectually arduous experience was drawing the French and German together. '*I was missing out*', he exclaimed: not missing out on the information, but on the *interanimation*. Although the role of interpreters working between English, German, French and Spanish had been indispensable, these crucial intermediaries could not deliver the emotion.

A DUTCH PERSPECTIVE

Sulzer Infra Netherlands (SINL) employs 400 people in four locations and regards itself as well integrated into the Sulzer Infra group of companies. The two informants had both attended the seminar in Martigny. One is the manager with responsibility for safety and quality control; the other is financial controller for SINL. The latter had been with the company for ten years and already had an extensive in-company network in Europe.

When the Dutch managers arrived for the seminar in Martigny, they put on SINL jumpers with *One Winning Team* written on them. They wanted to make certain that people knew who they were in the sessions. The informants' reactions to the seminar were contrasting, but generally positive. Both agreed that previously in-company training programmes had not been inspired or inspiring. According to the financial controller, this was by far the best event of its kind arranged by the company. 'The seminar had a heart', was how he put it. However, the engineering manager more than once used the word 'passive' to describe parts of the seminar.

The first main session in which the directors of the company had invited questions from the participants had not been very productive, they said. According to one informant, people asked 'nice questions' and got 'nice answers'; the questions were nothing like what they were discussing in their national groups and *ad hoc* teams. The presentation by the company president was 'interesting, but rather dry'. He and his fellow directors were seen as 'stars that are shining brightly'. One informant thought that the directors should not be separated physically from the participants and that a way should be found for them (the directors) to enjoy closer, personal relationships. This comment surprises Flooris van der Walt, the head of the Sulzer Infra Academy, who had deliberately planned the question-and-answer session so that the senior managers were not on the podium and were seated on the same level of the participants – 100 of them – who were arranged in a huge horseshoe. As van der Walt wryly commented: 'Unfortunately, even with the best arrangements, there will always be somebody who feels missed out.' But the other informant had contrasting impressions. The speech by the company president had been genuinely inspiring; it made him feel good to work for the company.

On the second day, one of the Dutch managers found things better from his point of view. They came with one thing in mind – to learn and network to improve personal performance, but also to help contribute to the culture of *One Winning Team*. Everything was judged from that stand-point. Both felt that some of the sessions and exercises 'lacked practical input'. Against that, they had received a lot of valuable information about the company 'whilst seated', but they missed what they termed 'practical information'. They also considered that a weakness of the entire seminar concept was the fact that there was no system (as far as they were aware) of follow-up: to find out what use participants got out of the seminar and how this could be fed back into the company on a Europe-wide basis.

The engineering manager described the seminar experience as 'a bit theatrical', even though his overall impressions were positive. He, the more sceptical of the two informants, was nevertheless a supporter of the use of music: it was, in his somewhat arresting phrase, 'good for making the mind jump'. He also found refreshing the keynote speech by the director of music: indeed, it was 'more refreshing' to hear about the management of a chamber orchestra than the standard platitudes of senior industrial managers. The financial controller first of all reacted negatively to the musical interludes at the seminar, then he took to them. He regularly plays the CD in his car 'as a nice souvenir' of the seminar.

The other informant again had rather different impressions. The entire pro-gramme was 'well-organized, not over-organized'. The networking side was, from the point of view of both informants, satisfactory. The financial controller made valuable contacts with colleagues in Germany, Austria, Spain and the UK, with whom he has been in regular contact ever since. For him, the contact-making side of the event was 'excellent'. But both he and the engineering manager agreed that there should have been more time for socialization. The engineering manager thought that this time could have been created within the overall event. The financial controller thought that an extra half-day with a team-building event 'in the mountains' would have been valuable. The engineering manager thought that 'the main purpose of attending is to get to know people rather than more things about the company'. But, of course, it wasn't. Perhaps, not surprisingly, he therefore felt that the overall programme was 'somewhat overdone' and not flexibly structured to permit greater interpersonal connecting. Against that, he greatly enjoyed the group painting exercises.

Both of the Dutch managers speak German, which is in general terms a big advantage. They speak in German at the company headquarters in Switzerland and often use the language when Swiss colleagues visit them in the Netherlands. Sulzer, he said, 'is not like Philips. German is more the company language than English.' To emphasize that point, when on the first day of the seminar the company president and directors address the participants, they do so in German, which is simultaneously interpreted into English, French and Spanish. Was it a disadvantage if German was so prominent as the working language of the company? 'No', came the reply of the engineering manager, 'as long as you know German'. It should be noted that Sulzer Infra does have an official company language, and that is English. It is the language of international communication within the company except in those cases where, for practical purposes, it makes sense to use another language. For example, Dutch and Swiss colleagues might use German with each other when telephoning or using e-mail to clarify general matters. The company policy is to generate all key company documents in English first and then make translations, if necessary, into other languages used throughout the company in Europe.

A CROSS-CULTURAL PERSPECTIVE

From a cross-cultural perspective one of the challenges is to make the company less conscious of national stereotypes or individual perceptions, which have little to do with reality. Flooris van der Walt, the head of the Sulzer Infra Academy, was perfectly aware of this. But he also knew that the quickest way to reduce the negative aspects of stereotypes was to encourage people to socialize and network and then, outside the slightly artificial ambience of a seminar, to work together. The UK managers confirmed that nationality became a side issue once there was active cooperation linked to a specific project. The weaving of music and painting games into the fabric of the seminars was done explicitly to engage people's minds and hearts into a collective experience, which might, and did, transcend cultural and linguistic factors.

But language was a problem. The UK managers only spoke English and they recognized that this was not just a general disadvantage, but a professional one. They found that many of their colleagues were able to operate in at least two languages, but they could only manage one. Then, as one of them realized, this was not such a big advantage in some international meetings, if you remembered to modify your spoken English by slowing down the speed of delivery or avoiding obscure words. In this connection it was noteworthy too how one of the managers was aware of missing out on the emotional side of personal interactions because he did not have to struggle with a foreign language. From this particular situation we can obtain a useful insight, but it is impossible to say how general it might be. The two Dutch managers spoke English and German: English was the language for general Europe-wide, team-based activity; German was for communicating with counterparts at corporate headquarters in Switzerland.

In the scenario in question, the communication experience engages the emotions with a sense of professional deficiency. The UK manager whose experiences we are describing felt personally limited through his encounter with two colleagues, each with a different mother tongue. The situation suggests that there is more to cross-cultural communication than passing information unambiguously across language and cultural barriers, and that there is more to foreign language capability than the standard communicative competence in that language. The British man was losing out in interanimation because he was not able to extend emotional solidarity to his colleagues. They were doing something in a communicative situation in which he could not act. He was the man who interestingly observed that it was occasionally necessary to 'speak louder' in English – a plea of failure as much as a psychological ploy to break into and perhaps dominate a conversation. This UK reaction brought from van der Walt the comment that, whilst this British manager was feeling linguistically inhibited, other participants were showing determination to communicate cross-culturally 'in broken English'.

Concerning the seminar as a forum for networking, reactions from the five informants were mixed, but generally positive. On balance, the tasks which aimed to mix up national groups worked, but there was a general feeling that more time was needed to consolidate the contacts before the seminar came to a close. Although there was a difference of opinion about the question-and-answer session with the directors, there was agreement that the presentation by Karl Bochsler, the company President, who spoke about how his personal development was linked to his life with and for Sulzer Infra, had been a success. The fact that his speech was delivered in German and had to be translated did not detract from the importance of the performance.

A KNOWLEDGE MANAGEMENT PERSPECTIVE

The concept of the Sulzer Infra Academy and the experiences of the UK managers reinforce the more or less accepted conviction that knowledge as the possession of individuals tends to be more easily leveraged in scenarios which encourage personal forms of intense interaction. As was noted by one of the UK informants, the seminars are deliberately emotive. What Sulzer Infra makes clear, and what the Novo Nordisk experience bears out, is that it is very difficult to separate the act of transferring knowledge from the cross-cultural know-how needed to effect that. This tends to support the plea of one of the UK managers that participants in the seminar need special preparation. But against that, it is necessary to recall that Sulzer Infra CBX is a relative newcomer to the Sulzer Infra family. The recorded instances of CBX's reluctance or even inability to adjust to its new parent suggest that, until it feels psychologically integrated with the parent company, knowledge transfer processes may prove difficult to effect. Paradoxically, this is why participation in the seminars, about which CBX has such mixed feelings, is of considerable importance.

As was noted above, the Sulzer Infra Academy is a relatively new institution and, if training (in the broadest sense of the word) has not been a priority in the company for a number of years, the processes may be too advanced at the moment. The point is a serious one, and, if we are to believe another informant, the Sulzer Infra Academy may have, in effect, to redesign its own success criteria to enable its participants to take out the best of it.

One of the most important findings of this case study related to the experience of the UK manager who missed not being able to struggle in a foreign language. This emotional rather than intellectual reaction suggests that interpersonal knowledge transfer, and perhaps especially in cross-cultural scenarios such as the Sulzer Infra Academy seminars, needs a conducive atmosphere. As already stated, the seminar was planned as an emotional experience, but how individuals themselves interacted could not be controlled, and yet this was plainly a crucial element of the entire experience. The important thing, therefore, about the Sulzer Infra seminars is that they try to be a kind of rehearsal for cross-cultural business interactions, in which the emotional experience of cross-cultural interactions is an inextricable feature of the process of intercommunication.

Apart from Flooris van der Walt, four of the five informants for this case study were qualified in science or engineering. The fifth was the Dutch financial controller. Of these five, it can be stated that the financial controller was the one who got most from the seminar. He, of course, had a wide in-company network, so for him the seminar was as much about consolidating old contacts as initiating new ones. But the striking feature about the engineers' reaction was the degree to which they wanted the seminar to be 'practical'. This suggests, and the point is made tentatively, that engineers may have different needs within a group learning activity of the kind mediated by the seminar. That one of the engineers referred to the seminar in Martigny as a theatre is of some significance.

One wonders how the marketing people react to it. The point is important. It should, however, not be overlooked that during the last few years Sulzer Infra placed comparatively little emphasis on in-company education. Training was, by all accounts, routine and pedestrian. The establishment of the Sulzer Infra Academy puts in-company education at the centre of the company renewal strategy – and it has a lot of lost ground to recover. The seminars and other events organized by the Academy are, in effect, experiments. But so far the experiment appears to be succeeding. No informant suggested that the idea behind the seminar was ill-founded; no one thought the event a waste of time and money, though there were suggestions on how to improve it. The way ahead is surely for the Sulzer Infra Academy to listen to these voices and build them into new in-company education formats. In this way the company can help the Academy to create its own environment for learning, networking and knowledge-sharing.

PARTICIPANTS' FEEDBACK

The big question is, of course, how successful is the concept of the seminars with those who attend. In early 2001 the 120 participants in a seminar similar to the one described above were asked to evaluate it. Participants were invited to respond to questions about their participation and how they valued the experience. One question was: Do you have the feeling that, now you have attended the seminar, you have a better idea of the Sulzer Infra Vision and Strategy? Here is the response:

Yes: 117   No: 3

Another question was: Has the seminar helped you to identify with Sulzer Infra as a place of work and to feel motivated? The response:

Yes: 106   No: 14

A third question was: Would you recommend the seminar to a colleague? The response:

Yes: 119   No: 1

Among the individual comments were these:

- Informative and enthusiastic presentations drove the Vision home

- The seminar demonstrated better than documentation the commitment throughout the company to work as *One Winning Team*

- Not just passive listening, but lots of interaction and involvement

- Having worked for Sulzer for many years, the charter of *One Winning Team* is probably the best thing that has happened to encourage enthusiasm

- I saw at first hand representatives of Infra from other countries working together, overcoming barriers, aiming to improve company profile and reputation

- Every participant is asked to present HIS or HER contribution

- Good opportunity for meeting people, which in turn promotes cross-border cooperation

- It has really inspired me to work towards joint goals

- The form, organization and facilities were outstanding

- Borderless multilingual communication

- The emerging feeling of belonging

The feedback from the participants is overwhelming. The Suzler Infra Academy has established itself as a major change agent in the company and is beginning to transform it into a knowledge-based organization in tune with its cross-border business activities in Europe. In the feedback from the participants there were several positive references to the contribution at the seminar of the company president Karl Bochsler. The message is simple: when companies are experiencing great change, the role and visibility of the chief executive are crucial. The seminars organized by the Sulzer Infra Academy have proved to be a key vehicle for the president to symbolize the company Vision, demonstrate leadership, and make every individual feel that he or she can contribute to the future success of the company.

AND WHAT ABOUT THE MUSIC?

As reported earlier, each participant in a seminar obtains a CD of music selected for the event. When asked if they ever played the music subsequently, two of the three UK managers said 'no'. But one mentioned that at the airport they were standing by a group of their German colleagues who were humming and singing one of the songs. The British man and his colleagues joined in the music-making: 'They were good blokes' – they being the Germans.

NOTES

1. This approach has been fully vindicated. In 2000 the company was awarded major contracts with AT&T and DigiPlex for providing infrastructure consulting services to these companies' data centres located in several European locations.

2. The CD (playing time 58 minutes) contains short pieces by well-known composers such as Corelli, Vivaldi, Mozart, Dvorak, Puccini and Johann Strauss, and lesser known composers. All the pieces can be described as relaxing with the exception of some jaunty airs by Marin Marais (1656–1728), which were played at the very beginning of the seminar.

3. Know-how Ring is the translation of the German term *Wissensring* (lit. knowledge ring).

4. The German word for facilitator used by the company is *Moderator*.

REFERENCES

The following documents from Sulzer Corporation were consulted:

A charter for *One Winning Team*
Infra Mail: 100 winning teams – Facilitators trained (D. Bright)
P-Team kick-off workshop schedule and other documentation on P-Teams
Sulzer Infra: Our leadership principles
Sulzer Infra: International Management Career Program
Sulzer Infra Jahresbericht (Annual report) (1999)
Sulzer Infra: Vision and Strategy 2002 (2001)
Sulzer Infra: The Infra Academy (2000)
Sulzer Geschäftsbericht (Annual Report) (1999)
Sulzer Infra CBX Briefing. E-commerce – here comes the future (March 1999)
Sulzer Infra CBX brochure
Interview with Karl Bochsler, President of Sulzer Infra, reprinted from *Premises and Facilities Management* (November 1999)

Part III

Redesigning cross-cultural management as a knowledge domain

'Achieving the optimum balance between what the firm knows and what it needs to know at any one time is the knowledge equivalent of cash flow management.'

Alan Burton-Jones, *Knowledge capitalism* (1999)

10 Cross-cultural management at interfaces and in networks

'Learning continually disturbs the *status quo.*'

Colin Cherry, *On human communication* (1980)

'To grasp the nature of the culture we live with now, we must also take an interest in the management of meaning by corporate and institutional actors, not least by the state and the market-place.'

Ulf Hannerz, *Transnational connections: Culture, people, places* (1996)

OBJECTIVES

- **Supplies reflections on the four case studies.**
- **Discusses some commonly held and contrastive features of the four informant companies.**
- **Analyzes how each company characteristically manages cross-cultural interfaces.**
- **Highlights cross-culturally significant features of the companies' organizational learning and networking.**
- **Suggests that the cross-cultural management of the transfer of knowledge, values and experience is a form of group translation, called *interactive translation.***
- **This translation work is conceived as a group activity requiring a cross-cultural skill called *participative competence.***

INTRODUCTION

It is now time to take stock. In this and the following chapters our task will be to review and reflect on the nature and remit of cross-cultural management on the basis of the experiences of the four informant companies. In this particular chapter we consider the experiences of the four informant companies from a cross-cultural management perspective, that is to say from a perspective consistent with the working definition of cross-cultural management previously introduced:

> The core task of cross-cultural management is to facilitate and direct synergistic interaction and learning at interfaces, where knowledge, values and experience are transferred into multicultural domains of implementation.

This may be referred to as a broad formulation of cross-cultural management, as opposed to the traditional, narrow one, which focuses disproportionately on the management of cultural differences – or rather on the potential occurrence of cross-cultural clashes. As was made clear in earlier chapters, the narrow formulation is inadequate for analyzing the kind of experiences mediated in our four case studies because it does not allow for the possibility of regarding culture as an organizational resource. Nor does it see it as an object of organizational knowledge.

Using the broader understanding of cross-cultural management, some general aspects of the four informant firms' corporate thinking and behaviour are considered. We then compare and contrast the four companies' style of management of cross-cultural interfaces, their networking characteristics and culturally significant features of organizational learning. The chapter concludes with a proposition for a radical way of understanding cross-cultural management. It will be contended that cross-cultural management is *a form of translation activity* in a literal and metaphorical sense. But it will be left to subsequent chapters to develop this notion.

REFLECTIONS ON THE CASE STUDIES

In chapter 5 it was pointed out that an alternative name for the case studies could be corporate knowledge histories. This term was chosen to reflect the fact that the material in the case studies – at least in two cases – covered events in company history going back several decades. The two companies concerned are Matsushita and LEGO. Although the accounts of Novo Nordisk and Sulzer Infra do not delve so far into the companies' histories, the information about the Facilitators, on the one hand, and the creation of, and logic behind, the Sulzer Infra Academy, can only be fully appreciated in the light of the business situation facing those companies in the early 1990s. All the case studies took account of relevant historical factors, and examined their recent and contemporary behaviour from a knowledge management perspective.

There was of course a subjective element given the role of the writer-domain expert (myself). As with the MIT learning histories, the case studies *could* be used within the companies in question to facilitate learning processes in order to stimulate innovation and promote change. Thus there are reasonable grounds for calling the case studies corporate knowledge histories. Each case study contained an analysis from a cross-cultural management perspective and a knowledge management perspective.

The challenge now is to examine the totality of cross-cultural behaviour in order ultimately to develop concepts for redesigning cross-cultural management. This totality of behaviour constitutes 'thick' knowledge, heaving with embeddedness (if embeddedness can be so described). It will be recalled that thick knowledge was described as very rich, very wide-ranging and arcane. Its reduction to thin knowledge will take up the greater part of the remainder of this book and in the process new concepts, stemming in part from comparisons of the four companies' cross-cultural behaviour, will be generated. At least I think the concepts are new. This process of knowledge reduction will be elaborate.

This chapter and the next will examine the totality of behaviour from a cross-cultural management perspective consistent with the guiding definition. These chapters will, as noted above, develop the idea of translation as a notional bridge linking the two perspectives. By chapter 12, which will develop the knowledge management perspective, a major knowledge reduction will have taken place despite the fact that the process will require thousands of words.

But in the end the reduction will come first in chapter 12 and then in chapter 13: all the complexities of the recorded cross-cultural management behaviour will be transformed into models. The purpose of a model is to represent reality or a portion of reality in as objective a way as possible and have predictive power. But models are useless if those who scrutinize or purport to use them do not understand what knowledge and assumptions have been compressed into them. The models, which incorporate 'culture-as-knowledge' are new to cross-cultural management as an academic discipline and practice. But there is no Hofstedian inviolability about them. They are to be challenged and improved.

THE FOUR COMPANIES AND THEIR CONTEXT IN THE GLOBALIZED ECONOMY: COMMONLY HELD AND CONTRASTIVE FEATURES

The four informant companies are TNCs who are leaders in their respective business sectors. Novo Nordisk is strong in two main business areas: biotechnology and pharmaceuticals. The global businesses of Matsushita, each huge in its own right, cover four main areas: consumer electronics and electric appliances, information and communication equipment, electrical and electronic components, and video and audio equipment. LEGO's business fall into four areas: toys, software, merchandizing and theme parks. Sulzer Infra, which specializes in supplying infrastructural solutions to the construction industry, is the smallest of the informants in terms of number of employees, turnover and markets served. Its business is mainly in Europe, whereas the activities of the first three companies are global. Sulzer Infra is also the only company in the sample that does not manufacture. Table 10.1 summarizes each company by headquarters, turnover, number of employees and business sectors.

Table 10.1   Summary of essential business data on the four informant companies

Company: **Novo Nordisk**
Headquarters: Denmark
Turnover: $1,800 million
Number of employees: 15,000 in 61 countries
Business sectors: biotechnology, health-care

Company: **Matsushita Electric**
Headquarters: Japan
Turnover: $65 billion
Number of employees: 290,000 in 40 countries
Business sectors: consumer electronics, electrical equipment, communication equipment, video and audio appliances

Company: **LEGO**
Headquarters: Denmark
Turnover: $1 billion
Number of employees: 7,800 in 29 countries
Business sectors: toys, games, theme parks, merchandizing

Company: **Sulzer Infra**
Headquarters: Switzerland
Turnover: $1 billion
Number of employees: 5,000
Business activity: infrastructural solutions for the construction industry

Despite the formal differences among the four companies, they hold a number of features in common, which are listed below. From the case studies it can be seen that all four TNCs:

- Regard globalization as a fact of modern business life, requiring new ways of working

- Are major players in one or more business sectors

- Are involved in developing or applying technological solutions

- Employ a workforce that is multinational

- Are increasingly conducting work on the basis of project teams on a regional (e.g. European) or worldwide basis not just for interfacing with customers, but for tackling in-company tasks

- Have well-developed management and business philosophies, which are claimed to be viable in the new geo-economy

- A top management that claims to be open to foreign ideas and influences and supports localization

Against that, we may note some significant points of contrast among the four companies:

- One company has an explicit aim to become a knowledge-based learning organization (Sulzer Infra)

- One company is using a core business philosophy which has remained more or less inviolate since before the emergence of the global economy (Matsushita)

- One company has made a major departure from its traditional product line in the last five years (LEGO has moved into the software end of the toy market)

- Two companies have developed systematic procedures for the company-wide transfer of knowledge, values and experience (Novo Nordisk via the Facilitators; Sulzer Infra via the Sulzer Infra Academy)

- One company explicitly regards localization in terms of empowerment (Novo Nordisk)

- Two companies are strongly dominated by top managers from the country of the headquarters (LEGO and Matsushita)

- Only one company does not use English at corporate headquarters as virtually interchangeable with the national language (Matsushita)

- Only two companies have invested substantially into new methodologies and organizational arrangements to promote company-wide interactive learning and the transfer of knowledge and experience (Novo Nordisk through the Facilitators and Sulzer Infra through its corporate university, the Sulzer Infra Academy)

- Only one company espoused a stated policy of suppressing cultural dominance from corporate headquarters (LEGO)

In addition we can note that each company is influenced by factors which give its own species of globalization a distinctive character. For example, Novo Nordisk is motivated by a desire not to become the victim of a hostile take-over bid or to be forced into a risky merger. As a pharmaceutical business, the company not only applies rigorous ethical standards to the manufacture and marketing of its products, but also has a policy of openness regarding its social and environmental responsibilities and actions. In its own way, too, LEGO articulates ethical concerns, being committed to the conviction that children anywhere have the *right* for their childhood to be respected.

Regarding the Matsushita Corporation, this company can only be understood in terms of the powerful influence of the founder's legacy on the company's style of management and way of doing business. To this point we might add its competitive obsession with its arch-rival, the ever-innovative Sony. Sulzer Infra, the smallest company in the sample, is in a market in which the clients want fewer interfaces with the suppliers and expect those suppliers to take responsibility and help them with solutions.

With those general comparative and contrastive points in mind, we can turn to an analysis of those companies' own universe of cross-cultural management interaction. In the three following sections this behaviour will be discussed in terms of three facets: (a) the management of interfaces, (b) networking and organizational learning, and (c) the transfer of knowledge and best practices. Organizational learning and networking can be considered as separate activities for theoretical purposes, but they are treated here under the same heading because, as the analysis will make clear, it is difficult to separate them in practice. After reviewing cross-cultural matters of interest with respect to each company, there is a short contrastive analysis of the firms' performance and behaviour.

THE MANAGEMENT OF CROSS-CULTURAL INTERFACES

A key word in our guiding definition of cross-cultural management is 'interface'. This is an advantageous term in that 'interface' implies a point of contact, a common boundary. There is no suggestion that an interface is robust or permanent, nor does it in principle have to be permeable. An interface can be a physical location or a metaphysical one – virtual, in modern parlance. Modern business activities are much concerned with the setting-up, management *and* dissolution of interfaces, especially in their international operations where specific groups of people from different countries need to be brought together. It will be recalled, for example, that BP, as part of its knowledge management system, even developed the notion of the virtual coffee break. As we shall see, the concept of the interface will enable us to analyze our informant companies' cross-cultural interactions from unusual perspectives.

Novo Nordisk

It will be recalled that the key task of the Novo Nordisk Facilitators was to provide 'a structured, planned assessment of the status of implementation of the Novo Nordisk Way of Management with a unit, or within a project or process, with the aim of developing agreed actions for improvement'. In line with this, the process of facilitation was focused on two main objectives:

- Assessment of the status and application of the Novo Nordisk Way of Management

- Ensuring a balance between business objectives and targets and the methods by which these business objectives are met

From the point of view of management of cross-cultural interfaces there are two areas of significance about the activities of the Facilitators: first, their self-management as a multicultural, multilingual team; and, second, their interactions with units. Taking the first point, we must note that the Facilitators are not only diverse in their national and linguistic backgrounds, but also represent diversity of educational background and professional affiliations. They operate in sets of two. In the three years since the Facilitator concept was implemented in 1997, 200 facilitations have been conducted.

The facilitation was in a narrow sense the interface to be managed: each facilitation was of short but intense duration, in which mutual trust had to be established, common ground staked out, problems aired and solutions proffered. But the quality of the interface – its transparency, its durability and its capacity to permit the essential interanimation – varied from facilitation to facilitation according to the local setting of the unit in terms of business culture, operational scope of the unit, and the specialist nature of the unit. Therefore the language of facilitation needed to accommodate a relevant professional discourse (for example, legal, marketing, enzyme-specific discourse). In short, the striking feature of the Facilitators was the sheer number of, and diversity within, cross-cultural interfaces they handled. But it should not be forgotten that the management of these cross-cultural interfaces cannot be appreciated without noting the Facilitators' own style of self-management, about which three key points should be made.

First, their interactions with each other were based on professional respect. They regarded themselves as equals; no single Facilitator ever emerged as an official spokesperson, let alone leader. Second, once they actually began to work together, they created their own occupational discourse, a language of facilitation, which they used in facilitations and in the production of their own documents about their activity. Third, because every facilitation they conducted was a unique and non-replicable experience (non-routine in knowledge management jargon), so each facilitation was in effect a rehearsal for the next one: a collective creative process in which Facilitators and units feel able to make or admit mistakes.

All 14 Facilitators spoke a language additional to their native one, using English as their principal language of professional communication. Each and every Facilitator was completely committed to Novo Nordisk and identified with the rationale of the Facilitator concept. There is no doubt that professionally speaking the organizational culture of Novo Nordisk was far more important to them than the sense of belonging to their own native culture. In their work with all other members of the team, as well as in their duos, the Facilitators were continually transferring knowledge and experience.

In their interactions with units the critical task was to gain trust and to present themselves as good listeners. They frequently had to adjust to local nuances of behaviour, for example, observing dress codes, which vary from culture to culture. In Asian countries they noted how it important it is not to deal with a senior person in a casual or informal way in front of junior people. In so far as the Facilitators experienced 'culture clashes' at all, it was Asian countries which came to the fore. The Asian colleagues, it seemed, expected a tutorial approach from people appointed by head office, but got something refreshingly different. In general, management of cultural differences, as popularly understood, was not a big issue for the Facilitators. They managed cross-cultural interfaces with a combination of intelligence and tact. Their inclination to be listeners made them learn for other Facilitators and for the company. We shall come back to this point later in this chapter.

Matsushita

The issue that served as the focal point of the case study concerning the Matsushita Corporation was the serviceability of the company's philosophy, which was created in the late 1920s, in the era of the global economy. What emerged was a portrayal of tensions, frustrations and misunderstanding resulting from differences between Japanese business organizational behaviour and practices in various company locations, especially in Europe and the USA. As noted in the case study, there is a long history of perceptual mismatches between Japanese management and local staff in general, so the Matsushita Corporation is continuing an established tradition. But the case of this huge concern has unusual dimensions owing to the all-pervading influence of the 'sacred' company philosophy, which the present corporate management in Japan has so much difficulty diluting, modifying and generally updating, even for Japanese employees.

It is not an exaggeration to say that the critical interface within the Matsushita Corporation is that which brings together, yet separates or compartmentalizes the Japanese and non-Japanese employees. This interface passes through the company like a geological fault-line. The general and long-standing reluctance to promote foreign managers into positions of *real* authority says it all. As a result, of the four case studies, the one concerning the Matsushita Corporation appears to be the one in which cultural differences, even spilling over into clashes (especially in the USA), come most significantly to the fore. In the case study we highlighted three factors which appear to make the management of cross-cultural interfaces within the Matsushita Corporation especially demanding:

- The mistrust of foreigners

- Language/communication problems

- The dichotomy of company discourse

I will not repeat the discussion of the cross-cultural issues, confining myself to two observations: first, these three factors have a dramatic impact on knowledge-sharing in the Matsushita Corporation, as we shall expound in the next chapter; second, this huge Japanese company tends to *disconfirm* the conviction that cultural differences arise as issues when other things are already going wrong. This is because cultural difference is already an issue in Japan's cross-cultural interactions. The *sine qua non* of being Japanese is that their culture is significantly different from other cultures and therefore that Japan, the Japanese way and Japanese thinking are liable to be misconstrued – not just misunderstood – by foreigners. The foreigners, for their part, have tended to fall for this argument and so a vicious circle has evolved. It would, however, be mistaken to see *all* Japanese companies as being locked into this spiral. Sony, Canon and Hitachi are three well-known corporations whose internationalization policies are linked to the 'de-Japanization' of company thinking, attitudes and decision-making at the corporate centre.

LEGO

We may say that LEGO's management of cross-cultural interfaces is predicated on three considerations:

- The company's overall style of management is an attempt to be, in a national–cultural sense, neutral

- The identity and values of the company, through its powerful brand image and respect for children, transcends cross-cultural differences

- The headquarters of the company, with a very strong contingent of Danish managers, is open to influences from subsidiary companies outside Denmark and deliberately encourages the establishment of mixed Danish/non-Danish work groups in order to promote what one senior manager called 'shared mental space'

In the case study we were mainly concerned with the interface between LEGO corporate headquarters and LEGO Media International in London. As such, the comments that follow should not be construed as pronouncements on other cross-cultural relationships within the LEGO group of companies. It will be recalled that LEGO in the USA takes a rather different view of the LEGO brand than in Europe. This in itself suggests an interface of a different quality. The comments of European employees make it plain that they like working for a company which has high, child-oriented ethical standards, which permeate not only business methods, but also production methods. Nothing is, as it were, too good for children. It is in fact hard to escape the impression that LEGO's European employees identify with these features very powerfully indeed. It is also hard not to escape the impression that employees are united in an infectious enthusiasm for the company and its products. Fortunately, 'the company' appears to be able to manage this.

As we noted in the case study, a member of the LEGO Company's executive management declared that the company was committed to cross-cultural learning. This policy and its operations reveal the nature of LEGO's style of cross-cultural interface management. First of all, this was no head office palliative. Something happened. Notably, the London colleagues were encouraged to compose their own mission statement and supporting values, using those traditional LEGO values that they wanted and excluding any that did not seem to apply. This took place in the absence of restriction from headquarters in Denmark. As a result, *'exuberance'* became a key word for developing and promoting LEGO software. This was a word, which, according to LEGO International Media in London, was not associated with toys.

This is a remarkable instance of cross-cultural interface management in which the headquarters of an internationally very well-known company allow a *newly formed* local subsidiary to create a mission statement with such discretion. However, this process did not occur with head office turning a blind eye. The young talented software personnel were inculcated with LEGO traditional values, which were apparently 'internalized' after a couple of months. A further result of the cross-cultural learning was that the word *'fun'* was adopted in the LEGO Company's main mission statement.

Sulzer Infra

Sulzer Infra is learning how to manage two types of interface: first, the in-company interfaces which link the European offices; and second, the interface with clients with their new demands, as noted above. The Sulzer Infra Academy, through its seminars and other activities, provides a mechanism for its employees to learn how to handle both. The seminar is a carefully planned event. It is a kind of experiment designed to reduce personal and professional barriers among the individuals who take part. Musical interludes and group exercises such as painting encourage people to find solidarity. A major consideration is that the seminar also provides participants with skills for participation in multicultural teams.

The company does face a problem of internal language barriers. Although English is the *de facto* company language in the international sense, German is the language of headquarters and not all executives are entirely at home in English. So it is that at seminars interpreters are on hand in four European languages: English, German, French and Spanish. The overall situation can be explained by the fact that up to the mid-1990s all the constituent companies of Sulzer Infra tended to work in their own countries. This fact should be linked to the consideration that several employees who interface with clients are engineers who until the Europeanization of the company did not need to use English in a particularly proactive way.

This of course does not apply to the company's UK employees. But, as we saw in the case study, those UK people did not necessarily enjoy a linguistic advantage. Indeed, we cited the experience of one manager, who regarded his own linguistic limitations as (a) a professional weakness because many of his counterparts knew two languages, and (b) a constraint on identification with foreign colleagues. The British experience can be contrasted with the Dutch one. The two Dutch informants both spoke and used German, especially in their contacts with head office in Switzerland.

CROSS-CULTURALLY SIGNIFICANT FEATURES OF ORGANIZATIONAL LEARNING AND NETWORKING

Novo Nordisk

There is little doubt that the Facilitators are a principal agency within Novo Nordisk for creating conditions and an atmosphere that promotes cross-cultural collaborative learning. They act as catalysts for network development by linking together units which can share knowledge and experience. But, as noted above, the *sine qua non* of these processes is that the Facilitators secure the trust of units through the world. Being listeners rather preachers, their non-censorious approach has had considerable impact on the company as an international organization.

As we noted, the Facilitators represent a significant human resource investment. The substantial running cost ignores the costs associated with personnel who have left positions to become Facilitators. Again, the point is made that the Facilitator concept has 'Scandinavia' written all over it. The concept, whilst looking straightforward on paper, can probably only take root in a corporate culture that is egalitarian in orientation and willing to suspend hierarchy to get things done. A significant feature of the Facilitators' work is that they continually extend their in-company network and act as catalysts in bringing into direct intercommunication parts of the company which hitherto would not have known that there was valuable knowledge and useful business practice to share.

Matsushita

Cross-cultural learning in the Matsushita Corporation is complex. It seems to take foreign (i.e. here Western) employees some time to adjust to working for this Japanese company, with its all-powerful corporate culture. It is probable that the adjustment is more demanding for the more senior ranks in the company, that is those working closely with Japanese managers at higher levels of responsibility and according to national background.

The case study did not interview foreign nationals from countries like Malaysia, Indonesia or Singapore, and it is possible that they, imbued with an oriental outlook on life, find it easier to secure the right cultural fit for themselves than some Americans and Europeans do. It was telling in the case that at a US subsidiary an American personnel manager refused to run an induction course until employees at executive levels had been with the company for six months.

The personnel manager had qualifications in Japanese studies, so she was a key facilitator in communicating the what and – more importantly – the why of the company logic. A purely impressionistic conclusion is that US managers were more sceptical and mystified by the Matsushita style of management and doing business than their European counterparts. The Americans felt that they knew much more about the American market and the way to do business in the USA than *any* transplanted Japanese manager.

The frustration was sometimes palpable. In one case, an American manager was angered that the Japanese management's unwillingness or inability to provide Panasonic products in bulk to a major retailing group from a single supply source was losing the company millions of dollars of business each year. In another instance, a report that took more than a year to compile by two US managers on business strategy, and that entailed visits to Matsushita facilities throughout the country, was sent to the company's US headquarters in New Jersey and nothing happened. Against that, I was told by a senior Japanese manager that the company wanted to give more power to foreign managers, but it was 'very difficult' to trust them.[1]

Of course, these are isolated incidences in one of the world's largest companies, but the attitudes and behaviours unearthed in the case study are fully consistent with the general output of two decades of writing on Japanese management overseas. But in the Matsushita case the managers interviewed in the USA, Australia and Europe were all united in one opinion and one impression: that the company, for all its size and market power, was very conservative in outlook. It will be recalled that one European manager described the company as 'old and tired'. This suggests that cross-cultural learning – the Japanese about European and American frustrations, and American and European learning about Japanese ways and ideals – is still an arduous process after 20 years and greater business interaction.

In Europe the company is making great strides to integrate business activities across borders: It has also set up a European works council. Yet whilst the company is so strongly dominated by one nationality, which both symbolizes and perpetuates the Japanese way and the Matsushita way, the conditions for effective cross-cultural learning and networking for organizational renewal may militate against the best efforts.

LEGO

As we have noted, since the 1950s LEGO has seen itself as an international company with an international outlook. It has consistently played down its Danish roots. Yet, when LEGO Media International was founded in 1996, the recruits to the new venture were rapidly aware that there *was* a distinct management style emanating from corporate headquarters. Not only that, but these recruits – mainly, but not exclusively British – regarded the management style as conservative. It is to the LEGO Company's credit that the top management in Denmark responded in such an enlightened way. Without this possibly unexpected reaction from the newly appointed colleagues, the company may well not have seen the need to establish a policy actively to promote cross-cultural learning with the LEGO group of companies. As mentioned above, the interaction between company headquarters in Denmark and LEGO Media International in London proved to be a mutual learning process. But this was predicated – and this cannot be over-emphasized – on the willingness of LEGO top management to learn. Once they were prepared to learn, it became an active policy.

Sulzer Infra

Sulzer Infra makes an interesting contrast with Novo Nordisk. The Danish company developed its team of Facilitators, its change agents who go out to company units worldwide. Sulzer Infra has centralized the equivalent function through its corporate university, the Sulzer Infra Academy. The activities of the Academy focus sharply on the ambition of making Sulzer Infra a knowledge-based company, which acknowledges that the company must rapidly develop Europe-wide learning and networking. The seminar is designed to facilitate these actions, which are clearly seen as mutually supporting. Among many special features is the presentation by the company president, who identifies his life with the company philosophy.

One feature of an event like the seminar is that the making of new, *directly useful* contacts is a random process. Of the three UK managers interviewed for the case study, the one who plainly got most out of the entire experience from a professional point of view was the one who found a very interested listener for his ideas on business software. As far as he was concerned, there were 'no boundaries in the company'. This apparently chance meeting, although of the kind that the seminar aims to create, was nevertheless fortuitous. The Sulzer Infra Academy is still a fairly young institution. So far its seminars appear to be encouraging in-company networking throughout Europe. At the moment it is still too early to say to what extent the networking is being converted into learning. But the signs suggest that this is happening.

CONTRASTING THE FOUR COMPANIES' CROSS-CULTURAL MANAGEMENT BEHAVIOUR

Taking the cross-cultural behaviour of the four companies as a whole, there are some striking contrasts. First, the company that is consistently the most ethnocentric in the management – if not *control* – of this behaviour is the Matsushita Corporation. Despite the fact that localization – that is empowerment to local managers – is a widely preached doctrine within the company, and despite the fact that it has been recognized by a former president and chairman of the company that the company division structure makes overseas operations 'extremely difficult' (Matsushita, 1996), the company appears not to have found a way to trust its foreign managers, at least in some European countries and the USA.

The conviction mediated via the founder, Konosuke Matsushita, that the company's way of doing business was universal in application, has become a sacred truth in, as it were, the Japanese half of the company. But, problematically, this same conviction has become a reinforcer of ethnocentrism. As is often the case with large, conservative, Japanese companies, the management of the Japanese workforce by Japanese managers is not necessarily harmonious, but people tend to know where they stand in relation to each other. That is the essence of Japanese socialization, which begins at home and is inculcated at school so that, when they join big corporations, young Japanese know how to behave. Europe and America tend not to produce such compliant people, so they can, from a Japanese point of view, be difficult to manage. A Japanese ploy is to encourage local personnel to make recommendations, but then not do anything with them. Part of the problem is not just between local managers and expatriate Japanese managers in the same country. Those expatriate managers have to explain things to their superiors in corporate headquarters. The expatriate Japanese manager is caught between two stools, but being a good Japanese there is only one direction in which he can bend. He may try to negotiate on behalf of the local managers, but his *obligation* to headquarters is greater than his commitment to local staff. The result is a lack of Japanese trust and frustration at the local level.

The approach of the two Danish firms, Novo Nordisk and LEGO, is quite different. Their commitment to localization is a key element in their strategy. But there are differences. Novo Nordisk, the more sophisticated company, sees localization in terms of empowerment and the release of good practices from unit to unit. The Facilitators are the active agents of this policy. LEGO is more concerned about localization as a source of ideas. It does not have a mechanism of such explicit enforcement, preferring to give local units plenty of discretion, believing that the LEGO group's cohesion stems from a commitment to, and identification with, the company values, which place the well-being of children at the core. This strategy appears to work, and plainly both LEGO Media International in London and LEGO Lab San Mateo in California find that they have plenty of scope for creativity both in product development and marketing.

The evidence suggests that the new ventures are startling corporate headquarters in Denmark with ideas. As was noted in the case study, corporate headquarters was not perceived by LEGO Media International as a source of creativity, owing to the dominance of Danish nationals there. In this sense LEGO shares with Matsushita a certain ethnocentrism, but the Danish concern is almost certainly more open to business ideas from its international subsidiaries. It is, incidentally, somewhat ironic that, although LEGO has had for many years a policy of national non-assertion, the company has only in the last few years genuinely opened itself up to foreign influences. These various observations support an increasingly held conviction that dominance by one national group at the top of a company or by those nationals in foreign subsidiaries can inhibit organizational learning and knowledge-sharing (Barham and Heimer, 1998; Rosenzweig, 1988; Schneider and Barsoux, 1997; Taylor, 1999).

If LEGO and Matsushita have something in common that affects their cross-cultural behaviour and performance, Sulzer has an interesting feature with Novo Nordisk. Both have company presidents who make themselves visible to their in-company constituencies as being strongly committed (Rosen, 2000).

THE UNSEEN ACTIVITY BEHIND THE LEARNING AND NETWORKING

In the case studies culture seldom emerges as the universally pernicious force that some writers like to describe, with images of terminal disease and earthquakes – alas for them. The only consistent instance of serious frictions and tensions arose with respect to the Matsushita Corporation and with particular reference to its US managers. Generally speaking, culture, primarily in the sense of national culture and cultural difference, is not experienced as an aggravation. What did emerge, however, is the distinctive ways in which cultural differences (in the accepted sense of the expression) manifest themselves, in the way that the companies devised systems and structures to cope with these, and used the experience gained in cross-cultural interactions as a source of organizational learning.

Two companies in the sample, Novo Nordisk and Sulzer Infra, explicitly attempted to use this cross-cultural experience to create changes to the internal company culture. But neither company went in for mechanistic cultural change, whereby 'all that management must do is to re-code, or re-wire the organization; informing people of the newly desired collective beliefs so that changes in belief systems may occur' (Harrison, 1995). This kind of approach may have a greater chance of succeeding in a fairly sanitized monocultural environment like the headquarters of Matsushita Electric in Japan, where deference to company logic will be unquestioned, or of major US and UK corporations where it is assumed that the shibboleths of change, articulated in glossy corporate English, are cross-culturally neutral.

As we shall see, the international management of change in Novo Nordisk and Sulzer Infra is predicated on the assumption that (a) those shibboleths enshrined in mission statements or expositions of company vision are not so universally apprehensible within the company, and (b) that managers in local units, physically and possibly psychologically remote from corporate headquarters, should be permitted some discretion over the interpretation of them. In other words, both companies are accepting that these acts of symbolic translation are, in principle, both necessary and desirable. This kind of policy, which requires much trust in local managers and their staff, acknowledges that the organizational renewal required for the global, (increasingly) knowledge-based economy is directly linked to the company's willingness and capacity to integrate best practices and experience from as many in-company loci of common knowledge as possible. This does not merely change the organization; it renews it.

Knowledge-sharing, organizational learning and networking were described above as acts of transferring know-how, special expertise, company values, best practices, and so forth. But the experiences of Novo Nordisk, Sulzer Infra and, to a lesser extent, LEGO suggest that these were more than acts of transfer. Super-intending these processes was another activity, unnoticed and complex: acts of translation. This does not mean translation in the literal sense of rendering texts and utterances composed in one language into another language. Rather, it is used in an extended sense. The purpose of this intra- and inter-organizational translation activity is to create what Nonaka (1991) terms 'common cognitive ground' among entire workforces through teamwork and team learning, knowledge-sharing, and networking. In chapters 11 and 12 translation in the sense of interlingual transposition will be used to illuminate the extended concept, which, for clarity's sake, I will term *interactive translation*.

A Novo Nordisk facilitation or a Sulzer Infra seminar are good examples of this kind of translation, which has four interesting properties. First, interactive translation is predicated on people working in groups. Second, it helps to establish common meanings in an international company. Third, in order to engage in, and (in principle) gain the maximum benefit from, interactive transla-tion activity as a process, individuals *need to be able work in teams*. Thus, interactive translation calls for adeptness in cross-cultural communication, which I am calling *participative competence*. This latter concept is merely introduced here and will be considered more fully in the following two chapters, along with interactive translation. It will argued in due course that a major task of cross-cultural management is to facilitate participative competence, without which group-based learning and knowledge-sharing cannot take place. Fourth, interactive translation is a form of negotiation, whereby individuals working in groups attempt to make sense of the organizational realities in which they find themselves and agree their own roles *vis-à-vis* each other within them.

The idea of translation as a heuristic device for explaining forms of social and institutional change is not new to organizational scientists (see, for example, Czarniawska and Sevón, 1996), but translation appears to be used as a rather dry analogue to describe the dynamics of social change processes. If I am not mis-taken, the organizational scientists see translation as an *ex post facto* explanation of what has gone on in order to attribute structure and meanings to events. In this book I depart from the abstractions by emphasizing that translation – in this case, interactive translation – is *a form of cross-cultural work*.

It is the notion of interactive translation which creates the paradigmatic common ground between cross-cultural management and knowledge management. But before cross-cultural management can be so joined to knowledge management, we need a chapter of explanation. In chapter 11 attention will be directed to the language of management, for this language has several functions and has an important role in the international transfer of knowledge, values and experience. This discussion will prepare the ground for chapter 12, when the international transfer of knowledge will be presented as a form of interactive translation.

NOTE

1. As connoisseurs of Japan well know, when a Japanese says that something is 'difficult', it really means it is virtually impossible.

REFERENCES

Barham, K. and Heimer, C. (1998). *ABB – the dancing giant*. London: Financial Times Prentice Hall.

Cherry, C. (1980). *On human communication: A review, a survey and a criticism*. Cambridge, MA: MIT Press.

Czarniawska, B. and Sevón, G. (eds) (1996). *Translating organisational change*. Berlin: de Gruyter.

Hannerz, U. (1996). *Transnational connections: Culture, people, places*. London: Routledge.

Harrison, R. (1995). *The collected papers of Roger Harrison*. London: McGraw-Hill. Also quoted in Collins, D. (2000). *Management fads and buzzwords*. London: Routledge.

Matsushita, M. (1996). *The mind of management: Fifty years with Konosuke Matsushita*. Osaka: Matsushita Electric Industrial Company.

Nonaka, I. (1991). The knowledge-creating company. *Harvard Business Review*. November–December: 96–104.

Rosen, R. (2000). *Global literacies: Lessons on business leaderships and national cultures*. New York: Simon & Schuster. See, especially, the case study 'Build an expert culture of shared values: Mads Øvlisen and Novo Nordisk A/S (Denmark)', pp. 229–33.

Rosenzweig, P. (1988). Strategies for managing diversity. In: Bickerstaffe, G. (ed.). *Mastering global business: The complete MBA companion to global business*. London: Pitman, pp. 177–81.

Schneider, S. and Barsoux, J.-L. (1997). *Managing across cultures*. London: Prentice Hall.

Taylor, S. (1999). National origin and the development of organizational capabilities. In: Beechler, S. and Bird, A. (eds). *Japanese multinationals abroad: Individual and organizational learning*. New York: Oxford University Press, pp. 131–50.

11 Language: management's lost continent

'Internasional komerse isto un vast sujekt ké no isto posabel aratar in un kort leson.'

An example of Eurolengo. In: Andrew Large, *The artificial language movement* (1985)[1]

'A public speaker – be he a politician, a preacher or a charlatan – is able, with proper and correct Arabic, to captivate his audience. Frequently, an articulate speaker can keep a massive crowd spell-bound not so much by what he is saying as by how the words roll off his tongue.'

A., J. Almaney and A. J. Alwan, *Communicating with the Arabs* (1982)

OBJECTIVES

- Describes the concept of culture that this book is developing: culture as infinitely overlapping habits of common knowledge.
- Argues that common knowledge can only be realized by virtue of a serviceable common language of corporate endeavour.
- Discusses the language of management.
- Proposes three modes of management language.
- Notes that the frequently heard appeal for a *new* language of management is linked to a centuries-old quest to find a perfect universal language of discovery and validation.

INTRODUCTION

The previous chapter analyzed the behaviour and experiences of the four informant companies from a cross-cultural perspective which emphasizes learning, knowledge-sharing and networking. It was proposed that cross-cultural management is a kind of interactive translation which both facilitates and modulates the intra- and inter-organisational transfer of knowledge, values and experience. This chapter will probe more deeply into this proposition. The first task, however, is to explain further the concept of culture which was introduced in chapter 5: 'culture is varieties of common knowledge'. The point has been reached where it is necessary to advance a notion of culture that is intended to suit the kind of cross-cultural management phenomena that we have been dealing with, and that is also compatible with the concepts of knowledge management. Then comes a discussion of the notion of interactive translation. This particular discussion will involve reference to language and sets the scene for a lengthy treatment of the notion of the language of management. For conceptual purposes this is regarded as comprising three modes which (a) formally describe management tasks, (b) mobilize human resources through learning networks, and (c) serve as a repository of company knowledge, lore and vision. It will be argued that cross-cultural management entails the interactive translation of all three elements, whereby knowledge can be converted into new outlooks and behaviours.

In this chapter there will be some reference to aspects of translation theory and practice, as well as linguistics, to draw the appropriate analogies and make pertinent explanations. Unavoidably, readers who have not experienced the frustrations and exhilarations of the intellectually demanding feat of translating may be disadvantaged when reading this chapter. But those without this experience should not feel at a complete disadvantage. Translation theory is being used sparsely to shed light on interactive translation, and everyone has experience of this form of translation in everyday communication. As the anthropologist Edmund Leach (1982) has noted: 'We spend our whole time interpreting the results of the past expressive actions of other people.' In a similar vein, Steiner (1975) has memorably pronounced that *'inside or between languages, human communication equals translation'* (original emphasis).

A MODIFIED CULTURE CONCEPT

One of the starting-points of this book lay in a conviction that the cross-cultural environment of the modern business world can no longer just be seen as comprising national cultures, which are the focal points of distinctive values, languages, management styles, and ways of doing business. Perhaps 20 years ago one could see the world like that, but the business world at the outset of the new millennium is mixing up people from all manner of linguistic, (national) cultural, educational and professional backgrounds on a scale and with an intensity unprecedented in human history. Furthermore, as we noted in the discussions of about modern business, the TNCs themselves operate as if the world economy were borderless.[2] The 'new' cross-cultural management which this book is advancing is trying to come to grips with the geo-economy with all its complexities of interconnectedness, which, quite apart from anything else, is changing the nature of human contact and human cooperation as it is mediated by world-spanning corporations.

The upshot is that culture – that is to say, culture in the popular sense – is no longer just 'out there'; infinite manifestations of it are, to a greater or lesser extent, being internalized by the world's companies in myriad forms and transmuted consciously and unconsciously in policies, plans and actions. These internalization processes involve millions and millions of people in direct and indirect communication around the world every day. As they work together in groups and teams, in their networks and at their interfaces, they create both a specific cultural identity and a common purpose distinctive to their understanding of, as well as to their function in, the corporation and the projects upon which they are engaged. Thus, in their groups and teams the people create habitats of common knowledge and shared meanings, membership of which is partly vouchsafed by affiliation to an organization and by collaborative endeavours with others to achieve organizational goals.

The study of the four TNCs in our sample make it clear that each firm in its own way is trying to link up varieties of common knowledge throughout its entire worldwide operations. The process may be described as *acts of interactive translation which are taking place in order to make common knowledge here available and intelligible there.* We can therefore propose that cross-cultural management is the art of combining varieties of common knowledge through interactive translation. In order to develop this modified concept of cross-cultural management, it will be necessary to come to an understanding of translation both as a process and as an analogy. This understanding will be mediated in this chapter and the following one.

The idea of common knowledge is useful because there are different kinds. But common knowledge is dispersed messily both throughout organizations and the wider networks which encompass their stakeholders. Some kinds of it can be widespread throughout a company, but other kinds are held exclusively by a few. An example of the first might concern a company scheme which offers scholarships or travel grants to the children of employees. An example of the other kind may be specialist know-how, which is the province of R&D people, or a customized purchasing procedure in a client's company, or a new company policy under discussion among a restricted number of people. A contrasting example may be the way business is done in Korea, which will be known mainly by staff working in a company's Seoul office and they are likely mainly to be Koreans sharing the common knowledge. But for the sake of argument let us ignore the fact that some kinds of common knowledge are confidential and regard a large corporation as composed of a number of loci of common knowledge, which represent varieties of valuable, but possibly untapped resource bases to each other.

It now becomes possible to understand culture as infinitely overlapping and perpetually redistributable habitats of common knowledge and shared meanings. Accordingly, the task of cross-cultural knowledge management lies in the redistribution of common knowledge, in connecting centres and sources of common knowledge *through the creation of a serviceable common language of corporate endeavour.* This language, which will be discussed below, is the lubricant of the transfer of knowledge, values and experience from one source of common knowledge to others. We may call it the language of management, a complex amalgam of code and discourse, which is discussed more fully below. This language is also a source of symbols, with which it clothes company values and encodes attitudes and behaviour that the company wishes its employees to share. It is the language which supplies the content and context for interactive translation.

When companies say that they wish to get everyone 'to speak the same language', this language is a metaphor for the state of sharing a common purpose. The common language develops and replenishes itself through acts of interactive translation which inform every act of communication. Although it is perfectly possible to talk about interactive translation even in a purely monolingual setting, the concept has extra potency with respect to big, internationally operating organizations which employ thousands of people working in languages other than the native one. Furthermore, certain kinds of common knowledge – like the way business is done in Korea – are protected by formal language barriers of variable permeability. So interactive translation is not just a metaphorical concept. In everyday corporate practice it involves interlingual translation: the cognitive movement of knowledge, ideas and experience among different languages.

For convenience, I am proposing to term this so-called serviceable common language of corporate endeavour 'the language of management'. By this expression I do not mean so much 'the language of managers' as the codes or discourses that managers create for, or share with, those whose endeavours they manage or, rather, facilitate. Before discussing the language of management, it is necessary to clarify the key term 'interactive translation'.

INTERACTIVE TRANSLATION

The theory of translation focuses on two key aspects: translation as a process and translation in terms of the final product (Sager, 1993). Translation as process is much preoccupied with the translator (that is, his or her competencies and methods). Translation in terms of the final product is also concerned with that and its effects on readers and audiences. A very considerable concern of professional translators is the matter of quality – what constitutes a good, reliable or adequate translation. Countless books and articles have been written on these topics. In this book it is necessary to delve into those aspects of the theory and practice of translation which contribute to a greater understanding of cross-cultural knowledge transfer. But in this extended sense of translation, the same fundamental question arises. What, intra- or inter-oranizationally speaking, constitutes a good translation?

Pinchuk (1977) is no doubt correct when he says that 'the notion that translation involves merely replacing words in one language with words in another is probably the most commonly held one by the general public.' But theorists of translation would regard such a popular notion as ill-informed and seriously inadequate. As Vermeer (1992) has noted: 'In recent years we have come a long way from the traditional approach to translation as a mere linguistic transcoding of a text "from one language to another" (Waard and Nida, 1986)'. Then he adds: 'it has become common sense to integrate translation into a wider network of social relations' (Vermeer, 1992). This socially aware concept of translation is a very useful staging-post between translation in the standard linguistic sense and the wider concept of interactive translation, which can help throw light on the cross-cultural transfer of knowledge, values and experience.

Vermeer's idea implies that receivers of translated material are part of the translation process. Let me explain that. Imagine that I am reading an English version of Tolstoy's *War and Peace*. In fact I am not just reading it. *I am translating the translation to myself as I read it*. This is a simple form of interactive translation. In the corporate world interactive translation involves lots of people. Their encounters with each other – for example in a team or during an exercise at a Sulzer Infra seminar – are more than discussions. These are acts of communication in which each person (in theory) alters an outlook, or decides to change a way of working or dealing with an awkward situation, or acquires information about a time-saving procedure. The individual translates everything in terms of his or her frame of reference. This individual translation is then woven back into the interactions with the translations of others, in a perpetual melding of people, processes and perspectives.

The participation in these processes of interactive translation is a learning process in its own right. A very good example from the case studies concerns Novo Nordisk. Every single act of facilitation is an interactive translation necessitating 'pre-learning' (i.e. learning from other facilitations) and on-the-spot learning of know-how to interact with this particular group of people in these particular circumstances. But the clients of the Facilitators need to learn how to interact with *them*. For the necessary synergy to take place, both sides need participative competence, the *sine qua non* of interactive translation and, as we shall later see, of knowledge transfer.

The importance of participative competence is incalculable for cross-cultural activity of any kind. Not only does it help promote knowledge-sharing and organizational learning, but it also makes individuals feel that they can make a positive contribution. A major task of cross-cultural management is to foster participative competence, for much works against it. But that is to get ahead of the story. We can in fact go no further until we address 'the great human fact of Language' (Entwistle, 1974) in one of its spectacular contexts: the modern corporation.

LANGUAGE AND MANAGEMENT

Let me begin this section by reinvoking the words of Colin Cherry (1980), which I quoted in the preface: 'Language makes a hard mistress and we are all her slaves. Anyone who would consort with her, to study and understand her, lays himself open to a severe discipline and much disappointment.' All too mindful of the dangers ahead, I propose to discuss language as an aspect of management behaviour and a facet of organizational life sufficient for the purpose of developing the notion of cross-cultural management as a form of knowledge management. The approach will be to discuss the notion of the language of management, which will be treated in a pragmatic way and not in a formal, scientific sense. Three modes of the language of management will be highlighted: as a descriptor of management tasks, as a network facilitator, and as the repository of company wisdom, lore and vision. Reference will be made to the four informant companies' behaviour for clarification of these aspects of the language of management.

There is no scientifically agreed definition of language. Indeed, the formal description of language, which must among other things comprehend the description of the history and features of all human languages living and dead, is beyond all intellectual possibility. In the words of one of the world's foremost linguists and literary scholars, George Steiner (1975): 'The application of the concept of exact science to the study of language is an idealized simile.' The *Collins Dictionary of English* (1990) lists eight principal meanings associated with the word language:

> **1.** A system for the expression of thoughts, feelings, etc., by the use of spoken sounds or conventional symbols. **2.** The faculty for the use of such systems, which is a distinguishing characteristic of man as compared with other animals. **3.** The language of a particular nation or people: *the French language.* **4.** Any other systemic or nonsystemic means of communicating, such as gesture or animal sounds: *the language of love.* **5.** The specialized vocabulary used by a particular group: *medical language.* **6.** A particular manner or style of verbal expression: *your language is disgusting.* **7.** *Computer technol.* See **programming language. 8.** Speak the same language. To communicate with understanding because of common background, values, etc. (original emphasis)

Language, then, is dauntingly complicated. In the following discussion very little attention will be paid to the language of management as cognitive experience. The treatment will be pragmatic, that is it will concern itself with 'the circumstances under which individuals use language, and the potential or functions of the language they use' (Sager et al., 1980). The language the management is what linguists term 'a language of special purpose' (or, simply, 'special language'): that is to say, a domain-specific subset of 'general language' which facilitates professional communication among specialists.[3] The most distinguishing feature of a special language is its generation and use of a domain-specific lexis, whilst recognizing that the use of this lexis by the individual is socially, i.e. organizationally, determined according to factors such as the status, professional competencies and location of interaction (see Sager et al., 1980). Regarding management as a special domain, the language of management is defined as:

> a set of linguistic symbols, manipulable in a given language (such as English, German, Japanese, Russian etc.), and incorporating standardised terms and informal elements (such as oblique reference, humour, pretence, etc.), necessary for the conceptualisation, description and execution of management tasks and sharing of management information. (Holden, 1996)

This definition considers the language of management in universalistic terms, whilst accounting for local variations and acknowledging subliminally that it is a form of language much concerned with creating an impression. Implicit in the definition is that the social usages, grammatical features, and lexical resources associated with individual languages of management – such as English, German, Japanese, Russian, etc. – vary in complex ways. Consider these observations. It is a fact that American management language is characterized by its 'sheer extent of codification and preformulation' (Hampden-Turner and Trompenaars, 1993) and penchant for 'snappy neologisms' (Torrington and Holden, 1992). This is in complete contrast with the situation in Russia, where:

> entire areas of management vocabulary have got to be invented and institutionalised, replacing the impoverished and discredited lexicon of Marxist-Leninism. But even if the language of socialism is waning in influence, because the state is no longer in a position to use this language as an element of social coercion and political direction, the Russians in general do not seem to be interested in assimilating the language of the market economy. (Holden et al., 1998)

Japanese, like American English, is in a seemingly permanent state of 'acquisitive brilliance' (Steiner, 1975). Thus, in Japan, managers do not merely have all the words they need, whether from their native word-stock or acquired from (American) English. They sometimes use foreign words and the nominally equivalent Japanese term for quite separate denotations. To take an example relevant to this book: the Japanese, it seems, have added *narejji manejimento* (knowledge management) to their enormous corpus of English-language-derived business vocabulary, but use an indigenous term *chishiki keiei* to mean something rather different. With *narejji manejimento* the Japanese tend to refer to the proceduralized management of knowledge, whereas their own expression both embraces and emphasizes knowledge creation, transfer and application via Japanese-style socialization.[4] Japanese managers use the 'unique' Japanese language,[5] which encodes social distance with great precision, whilst permitting messages to be communicated 'through the use of context, not solely by the self-complete grammatical code' (Nonaka and Takeuchi, 1995).

The German manager does not have such an exquisite medium at his disposal. He uses the German language, 'that glorious but all-too-powerful instrument' (Garton Ash, 1997), which encodes 'timeliness, tidiness and proper form' (Viney, 1997) under that sublimely untranslatable word *Ordnung*. German, it is true, is elaborate and, like a Mercedes car, is splendidly over-engineered, a precision instrument of great robustness. As Pinchuk (1977) has noted, the German language is in its syntax 'not economical, but it is less susceptible of misunderstanding'. And that *might* give a clue to the German management behaviour.

The relationship between language and society is a fascinating subject. The relationship between individual languages of management and their native domain is equally fascinating, but minefields await those who pursue the quest. However, the issue will be aired again, albeit briefly, in chapter 12. Suffice it to say for now that each language of management conjures up a different *ideal* world of management. It is tempting to contrast a picture of this world mediated via the German language with one mediated via Japanese. The German ideal world is one of orderliness and organization; the Japanese world is one of harmonious relationships. Hence, different languages, different world-views, different approaches to management. But no more 'dangerous' speculation: the main task now is to attempt to characterize the language of management in functional terms.

For our purposes, the language of management is considered as comprising three modes in pragmatic space: as a descriptor of management tasks, as a network facilitator, and as the repository of company wisdom, lore and vision. For the first aspect the intellectual debt is to the cybernetician (and founding father of operational research), Stafford Beer (1966).[6] The second mode posits language as a mobilizer of people into networks for promoting organizational learning and knowledge-sharing. The third aspect is, as we shall see, a continuation of a quest for an unambiguous and universal code of communication. In the daily life of organizations these three aspects of language can be completely intermeshed, but the proposed tripartite division is intended to throw light on the relationship between language and interactive translation.

Language as a descriptor of management tasks

For Beer (1966), the formal mode of the language of management is the rigorous description of management activities.[7] This formal language refers predominantly to quantity, probability, and quality. Quantity refers to anything which can be measured formally and scientifically such as inventories, a production process, stock market ratings, or changes in the labour market. We may take probability to refer to the formal language for discussing and evaluating risk. If you prefer, this is the language of SWOT analysis. By quality, Beer refers to the adequacy of the formal language to map reality.

These three elements of formal language provide a kind of matrix 'for discussing the business with an objective language of fact and its models of reality and reality itself' (Beer, 1966). Thus the formal aspect of the language of management is concerned with management tasks and their formal description. It is the language associated with two fairly formal areas of company operations: strategy formulation and decisions (but not necessarily decision-making).

Of the three modes of management language, this may be the easiest to translate in the literal sense: to render accurately its terminology and quantitative formulations in another language. But even so that can only be safely said of languages in intercommunication which use the same conceptual bases, the same conventions of notation, and have the necessary and equivalent lexical resources, and whose users (i.e. managers) share similar operational experiences.

Formal language is more or less easily translatable among West European languages, which includes American English, and two oriental languages, Japanese and Korean, thanks to (a) the American influence over the two countries since the Second World War, and (b) the high proportion of Japanese and Korean students who have studied at business schools in the USA. But the translation of 'simple' words like management or marketing into West European languages is not always straighforward; which is why one encounters in Germany 'der Manager' and in France 'le marketing'.

Once one passes into the post-socialist countries of Eastern Europe and the former USSR, then the quest for semantic equivalence is a nightmare, as the languages concerned have still not developed their lexical resources to cope with Western management terminology (Holden et al., 1998). Japan, it might be said, has developed its own discourse of production, which is hard to render formally in English, partly because production in Japan is both a technological process and a social activity. The case studies produced no instance of a problem of translation in this mode of language. However, the interviews with Novo Nordisk revealed that the related terms 'Facilitator' and 'facilitation' were not easily expressible in languages like Japanese, Chinese or Korean.

Language as a network facilitator

This function of management language mobilizes people into networks for knowledge-sharing and team learning. This aspect of management language is much more difficult to specify. It creates interactive synergies, facilitates interpersonal communication, influences outlooks, releases new behaviours. This is the kind of company-wide language that Sulzer Infra and Novo Nordisk attempt to create and maintain through their seminars and facilitations respectively, whereby personal networks within the company are widened and deepened. It is the *informal language of know-how, the carrier of best practices*. It makes use of and even elaborates the language of company knowledge, procedures and vision, which is discussed presently.

It is a language which LEGO appears to be able to call forth through the appeal of its identity. It is an aspect of language which seems to elude the Matsushita Corporation outside Japan, for it cannot make use of the Japanese language for this purpose with its many thousands of non-Japanese employees. Overall, this mode of the language of management facilitates the interactive processes of translation.

As a language of mobilization and networking, it engenders and is engendered by *participative competence*: the facility to engage in discussions productively in, say, a group project, even using a second language, to contribute equitably to the common task, to be able to share knowledge, communicate experience, and stimulate group learning. In an apt phrase Schneider and Barsoux (1997) talk about the challenge of 'eliciting' participation, noting that 'anglophones, those most likely to preach empowerment or to favour brain-storming, tend to dominate group discussion, ignoring [the fact] that the differences in ability to speak English create an unequal playing-field'. This is reminiscent of the Anglo-American tendency to muffle other voices in the field of economics. As Fallows (1995) has wryly noted: 'The Anglo-American theories have won the battle of ideas – wherever that battle has been carried out *in English*' (added emphasis).

It is in this area of management language, which operates at interfaces (including a computer screen) and in networks, that interactive translation plays a critical role. Interactive translation, *predicated on participative competence*, releases the synergies, as suggested above. The hall mark of 'a good translation' is whether the individual has consciously and visibly gained in participative competence so that networking becomes higher-grade communication by adding value to the information flows.

Language as a repository of company knowledge and vision

This is the subjective language in which the company describes itself to create or confirm an image or impression pertaining to its overall way of doing business – the way it treats its employees, its vision statement, its policies on a wide range of issues from safety at work to pension schemes, from the handling of grievances to induction programmes for new employees. The language is formally conceived in written form and in a large international company may be translated into several languages. This language informs and updates knowledge about the company. It is manifested, for example, in company-wide mails, the company's intranet, company posters and in-house publications. But this language is also symbolic and subjective, supplying concepts and vocabulary of interaction. In its written form this mode of language is a kind of linguistic textbook for the company. Companies want their staff to use these words in their spoken discourse: doing so is a badge of shared affiliation and purpose. It confers what Barham and Heimer (1998) call 'collegiality'.

In the Matsushita Corporation Japanese employees will studiously learn about the life of Konosuke Matsushita; they will learn his sayings by heart, not to mention the basic management principles. In Sulzer Infra the concept of *One Winning Team* is not just three words: it distils the vision and purpose; it is associated with the seminars, which are intense events of interactive translation. In Novo Nordisk the term 'facilitation' was almost synonymous with 'management snooping' until the facilitation process started. Now it is largely seen as synonymous with empowerment and localization. LEGO uses the word 'children' to release synergies through interactive translation. One problem that Matsushita has is that it seems unwilling to exploit this aspect of the company management language to extend participative competence to its non-Japanese employees. Matsushita fears revisionism and so interactive translation in that huge organization seems to be restricted.

The language of management: summarizing the dimensions of translation

The typology, just described, by which the language of management is portrayed as being made of three modes, makes clear how complicated it is to describe and represent linguistic phenomena formally. The division into three is manifestly oversimplified, but it nevertheless serves an important purpose in appreciating the concept of interactive translation. Table 11.1 summarizes the three modes of the language of management and the associated translation significance.

The tasks of cross-cultural management make use of the language of management in each of three modes, but of particular interest is the network facilitator mode, which is concerned with facilitating interactive translation and participative competence. This suggests that there is more to so-called cross-cultural (or intercultural) communication than 'appropriate communication across cultures' (Mead, 1994). But it could have rather more 'to do with releasing the right responses than with sending the "right" messages' (Deresky, 2000). This important issue will be picked up again when we come to discuss cross-cultural communication in the next chapter.

Table 11.1 indicates that each of the three components of management language can be related to specific translation tasks which in turn influence not so much the transfer as the *transferability*[8] of knowledge. A particular conceptual problem, especially for those readers who are interested in knowledge management, is that neither the tripartite typology nor the table derived from it provide nice,

Table 11.1 The components of management language and associated translation tasks

Aspect of management language	Translation significance
Descriptor of management tasks	Source of objective facts about the company
Mobilizing and networking	Interactive translation for networking and learning via participative competence
Repository of company knowledge	Supply of 'subjective' concepts and vocabulary for interaction

neat envelopes for knowledge which is tacit and knowledge which is explicit. This tricky issue will be taken up in the next chapter.

IN SEARCH OF A LANGUAGE OF EXCELLENCE

It is commonplace to hear and read about the word 'language' referring to the state of sharing in enhanced communication and heightened perceptions in company contexts. If we speak 'the same language', we identify with the company goals and set our thinking and actions, within the remit of required tasks, to harmonize with the actions of others. Language is in this sense a metaphor, its symbolic powers serving to *unite* people with a sense of common purpose. Seen in this way, language is a very potent expression of company wisdom, lore and vision.

The case study of the Matsushita Corporation provides a supreme example. All that company's wisdom, lore and aspiration turns on the words of the company founder and subsequent interpretations which reinforce rather than replenish and certainly not criticize the sacred utterances. As we noted in the case study, it is very difficult to rearticulate this Matsushita language in Western languages and this, as was argued, acts as a barrier between the company's Japanese and non-Japanese employees. The pre-packaged Matsushita language blocks genuine company-wide discourse (and it is possible that other Japanese corporations have similar problems too). We must wait and see whether the watch-words of the newly appointed president – speed, simplicity, strategy, sincerity and smile – will reduce the Japanese/non-Japanese divide in the company.

Despite the fact that managers do extraordinary things with language, that it is an empirical fact that managers spend a considerable portion of their professional time *talking*, and that their very careers depend on how they use language, management writers in the main do not pay much attention to this most familiar, yet remarkable phenomenon.[9] As the great American linguist, Leonard Bloomfield (1979) noted: 'Language plays a great part in our life. Perhaps because of its familiarity, we rarely observe it, taking it for granted, as we do breathing or walking.' In the world of management the word 'language' causes the eye to glaze over, but the word 'communication' causes them to light up. The great management thinker, Peter Drucker (1962), once observed that distribution was the 'Economy's Dark Continent'. By analogy, we may say that language is not just management's dark continent, but its *lost* continent.

The significance of language as a potent symbolic feature of organizational life was noted, possibly for the first time by mainstream researchers, nearly 20 years ago. In 1982 Peters and Waterman published *In search of excellence*, which may claim to be the most influential management book of all time. Probably, most readers of the book did not realize how much Peters and Waterman referred to language. I reproduce below the statements on language.

Language and the search for excellence

'Above all, the *intensity itself*, stemming from strongly held views, marks these companies. During our first round of interviews we could "feel it." The language used in talking about people was different.' (p. 16)

'The enquiry ran into two formidable roadblocks. . . . Second, the attack ran into a language problem. . . . It was an attack on rationality and logical thought *per se*, thus implicitly encouraging escape into irrationality and mysticism.' (p. 41)

'Leadership is about many things. . . . It is meticulously shifting attention through the mundane language of management systems.' (p. 82)

'The transforming leader is concerned with minutiae, as well . . . he is concerned with the tricks of the pedagogue, the mentor, the linguist – the more successfully to become the value shaper, the exemplar, the maker of meanings.' (p. 82)

'We need new language. We need to consider adding terms to our management vocabulary. . . . We need new metaphors.' (pp. 106–7)

'At P&G the language of action – the language of systems – is the fabled *one page memorandum*.' (p. 150)

'Yes, TI is a systems-driven company; ex-Chairman Haggerty spent a decade instilling what he calls "the language" of the Objectives, Strategies and Tactics system.' (p. 153)

'Service-intensive companies use the same language in describing themselves. She [Dinah Nemeroff of Citibank] notes, "They discuss service issues in identical words."' (p. 165)

'The service-through-people theme at Disney starts, as it does in many of the excellent companies, with a special language.' (p. 167)

'As we step back from the analysis of people and productivity, we find a number of striking themes running through the excellent companies' data. First is language. *The language in people-oriented institutions has a common flavour.* . . . We doubt that "The HP Way" meant very much to anyone in Hewlett-Packard when the language was first introduced. As time went by, we suspect that the phrase took on deeper and richer meanings in ways that no one would have suspected.' (p. 260)

'Most impressive of all the language characteristics in the excellent companies are the phrases that upgrade the status of the individual employee.' (p. 261)

Some references to language in *In search of excellence* (Peters and Waterman, 1982, original emphasis)

Peters and Waterman make no attempt to explain the word 'language' in a formal way. But four interrelated things stand out. First, it is clear from this list that language is a consequence of interactions throughout a company, and these interactions are guided by management, which is characterized by the *'apparent absence of a rigidly followed chain of command'* (Peters and Waterman, 1982, original emphasis). Second, the special language of 'excellent' companies is not conscientiously created; it is a product of cooperation, which employees identify with and find motivating. Third, the special language is a very significant feature of the corporate culture. And fourth, language equals *code*.

Despite the fact that Peters and Waterman use the word language in such a heavily coded way, they can be credited with a major attempt to 'refashion (some would say, debase) the "grammar" and lexicon of management' (Collins, 2000). If that is true, then it is somewhat ironic that the word 'language' is only referenced once in the index of *In search of Excellence*, and then only to refer to a book with the word 'language' in the title. There is something of further interest revealed in the Peters and Waterman pronouncements on language. They call for a new language, a new vocabulary and new metaphors to describe 'excellent' management. That may have been an unusual plea 20 years ago, but no longer. In *The fifth discipline* (1990), a core text on organization learning, Senge calls for a new language of relationships. Western languages, he claims, tend to make people think in straight lines. So we need 'a language made up of circles. Without such a language, our habitual ways of seeing the world produce fragmented views and counterproductive actions' (Senge, 1990).

For her part, Hoecklin (1995) states that 'the old definitions of international business are now defunct'. As a result, she claims, 'many companies are searching for a new language'. Consider this call to arms by Rosen, the author of *Global literacies* (2000):

> What's needed in this new, increasingly complex world is a new language of global business, a language where leaders see world's business challenges as opportunities, think with an international mindset, act with fresh global-centric leadership behaviors, and mobilize world-class companies.

In their idealization and elevation of language, both Peters and Waterman (1982) and Rosen (2000) appear to be united. But there is more to their utterances than idealization of language. This calls for an explanation, which is worth a short digression. These authors' appeals for a new language – or code – can be seen as a continuation of the enduring utopian quest 'to construct an ideal language ... without the procedures and confusions of ordinary discourse' (Steiner, 1975). Such a quest for a perfectly unambiguous language – or code – can be traced back to Ancient Greece in the first century BC (Large, 1985). The dream has been the creation of a universal language which would be unambiguous and have the facility to describe things *as they truly are*. According to Cherry (1980), the great French philosopher Descartes (1596–1650) 'had considered the possibility of creating an artificial, universal language, realizing that the various languages of the world were, by virtue of their complex evolution, utterly illogical, difficult and ambiguous'. Which is exactly how languages are today of course. In the seventeenth century the quest was, to quote a famous advocate of linguistic universalism, the English churchman and scientist, John Wilkins (1614–72), for both 'a general Language, as should be equally speakable by all People and Nations' (in Large, 1985). Such a language was also to serve the needs of international scientific communication. There is no doubt too that the very idea of an 'equally speakable' language sprang from 'the empirical conviction that the human mind actually does communicate across linguistic barriers' (Steiner, 1975).

Since the seventeenth century some hundreds of artificial languages have been created, the most famous of which is Esperanto. Interestingly, one such universal language, invented at the end of the eighteenth century, even attracted the attention of businessmen, who wrote letters to the French inventor using him to bring his scheme into full operational use (Large, 1985). This may be the first attested case in history of businessmen being interested in an artificial universal to facilitate commercial communication. Before that of course the businessmen and traders of the world were long accustomed to agreeing to use one language to further regional trade (see Moore and Lewis, 1999 concerning the ancient Mediterranean world; Taylor, 1981 and Wendt, 1963 concerning trade contacts between European settlers and North American Indians).

It is one thing to call for a universal language of commerce, and quite another to call for a universal language of management. The cybernetician, Stafford Beer, who was quoted above, may not have known Descartes' views on the limitation of language, but he was perfectly aware that modern English as a language of management had its shortcomings. In his book *Decision and control* (1966), Beer noted: 'It seems to me high time that management, which is now a profession on which turns the future of every company, every country, and indeed of the world itself, should accept the need for a more advanced language than basic English.' For Beer this advanced language has the characteristics of scientific language. Pinchuk (1977) describes scientific language as follows:

> Scientific language is used in research papers and in the exposition of hypotheses and theories. It is normally very formal in style and its vocabulary is highly standardized. But there is considerable range within this variety and it can be of a high literary standard. Scientific vocabulary includes rigorously defined words and words not usually found in everyday word stock. It avoids emotional associations and seeks transparency.

This does not seem to be the language that Peters and Waterman, Hoecklin, Rosen and no doubt others of similar persuasion have in mind. Not for them a cerebral language, but a complicated awkwardly transcendental language both of action and description, a metaphor, a code for higher shared purpose. It is a language which shapes and is shaped by networking, collaborative learning and knowledge-sharing. In day-to-day business these activities are performed by people who may be attached to one or more culture in the sense described and for a greater or lesser duration (Schneider and Barsoux, 1997). The location of these activities can be somewhere physical or virtual. A high proportion of the work is conducted by teams of specialists drawn, in principle, from any part of the organization. Often such teams are 'diverse'. Their *raison d'être* is to achieve articulate interanimation, a process and an outcome which transcends 'culture' as conventionally understood.

The task of cross-cultural management is to devise, support and implement activities which sustain articulate interanimation for knowledge-sharing. Firms use all manner of techniques to achieve these ends. Novo Nordisk uses Facilitators; LEGO has instituted its millennium meetings; Sulzer Infra uses seminars via its Academy. Matsushita has regular meetings of managers in key regions such as Europe to discuss cross-border cooperation within the company. Around the world there are well over 1,000 corporate universities, many of which are investing considerably in global learning programmes (Deiser, 1998; Meister, 1998; Vine and Palsule, 1999). Organizations are daily creating, changing and experimenting with cross-cultural collectivities. All these activities involve forms of interactive translation to create cross-cultural synergies, new outlooks and behaviours, not to mention new organizational structures. The time has come to consider the implications of these ideas from a knowledge management perspective.

NOTES

1. Eurolengo was the brain-child of Leslie Jones, who published his scheme in his book *Eurolengo, the language for Europe: A practical guide for business and tourism* (Newcastle-upon-Tyne: Oriel Press, 1972). This quotation is not accompanied by a translation into English. Readers are invited to devise their own translation. Those with a knowledge of Spanish would appear to be advantaged.

2. The word 'borderless' features of course in the well-known book by Ohmae, *The borderless world* (1990).

3. Beer (1966) makes this observation on special languages: 'Thought blocks, aided very powerfully by special languages (that is, trade terms and works jargon) prevent our defining a process as anything other than it has always been.'

4. This information was provided by a graduate student of Japanese studies at Copenhagen who is preparing a dissertation on knowledge management in Japan.

5. Connoisseurs of Japan will know that the word 'unique' is meant ironically. For a masterful discussion of the Japanese preoccupation with their specialness, see Dale, (1990).

6. Beer (1966) makes a distinction between formal language and network language. For him, the latter concept is a meta-language, the language for describing relationships within networks. I am not using the term in this sense.

7. There is another formal mode of management language: what Revans (1965) calls the language of the management academy, 'a code of depersonalised abstractions, such as economic theory and network analysis, taught by experts' (quoted in Lessem and Neubauer, 1994). I consider this is to be a form of academic discourse related to, but distinct from, the formal mode of the language of management.

8. Bird, Taylor and Beechler (1999) discuss the 'transferability of learning' – 'the extent to which it can be transmitted to others' – in Japanese overseas affiliates.

9. According to Larkin and Larkin (1994), senior managers spend 80% of their time in direct communication with middle managers when it is necessary to introduce change processes.

REFERENCES

Almaney, A. J. and Alwan, A. J. (1982). *Communicating with the Arabs: A handbook for the business executive.* Prospect Heights, IL: Waveland Press.

Barham, K. and Heimer, C. (1998). *ABB – the dancing giant.* London: Financial Times Prentice Hall.

Beer, S. (1966). *Decision and control: The meaning of operational research and management cybernetics.* Chichester: John Wiley & Sons.

Bird, A., Taylor, S. and Beechler, S. (1999). Organizational learning in Japanese overseas affiliates. In: Beechler, S. and Bird, A. (eds). *Japanese multinationals abroad: Individual and organizational learning.* New York: Oxford University Press, pp. 235–59.

Bloomfield, L. (1979). *Language.* London: George Allen & Unwin.

Cherry, C. (1980). *On human communication: A review, a survey and a criticism.* Cambridge, MA: MIT Press.

Collins, D. (2000). *Management fads and buzzwords.* London: Routledge.

Collins Dictionary of the English language (1990) (ed. P. Hanks). London: Collins.

Dale, P. (1990). *The myth of Japanese uniqueness.* London: Routledge.

Deiser, R. (1998). Corporate Universities – Modeerscheinung oder strategischer Erfolgfaktor? *Organisationsentwicklung* 1: 37–49.

Deresky, H. (2000). *International management: Management across borders and cultures.* Upper Saddle River, NJ: Prentice Hall.

Drucker, P. (1962). *Fortune.* Quoted in Baker, M. J. (1985). *Marketing: An introductory text.* Basingstoke, UK: Macmillan.

Entwistle, W. J. (1974). *The Spanish language.* London: Faber & Faber.

Fallows, J. (1995). *Looking at the sun: The rise of the new East Asian economic and political system.* New York: Vintage Books.

Garton Ash, T. (1997). *The file: A personal history.* London: Flamingo.

Hampden-Turner, C. and Trompenaars, F. (1993). *The seven cultures of capitalism: Value systems for creating wealth in the United States, Britain, Japan, Germany, France, Sweden and the Netherlands.* London: Judy Piatkus.

Hoecklin, L. (1995). *Managing cultural differences: Strategies for competitive advantage.* London: Economist Intelligence Unit/Addison Wesley.

Holden, N. J. (1996). The reorientation of management language in Russia and Poland in the transition to the market economy: A neglected perspective. In: Somers, H. (ed.). *Terminology, LSP and translation: Studies in language engineering in honour of J. C. Sager.* Amsterdam: John Benjamins, pp. 47–65.

Holden, N. J., Cooper, C. L. and Carr, J. (1998). *Dealing with the new Russia: Management cultures in collision.* Chichester, UK: John Wiley & Sons.

Large, A. (1985) *The artificial language movement.* London: Basil Blackwell/André Deutsch.

Larkin, T. J. and Larkin, S. (1994). *Communicating change: How to win employee support for new business directions.* New York: McGraw-Hill. Also cited in: Helder, J. and Pjetursson, L. (1999). *Modtageren som medproducent: Nye tendenser i virksomhedskommunikation.* Copenhagen: Samfundlitteratur.

Leach, E. (1982). *Culture and communication: The logic by which symbols are connected.* Cambridge: Cambridge University Press.

Lessem, R. and Neubauer, F. (1994). *European management systems: Towards unity out of cultural diversity.* London: McGraw-Hill.

Mead, R. (1994). *International management: Cross-cultural dimensions.* Oxford: Blackwell.

Meister, J. C. (1998). *Corporate universities: Lessons in building a world-class workforce.* New York: McGraw-Hill.

Moore, K. and Lewis, D. (1999). *Birth of the multinational: 2000 years of ancient business history from Ashur to Augustus.* Copenhagen: Copenhagen Business School.

Nonaka, I. and Takeuchi, H. (1995). *The knowledge-creating company.* New York: Oxford University Press.

Ohmae, K. (1990). *The borderless world: Power and strategy in the interlinked economy.* London: Collins.

Peters, T. J. and Waterman, R. H. (1982). *In search of excellence: Lessons from America's best-run companies.* New York: Harper & Row.

Pinchuk, I. (1977). *Scientific and technical translation.* London: André Deutsch.

Revans, R. (1965). *Science and the manager.* London: MacDonald.

Rosen, R. (2000). *Global literacies: Lessons on business leaderships and national cultures.* New York: Simon & Schuster.

Sager, J. C. (1993) *Language engineering and translation: Consequences of information.* Amsterdam: John Benjamins.

Sager, J. C., Dungworth, D. and McDonald, P. F. (1980). *English special languages: Principles and practice in science and technology.* Wiesbaden: Oscar Brandstetter Verlag.

Schneider, S. and Barsoux, J.-L. (1997). *Managing across cultures.* London: Prentice Hall.

Senge, P. (1990). *The fifth discipline: The art and practice of the learning organization.* New York: Doubleday.

Steiner, G. (1975). *After Babel: Aspects of language and translation.* London: Oxford University Press.

Taylor, A. R. (1981). Indian lingua francas. In: Ferguson, C. A. and Heath, S. B. (eds). *Language in the USA.* Cambridge: Cambridge University Press, pp. 175–95.

Torrington, D. and Holden, N. J. (1992). Human resource management and the international challenge of change. *Personnel Review* 21(2): 19–30.

Vermeer, H. J. (1992). Translation today: Old and new problems. In: Hornby, M. S., Pöchhacker, F. and Kaindl, K. (eds). *Translation studies: An interdiscipline.* Amsterdam: John Benjamin.

Vine, P. and Palsule, S. (1999). Corporate universities: Back to school. *British Journal of Administrative Management* March/April: 18–21.

Viney, J. (1997). *The culture wars: How American and Japanese businesses have outperformed Europe's and why the future will be different.* London: Capstone.

Waard, J. de and Nida, E. A. (1986). *From one language to another: Functional equivalence in Bible translating.* Nashville/Camden/New York: Thomas Nelson. Also cited in: Vermeer (1992).

Wendt, H. (1963). *It began in Babel: The story of the birth and development of races and peoples.* London: Weidenfeld & Nicolson.

12 The art of translating common knowledge

'Knowledge is of two kinds. We know a subject ourselves, or we know where we can find information upon it.'

Samuel Johnson (1709–84)

'Traditionally evaluation of the translation product is based on text comparison in order to determine degrees of fidelity, accuracy, completeness and felicity.'

Juan Sager, *Language engineering and translation* (1994)

OBJECTIVES

- Develops the link between translation in the formal sense (i.e. between languages) and the cross-cultural transfer of knowledge.
- Characterizes the cross-cultural knowledge-sharing activities of the four informant companies.
- Distinguishes and specifies three modes of cultural knowledge.
- Discusses the transferability of knowledge in relation to three aspects of translation: ambiguity, interference and equivalence.
- Proposes that organizational atmosphere is crucial for the transfer and diffusion of cross-cultural knowledge.
- Uses various models to portray the interplay of processes such as the creation of atmosphere and interactive translation.

INTRODUCTION

The last chapter developed the notion of cross-cultural management as a form of interactive translation. A key idea was that cross-cultural management facilitates the translation of common knowledge. This approach not only supplies for scholars of cross-cultural management a new, fertile analogy and conceptual basis for investigating the field, but it provides a valuable point of departure for gaining insights into the international *pace* cross-cultural transfer. The task of this chapter is to explore the notion of international knowledge transfer as a form of cross-cultural translation. The first section will make reference to authors who have already noted that knowledge transfer is a form of translation. Then the cross-cultural management experiences of the four informant companies will be analyzed from a knowledge management perspective. This will lead to a general discussion about the practical and theoretical problems of international transfer of knowledge. For convenience the word 'knowledge' will be used in this chapter to cover organizational knowledge, know-how such as best practices, and professional experience, unless it is necessary to make clear distinctions among these categories.

TRANSFER AND TRANSLATION

With reference to the skills enhancement of expatriate executives for assignments in other countries, Hurn (1996) describes the process as follows: 'Essentially the process involves "translating" one's knowledge from one's own cultural context to the context of the host culture and the personal framework of the counterparts and local workforce.' But more revealing is the fact that the knowledge management literature occasionally refers to the process of transferring knowledge as a kind of translation. Dixon, a leading writer in the field, notes that as a result of the knowledge transfer process 'knowledge is translated into a form usable by others' (Dixon, 2000). For his part, Garvin (1998) suggests that firms that are most advanced in organizational learning are those which 'become adept at translating new knowledge into new ways of behaving'. It is perfectly evident that these authors are not using the term *translate* to mean something rather more than mere transfer. Both Dixon and Garvin are surely referring to what Nonaka and Takeuchi (1995) call 'knowledge conversion': the rendering or re-expression of knowledge such as skills in one form (i.e. tacit) into another (i.e. explicit) through a process of socialization which is 'a process of sharing experiences' (Nonaka and Takeuchi, 1995).

In the kind of cross-cultural context which have been described in this book, 'translation' is a very useful word to use to explain the cross-cultural knowledge conversion. In the transfer of knowledge, the quest must always be to find 'common cognitive ground' (Nonaka, 1991) among knowledge-sharers. It is obvious that finding this common cognitive ground can be more demanding, more subject to 'heightened miscommunication and misunderstandings' (Schoenberg, 1999), when its creators and users form a multicultural group, whose members do not share a common language – figuratively and literally – with equal facility in knowledge-sharing contexts.

The value of describing cross-cultural knowledge transfer processes as a form of translation is not just a handy analogy or metaphor for highlighting and analyzing aspects of knowledge conversion and transfer; the fact is that in knowledge-sharing contexts real acts of translation *are* taking place among participants. An aim of this chapter will be to use some concepts from translation theory to highlight constraints on the international transfer of knowledge.

As was noted in chapter 11, we can regard the international transfer of knowledge as a form of cross-cultural translation, but we should also note that cross-cultural know-how, in its own right, is an inalienable element in any transfer process that involves human beings in interaction. In this context, international knowledge transfer may be regarded as the process of translating any knowledge from any source of common knowledge into a common language or code for dissemination and possible application throughout an organization's internal and external networks. The translation may be received cognitively in the form of an updating of existing knowledge or modification of outlook. But the knowledge may also be converted into new behaviours and actions.

To continue the discussion of common knowledge from the last chapter, we may say that it corresponds roughly to the well-known description of culture 'as the way we do things around here' (Deal and Kennedy, 1982) – that 'awful definition', as Collins (2000) rightly points out. But in this book it has a rather more precise designation, which is consistent with the characterization of Dixon (2000), for whom common knowledge is 'only one of the many possible types of knowledge that reside in an organization: the knowledge that employees learn from doing the organization's tasks'. She goes on:

> I call this kind of knowledge 'common knowledge' to differentiate it from book knowledge or firm lists of regulations or databases of customer information. Some examples of common knowledge are what an organization has learned about how to introduce a new drug into the diabetes market, how to increase refinery reliability, how to reduce materials cost on capital projects, and how to control the amount of pitch in wood pulp.

Dixon is at pains to stress that in the world of organizations common knowledge is more or less synonymous with know-how 'rather than the "know what" of school learning. Moreover, it is known how that is unique to a specific company.' This is acceptable, but it is important to emphasize that common knowledge is sometimes only unique to a specific company in so far as it is available at a given location within the corporation itself. This does not mean that such knowledge is common to the entire company. In a TNC this knowledge is globally scattered, awkwardly local. As the case studies have shown, a key challenge is to leverage *localized* common knowledge peculiar to other parts within the same company often in another country. There can be many barriers inhibiting this process, as we shall discuss below.

One more important point needs to be made about the knowledge-leveraging processes which the case studies have highlighted and which are about to be analyzed. The point concerns the distinction between physical space and virtual space in the knowledge management processes. The case studies provided several examples of the two modes. Novo Nordisk facilitations and the seminars of the Sulzer Infra Academy are clear examples of knowledge management in physical space in the sense that both take place in locations of human interaction. But all four companies were also engaged in knowledge management in virtual space, that is 'by use of telephone, e-mail, teleconferencing, computer-based collaborative tools, newsgroups, e-learning, databases and on-line communities of practice [so that] employees can . . . interact in a fast and seamless fashion between distant locations' (Rasmussen, 2000).

In the analysis which follows, this distinction between physical and virtual space will not be observed, as the research design never envisaged the investigation making use of it. But what the anlysis will eventually make clear is that what Nonaka (1998) called 'common cognitive ground' appears to be more difficult to attain when that knowledge is to be dispersed among locations that are not just 'distant physically, but also "distant" culturally, economically, technologically, and so on' (Doz and Santos, 1997). Distance in this psychological or psychic sense has been defined as 'factors preventing or disturbing the flows of information between firms and markets. Factors include differences in language, culture, education levels, political systems, etc.' (Turnbull, 1990). It is of crucial importance to emphasize that this form of distance is not constant, but varies according to context, the personalities and competencies of persons in interaction, organizational strategy, openness to innovative impulses, and so forth.

THE TRANSLATION OF CROSS-CULTURAL MANAGEMENT KNOWLEDGE IN THE FOUR INFORMANT COMPANIES

Novo Nordisk

In the case of Novo Nordisk, the knowledge management activities must be seen in relation to a company quest to improve the transfer of best practices, whilst adhering to the Novo Nordisk Way of Management, which emphasizes localization and empowerment. As noted earlier, these activities are characterized as:

- Absorbing and documenting 'new' knowledge about the company from the point of view of units, each with a different embedding in three interacting levels of culture: national, corporate and professional

- Adapting personal behaviour and communication styles to suit local conditions

- Sharing 'facilitation know-how' with other Facilitators

- Prioritizing acquired knowledge

- Converting knowledge into suitable formats for transfer to potential beneficiaries in the company

- Combining their existing professional knowledge with that of other Facilitators in duos or on a group basis

The main task of the Facilitators is to act as change agents by ensuring conformity with the Novo Nordisk Way of Management and other company policies, and identifying examples of best practice which might only be known in specific units, but which could be of benefit in other areas of the company. This approach raises a very interesting point from the knowledge management perspective. The Facilitators obtain information about best practices and valuable experiences not by probing for them, but by using the facilitation more as an *indirect* mechanism for releasing this knowledge. In other words, the facilitation approach tends to prevent them from assuming in advance what knowledge may be lying in wait for them.

The fact, too, that Facilitators work in duos is significant. It widens the knowledge catchment horizon. First of all, no two Facilitators have the same professional or organizational background. Second, a very high proportion of duos involve persons from different parts of the world who have their own particular international experiences with the company. As a system for capturing what might be called rich, 'soft' knowledge and releasing it via the company headquarters in Denmark, the Facilitator concept seems to be without peer. By the expression 'soft' knowledge, I mean rather more than tacit knowledge. I use the 'soft' to refer to knowledge that is easily elusive, that must be understood in its context of origination, and that needs delicate handling. It is knowledge whose softness must be appreciated by its receivers or users. Otherwise it will decompose.

Matsushita

Matsushita is one of the world's biggest companies. Every single day knowledge, experience and values are moving around the company. The case study did not explicitly study those processes, but it is nevertheless possible to make some observations about how the company manages what might be called its 'in-company knowledge relationships'.

The case study, it will be recalled, was presented as a learning history. The kind of knowledge it generated has various applications. It can serve as a basis in its own right to supplement existing knowledge on (a) Japan, (b) Konosuke Matsushita, or (c) the Matsushita Corporation. The knowledge can, in principle, be used by the company itself for improving knowledge-sharing and driving *genuine* localization forward. It can be used to qualify the well-known case study of Nonaka and Takeuchi (1995) about the Matsushita daughter company which developed a new bread-making machine. These authors suggest that the development of this device was in no small way attributable to the company's ability to create and share knowledge. In contrast to that, the case study suggests that the entire corporation as a globalized entity has problems with knowledge management when its non-Japanese employees are involved in knowledge generation and knowledge-sharing.

Owing to limited knowledge-sharing between the two classes of employees, the current style of knowledge management as a worldwide activity at Matsushita can be characterized as:

- Stimulating substantial redundancies in knowledge production

- Concentrating a disproportionate amount of knowledge for decision-making in Japanese hands

- Inconsistent success in securing best practice from outside Japan because best practice is held only to emanate from the place of origin of the Matsushita philosophy and value system, that is Japan itself

When the company began to internationalize in the early 1950s, its entrenched ethnocentrism served it well; and even more so in the 1970s and 1980s, when Japanese companies like Matsushita presented to the rest of the world a dazzling montage of management mystique, innovative products (especially in consumer electronics), and ambition to win the rest of the world's admiration for Japanese achievement. Whilst its arch-rival Sony, already a company far more internationalized than Matsushita in outlook, is reinventing itself for the 'network-centric society of the 21st century' (Oshika, 1999), it seems that Matsushita is still struggling with its entrenched ethnocentrism. The dilemma for the company (and I understand that this is now under active debate in the company) is how to reinvent itself without seeming to disregard the precepts and philosophy of the legendary company founder.

As was stressed in the case study, the Matsushita Corporation is unusual even by Japanese standards, but from the point of view of knowledge management as an international activity ethnocentrism is the warning light. This raises a further general point that firms that are not in any case skilled in managing diversity may also be disadvantaged when it comes to practising international knowledge management. There are those who claim that European firms are better at handling diversity than US and Japanese firms precisely because Europeans have greater collective experience of operating in culturally and linguistically heterogeneous contexts (Rosenzweig, 1988; Viney, 1997).[1] Against that, it should not be overlooked that Matsushita comes from a country with a centuries-long history not only of acquiring knowledge from abroad, but also of institutional learning (Lorriman and Kenjo, 1994; Sansom, 1977; Westney, 1999). The challenge now is not to acquire it for internal assimilation, but for its redistribution through the entire worldwide organization to stimulate collaborative knowledge-sharing and learning.

LEGO

Transfer of knowledge with the companies making up the LEGO Group is driven by a commitment to make LEGO the world's most familiar brand name to families by 2005. Of all the four companies studied in this book, only LEGO focused knowledge transfer on such a clear-cut commercial target. Its practices are strongly related to LEGO's style of management of cross-cultural interfaces, as noted in chapter 8:

- The company's overall style of management is, in a national-cultural sense, neutral

- The identity and values of the company, through its powerful brand image and respect for children, transcends cross-cultural differences

- The headquarters of the company, which has a very strong contingent of Danish managers, is open to influences from subsidiary companies outside Denmark and is deliberately encouraging the establishment of mixed Danish/non-Danish work groups

As was noted in the case study, LEGO – for its self-marketing as an international company – has only in the last few years been genuinely open to foreign ideas. The opening up of LEGO Media International in 1996 was plainly decisive. Once it recognized the value of cross-cultural collaborative learning, LEGO made some valuable discoveries: first, the UK software developers found inspiration in the LEGO's design practices for conventional toys; second, the UK team found it straightforward to accept that socially undesirable software games were out of court; and, third, the collaboration led to the introduction of a new concept: fun. Of the four case studies, the LEGO experience provides the best and clearest examples of cross-cultural collaborative learning as a positive influence on product development.

Now the company's learning and knowledge management activities are predicated on the notion of 'shared mental space', whereby the firm aims to reduce psychic barriers to the transfer of knowledge on a cross-cultural basis. We suggested that the LEGO style of not imposing Danish management values was a notable feature of this approach. Overall, the in-company networking and learning is intensive and is face-to-face as much as possible. However, the interactions between LEGO headquarters and the LEGO Lab San Mateo in California were strongly supported by various forms of technological facilitation, owing to the time difference between the two centres.

Sulzer Infra

The Sulzer Infra case study has focused overwhelmingly on one activity, which has been especially designed for releasing cross-border knowledge transfer and mutual learning: the seminar. But it should be emphasized that the following comments about knowledge management focus on the seminar and may not reflect practice throughout the company at large.

The concept of the Sulzer Infra Academy and the experiences of the UK managers reinforce the more or less accepted conviction that knowledge, as the possession of individuals, tends to be more easily leveraged in scenarios which encourage occasionally intense interaction. As was noted by one of the UK informants, the seminars are deliberately emotive. After all in a seminar of 100 people, perhaps each individual knows only 20% of the other participants. A seminar is an event to convert strangers into contacts, into new linkages and nodes in personal in-company networks throughout Europe. The short-term evidence is that it works.

One of the most important findings of this case study related to the experience of the UK manager, who felt he missed out because he was unable to struggle in a foreign language. This emotional rather than intellectual reaction suggests that interpersonal knowledge transfer, and perhaps especially in cross-cultural scenarios such as the seminars, needs a conducive atmosphere. As already stated, the seminar was planned to some extent as an emotional experience, but how individuals themselves interacted could not be controlled, and yet the emotion was plainly a crucial element of the entire experience. Perhaps the most important thing about the Sulzer Infra seminars is that they, in a sense, try to be a kind of rehearsal for subsequent cross-cultural business interactions involving people in in-company teams and at interfaces with clients.

What the Sulzer Infra makes clear, and the Novo Nordisk experience bears out this point, is that it is very difficult to separate the act of transferring knowledge from the cross-cultural know-how needed to effect that. This has importance consequences for the transferability of knowledge and needs to be built into any model of international knowledge transfer in which there is human interaction. Lastly, we should not forget that CBX, the British subsidiary of Sulzer Infra, is a relative newcomer to the group, and it was plainly not well integrated. This suggests that in-company knowledge-sharing may be hard to achieve in cases where a new subsidiary or other new entity within an internationally dispersed group has not fully absorbed the general way of company thinking and the logic behind it.

CROSS-CULTURAL KNOWLEDGE MANAGEMENT: STICKINESS AND ABSORPTIVE CAPACITY

Now that the cross-cultural knowledge management activities of the four informant companies have been discussed, it is feasible to draw some general implications. In this section we return to the concepts of stickiness and absorptive capacity, which were introduced in chapter 4. Stickiness refers to the problems of detaching knowledge from its context and transferring it so that it does not lose its essential properties. Stickiness is the equivalent to what gets lost in the translation. Absorptive capacity affects how easily the recipient can understand knowledge. It is generally accepted that existing knowledge of a particular knowledge domain or subject area promotes absorptive capacity. We are now in a position to compare the data on knowledge transfer behaviour of the four informant companies and note the factors which constrain or facilitate knowledge transfer.

Stickiness

The knowledge management literature is replete with examples of stickiness. Davenport and Prusak (1998) cited these constraints as: lack of trust; different cultures, vocabularies, frames of reference; lack of time and meeting places; knowledge owners as the prime beneficiaries of status and rewards; lack of absorptive capacity in recipients; belief that knowledge is a prerogative of particular groups – the not-invented-here syndrome; intolerance for mistakes or need for help. In their totality, the case studies all produced examples of these factors. Sometimes, of course, the stickiness was built into the company system. Sometimes it was created in the process of detaching the knowledge from its context. Sometimes it occurred in the transfer process proper. The following sticky factors emerge from the experiences recorded in the case studies:

- Ethnocentrism (Matsushita and, in the recent past, LEGO)

- Language problems (Matsushita and the competing roles of English and Japanese; Sulzer Infra and the slightly competing roles of German and English)

- Vagueness surrounding identification of objectives and related procedures for implementation (Matsushita on globalization and localization)

- Lack of a unitary language or discourse (Matsushita and, to a lesser extent, Sulzer Infra)

- Its identification with a dominant national group that was out of touch with local thinking and attitudes (Matsushita and, to a lesser extent, LEGO)

- The perceived limited relevance of the company philosophy to business conditions (Matsushita)

- The establishment of a company institution (such as a corporate university) to combat stickiness may reveal other forms of stickiness (Sulzer Infra and the problem of integrating new subsidiaries into the company way of thinking)

These factors may be intensified negatively if there is:

- A belief that headquarters does not understand local feelings and thinking

- A lack of HQ interest in learning from local units

Absorptive capacity

Absorptive capacity is the other side of the coin. For people interested in developing concepts for good practice in the international transfer of knowledge. The following factors emerged as facilitating absorptive capacity.

251

- Cross-cultural learning has a greater chance of succeeding when the nominally national senior group in knowledge exchanges is not too concerned about imposing its values and thinking on others

- Top management must be competent in the English language

- Cross-cultural learning must stimulate new knowledge, i.e. the kind of knowledge that is unlikely to be generated from corporate headquarters

- There needs to be a sharp focus on the key knowledge to be transferred

- There needs to be visible top management commitment

- There needs to be substantial investment and a long-term commitment harnessed to the company vision and the reality of business conditions

- Initiatives must be developed that bring together persons of different cultural (ethnic), linguistic and professional backgrounds for mutual learning and knowledge-sharing

- A common ground for networking must be created

- A special task force (such as the Novo Nordisk Facilitators or the Sulzer Infra Academy) must be established to harmonize initiatives and serve as a channel for (re-)distributing knowledge

- Knowledge transfer must be linked to collaborative cross-cultural learning

- A clear-cut policy must be driven from the centre

- There needs to be respect for top management

- There needs to be a commitment to organizational learning and the sharing of knowledge and best practices

- Structures to facilitate networking across borders, and regardless of hierarchy, must be promoted

- There needs to be an ability to handle multicultural groups

This list is long and ungainly. The factors cover a range of issues: attitudes, organizational structures, a willingness to experiment, the role of top management, an ability to manage multicultural teams. Many of the factors are plainly common sense: the essence of good management. But we need more than lists to understand processes. In addition to the categories of stickiness and absorptive capacity, knowledge management experts are inclined to make a distinction between knowledge which is tacit and knowledge which is explicit. We now have a wealth of information that has been generated by the case studies and their subsequent analysis of the firms' behaviour from first a cross-cultural perspective and then a knowledge management perspective. Although it would be possible to classify the types of knowledge for nominal purposes into the tacit and explicit categories, it is not certain how useful this would be.

What is important about the lists of factors according to stickiness and absorptive capacity is what they reveal about the problem of creating that common cognitive ground within globally dispersed companies. There is every reason to hypothesize that there exist specific correlations between degrees of absorptive capacity and distance framed in psychological (or psychic) and possibly technological terms: in other words, the greater the distance, the smaller potentially the absorptive capacity.

The most clear-cut example of the former 'truth' is the case of Matsushita, in which the Japanese dominance, duality of discourse, and the conservatism of the company philosophy and other company-specific and Japan-specific factors all conspire to inhibit the transfer and translation of knowledge. By contrast, the experience of Novo Nordisk suggests that, if a firm actively seeks to reduce distance, it appears to promote absorptive capacity. As noted above, distance is not a constant, but an amalgam of ever-changing influences that are both internal and external to organizations. These various notions are presented in Figure 12.1, which presents distance and absorptive capacity in relation to ease and difficulty of knowledge-sharing.

It has to be borne in mind that the knowledge presented and discussed in the case studies and subsequently has in one way and another been culturally influenced at the point of origination and then subjected to a cross-cultural

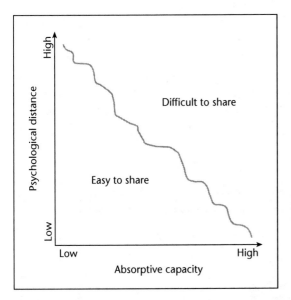

Fig. 12.1 **Absorptive capacity and distance in relationship to knowledge-sharing**[2]

transfer process – and every single scrap of knowledge has reached you via *my* head. Spectres of epistemology and validity now come into the frame. In order to short-circuit an epistemological discussion, about which there can in the end be no final conclusion, I propose in the following section to introduce a tripartite division of cultural knowledge. In the meantime I remind the reader of the truth of the quotation of Dr Johnson which heads this chapter: it all depends on what we know rather than on whether what we do not know is in tacit or explicit form.

THREE DOMAINS OF CULTURAL KNOWLEDGE

The time has come to attempt to specify cultural knowledge, which as been defined by Phillips (1996) as follows:

> A set of assumptions shared by a group of people. The set is distinctive to the group. The assumptions serve as guides to acceptable perception, thought, feeling, and behavior, and they are manifested in the groups' values, norms, and artifacts. The assumptions are tacit among members, are developed through and evolve, and are learned and passed on to each new member of the group.

This definition is an elaboration of the famous Kroeber and Kluckhohn definition (see chapter 2) with a twist of knowledge management. Its essentialist nature is not helpful. The retrospective proof lies in the fact that the assumptions guiding the definition would not have teased out the rich information, just highlighted, on the four cross-cultural management behaviours from a knowledge management perspective. To break away – again! – from the essentialist straitjacket, I am going to propose a tripartite classification, but emphasize at the outset that the categories should by no means be seen as hermetic. They overlap and complement each other. The classification is as follows: general cultural knowledge, culture-specific knowledge and cross-cultural *know-how*. The distinction between knowledge and know-how is, as we shall see, important. Figure 12.2 below suggests that general cultural knowledge and specific cultural knowledge are passive, but both domains, which overlap in pragmatic space, are converted into active – implementational – know-how when two cultures interact.

General cultural knowledge:

- Refers to freely available knowledge about cultures

- Is explicit and is already available in online or printed reference sources such the world wide web, encyclopædias, country surveys in newspapers, and so forth

- Can be formally classified

- Can be 'thick'

- Is objective in the general sense of the word

- Can also be of the periodic table variety (see chapter 3)

In alternative terminology, this knowledge can be expressed in the descriptor mode of language (chapter 11). But, as an example will presently reveal, knowledge which belongs to the general cultural variety may need to be explained with reference to knowledge outside the nominal domain.

Specific cultural knowledge:

- Is that which is peculiar to a given source of common knowledge

- Is subjective in the sense that it is selected for relevance to the firms' operations

- Has variable potential according to the purposes to which it is put

- Can be 'thick', but may lose vital properties (such as insights) in 'thin' representation

- Can be tacit and explicit according to the convention, but perhaps more crucial is the degree of relevant pre-existing knowledge on the part of those who gather it and interpret it

Examples which have appeared in this book include: Japanese automotive production know-how; the legacy of Konosuke Matsushita on the business empire bearing his name; the European construction market; the LEGO identity; a seminar organized by the Sulzer Infra Academy; the nature of *guanxi* in Chinese social and business interactions; and Russia's complicated anti-Westernism.

Although specific knowledge is in public sources, including the Internet, its key property from our point of view is that it has specific, but variable relevance for a company and its objectives. This class of knowledge is often used by experts for specialist tasks such as creating a marketing plan, creating a report on a business sector, or evaluating technical information. The general cultural knowledge is the embedding for the specific cultural knowledge. In the case studies, the Matsushita philosophy (specific cultural knowledge) was presented in the wider context of Japan's twentieth-century history (general cultural knowledge). In practice, it is difficult to separate these two kinds of cultural knowledge, as examples below will demonstrate, but the distinction between the two forms of cultural knowledge and cross-cultural know-how is crucial. Figure 12.2 tries to capture this distinction graphically.

Cross-cultural know-how:

- Is practical knowledge applied in cross-cultural interactions and continually updated with experience

- May be derived from the two other kinds of cultural knowledge, but this kind of know-how is often subjective and experiential, often having a very high tacit content

- Is knowledge that is passed from head to head

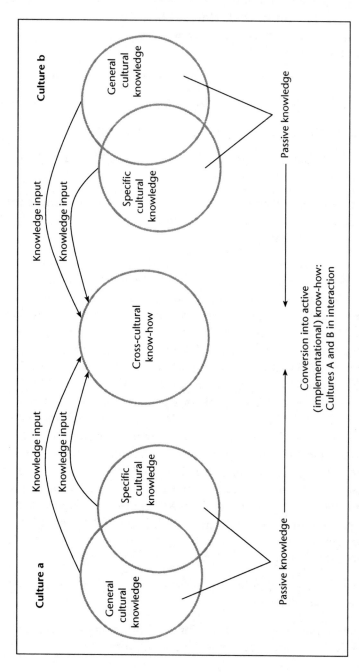

Fig. 12.2 Three domains of cultural knowledge: interdependence and distinction

- Facilitates interaction, informs participative competence and stimulates cross-cultural collaborative learning

In the case studies, cross-cultural know-how is the knowledge that Daimler lacked (and may now have acquired) in its dealings with Chrysler managers when the German company took over the American concern. Cross-cultural know-how is an amalgam of knowledge and knowing, knowing being the extra knowledge that is needed to make the knowledge useful in applications. It is, in a sense, knowledge in action (Rasmussen, 2000). Taken together, all three forms of cultural knowledge can be used as an organizational resource. It is a form of knowledge that is articulated in the mode of management language characterized as network facilitator (chapter 13).

In Figure 12.2 cross-cultural know-how is represented as a pivot between two business cultures which are in fact each subsets of cultures A and B. Both general cultural knowledge and specific cultural knowledge (both forms of knowledge are passive) are converted into active, implementational know-how in order to execute effective cross-cultural interaction. The knowledge associated with general culture and specific culture is a form of potential: it is the wire without the electricity going through it. Cross-cultural know-how is created when this potential, *coming from both cultures simultaneously*, is converted into implementational form (e.g. 'extra' competencies needed for handling negotiations in China or integrating personnel in a merger). If the resulting know-how is well used, it is a resource which can become an organization's core competence (see chapter 13).

Figure 12.3 captures the tripartite division of cultural knowledge, showing three facets of the knowledge in terms of transferability: its relative explicitness and tacitness; the degree to which technological and human intervention is used to capture and apply the knowledge; and the degree to which the knowledge is *mappable*. By transferability I mean both the act of transfer by human or technical means as well as its perceived relevance and actual apprehensibility at the receiving end. Mappability may be seen as a measure (or test) of the possibility to model a specific knowledge transfer process: to reduce complexity to its essential significant components for explanatory and predictive purposes. Maps, everything from production flow diagrams to organization charts, are used by knowledge management workers (Davenport and Prusak, 1998), but they also create their own maps and models which attempt to capture the objective reality of knowledge flows.

The mapping of intra- and inter-organizational cross-cultural behaviour *as knowledge* is very difficult, as it needs the cooperation of two kinds of domain expert who professionally seldom, if ever, meet: specialists of culture and knowledge workers. But the practice should be strongly encouraged, not least within firms contemplating mergers or acquisitions, in which one of the main

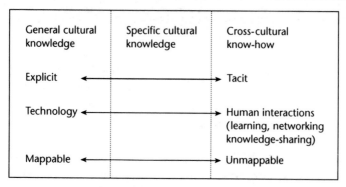

Fig. 12.3 Tripartite division of cultural knowledge with respect to transferability of knowledge

tasks to is create a giant new pool of common knowledge. (Do companies see it that way?) The mapping of such a pool of common knowledge might persuade firms to drop their seemingly disastrous love affair with cultural fit – 'one of the "black holes" in cross-border mergers that often accounts for expectations not being met', and carefully avoided by companies such as the Swiss–Swedish electrical engineering giant, ABB (Barham and Heimer, 1998).

Figure 12.3 is itself a kind of map. It has no sophisticated pretensions, but the notion of mappability may be worth exploring, if only because mappability is a kind of measure of clarity of understanding of a situation or challenge. To grasp the significance of what this model is trying to say, it is important to appreciate that it is impossible to make an absolutely clear-cut distinction between tacit knowledge and explicit knowledge, so the model does not indicate a point where the one mode becomes the other. The degree of tacitness, for example, is determined by factors such as previous knowledge and experience of the three domains, the purpose for which the knowledge might be valuable, or its transferability to potential users.

A simple example concerns culturally specific explicit knowledge which is more or less incomprehensible to outsiders to the culture. Consider the case of information contained in 'a text in a strange language [which] sets up an abrupt change in our experience, a discontinuity, and we can make nothing of it' (Cherry, 1980). The text might be an article or report in German or Japanese from which non-readers of those languages are excluded. We may say that the form of the text in a foreign language is arcane, but its content is explicit. It is as a document even transferable. For its potential to be assessed, the document needs *convertibility*. Convertibility is not solely a property of the text in terms of ease of translation. It also refers to its perceived utility and the availability of domain experts (of whom one would be a translator) to reveal its import to the final user. It is not the act of translation alone that makes tacit knowledge become explicit: it is the wider conversion into users' existing knowledge domains.

Here is a hypothetical example which shows up the limitations of rigidly compartmentalizing general cultural knowledge from the specific variety. Let us suppose that we are gathering information on a country in the Arab world. We know that Islam plays a vastly significant role not only in general social life, but also in all business interactions in that country. The knowledge of the core fact is explicit, but when we learn that Islam is 'a universal doctrine designed to perfect Christianity and Judaism' (Almaney and Alwan, 1982), we need more specialist knowledge. The ramifications are a closed book until explained by a domain expert. Similarly, it is virtually common knowledge in the corporate world that Japanese business activity is predicated on relationships, but the logic behind the system can be highly baffling for foreign business people (Beechler and Bird, 1999; Fallows, 1995; Gerlach, 1992). Again, the general knowledge needs explanation by a domain expert.

Another way of throwing light on this state of affairs is by making use of Schein's model of the typology of culture into three levels, which was introduced in chapter 1. The three levels of artifacts, values and assumptions represent various degrees of embeddedness, transferability and convertibility. Figure 12.4 juxtaposes these three levels of culture against general cultural knowledge and specific cultural knowledge. Presently, examples will be given of knowledge at each level and in the two modes with respect to Japan.

Why is cross-cultural know-how not part of the model? The answer is that general cultural knowledge and specific cultural knowledge are considered to be externally derived. They come into the organization with various understandings and perceptions of the associated artifacts, values and assumptions. Cross-cultural know-how is primarily internally created expertise for collaborative learning, networking and knowledge-sharing. This kind of know-how is nominally tacit. When it becomes institutionalized know-how, then it becomes knowledge informed with company-specific artifacts, values and assumptions.

General cultural knowledge	Artifacts (visible but often undecipherable)	Various degrees of embeddedness, transferability and convertibility
	Values (greater level of awareness)	
	Assumptions (taken for granted)	
Specific cultural knowledge	Artifacts	
	Values	
	Assumptions	

Fig. 12.4 General cultural knowledge and specific cultural knowledge *vis-à-vis* Schein's levels of culture

This, of course, is the process that Nonaka and Takeuchi (1995) described (see chapter 4). Know-how, which reflects a company-specific capability and which cannot be readily imitated or substituted, can then be seen as a core competence. The link between cross-cultural know-how and core competence will be explored further in chapter 13.

As emphasized above, this tripartite classification of two forms of cultural knowledge and know-how has its limitations. In operational practice they are fused, complementing and augmenting each other. But the value of Figure 12.4 is that it permits a potentially useful classification of organizational cultural knowledge into six distinct classes: this is plainly more satisfactory than ascribing this knowledge to tacit and explicit categories.

To conclude this section, I will attempt to show the difference between general cultural knowledge and specific cultural knowledge. Japan will be used as the point of reference for the former; the Matsushita Corporation for the latter. The raw information is presented in Figure 12.5. Brief explanations of the identified factor of each level are provided. It will be noted that the artifacts depend on explanations being supported by information from the deeper levels. It goes without saying that the features about the Matsushita Corporation cannot be fully grasped without reference to general cultural knowledge of Japan.

	Level of culture	Related phenomena
General cultural knowledge JAPAN	Artifacts	Customer
	Values	Education
	Assumptions	Obligation
Specific cultural knowledge MATSUSHITA CORPORATION	Artifacts	*Meishi* (business card)
	Values	Matsushita values
	Assumptions	Univeral applicability of K. Matsushita's business philosophy

Fig. 12.5   Japan and the Matsushita Corporation: three examples of general cultural knowledge and specific cultural knowledge

JAPAN: THREE EXAMPLES OF GENERAL CULTURAL KNOWLEDGE

Customer

It is well-known in Japan that 'the customer is god' ('O-kyaku-sama wa kami-sama desu'). Its adulatory tone immediately suggests that this famous aphorism does not correlate culturally with the Western maxim 'the customer is king'. Many Western writers on doing business in Japan are quick to latch on to this divine status in a bid to remind foreign firms that Japanese customers expect the highest possible levels of service and attention. But the most telling part of the Japanese expression centres on the meaning of the word 'customer'. In Japanese the word is 'O-kyaku-sama'. The semantic essence is in 'kyaku' whose generic meaning is, not customer, but *guest*. In other words, customer has a meaning derived from guest. The particles *o-* and *sama* are both honorific forms. The first is usually translated into English, somewhat awkwardly, as 'honourable'. The second particle is a very polite form, virtually impossible to translate by a single word, but it has the flavour of 'much respected one(s)' or perhaps 'most gracious one(s)'.

This incursion into Japanese linguistics is important, for now we know that customers are not only divine in Japan but also that their patronage does great honour to a purveyor of goods and services. This patronage does not necessarily imply that customers have to buy anything; their mere presence on the premises of the establishment concerned is sufficient to accord them shimmering courtesies and respectful bows – even if in the end they decline to purchase anything. From this we may deduce that how customers or 'honourable guests' are addressed is of extreme importance to any kind of shop, service organization or company. The practice, of course, goes to the centre of Japanese social organization and the centuries-long preference for harmonious interaction, entailing manifestations of respect for one's elders and betters, and a readiness to be of service to anyone where socially appropriate (an important qualification) (Holden and Burgess, 1994).

Education

Education has enormous importance in Japan (Beauchamp and Vardaman, 1994; Lorriman and Kenjo, 1994). One of its main purposes is to cultivate young people for harmonious interaction with all other (Japanese) people. The Japanese, an eminently teachable nation, acquire this all-important social skill, but it might be argued at a high cost to Japan. Other aspects of the education system emphasize rote learning: reflection and constructive criticism are not encouraged. The result was a marvellous workforce for Japan in the electric 1970s and 1980s (Jackson, 1993). Since the 1990s Japan needs creative people. Japan's ultra-conservative Ministry of Education has never been geared for that. It is said, incidentally, that in Japanese schools children reading the standard school textbook for a given subject will turn over the same page at exactly the same time!

Obligation

One of the sources of all social and economic action in Japan is the all-pervasive sense of obligation, which underpins all relationships. Obligated relationships are at the heart of Japanese business organization and concepts of corporate governance.

Whilst there may be exceptions to prove the rule, one may say that firms in Japan will do business with each other even though for one party it may not be economically advantageous. If it is a pre-existing relationship and the one company has been a regular customer or has supplied technological expertise over many years, then the other must fulfil its obligations.

The webs of relationships that keep the system working cut across every aspect of Japanese life to the extent that the distinction between business life and 'non-business' life becomes very blurred, if not non-existent. If in most Western economies the market is seen as the great mechanism for economic activity, in Japan the mechanism is created through a mind-boggling interplay of obligated interpersonal ties and inter-organizational alliances, in which human relations (*ningen kankei*) reign supreme (Gerlach, 1992). For operation in this kind of society the Japanese need social negotiation skills of an exceptionally high order, and these become business negotiating skills of an equally high order.

MATSUSHITA: THREE EXAMPLES OF SPECIFIC CULTURAL KNOWLEDGE

Business cards

The Japanese business card (Jap. *meishi*, lit. 'name-card') has been well described as 'the most ubiquitous of Japanese accessories' (Seidensticker, 1983). It is a fine example of an artifact behind which stand all manner of subtleties and assumptions. The *meishi* plays a key role in introductions. In major Japanese corporations young recruits will receive instruction in how to present their own business cards and receive them from others. Such instruction involves guidance on bowing (depth and duration) and accompanying polite language, which can be ratcheted up or down to suit the importance of the occasion and of the other party. When a Japanese presents his business card, he recommends both himself and his company, of whom he is a walking symbol. You will never see a Matsushita employee exchange his business card with anyone in a casual manner.[3] Nor, incidentally, will a Matsushita employee – at least in Japan – receive his or her *meishi* and lapel badge until the successful completion of the company's induction course.

Matsushita values

The Matsushita values that were shaped some 70 years ago are an extraordinary blend of traditional Japanese values, business pragmatism and an equally extraordinary personal vision. Even today, the values of the company have remained uncontested. They are virtually holy writ. The Japanese employees are not encouraged to challenge the values. Rather, they are inclined to accept them as suitable guidelines on company thinking and behaviour. For them, the Matsushita values ensure conformity and continuity; they are the basis of the common language throughout the company's operations in Japan. Do not forget that conformity is not a dirty word in Japan. It is the *sine qua non* of group spirit and this spirit can triumph over all the odds.

The Matsushita values, which directly and indirectly influence the lives of nearly 300,000 employees worldwide and conditions its relationships with thousands of customers, suppliers and other stakeholders, are the rock upon which the company stands. Despite the fact that several commentators have noted the very conservative nature of the Matsushita Corporation, it has long been among the 30 largest companies in the world; its products, under the main Panasonic and Technics brands, are universally known; and about half its total workforce is non-Japanese. In this respect internal resistance to change from the very top of the company is understandable.

Universal applicability of K. Matsushita's business philosophy

Konsuke Matsushita's management values are also the basis of a business philosophy which took shape in the early 1930s, well before the company had business involvements outside Japan. The post-war transformation of the Matsushita Corporation from a national company to an international one – or even a global one – can well be said to have taken place thanks to the applicability of the original business philosophy to universal business conditions. Like the values, these are not contested by Japanese employees, but, as was noted in the case study, they are not whole-heartedly accepted by local managers in Europe and the USA.

This philosophy is considered truly universal by the Japanese employees and especially by its senior managers, many of whom will have personally experienced tensions with Western managers. But I do not think that it is an exaggeration to say that the Japanese position would be that there is nothing wrong with the philosophy, only with the foreign employees, who by virtue of not being Japanese, cannot appreciate its essential truth. Thus the business philosophy becomes, at the deeper level, something else: a source of ethnocentrism.

The above information on Japan and the Matsushita Corporation is arguably interesting knowledge to a firm that might be contemplating a business relationship with the Japanese company. As anyone familiar with Japan will know, it is grossly incomplete, representing a massive concentration of information for explanatory purposes. From a knowledge management perspective, the information presented was an almost diabolical mixture of the tacit and explicit, the mappable and unmappable, and seems to be the sort of knowledge that needs a domain expert. These represent big challenges to the knowledge management community because it is knowledge like this – largely unmappable and not easily reducible – that in turn supplies the foundation for the all-important core competence. We will look at the issue of core competence again in the following chapter. In the meantime, we address the knowledge management challenge from the point of view of transferability.

TRANSFERABILITY AND TRANSLATION

Stickiness may be seen as a factor which directly influences transferability. Dixon (2000) has noted that transferability (a term she does not use) is affected by three factors:

- The intended receiver of the knowledge in terms of similarity of task and context

- The nature of the task in terms of how routine and frequent it is

- The type of knowledge that is being transferred

These factors are entirely consistent with the points I have been making, but the fact that the knowledge transfer process has been represented in this book as a kind of translation process allows us to make further use of the analogy to explain the nature of constraints on knowledge transfer and transferability. Taking a cue from Pinchuk (1977), who writes on the art of technical and scientific translation, we can make use of three 'pitfalls' which can affect the quality of a translation. The idea of quality of translation is very complicated, not least because this factor can be influenced by the nature of the source and target languages. Without going into detail, we can follow Pinchuk (1977) and suggest that translations can be graded along the following lines for accuracy:

1. General idea of original conveyed
Enough to indicate, for example, whether information is relevant or irrelevant and whether translation is worthwhile. This is not a simple matter, and unfortunately sometimes it is impossible to know this until a full translation has been made.
2. Information content conveyed sufficiently for action to be taken
3. Most of the information conveyed
4. Virtually all the information conveyed. (Pinchuk, 1977)

Factors that influence accuracy include the translator's own skills and resourcefulness, knowledge of the subject area, the transferability of meaning between languages according to grammatical, lexical and stylistic considerations, and so forth. Those readers who have translated from one language to another will appreciate how intellectually demanding translation can be. Only the most skilled of translators can convey in English the subtlety of the dynamics of Japanese interpersonal relationships, in which bluntness can be masked behind exquisite politeness, in which the social distance between two interlocutors is conveyed not just by special words, but by grammatical forms which are carefully calibrated to ensure that the appropriate level of deference conveyed by the one is matched by the appropriate level of gracious civility bestowed by the other. If translation is a form of knowledge modification, then the translator's skill lies in understanding how a modification of knowledge, without destroying its integrity, can enhance the transferability of the original in another language. It is conceptually the same challenge with the cross-cultural transfer of management knowledge.

At this point, in order to make the analogy between translation and knowledge transfer more powerful, we can turn profitably to translation theory for insights into the constraints on the international transferability of knowledge. The translator habitually deals with three constraints as he or she attempts to render a text from a source language into a target language:

- Ambiguity (confusion in original text)

- Interference (intrusive errors brought forward from one's own linguistic and cultural background)

- Lack of equivalence (the absence of direct matches in the target language)

Each of each terms will be discussed from a general translation point of view and then used as analogies to explain constraints on the international (cross-cultural) transfer of knowledge. From the point of view of communication theory, these three constraints on translation may be regarded as 'noise'. In a technical sense, noise is 'any disturbance or interference, apart from the wanted signals or messages selected and being sent' (Cherry, 1980). In translation, noise is anything that distorts the translation process and influences variously the accuracy of the final product. So, by analogy, in the intra- or inter-organizational transfer of knowledge, noise is anything that distorts this process and constrains the convertibility of knowledge.

Ambiguity

To the translator the word 'ambiguity' is a precise term. It refers to words or expressions that are capable or being understood in two or more ways. If we assume that the translator is dealing with texts in which – say, unlike the novels of Kafka or Eco – ambiguity is a feature of the original, then his task is to ensure that the translated version does not give rise to *unintended* ambiguity. In the organizational sciences, ambiguity is a over-worked word, referring to any general vagueness or uncertainty.

In writings on culture and international management it is customary to urge 'tolerance of ambiguity' as a cross-cultural competence. It is a characteristic of cross-cultural writing not to define the word closely, which means, perhaps not inconveniently, that the word remains ambiguous. We can all understand it as we wish. In his book *International management: Cross-cultural dimensions* (1994), Mead has 13 indexed references to 'ambiguity' and has a section on 'avoiding conflict by exploiting ambiguity' and another on 'interpreting ambiguity', but the word itself is not defined; or rather it is, but only elliptically.

What we do find are definitions and characterizations of tolerance to ambiguity. Guirdham (1999), who in fact discusses ambiguity and language, describes tolerance of ambiguity as involving 'managing the feelings associated with unpredictability'. For Harris and Moran (1996) it 'refers to the ability to react to new, different and at times unpredictable situations with little visible discomfort'. To Hofstede (1994) and his followers tolerance of ambiguity is associated with uncertainty avoidance, which is premised on a wish to avoid future unpleasantness. Hofstede (1994) suggests that uncertainty avoidance is a key variable in differentiating (national cultures). In their book *Culture clash* (1995), US authors Seelye and Seelye-James have this under 'U' in their index: *Uncertainty avoidance vs Tolerance of ambiguity*. It is impossible not to read about tolerance of ambiguity and not come to the conclusion that these authors take the essentialist view of culture, so ambiguity is presented, in effect, as a kind of culture shock.

In the case studies, not one informant (to the best of my knowledge) ever used the word 'ambiguity' to describe any sense of personal or shared uncertainty. This is not to say that individual informants did not experience uncertainties or encounter unpredictable situations. I list from the case studies some examples of ambiguity that affected transfer and transferability of knowledge. In the case studies there were a number of ambiguous situations which have general implications for the transfer of knowledge:

- Uncertainty about how to cooperate with change agents (units *vis-à-vis* Novo Nordisk Facilitators)

- Uncertainty about change strategy (UK managers *vis-à-vis* the Sulzer Infra Academy)

- Problems of communicating company policy and thinking across language barriers within the company (Matsushita; to a lesser extent Sulzer Infra at seminars)

Interference

In translation theory (and practice) interference refers to the transfer of usages peculiar to the source language to the target language. This happens when words look the same in different languages, but mean something else. Here are some confusables between English and French. The French word *licence* does not always coincide with its apparent counterparts in English. It can mean, among other things, a university degree or membership of a sports federation (Thody and Evans, 1985). *Conjurer* has nothing to with sleight of hand in French. It can variously mean to entreat, to exorcise (demons) or to stave off (danger) (Thody and Evans, 1985). Conversely, the English word 'banger' might suggest to an unwitting

French translator a type of firework. But it might in a particular context refer to an English sausage, for which, by the way, an attested French translation is 'préparations de porc, recette britannique (pork speciality, British recipe)' (Gaskell, 1999).

But interference does not just affect translators. Almost all learners of foreign languages are influenced to a greater or lesser by the pronunciation, grammatical structures and vocabulary of their own languages. These facets are carried into the foreign language. These are received as 'errors' in the target language, marking the speaker as a foreigner. Sometimes these 'errors' may be so severe as to make a person unintelligible or to create literal ambiguities. For example, a French speaker with an unsure command of English may say: 'I work here since three years' (= 'I have been working here for three years'). A German also with a relatively weak command of English might say: 'I worked here for three years'. In this case he means 'I worked there three years ago' (German 'vor', meaning 'ago' being confused with, and pronounced the same as, the English word 'for' as a temporal adverb).

Sometimes the interference can have its amusing side. Often foreigners have difficulty distinguishing between the English 'u' sound and 'a' sound (for example, in 'butter' and 'batter'). I once overhead this conversation between a Russian and an English person. The latter: 'We have a lot of Russians in England.' The former (shocked): 'You still have rations in England?' (for Anglo-Russian management confusions, see Holden et al., 1998).

It goes without saying that this kind of confusion creeps into millions of cross-cultural conversations worldwide every day. Most are overcome or ignored. Some may have more complicated consequences. For examples, Japanese speakers of English are influenced by Japanese notions of politeness. Rather than categorically refuse a request, a Japanese might say: 'I'll think about it' (which means 'there is no way I am going to do anything about it'; or, often with a great sucking of breath between clenched teeth: 'That's very difficult', meaning that something is a sheer impossibility. As Nathan (1999) has pointed out, there is 'no language better suited to obfuscation than Japanese'. Often, Japanese speakers of foreign languages carry the obfuscation into new sociolinguistic domains where, for the most part, the foreign interlocutors do not understand the *rules* of obfuscation.

These last Japanese examples are useful in that they make a bridge from linguistic interference to behavioural interference. The Matsushita Company provided several examples of Japanese cultural interference, and it is even discernible in Novo Nordisk and LEGO. Both firms, especially the latter, make a great show of being culture-neutral in their management style. But, ironically, this is itself a cultural trait. LEGO only became less Danish when it proactively cultivated foreign ideas. A reluctance to take localized and other forms of ethnocentrism may be taken as a form of interference. It can be argued that the activities of the Novo Nordisk Facilitators are a form of intervention.

No doubt there have been a few occasions where a facilitation has been seen as unwelcome intervention. In everyday speech the word 'interference' tends to imply unwanted intervention. In this linguistic and cultural realm, interference is part and parcel of behaviour and language use that is often unconsciously carried over into a new cultural environment. The skill lies in becoming conscious of unwitting behaviour, which may stand out sharply in a new cultural environment (like seeing two Japanese bow politely to each other in the centre of Copenhagen) and knowing how it affects interactions at the local end.

Lack of equivalence

Equivalence can be a very useful concept for knowledge managers.[4] I will discuss the term in relation to translation theory and language and then apply it to cross-cultural interactions, using the material from the case studies as examples. As Sager (1994) has noted: 'Translation consists of producing in the target language the closest natural equivalent of the source language message, firstly with respect to meaning and secondly with respect to style.' What is meant by equivalence has been the subject of much scholarly debate, but according to Sager (1994) 'it is generally recognised that the relationship of a source and target is one of cognitive, pragmatic and linguistic equivalence.' This provides us with a useful insight into the cross-cultural conversion and transfer of knowledge.

By way of considerable simplification, we may say that human languages differ from each other formally in four principal ways: in their syntax (the way in which words are arranged and combined 'grammatically'); in their morphology (which refers to the study of ways in which the forms of words change according to context (i.e. walk, walked, walking; big, bigger, biggest); in their lexis (which refers to the vocabulary items of a language); and in their phonology (which refers to the speech sounds of a language). Anyone who has studied foreign languages will be aware of the complicated ways in which these four 'systems' deviate from each other in different languages.

To quote once more great American linguist, Edward Sapir (1956): 'No two languages are ever sufficiently similar to be considered as representing the same social reality. The worlds in which different societies live are distinct worlds, not merely the same world with different labels attached.' In other words, there is not only distance among languages, owing to similarities and differences in the four basic systems of language, but distance as a function of language, as a repository of knowledge, experience and impressions and a device for facilitating social interaction. The challenge for the translator in finding equivalence is not just to render the words of one language into a second one, but also to re-express psychological and related factors within the terms of reference of that second language.

The translator of technical texts must find the precise equivalents of formal specialized terms, if they exist in the target language. If they do not exist, he or she may decide that a sentence or even an entire text, dependent on a key word, may be *untranslatable*. One option may be to abandon the project. Another (possibly in conjunction with the writer of the text) may be to create a specific paraphrase. This requires resourcefulness, as does the translation of poems, whose rhythms and rhyme test the translator to the ultimate degree.

Here are some examples. The very word 'manager' in (American) English does not find straightforward counterparts in modern European languages. In French and German, one encounters 'le manager' and 'der Manager' respectively. There is a tendency in such languages to depersonalize manager into an abstract noun meaning management, for example French 'la gestion', German 'die Unternehmungsführung'. The Danish word 'ledelse' carries connotations of 'leading', but without a soupçon of the grand American sense of business leadership. The word 'marketing' is not easily translatable into various languages of the former socialist word, not to mention Japanese (Holden, 1998). Hence the word 'marketing' remains in English form in such languages, each one overlaying distinctive nuances.

Whilst Arabic may have countless words for particular formations of sand and Inuit languages all manner of words to describe kinds of snow, (American) English is triumphant in the number of words and expressions – many of which are pure euphemisms – for describing forms of reorganization and the dismissal of employees. There is, it seems, no limit to what Collins (2000) terms 'the lexicon of downsizing', to the number of ways you can be told that you have been 'de-hired'.

If we regard the transfer of knowledge as an interactive translation, then it follows that the purpose of international knowledge transfer is to find cross-cultural equivalence: the state of achieving harmonization of view, purpose and priorities. But before turning to the experience of the four informant companies, let me present a clear example of cross-cultural equivalence and the difficulties of achieving it in the arduous endeavour of communicating Western management know-how into the Russian frame of reference. The quotation, emphasizing the Russian desire for equivalence as distinct from equality, is based on personal experiences in Russia from 1991 to 1996. Everything I read about Russia today does not suggest that the quoted information is out of date, nor will go out of date in the near future:

> At the heart of this desire for equivalence is a Russian conviction that Russians are no less intelligent, educated or competent than people elsewhere, but Russia has a lot of problems which make it difficult at the moment to harness all her talents. At the same time, Russia still has undisputed potential as an economic and technological powerhouse. It is, the Russians will point out, the selfsame potential which transformed a largely backward agricultural country into the second most powerful country on earth in a matter of decades; was instrumental in defeating Nazi Germany; launched the world's first artificial satellite; created a scientific establishment which

in its hey-day (in the 1970s) comprehensively rivalled achievement in the Western world (Graham, 1993); and presented over many decades a fully-fledged alternative model of global economic development.

The fact that the communist leadership sacrificed millions of Russians and non-Russians in the gulag (see Conquest, 1992), kept the rest behind the country's borders and deprived them of what we consider to be basic necessities of life over several decades – all this does not diminish the argument. The Russian businessman who used the example of Russia's launch of the first sputnik (in October 1957) to impress a would-be joint venture partner from the UK is using a past – and world-famous – technological achievement to demonstrate *contemporary* potential. He knows that his enterprise is not technologically equal to the UK firm now, but it has the potential to be. This 'posture' requires of a foreign business partner a recognition of equivalence in the situation. Awareness of a Russian *need* for equivalence is one thing, but building this need into a viable business arrangement is something else.

Thus the advice that 'Western managers should expect to approach their Russian counterparts as equals' sounds sensible enough, but is misplaced. Likewise, the assumption guiding a cross-cultural management programme in Moscow, which allows 'Russians and Americans to learn from one another and preserving the best from both cultures' (Duneyeva and Vipperman, 1995) seems to miss an essential component of the Russian mindset. To make the distinction between equality and equivalence absolutely clear: there is only one time-honoured way in Russia of achieving *equality* with foreigners – at least in the short term – and that is to ply and quite possibly anaesthetise them with vodka. (Holden, et al., 1998)

Of all the countries making up the former socialist world, Russians as a national group may constitute the greatest challenge in terms of achieving equivalence. This may be seen as a natural reaction of a once powerful country that, since the collapse of the communist system in 1991, has been experiencing a triple transition: from dictatorship to democracy; from centralized economy to free market; and from four-century-old empire to nation-state (Yergin and Gustafson, 1994). But other smaller states are also aware that the West does not seem to understand them on their own terms. They do not feel treated as equals because the West does not know how to find equivalence, the art of finding isomorphic structures, world-views and aspirations. Part of the problem is that many who undertake management training projects in East and Central Europe do not have the knowledge background, not just of individual countries, but of the entire region.

The Novo Nordisk Facilitators, on the one hand, and the seminars of the Sulzer Infra Academy, on the other, are experiments for achieving cross-cultural equivalence among a culturally diverse workforce. There is far more to this than reaching for 'cultural literacy': the ability to value and leverage cultural differences (Rosen, 2000). Cross-cultural equivalence stems from harmonizing the linguistic, cognitive and pragmatic elements at interfaces – to cite our definition – where knowledge, values and experience are transferred into multicultural domains of implementation. This is the essence of the management of diversity, a matter that will be considered more in the next chapter. In the case studies, the company having the greatest difficulty creating equivalence was Matsushita.

CROSS-CULTURAL COMMUNICATION

Cross-cultural communication is a topic that receives a good deal of attention in books and articles on cross-cultural management, but it is weakly developed as an academic subject area. Limaye and Victor (1995) rightly argue that the field lacks a 'rich conceptual basis', is too dependent on anecdote and linear models of communication, and rests lop-sidedly on assumptions of communication that are steeped in Western culture. One might add that the area is snagged on cross-cultural negotiation, which manages to investigate everything (as it were) except the crux of the business. Cross-cultural communication, not surprisingly, is the quintessential pasture of cross-cultural do-gooders.

American authors Harris and Moran (1996) write about cross-cultural communication in these terms:

> Recognizing that what is involved in one's image of self and one's role, personal needs, values, standards, expectations, all of which are culturally conditioned. Such a person understands the impact of cultural factors on communication, and is willing to revise and expand such images as part of the process of growth. Furthermore, he or she is aware of verbal and non-verbal differences in communication with persons from another culture. Not only does such a person seek to learn another language, but he or she is cognisant that even when people speak the same language, cultural differences can alter communication symbols and meanings and result in misunderstandings.

Note that although Harris and Moran's book is called *Managing cultural differences*, there is nothing in their formulation of cross-cultural communication which pertains explicitly to any task of management. This is symptomatic of a tendency, which I hope this book has avoided, of conflating cross-cultural management with cross-cultural communication. All authors on cross-cultural issues stress the significance of language in terms of verbal and non-verbal modes, the desirability of foreign language capability, but it is recognized that 'narrow' linguistic competence must be supplemented by communicative competence.

In cross-cultural situations linguistic competence refers to a person's knowledge of the rules of a foreign language to produce and understand sentences (based on Crystal, 1980).[5] Communicative competence expands this by emphasizing social competence, which refers to the speaker's ability to use his knowledge of the language in a way that is appropriate to the context of interactions. This competence requires actors to know how to use direct and indirect speech, how to balance the formal with the informal, according to circumstances (Claes, 2001). In other words, communicative competence comes with familiarity, with knowing the rules of interaction embedded in particular cultures. Such competence may take years to acquire; perhaps 20 or more in the case of a foreigner who aims at 'total' communicative competence in Japanese, a language unusual for the way which social distance is grammatically encoded.

In the world of business communicative competence can also relate to how one uses English as a native language or second language. Many native speakers of English have less communicative competence than they think in certain cross-cultural encounters. A tendency not to slacken the speed of verbal delivery, to speak in convoluted sentences (which rarely happens with good speakers of English as a second language!), to pepper speech with obscure words, similes and metaphors or references to phenomena outside the experience of the listener, all can make communication hard work for the non-native speaker of English. In the process goodwill can be lost, atmosphere spoiled. Nor should it be assumed that communicative competence necessarily involves active use of language. In an appeal to restrain American business people from numbing their Japanese business partners with sheer talk, Zimmerman (1985) urged his countrymen to curb garrulousness by the seemingly unusual expedient of actually keeping their mouths shut.

In books and articles on cross-cultural communication language is usually treated expressively in its communicative function and as a medium for transmitting clear messages. There is an implicit assumption that communication takes place between two parties. This is a regrettable misconception. Communication in business is multipolar as well as dyadic, so it is best seen as a participative act involving several people as individuals and groups. This suggests that cross-cultural knowledge management necessitates its own way of looking cross-cultural communication and accordingly requires a modified communicative competence. This is in keeping with Claes and du Bois (2000), who remind us that 'the new paradigms of communication and management suggest that it will be necessary to re-examine and redefine what is meant by effective communication.' In line with that sentiment it will be argued in the next chapter that one of the key tasks of cross-cultural management is to identify and restrict the pernicious effects of 'the ultimate limiter of communication' (Cherry, 1980): noise in the system. This proposition will present 'effective communication' in a completely different light.

In the domain of knowledge transfer communication is not necessarily in the form of a dialogue between two people or two parties. It is a collective experience, and it can have many manifestations: participation in a LEGO Millennium Meeting, in a Novo Nordisk facilitation, in a Sulzer Infra seminar, in an in-company presentation on the Matsushita way of doing business. These encounters, and no two encounters are ever the same, bring together different people with different cultural and ethnic backgrounds, with different competencies in one or more foreign languages. Participants may be in teams: engineers with marketing people, or psychologists or accountants, each bringing a special professional language.

According to the requirements of projects, these people meet again – perhaps in a country foreign to them all. They are later disassembled, keeping their affiliations to other groups and possibly joining new ones. All the while they are in contact with the focal group as well as their own units, maintaining networks. For this kind of work, 'traditional' communicative competence is not enough. The key to understanding this multipolar communication activity is to realize that interactive translation is facilitated by participative competence. The concept of participative competence has already been introduced and it will come in for further discussion in the next chapter. I regard participative competence as the ability to interact on equal terms in multicultural environments in such a way that knowledge is shared and that the learning experience is professionally enhancing.

One of the key tasks of cross-cultural management is to nurture participative competence. In the case of intra- and inter-organizational communication involving multiple cultures, the detection and counterbalancing of noise is especially complicated. More will be said on that theme in the next chapter when we consider the cross-cultural manager as a communicator. For the time being, let us say that participative competence implies facets of 'normal' communicative competence, which presupposes knowledge of certain rules and structures communication pertinent to a situation. But whereas communicative competence focuses on interaction with 'the other', participative competence focuses on 'the others'. Claes (2001) specifies what these rules are. I reproduce these, using italics to indicate where I have converted 'other' to 'others':

- That the *others* are socially competent; they know the world, the environment, the references

- That the *others* know how communication is structured, and are able to make a distinction between the central and the peripheral

- That the *others* can infer messages, read between the lines

- That the messages are encoded in different ways, not just in language, so one must accept and learn the other codes

The last point is important. Participative competence is acquired and extended through continual learning, for which involvement in interactive translation is the main mechanism. It is up to the individual to use that competence resourcefully in new situations. In that quest, he or she faces the challenge of mitigating the effects of ambiguity, interference and relative lack of equivalence in *every* cross-cultural situation. It is perfectly clear that participative competence is a vital factor if one is to gain great benefit from attending a seminar organized by the Sulzer Infra Academy. But this participative competence is not the same as that which might be required for doing business in China where foreigner business people may be seen as 'barbaric, short-tempered and rapacious' (Blackman, 1997), and where 'every step of the business chain is decided by negotiation through the "spider's web": the network of people who give and receive favours to ensure favourable outcomes for their own group' (Blackman, 1997).

In Russia participative competence means knowing how to cope which what Hingley (1978), a noted translator of Chekhov, calls 'the Russian speciality', which is 'a tendency for a single individual or group to alternate between one extreme position and its opposite; or even, somehow, to occupy two or more mutually exclusive positions'. And the participative competence needed for the 'cross-cultural minefield' (*Financial Times*, 1993) called Russia is again quite different for operating in the Swedish–Swiss electrical engineering group ABB, which is 'a globally connected corporation, a loose-tight network of processes, projects and partners that can only be held together by highly committed people and strongly held principles' (Barham and Heimer, 1998). The point has been made. There is no need to extend the list. Against those realities it is surely clear now why a narrowly defined 'cross-cultural awareness' or why 'more knowledge about culture' are such pitifully inadequate appeals.

Figure 12.6 may be seen to represent cross-cultural management in its function as a facilitator of participative competence in the international knowledge

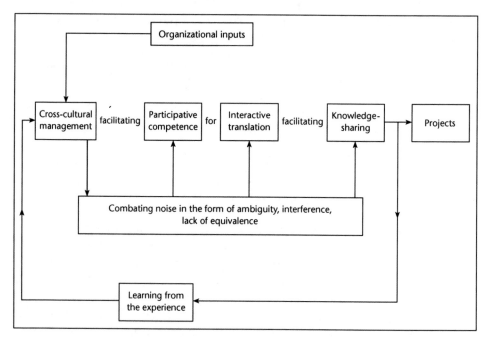

Fig. 12.6 Basic process model of cross-cultural management and knowledge transfer

management process. The model suggests that cross-cultural management has the task of combating noise which permeates the entire communication system and learns from the process 'for next time'.

A little later this model will be further modified so that it reflects more fully the knowledge transfer process. But before we can do that, we have to introduce another element of cross-cultural interactions: atmosphere. In this sense, the Sulzer Infra seminars are a professional kind of rehearsal for cross-cultural business interactions in which the emotional experience of cross-cultural interactions is an inextricable feature of the process of interanimation.

CROSS-CULTURAL COMMUNICATION: THE ROLE OF ATMOSPHERE

Atmosphere is the 'sum of feelings, intentions, will and interest' (Hallén and Sandström, 1989) that parties bring to an interaction.[6] It is an elusive, yet palpable quality of relationships which is 'derived from experience, which serves in turn as a determinant of expectations about future cooperation' (Holden and Burgess, 1994). Managers may not always have the cross-cultural *savoir-faire* for all situations involving interactions with multiple cultures, but there is always one thing they can do. They help create and sustain a conducive, collaborative atmosphere. They can do this by displaying social adroitness, professional competence, and by applying intelligence and tact to interactions. But, cross-culturally, there is no fixed formula. If I may speak from my own contrasting experiences of Japan and Russia, I would say that atmosphere is smoothed in Japan if you (the foreigner) display professional competence and personal modesty at the same time; a balance that does not come easily to those from assertive cultures. In the case of Russia the challenge is to convey *considerable* professional competence – Russians respect experts – but without giving the Russians the impression that you regard them as incompetent (Holden et al., 1998); another awkward balance to strike. To understand the importance of atmosphere and to be able to create it for fostering dialogue takes years of experience. The work is, of course, the diplomat's stock-in-trade and the would-be business practitioner must 'master both the cognitive and behavioral complexities' (Saner et al., 2000) required for this most important – and least recognized – of tasks in global business.

Recall the case of the DaimlerChrysler merger (chapter 1). In the end it was not so much a failure of American or German managers to understand their respective cultural values as a failure of top management to understand how to create an atmosphere conducive to collaborative cross-cultural learning (*Economist*, 2000). The importance of atmosphere is understood by Novo Nordisk and Sulzer Infra, whose respective systems bring together individuals regardless of position in the nominal hierarchy. Sulzer Infra tries to create a pan-European collaborative atmosphere at its seminars so that participants will be well disposed to each other in subsequent encounters in their project teams. Atmosphere is something which can, in principle, be managed, but the history of mergers and acquisitions shows that it is consistently mismanaged. By its nature atmosphere cannot be retrospectively imposed.

Now that the all-important notion of atmosphere has been introduced, it is possible to construct a model purporting to show the elements composing the process of cross-cultural transfer of knowledge. In fact two related models can be created out of the experiences of the four companies who served as informants for this book. The first model (Figure 12.7) shows a cyclic path leading from preparation to participative competence, interactive translation, knowledge-sharing and knowledge distribution. Atmosphere is shown at key phases. Note too that atmosphere is an element in the feedback loop. So that the model does not become unduly complicated, noise factors are not represented, but they should be understood as pervading the entire communication process.

The second model (Figure 12.8) emphasizes the role of atmosphere by placing it at the core of the entire cycle of activities. It is easy to envisage atmosphere, so represented, as having a halo effect throughout the processes leading to knowledge-sharing and beyond.

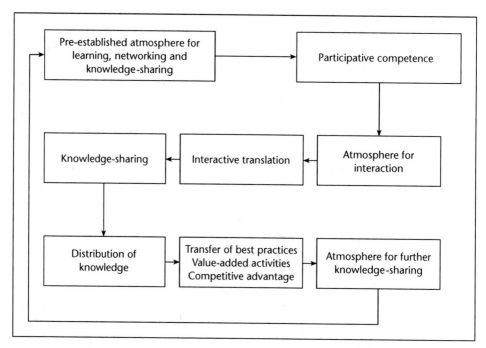

Fig. 12.7 The role of atmosphere in the cross-cultural transfer of knowledge

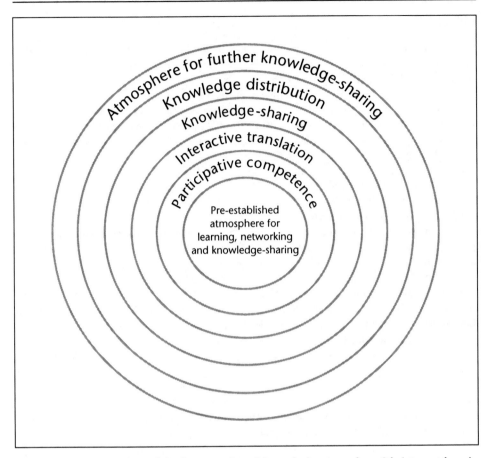

Fig. 12.8 Concentric model of cross-cultural knowledge transfer with 'atmosphere' at the core

CONCLUSION

This concludes the three chapters of analysis and commentary on the four case studies. The harnessing of cross-cultural management and knowledge management has certainly developed new concepts and models for understanding the domain of the former in today's world. We are at this point a long way from culture-as-essence and culture-as-difference and are within reach of achieving one of this book's main aims, which is to reformulate the field of cross-cultural management from a non-cultural standpoint. In the final chapter there are three key tasks: to specify more closely culture as an organizational resource; to present the reformulation of cross-cultural management; and, in the time-honoured way, draw various implications for students, researchers and practitioners.

NOTES

1. Rosenzweig (1999) makes the very important qualification that US firms approach diversity management from 'a point of relative employee homogeneity and try to promote greater diversity in racial and gender representation'.

2. My thanks are due to Kasper Rasmussen for the discussion and design of this model.

3. Seidensticker (1983) supplies the fascinating information that the forebear of the *meishi* is the French *carte de visite*. In the latter half of the last century, when Japanese officials were scouring the world – the USA, Britain, France and Germany in the main – for knowledge, one of their delegations encountered the *carte de visite* in France. A fine example of a Western artifact being so thoroughly Japanized that nobody would suspect an outside source for its provenance.

4. In *Marketing across cultures*, Jean-Claude Usunier (2000) devotes three pages to translation equivalence with special reference to translation of marketing questionnaires. See also Ricks (1992) for a selection of regrettable, if outdated, bad advertising translations.

5. The most amazing case I know of awesome linguistic competence being inexplicably not up to the job concerned the redoubtable James Murray, editor of the *Oxford English Dictionary*, arguably the greatest lexicographical achievement of all time (Winchester 1998). In his thirtieth year, in 1867, Murray applied for a post at the British Museum. In his letter of application Murray claimed 'a general acquaintance with the languages & literatures of the Aryan and Syro-Arabic classes' and 'more intimate acquaintance . . . with the Romance tongues, Italian, French, Catalan, Spanish, Latin & in a less degree Portuguese, Vaudois, Provençal and various dialects'. Apart from that, he was 'tolerably familiar' with Dutch, German, Danish as well as Anglo-Saxon and Moeso-Gothic, as far as Germanic languages were concerned. Murray knew 'a little Celtic', had 'a useful knowledge' of Russian. For philological purposes he knew Persian and Achaemenian cuneiform. He knew Hebrew and Syriac 'to read at sight the Old Testament', and 'to a less degree' Aramaic Arabic, Coptic and Phoenician. As his biographer notes: 'It somewhat beggars the imagination that the Museum turned down his job application' (Winchester, 1998). And for those who notice such things, Murray did not specifically admit to a knowledge of Classical Greek! To be taken as read, I expect.

6. In their book *Alliance competence* (2000), Spekman, Isabella and MacAvoy devote a chapter to 'the alliance spirit'. The components of this spirit are 'atmosphere of flexibility, commitment of mutuality, sense of solidarity, and preference for harmony'. Spirit is akin to atmosphere, but suggests an outcome of will or conviction. Spirit, unlike atmosphere, is non-negotiable.

REFERENCES

Almaney, A. J. and Alwan, A. J. (1982). *Communicating with the Arabs: A handbook for the business executive.* Prospect Heights, IL: Waveland Press.

Barham, K. and Heimer, C. (1998). *ABB – the dancing giant.* London: Financial Times Prentice Hall.

Beauchamp, E. R. and Vardaman, J. M. (1994). *Japanese education since 1945: A documentary study.* Armonk, NY: M E Sharpe.

Beechler, S. and Bird, A. (eds) (1999). *Japanese multinationals abroad: Individual and organizational learning.* New York: Oxford University Press.

Blackman, C. (1997). *Negotiating China: Case studies and strategies.* St Leonards, NSW: Allen & Unwin.

Cherry, C. (1980). *On human communication: A review, a survey and a criticism.* Cambridge, MA: MIT Press.

Claes, M.-T. (2001). Direct/indirect and formal/informal communication: a reassessment. In: Cooper, C. L. and Cartwright, S. (eds). *The international handbook of organizational culture and climate*. Chichester: John Wiley & Sons.

Claes, M.-T. and du Bois, P. (2000). Universelle ou différenciée? La communication d'entreprise dans L'interculturel'. In: Dupriez, P. and Simons, S. (eds). *La résistance culturelle: Fondements, applications et implications du management interculturel*. Brussels: De Boeck & Larcier, pp. 147–61.

Collins, D. (2000). *Management fads and buzzwords*. London: Routledge.

Conquest, R. (1992). *The Great Terror: A reassessment*. London: Pimlico.

Crystal, D. (ed.) (1980). *A first dictionary of linguistics and phonetics*. London: André Deutsch.

Davenport, T. H. and Prusak, L. (1998). *Working knowledge: How organizations manage what they know*. Boston, MA: Harvard Business School Press.

Deal, T. and Kennedy, A. (1982) *Corporate cultures: The rites and rituals of corporate life*. London: Penguin Books.

Dixon, N. M. (2000). *Common knowledge: How companies thrive by sharing what they know*. Boston, MA: Harvard Business School Press

Doz, Y. and Santos, J. P. F. (1997). On the management of knowledge: From the transparency of collocation and co-setting to the quandry of dispersion and differentiation. *INSEAD Working Papers*. No. 119–SM. Fountainebleau.

Duneyeva, D. and Vipperman, C. (1995). Similar but different. Why do Russian and American business-people, even when they speak the same language, so often seem to be engaging in a dialogue of the deaf? *Business in Russia*. June.

Economist (2000). Merger brief: The DaimlerChrysler emulsion. 29 July.

Fallows, J. (1995). *Looking at the sun: The rise of the new East Asian economic and political system*. New York: Vintage Books.

Financial Times (1993). A cross-cultural minefield. 2 August.

Garvin, D. A. (1998). Building a learning organization. *Harvard Business Review on management knowledge*. Boston, MA: Harvard Business School Press, pp. 47–80.

Gaskell, P. (1999). Laisser faire is not universally popular. *Financial Times*. 6 November.

Gerlach, M. L. (1992). *Alliance capitalism: The social organization of Japanese business*. Berkeley, CA: University of California Press.

Graham, L. R. (1993). *The ghost of The executed engineer: Technology and the fall of the Soviet Union*. Cambridge, MA: Harvard University Press.

Guirdham, M. (1999). *Communication across cultures*. Basingstoke, UK: Macmillan.

Hallén, L. and Sandström, M. (1989). Relationship atmosphere in international business. Working paper. Uppsala: University of Uppsala.

Harris, P. R. and Moran, R. T. (1996). *Managing cultural differences: Leadership strategies for a new world of business*. Houston, TX: Gulf Publishing.

Hingley, R. (1978). *The Russian mind*. London: Bodley Head.

Hofstede, G. (1994). *Culture and organizations: Intercultural cooperation and its importance for survival – software of the mind*. London: HarperCollins.

Holden, N. J. (1998). International marketing studies: Time to break the English-language stranglehold. *International Marketing Review* 15(2): 86–100.

Holden, N. J. and Burgess, M. (1994). *Japanese-led companies: Understanding how to make them your customers*. London: McGraw-Hill.

Holden, N. J., Cooper C. L. and Carr, J. (1998). *Dealing with the new Russia: Management cultures in collision*. Chichester, UK: John Wiley & Sons.

Hurn, B. J. (1996) Intercultural transfer of skills and knowledge. *Cross-cultural management: An international journal* 3(1): 33–6.

Jackson, T. (1993). *Turning Japanese: The fight for industrial control of the new Europe.* London: HarperCollins.

Limaye, M. R. and Victor, D. A. (1995). Cross-cultural business communication: State of the art and hypotheses for the 1990s. In: Jackson, T. (ed.). *Cross-cultural management.* Oxford: Butterworth-Heinemann, pp. 217–37.

Lorriman, J. and Kenjo, T. (1994). *Japan's winning margin's: The secrets of Japanese success.* Oxford: Oxford University Press.

Mead, R. (1994). *International management: Cross-cultural dimensions.* Oxford: Blackwell.

Nathan, J. (1999). *Sony: The private life.* London: HarperCollins.

Nonaka, I. (1998). *The knowledge-creating company.* Cambridge, MA: Harvard Business School Press.

Nonaka, I. (1991). The knowledge-creating company. *Harvard Business Review.* November–December: 96–104.

Nonaka, I. and Takeuchi, H. (1995). *The knowledge-creating company.* New York: Oxford University Press.

Oshika, Y. (1999). Sony out to reinvent itself. *Japan Quarterly* 47: 47–53.

Phillips, M. E. (1996). Industry mindsets: Exploring the cultures of two macro-organizational settings. In: Meindl, J. R., Stubbart, C. and Porac, J. (eds). *Cognition in and between organisations.* London: Sage Publications.

Pinchuk, I. (1977). *Scientific and technical translation.* London: André Deutsch.

Rasmussen, K. (2000). Knowledge management in multinational companies: The use of shared space in cross-cultural settings. Unpublished working paper. Copenhagen Business School.

Ricks, D. A. (1992). *Big business blunders.* Homewood, IL: Irwin.

Rosen, R. (2000). *Global literacies: Lessons on business leaderships and national cultures.* New York: Simon & Schuster. See, especially, the case study 'Build an expert culture of shared values: Mads Øvlisen and Novo Nordisk A/S (Denmark)', pp. 229–33.

Rosenzweig, P. (1988). Strategies for managing diversity. In: Bickerstaffe, G. (ed.). *Mastering global business: The complete MBA companion to global business.* London: Pitman, pp. 177–81.

Sager, J. C. (1994) *Language engineering and translation: Consequences of information.* Amsterdam: John Benjamins.

Saner, R., Yiu, L. and Søndergaard, M. (2000). Business diplomacy management: A core competence for global companies. *Academy of Management Executive* 14(1): 80–92.

Sansom, G. (1977). *The western world and Japan.* Tokyo: Charles E. Tuttle.

Sapir, E. (1956). *Culture, language and personality.* Berkeley, CA: University of California Press.

Schoenberg, R. (1999). Knowledge transfer and resource sharing as value creation mechanisms in inbound continental European acquisitions. A paper presented at the 19th Annual International Conference of the Strategic Management Society, Berlin, October.

Seelye, H. N. and Seelye-James, A. (1995). *Culture clash: Managing in a multicultural world.* Lincolnwood, IL: NTC Business Books.

Seidensticker, E. (1983). *Low city, high city: Tokyo from Edo to the earthquake.* Harmondsworth: Penguin.

Spekman, R. E., Isabella, L. A. and MacAvoy, T. C. (2000). *Alliance competence: Maximizing the value of your partnerships.* New York: John Wiley & Sons.

Thody, P. and Evans, H. (1985). *Faux amis & key words: A dictionary-guide to French language, culture and society through lookalikes and confusables.* London: Athlone Press.

Turnbull, P. W. (1990). Roles of personal contacts in industrial export marketing. In: Ford, D. (ed.). *Understanding business markets: Interaction, relationships, networks*. London: Academic Press, pp. 78–86.

Usunier, J.-C. (2000). *Marketing across cultures*. London: Prentice Hall.

Viney, J. (1997). *The culture wars: How American and Japanese businesses have outperformed Europe's and why the future will be different*. London: Capstone.

Westney, D. E. (1999). Changing perspectives on the organization of Japanese multinational companies. In: Beechler, S. and Bird, A. (eds). *Japanese multinationals abroad: Individual and organizational learning*. New York: Oxford University Press, pp. 11–29.

Winchester, S. (1998). *The surgeon of Crowthorne. A tale of murder, madness and the love of words*. London: Viking.

Yergin, D. and Gustafson, T. (1994). *Russia 2010 and what it means for the world*. London: Nicholas Brealey.

Zimmerman, M. (1985). *Dealing with the Japanese*. London: George Allen & Unwin.

13 Remapping the domain of cross-cultural management

'Can the enterprise somehow reconcile inner-direction with outer-direction, those things invented here with those not invented here? Can it internalize the outer world so as to act decisively and competently?'

Charles Hampden-Turner and Fons Trompenaars,
The seven cultures of capitalism (1993)

'A model is simply a reflection of whatever is the case, which is explicitly made available for experimentation.'

Stafford Beer, *Decision and control* (1966)

OBJECTIVES

■ **Summarizes the arguments developed in the book.**

■ **Suggests how culture can be conceived as an organizational resource and a factor of core competence.**

■ **Introduces the notion of the cross-cultural manager as a knowledge worker.**

■ **Remaps the domain of cross-cultural management.**

■ **Draws some implications for management educators and researchers, cross-cultural trainers, and knowledge management specialists.**

INTRODUCTION

In this last chapter I review first and briefly the evolution of the argument underpinning this book. Then I reflect on the understanding of cross-cultural management which has emerged in this book in order to put some conceptual boundaries around it. After that attention will switch to that elusive personage, the cross-cultural manager. If in previous contributions he or she has emerged as victorious in single combat with culture, this personage will appear in this book – no surprise by now – as a knowledge worker. I will venture to associate some competencies, based on the four case studies, with this new cross-cultural knowledge manager (or worker). The last section in the book will, in the time-honoured way, conclude with implications for various professional communities for whom this book may have a message.

SUMMARY REVIEW OF THE ARGUMENT

The preceding chapters may be taken to be an argument for reformulating cross-cultural management as a form of knowledge management. The paths that brought us to this point have been long and winding. The starting point was a dissatisfaction with the anthropologically derived concept of culture, the Hofstedian grip and cleaving to ideas and assumptions that are decades old which permeate so much writing on issues of culture and management with specific reference to international dimensions. It was reasoned that a new way of looking at cross-cultural management was called for.

The traditional assumption that cross-cultural management is about the management of cultural differences and being able to cope with culture shock was criticized for being both naive and out of touch with the modern business activity under a multiplicity of pressures and influences. It was argued that cross-cultural management was simply reinventing itself, making no significant conceptual advances, being largely locked in single-country and comparative approaches. The new economy, with its instantaneous communications, its global reach, the scale and complexities of companies' cross-border involvements, its emphasis on knowledge as firms' paramount resource, the (multicultural) team as the new workhorse of international business, all these things drove the book along.

By developing the notion of culture as an object of knowledge management, I have attempted to show how culture can be understood as an organizational resource. But I am only too aware of making a few tentative steps and I hope that others will take up the intellectual challenges. Culture is, as was noted in chapter 2, one of the most problematical words in the entire English language. My 'repackaging' of culture as a form of knowledge may not win everyone's approval. Some may say: 'Of course, culture is knowledge', adding 'But I don't like the way you handle culture as knowledge as an organizational resource, serving the needs of big business.' Others, representing the so-called 'culture shock prevention industry' will no doubt feel that I have not given adequate attention to major traditional topics such as cultural difference, value systems, or negotiation. But these 'omissions' are quite consistent with an approach that is avoiding the presentation of culture as colliding zones of adversarial oppositions.

Furthermore, my commitment to the knowledge management approach did not, I feel, necessitate so much treatment of these issues, except where I believe that something new was being proposed. It seemed more important to develop notions like interactive translation and participative competence. The modern world of business is, in effect, creating new kinds of cultures, which are perhaps better understood as infinitely overlapping and perpetually redistributable habitats of common knowledge and shared meanings. Cultures, conceived in this way, do call for a new conceptual framework. The knowledge management approach is but one.

From the beginning, the notion of cross-cultural management was conceived in terms of collaborative learning, the transfer and sharing of knowledge and experience. This was already a significant shift from cross-cultural management seen as the management of cultural differences, in which those differences are all too often represented as inescapable vortices of corporate undoing. Part of the shift entailed regarding culture, or rather cultural inputs, as an object of knowledge and cross-cultural management at the organizational level of analysis. This approach made it much easier to associate cross-cultural management with the writing about networks, learning and knowledge management as organizational processes. Incidentally, this approach, unshackled from culture-as-essence and culture-as-difference, also made it virtually superfluous to talk about cross-cultural management as activities *across* cultures. On the basis of the case studies, it is suggested that cultures are better conceived as intersecting zones of collaborative learning, pools of common knowledge.

These ideas influenced the approach to the empirical studies and the subsequent analysis of the four companies' cross-cultural behaviour. Analysis of the case studies generated two new concepts in cross-cultural management writing from a knowledge management perspective – interactive translation and participative competence. Against that, the analysis of knowledge management behaviour from a cross-cultural perspective suggested that the notions of tacit and explicit knowledge are not helpful categories to determine or describe the relative transferability of knowledge in cross-cultural ambiences. It was proposed that organizational cultural knowledge can be seen as compromising three facets: general cultural knowledge, specific cultural knowledge, and cross-cultural know-how. The last was seen as a constituent element of core competence: knowledge that is advantageously company-specific.

A major feature of the treatment of the international (cross-cultural) transfer of knowledge was to regard it as a form of translation; and that may be the most important contribution this book makes to the knowledge management literature. In so far as the international transfer (or translation) of knowledge is an activity mediated by human beings, no matter how much technology can support it, I argued that a major influence on these processes was atmosphere as both a precondition for, and valuable product of, cross-cultural interactions. Atmosphere is the balm which allows cultures to intersect smoothly, and allows pools of knowledge to overlap freely.

The argument has not just been propelled by words. I stressed the importance of modelling and mapping to give focus and direction to verbal dispositions about cross-cultural management behaviour. Hence I have developed models and maps which attempt to describe the distillations of reality, *as I see them*, of the described cross-cultural interactions. Readers may find them persuasive (a persuasive model is one that has predictive power). Others may find them just the opposite. But the important thing is that the models – and indeed everything else in this book – throw doubts in people's minds. Alas, the monumental work of Hofstede never did that (which was not the guru's fault, of course), and that is one among other reasons why cross-cultural management as an academic field has not yet found its intellectual feet. An academic field cannot grow if it is dominated by certainty. If there is certainty in an academic field, too many people have stopped thinking. It is not the case that cross-cultural management needs 'a new language', but it definitely needs an alternative vocabulary, the basic terms of which can be found in the glossary.[1] This book may be a catalyst and source of ideas to stimulate the process.

CULTURE, ORGANIZATIONAL CAPABILITIES AND CORE COMPETENCIES

Everything that needs to be said in this book is predicated on the way in which culture is to be regarded as an organizational resource. In the previous chapter three types of cultural knowledge were identified: general cultural knowledge, specific cultural knowledge, and cross-cultural know-how. In the everyday life of an organization these knowledge types blend, merge, augment each other, and they coalesce with organizational culture. In fact, the very act of coalescence constitutes a modification to the organizational culture. However, it does not serve any purpose to look upon an organization as a huge cultural soup, even if it is! The solution to our problem is to stay with the notion of cultural knowledge so that culture can be more clearly seen as a utilizable resource. One challenge is to model culture as an organizational resource.

Such a model, which has to be consistent with resource-based models of the firm, would enable us to develop a company-oriented perspective on culture. This means that we have a way of viewing the company as manager of cultural resources and potential harmonizer of so-called cultural diversity. However, is there such a resource-based model of the firm which also accommodates internal and external cultural factors? Fortunately, there is. Fink and Mayrhofer (2001) of the Vienna School of Economics, have come to the general rescue. They belong to a group of theorists who regard the company as a problem-solving organization, but recognize too that cultural factors are complex internal influences which strongly affect firms' governance and performance. These scholars have developed a resource-based model of the firm (see Figure 13.1).

Under this model, as they explain:

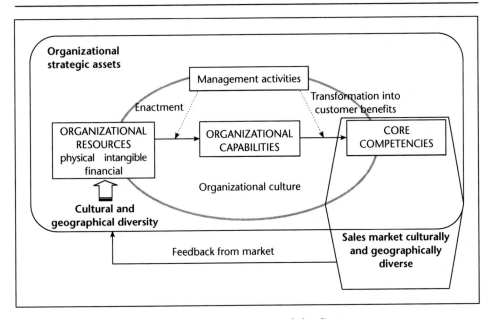

Fig. 13.1   Culture-sensitive resource-based view of the firm

Source: 'Intercultural Issues in Management and Business' by G. Fink and W. Mayrhofer in Cooper et al. (2001).

Organisational strategic assets contain all those elements that organisations can use in order to create customer value. *Organisational resources* are of potential use for the organisation and include all those factors which are available for the organisation. In a broad categorisation, one can differentiate between physical resources, e.g., location, equipment, financial resources, e.g., capital structure, credit lines, and intangible resources, e.g., human resources, organisational culture. Transforming various organisational resources into customer benefits is the core task of management. This is done through combining and aggregating various types of existing resources into *organisational capabilities*. (Fink and Mayrhofer, 2001, original emphasis)

Organizational capabilities:

have a profound effect on the processes of the organisations because they co-ordinate actions and are influencing, as well as rooted in, the basal, 'deep' layers of the organisational structure. *Core competencies* are the link, the intersection between organisation-specific strategic assets and customer benefits, in other words, between the internal sphere of the organisation and the external market. They are a result of managerial efforts to convert organisational capabilities into customer benefits in order to create a sustainable competitive advantage. Through the feedback of the sales market, the internal processes of the organisation, [by] creating customer benefits out of existing resources via organisational capabilities and core competencies, are shaped and modified. (Fink and Mayrhofer, 2001)

In this light, an organization 'must be viewed as a portfolio of competencies rather than a portfolio of businesses' (Prahalad and Hamel, 1990). However, Fink and Mayrhofer add to the complexity by stating 'a cultural perspective in at least two ways' from the point of view of an internationally operating firm.

Fink and Mayrhofer assume, with respect to the first of these perspectives, the significance of corporate culture as an organizational resource, noting that 'organisation cultures also reflect nationality, besides other given elements such as demographics of employees and managers' (Fink and Mayrhofer, 2001). In other words, an organizational culture can reflect several national cultures over and above all other elements. In this sense, all these national cultures represent a key resource. The organizational culture, which is informed by these various national cultures 'influence all internal processes of the organisation'. Furthermore, 'organisational efforts to create customer value through the transformation of resources into customer benefits are embedded into the culture of the organisation' (Fink and Mayrhofer, 2001). In other words, the quality and character of these organizational efforts is a reflection of the organization's own national and ethnic composition.

Their second cultural perspective recognizes that the organizations interact with several distinctive business cultures (such as 'markets') in their international operations. Fink and Mayrhofer (2001) note that: 'Given an increasingly, even global business environment stimulating cross-border activities, the problem of interaction between members of different national and cultural origin becomes more prominent.' However, effective planning and implementation of international strategies requires more than 'avoiding cultural shocks and mistakes in international intercultural management'. Accordingly, their culture-sensitive resource-based model of the firm acknowledges that the external cultural influences not merely interact with internal organizational culture, but make it possible for the firm to acquire 'a large array of different sources of knowledge' as inputs for policy-making and strategy formation.

Fink and Mayrhofer (2001) point out that in the international marketplace firms depend on a huge array of external experts: tax advisors, lawyers, bankers and advertising agencies. They 'have learned how costly it can become not to integrate this knowledge into their organisational capabilities'. At the same time, firms in the new global conditions require new kinds of specialist knowledge in the form of experience, good practices, valuable solutions. This knowledge needs to be evaluated, codified and diffused in the appropriate form to users who may be managers in local units through the world, agents and other market intermediaries, customers, stakeholders. So far this kind of knowledge, which is most amenable to electronic storage and distribution, is largely confined to technical knowledge. But, as global competition intensifies, cross-cultural knowledge will become more and more important, as suggested by Fink and Mayrhofer, in giving global firms the competitive edge.

In the model these is a dotted line, linking organizational resources and management activities, referring to 'enactment'. This term, which may need explanation, is associated with the social theorist, Karl Weick, who has argued that 'conditions in the environment cannot be separated from perceptions of the environment. This view places both uncertainty and the environment within the decision-maker's head' (Weick, 1969; cited in Hatch, 1997). Bird, Taylor and Beechler (1999) add this clarification:

> [Weick] noted that it is not the variation of the environmental stimuli *per se* to which organizations react, but rather organizations' peceptions of the stimuli. Stimuli pass through perceptual filters so that an organization responds not to what is but to what is perceived. In this sense organizations *enact* their environments.

Accordingly, enactment is a key filter of organizational learning. It conditions perception. Using the terminology of the model, we may regard culture as an available intangible resource. However, *culture is a dead resource until its value and utility are recognized as knowledge.* Once it is recognized as knowledge – for example, in the three forms identified – then it forms a part of organizational capabilities. In our case studies, Novo Nordisk and Sulzer Infra are the two companies that have the clearest view of culture-as-diversity as a resource. The Facilitators, on the one hand, and the Sulzer Infra Academy, on the other, are sophisticated devices for converting culture-as-diversity into organizational capabilities. The model suggests a transformation of organizational capabilities into core competencies, which are translated (to use that word deliberately) into customer benefits. But for our purposes it is necessary to reconstruct the Fink/ Mayrhofer model so that the core competencies *are* cross-cultural know-how. Before that task can be performed, it is essential to understand what is meant by the term 'core competence'.

'Core competence' is an overworked expression. It is one of the terms, like 'resources, capabilities, skills [for which] the conceptual framework is over-determined in that there are too many competing explanations for the phenomena identified' (Teece et al., 1991). The term 'core competence' is associated with intangible resources, strategic assets and various distinctive kinds of organizational capabilities. The word 'competence' overlaps semantically with 'capability' and 'skills' to the extent that the words seem synonymous. A useful characterization of core competencies is provided by Griffiths (1998):

- They are unique to the firm

- They are sustainable because they are hard to imitate or to substitute

- They confer some kind of functionality to the customer (in the case of products and some services)

- They are partly the product of learning and therefore incorporate tacit as well as explicit knowledge

- They are generic because they are incorporated into a number of products and/or processes

If we take core competencies to be a manifestation of 'the collective learning in the organisation' (Barney and Stewart 2000), then culture-as-diversity is both producer and object of collective learning. In this sense, it is a potentially rich source of new knowledge, ideas and perspectives on running especially strongly international companies, developing new products and services, implementing multicultural project teams, and interfacing with customers.[2] The cultivation of this rich source is the task of cross-cultural management in order to convert the knowledge, ideas and perspectives into cross-cultural know-how which is unique, hard to imitate, and adds value.

Core competence is, as Lessem (1998) points out, 'a bundle of skills and technologies that enables a company to provide a particular benefit to customers'. He adds that a core competence 'represents the sum of learning across individual skill sets and organizational units, that is a hierarchy of competencies', and can take years rather than months to acquire. Cross-cultural know-how is a core competence in precisely this sense: it is a store of learning for cross-cultural knowledge-sharing throughout companies' entire webs of relationships.

All this suggests that cross-cultural know-how as a core competence has got to be more than a delivery system of benefit to customers and stakeholders: in effect, it facilitates the flow of knowledge, values and experience from diverse cultural sources within and outside the organization and translates them into behaviour, concepts, products or service, which *in the way they are converted* make a critical contribution at the receiving end. The receiving end might be the gathering (actual or virtual) of Danish and US product designers working for LEGO, a Sulzer Infra seminar, a meeting of Matsushita with European Union telecommunications officials, Novo Nordisk sales representatives discussing a diabetic treatment at a hospital in Delhi.

In terms of the approach being advocated in this book, cross-cultural know-how is rather more than the best knowledge stored in an organization about how to interact with a multiplicity of receiving ends throughout its entire international business network. It also continually renews itself with knowledge from the network, which it converts into organizational capability and then into core competence. In the following section I will specify the components of this cross-cultural know-how as organizational core competence. It is a good deal more than speaking a foreign language or having an in-depth knowledge of a foreign business culture and its associated management style.

But with this short discussion on core competencies enough ground has been covered to reconstruct the Fink/Mayrhofer model so that it accommodates culture-as-diversity as a resource and posits cross-cultural know-how as a core competence (Figure 13.2). It will be noticed that 'enactment' has been modified to read 'interaction with key cultural knowledge inputs', these inputs being of the general knowledge and specific knowledge varieties, as defined in the last chapter. The word 'interaction' implies that the key knowledge inputs create change in organizational thinking and behaviour. The original model used the designation 'transformation into customer benefits'. In the modified model this is replaced by 'facilitation of interactive translation and knowledge-sharing'. These two modifications result directly from the findings in the case study.

Under the modified model cultural knowledge inputs enter the firm from domains of knowledge (e.g. a Novo Nordisk facilitation, a LEGO Millennium Meeting, a market report, etc.) and domains of business action (e.g. the customer market). Whether formally stored or retained in the heads of individuals, the inputs become an organizational resource, adding to pre-existing cultural and geographical diversity. As noted above, the cultural inputs, once recognized as having utility, are converted into capabilities relating to knowledge in three forms, the critical phase being the conversion of cross-cultural know-how into a core competence. Every single internationally operating company on this planet avails itself of general cultural knowledge, specific cultural knowledge and cross-cultural know-how. It cannot help acquiring these *to some degree*. But the critical question is: can it convert these inputs into capabilities and core competence? The answer is 'yes', but only if the organization sees the necessity, and the business logic,

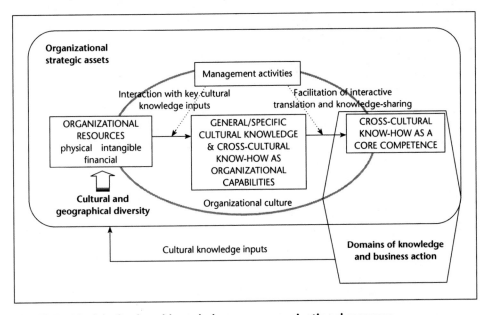

Fig. 13.2 Model of cultural knowledge as an organizational resource
Source: based on Fink and Mayrhofer, 2001.

has the managerial will, and can mobilize its entire workforce to see its international business interactions in a new light: that is, to see them as cross-cultural knowledge-sharing activities, ventures in cross-cultural collaborative learning.

This may sound pretentious, but consider things in this light. The most dramatic forms of cross-cultural encounter in today's business world are without a doubt associated with international mergers and acquisitions. The literature is pointing in one direction: there is a dismal record of failure or underachievement in the international sphere and there is a lot of post-merger panic and fire-fighting in the process (Gertsen et al., 1998; Spekman et al., 2000; Sudarsanam, 1995). To what extent 'culture' – a complex fusion of organizational culture and national culture – is a direct contributor to these disappointments is a moot point. But it seems fairly safe to say that companies poised to merge or acquire, but with a mindset fixed on strategic and cultural fit, have in fact failed to grasp that these great inter-corporate fusions *are exercises in the cross-cultural interchange of knowledge.*

The purpose of this section was to develop the notion of culture as an organizational resource, using the Fink/Mayrhofer model to support the explanation. It shows very clearly how culture changes its role in an organization from something vague – a general and diverse input – to something quite specific, namely a core competence. Novo Nordisk and Sulzer Infra, which have been investing in developing culture and cultural diversity as a knowledge resource, use this resource to support decision-making in their international business operations. LEGO, an otherwise very internationalized company, came to an equivalent realization rather late. In fact, it happened serendipitously when the company opened LEGO Media International in 1996, which probably created the biggest influx of outside business ideas into the company in its entire history.

Matsushita shows in many ways how a company dominated by thinking of one national group closes itself off from potentially valuable knowledge. The experience of the Japanese corporation is consistent with research findings which suggest that this is a serious problem for companies – not just Japanese ones – aspiring to develop a genuinely globalized mindset (Barham and Heimer, 1998; Hoecklin, 1995; Jeannet, 2000; Tayeb, 1996). Corporate managements that proclaim the virtues of diversity in the rest of the workforce might care to look at their own composition rather more closely.

With this clarification of cultural knowledge as an advantageous resource for internationally operating countries, we are in a better position to remap cross-cultural management both as an activity and a branch of the management (or organizational) sciences.

REMAPPING THE DOMAIN OF CROSS-CULTURAL MANAGEMENT

In chapter 2 it was stated that the domain of cross-cultural management was not easy to delineate. Part of the problem is that the scope of cross-cultural management is enormously broad, so broad in fact that it may not be able support new (i.e. post-Hofstedian) concepts and frameworks which have a chance of universal acceptance among proponents of the field, which is of course worldwide. Furthermore, cross-cultural management is awkwardly positioned against other more powerful disciplines, such as sociology, anthropology and organization theory, so that its voice (if there is one) is smothered. So the task of remapping cross-cultural management is a very difficult one.

With that, I advance the following propositions to stimulate new ideas about the domain of cross-cultural management. First, if cross-cultural management is to be a form of management, it must give direction and purpose to the cross-cultural activities of people and facilitate their interactions to achieve organizational goals. Second, if cross-cultural management is to perform these things, it must control financial and other resources. I emphasize these points because management is management. In too many contributions on cross-cultural management the impression is given that if you handle cultural differences in various organizational settings successfully, then that is management. It is not.

Based on the case studies, the analyses and the discussions in the previous three chapters, I am suggesting that the scope of cross-cultural management should relate to the *task* of cross-cultural management. The first task, it might be argued, is to acquire and use cross-cultural management know-how. It should not necessarily or indiscriminately relate to culture's periodic tables and lists (chapter 3) or to any prevailing notion of culture, 'an all-purpose concept which has as many meanings as the number of people who use it' (Holzmüller, 1997). The research in this book has suggested that the scope of cross-cultural management know-how relates to competencies in six tasks at interfaces of intense interaction:

- Cross-cultural transfer of knowledge, experience and values

- Collaborative cross-cultural learning

- Cross-cultural networking

- Interactive translation

- Development of participative competence

- Creation of collaborative atmosphere

The case studies revealed the sheer variegatedness of these interfaces, where knowledge, experience and values are transferred into multicultural domains of implementation. The six listed activities are not only the operational and intellectual terrain of cross-cultural management, but they also constitute its core vocabulary. All of these terms have been discussed in this book, and the case studies have supplied ample examples of each activity.

This conception of cross-cultural management, under these six tasks, introduces a number of innovations about the 'traditional' field. First, it accords the management of intra- and inter-organizational interactions a central position. Second, the management of cultural differences is subordinated to management of the cross-cultural processes of knowledge-sharing, networking and learning as collaborative activities; in other words, as part of teamwork. Third, particular significance has been attached to cross-cultural management as a form of knowledge work, whereby culture – in the shape of general cultural knowledge, specific cultural knowledge and cross-cultural know-how – is held to be an organizational resource. Underpinning this approach is a concept of culture which posits it as infinitely overlapping and perpetually redistributable habitats of common knowledge and shared meanings. Fourth, this concept of cross-cultural management is distancing itself from comparative management, a field which is a major purveyor of culture's periodic tables. This last point is important. It emphasizes that interactions are at the heart of the 'new' cross-cultural management.

The human and organizational activities which this conception of cross-cultural management makes its area of specialist interest are fusions – invariably hybrid, sometimes ephemeral – of diversities of behaviours, learning styles, mentalities, business logics, and approaches to decision-making and problem-solving in complex multicultural settings. The word 'fusion' should not necessarily be taken to mean that the process is a smooth one, but it has been chosen to suggest that these activities are *not* seen as taking place *across* cultures (see page 18 in chapter 2). Fusions entail interpersonal and cross-functional processes of compromise, adjustment, learning and *un*learning.[3] Cross-cultural management as a practice is the management of these processes; as an academic discipline it is the study of the creation, evolution, and management of such fusions of diversity in relation to organizations' policies, goals, strategies and achievements.

The six points above cannot be used as a check list without an appreciation of the 'logic' behind each one and how one competence relates to another in operational life. We may well live in an age when 'ideas travel at the speed of light-waves' (Czarniawska and Joerges, 1996), but it is a truth that the experience needed to *master* those six competencies will take an individual years. Business schools, which for the most part 'have neither the global presence nor the wealth of knowledgeable faculty' (Bradshaw, 2000), may do little to prepare future international managers, whose success *will* depend on things like their capacity to engage in interactive translation, to create a collaborative atmosphere or acquire participative competence. At this point it is timely to discuss the nature of cross-cultural management from two facets which operationally coalesce: as a communication activity and as a form of knowledge management. These topics will be discussed in the following sections.

THE CROSS-CULTURAL MANAGER

In chapter 2 it was noted that the cross-cultural manager was an idealized personage who embodies the capability to offset culture shock and so is adaptable to the circumstances of another cultural environment, this environment being frequently seen as another country, that is another national culture. The cross-cultural manager is, in effect, an international manager who knows how to cope with cultural differences (Hickson and Pugh, 1995). According to Torrington (1994), there are four distinctive types of cross-cultural manager:

- The fully international manager

- The expatriate

- The technical specialist

- The 'occasional parachutist'

But generally the cross-cultural manager must be inferred from authors' demarcation of cross-cultural management, which is seen as a branch of international management. Fatehi (1996), for example, is much concerned with cross-cultural management as an aspect of keeping multinational corporations (MNC) in operation and does not concern himself with cross-cultural managers as such. He sees MNC managers in terms of:

- 'Going native' (which is not the most felicitous choice of words) in foreign cultures

- Handling international communication and negotiation

- Cross-cultural motivation

- Exercising managerial leadership

- International human resource management

For Richard Mead (1994) culture is everywhere, so cross-cultural management is an all-pervasive aspect of international companies, and the cross-cultural manager is very much in single combat with culture. Schneider and Barsoux (1997) have a much more focused and balanced view of cross-cultural management. They see it as a practice in relation to organizational issues, strategy, and human resource management. Beyond that, cross-cultural management is concerned with the management of cultural differences by the *international* manager, who guides *multicultural teams* and helps run the *global* organization. Furthermore, they see cross-cultural management as being concerned with business ethics and social responsibility. Schneider and Barsoux (1997) also emphasize that the cross-cultural manager, because of this involvement in 'higher things', is a citizen of the world. In the current literature these authors present the clearest statement of using culture as a resource within internationally operating corporations.

Harris and Moran (1996) acknowledge that cultural awareness facilitates cross-cultural skill and knowledge, but write about cross-cultural management in terms of handling cultural diversity and difference. But they also conceive competence in cross-cultural management in terms of leadership: in globalization; in global communications; in global negotiations and strategic alliances; in cultural change; and in cultural synergy. It is, incidentally, noticeable that American writers are more prone than European authors to link cross-cultural management and global business leadership. The events of 11 September 2001 may tone that down in future.

There is nothing in my book which presents a view of cross-cultural management and the associated manager which goes against these various characterizations, but I allow myself to voice a couple of concerns. First, I certainly do not advocate 'going native'. Second, the pounding of the leadership drum may make good sense for attracting young Americans to courses on cross-cultural management, but on this side of the Atlantic this visionary view of business leadership as a facet of cross-cultural management sounds rather high-flown and pretentious (in some parts of the world it might be seen as tantamount to a declaration of American economic and technological colonialism).

As noted earlier in this book, the cross-cultural manager does not exist like a marketing manager or production manager. He or she is an idealized personage. Rather, the implication is that anyone who, regardless of his or her formal function, becomes engaged in situations involving some kind of professional cross-cultural activity, becomes a *de facto* cross-cultural manager (or communicator), exemplifying what good cross-cultural management practice is held to be. It is hard to see anyone ever holding the job title cross-cultural manager, but cross-cultural communications manager, cross-cultural knowledge manager or cross-cultural relations manager all have the whiff of plausibility, though I have personally never encountered these titles. In the case studies the closest living archetypes were surely the Novo Nordisk Facilitators, who are perfect exemplars of the kind of concept of cross-cultural management being advocated in this book. But, here, incidentally, lies a small irony. When I presented the first draft of my case study to Novo Nordisk, I was asked to change my references to the Facilitators as *managers*. They were internal consultants and change agents, I was told, but definitely not managers.

Thus we are left with a slight irony: it seems much easier to stake out the territory of cross-cultural management than to specify attributes of the cross-cultural manager which are genuinely distinct. However, as will be argued presently, the 'cross-cultural knowledge manager' – to emphasize his or her hypothetical nature with inverted commas – has the potential to become functionally distinct. Besides, the continued development of the world economy as 'knowledge capitalism' (Burton-Jones, 1999), with the concomitant drive towards localization, is going to make such people increasingly necessary.

As the competencies of the cross-cultural knowledge manager will take a long time to acquire and because business schools will have great difficulty in imparting them, the rewards for those competencies will be handsome. Under current logic, big firms regularly run the risk of losing millions of dollars in the case of a failed merger. Not only that: they are prepared for this contingency. Indeed, there is a very high statistical possibility of it coming to pass. So, one day, TNCs might discover that they need this new kind of knowledge worker and that investment is worth it. This brings us to the point where it is useful to say rather more about the cross-cultural manager – in whatever professional and organizational guise – as a global knowledge worker. But before coming to that, it is necessary to develop some points introduced in the last chapter about the cross-cultural manager as a communicator.

THE CROSS-CULTURAL MANAGER AS COMMUNICATOR

As noted in the previous chapter, the reformulated concept of cross-cultural management requires a new formulation of cross-cultural communication. Already, two weaknesses in the way in which cross-cultural communication is normally treated have been identified: first, the orientation of cross-cultural communicative competence to dyadic and not collective and multipolar communication scenarios; and, second, the failure to grasp that the key task of cross-cultural management communication is to limit noise in the system. This latter situation stems from the fact that 'experts' in 'traditional' cross-cultural management focus narrowly on acts of communication as performance in speech and linguistic capabilities. The argument here is that, whilst that is plainly important, the key communication task of the cross-cultural manager is to facilitate participative competence and that entails competence in limiting noise in the zones of cross-cultural interaction.

A further problem is that general writing about cross-cultural communication is so preoccupied with the linguistic-cultural dimensions of interactions that something very important tends to get overlooked: all the communicative interactions are ultimately connected with achieving business goals. Accordingly, cross-cultural communication should be seen as an element in the wider organizational communication environment. For convenience, I will refer to the related communication behaviour as business communication, which is:

> The totality of procedures, whereby a business enterprise seeks to initiate, influence and maintain relationships with its stakeholders and establish pathways to resources through networks. Under this concept relationships facilitate exchange processes between the business enterprise and its stakeholders, involving the transfer of money, products and services, and information and knowledge as well as values, experience and modes of behaviour. In these communication processes it is held that

the function of language is not only to serve as a carrier of information, but also (ideally) to contribute to an atmosphere of collaborative goodwill between the business enterprise and its stakeholders.

This delineation of business communication is of course consistent with the way in which cross-cultural communication has been handled in this book: less as interpersonal behaviour, more as networking behaviour for facilitating the transfer of organizational knowledge and experience. At the heart of the knowledge-based concept of cross-cultural management is the notion of enabling or facilitating rather than directing or giving instructions. The competence required is participative competence which is held to entail, in greater or lesser measure:

• An adeptness in cross-cultural communication for engaging in discussions productively in, say, a group project, even when using a second language

• An ability to contribute equitably to the common task under discussion

• An ability to share knowledge, communicate experience and stimulate group learning

To develop capability in these three areas is central to any concept of the cross-cultural manager as communicator. His or her role, if you wish, is not just to help others communicate, but to impart a set of developmental skills (i.e. participative competence), which can make cross-cultural collaborative learning, networking and knowledge-sharing more productive. Networking, it will be recalled from chapter 3, is not to be seen as 'mere' contact-making, but as activity of creating pathways to resources, competence and capability needed by an organization to sustain its viability and to manage the resulting information channels. Networking links knowledge communities throughout the TNC's webs of relationships, nurtures collections of lineages sharing the company identity, mission and strategy, and stores any knowledge elicited from networks for possible future use. A network is an investment in time and effort. In countries like Japan and China, networking requires social skills of an exceptionally high order; lose your network, lose your life.[4] People in such countries have developed those skills over centuries. In the modern-day networked business life, Western corporations have more to learn from Eastern countries than they perhaps appreciate.

The main medium for the cross-cultural manager as communicator is the mode of language which was designated as facilitating networking and mobilizing synergies (chapter 12). The kinds of skills of communication and motivation that are required to facilitate participative competence require linguistic skills of a high order, whether in English or in other common language. As participants may have unequal facility in the language in question, the cross-cultural communicator must learn the skills of modulating this language in various ways: slowing down normal speed of speech delivery, using simplified grammatical forms, avoiding obscure phrases of references, pausing between utterances, eliciting questions and opinions, and so forth. There is nothing new in these formulations, but if you are addressing a group comprising a German, a Dane, an American, a Chinese and a Japanese, then the challenges begin. Consider this hypothetical scenario.

You are moderating a discussion involving these people. The Japanese and the German may not want to be addressed by their first names. The Chinese and the Japanese may not want at all costs to be asked to give a *personal* opinion. There may be no holding back the German and the American, whose keenness to speak out may interrupt another person. The Japanese and the Chinese cannot easily understand the German's accent when he speaks English. They cannot understand the American, who refers to things in America as if everybody has been there. The Japanese, aching not to make a grammatical mistake in public, speaks very slowly and hesitantly. This annoys the Dane, who speaks in English rapidly (see also Schneider and Barsoux, 1997). This is not a propitious ambience for stimulating interactive translation, the prerequisite process for *real* cooperation. Have you, the cross-cultural manager/communicator, picked all this up and noticed how this has affected the group dynamics? If you have not, then the scene has been set for communication breakdown, and without anybody realizing exactly when and how the tensions, exasperations and misunderstandings, both cognitive and behavioural, have arisen.

What this hypothetical, but by no means implausible, situation shows is that the three forms of noise are clearly on display: ambiguity, interference and lack of equivalence. In the example these three forms of noise would have been clearly manifested within a matter of minutes. If they are not combated, they remain in the system: that is, they become embedded as counterproductive elements in the wider organizational system. Once that happens, these elements corrupt the organization's cultural resources and undermine its cross-cultural know-how as a core competence. And then, as we noted in chapter 4 on knowledge management, in cases where knowledge continually needs to be updated or it gets lost in the wider system, then the job of restoration means a reinvention of the wheel. It is in these terms that the cross-cultural manager/communicator should see his or her task. This is why 'normal' cross-cultural competence is not enough.

THE CROSS-CULTURAL MANAGER AS GLOBAL KNOWLEDGE WORKER

The reformulation of cross-cultural management presented earlier in this chapter suggests a slightly different role for the cross-cultural manager. Accordingly, he or she facilitates the six core-competence activities:

- Transfer of knowledge, experience and values

- Collaborative learning

- Networking

- Interactive translation

- Participative competence

- Creation of a collaborative atmosphere for these activities

But, if the cross-cultural manager is a genuine manager, then he or she needs a further competence: *business focus*. This is the sense of knowing where the company is going and why; and knowing how cross-cultural management activities relate to the organization, its goals and aspirations. Business focus is the ultimate guiding light of these activities, the logic of last resort, if they are to deliver value to the company and its stakeholders: to the company in terms of cross-cultural know-how as a core competence, and to the stakeholders in terms of benefits. Business focus *tempers* interactive translation. In other words, it gives this activity direction and boundaries. The relationship between business focus and the other activities is reproduced in Figure 13.3. In this model the zone of interactive translation, which is poised between the activities associated with cross-cultural management and the domain of implementation, is represented as being tempered by business focus.

These categories are fully consistent with a perspective which advocates cross-cultural management as a form of knowledge work. The question which follows from this is: how can we characterize the cross-cultural manager as a knowledge worker? There are two ways of answering this question: first, in terms of job requirements; second, in terms of educational background and competencies.

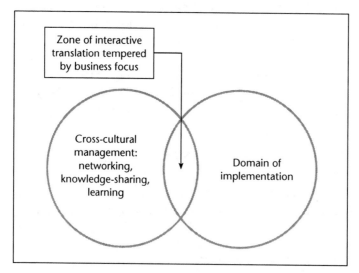

Fig. 13.3 Business focus and cross-cultural management

It has been suggested that knowledge workers need four professional attributes: problem-solving abilities, creativity, talent and intelligence (Kelley, 1990). The biggest challenge in this list is the first attribute. Representatives of the cross-cultural knowledge industry or its alternate pole, the culture shock reduction industry, can be too inclined to see cross-cultural problems in terms of their stock-in-trade: 'culture'. As has been argued in this book, this approach can decontextualize problems, focus on an isolated issue, and present, in effect, the wrong solution or a partial one. So, cultural experts, if they are to be of service to companies, need to widen and upgrade their knowledge about organizations and management. This is the *sine qua non* for such people. Knowledge of culture as delivered by its periodic tables (chapter 3) is, by itself, insufficient.

In the section above on best cross-cultural management practices, it is clear that the key task in cross-cultural management is to facilitate knowledge flows and organizational learning so that others in key functional positions can perform their jobs better not so much as individuals, but as members of compositionally diverse collaborative groups. In this sense, cross-cultural management manages cross-cultural know-how for other managers and decision-makers. Such people appear not to exist, yet there are overpowering reasons why they should. If General Motors had, for the sake of argument, a cross-cultural knowledge manager, then the transfer of production know-how from Japan might not have been so disastrous and counterproductive. Similarly, the merger between Daimler and Chrysler may have proceeded more smoothly. If the Matsushita Corporation had not lulled itself into believing that the company philosophy was universally applicable, it might have appointed a cross-cultural knowledge manager to devise systems for modifying the core beliefs without destroying their essence so that the psychological gap was closed between Japanese and non-Japanese employees *many years ago*.

The reason why cross-cultural managers have never emerged as an operational function of management is that companies had no way of systematically understanding culture. The advantage (I hope) of this book is that cross-cultural management can be explicitly linked to a major function, knowledge management, and that that, in itself, channels what it is necessary to know about culture. It might then be helpful for cross-cultural management specialists to see themselves as having expertise in the three areas indicated in the model of cross-cultural knowledge transferability (see Figure 12.3). A modified version of this model is reproduced as a map (Figure 13.4). A new shaded area has been added which represents the core domain of cross-cultural management, where high expertise is required. Thus the challenge of the cross-cultural knowledge worker is to be able to understand tacit knowledge in a given context, provide insights into the dynamics of human interactions and throw light on 'unmappable' problems.

Indeed, (paradoxically) the litmus test for a cross-cultural knowledge worker is whether he or she can map an otherwise unmappable situation! It is my

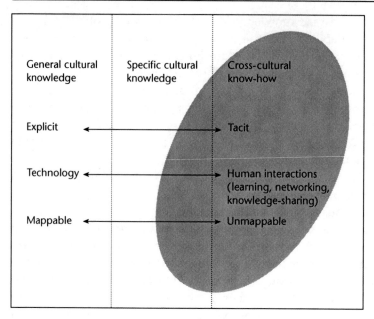

Fig. 13.4 The domain of high cross-cultural management expertise (shaded)

impression that people who present themselves as cross-cultural experts are essentially competent in the aspects of general cultural knowledge and specific cultural knowledge, but not in the third critical domain. It is one thing to be a cultural expert (they are two a penny), but quite another to be a cross-cultural expert of the kind that can map the seemingly unmappable.

The cross-cultural knowledge worker needs the following special attributes:

- A good general education, not necessarily in the business sciences, but certainly in subjects like philosophy, history, literature, mathematics and various sciences, and classical languages

- Some useful international experience which has *permanently* widened and deepened the mind, such as work, education or long-term residence in another country

- The know-how to apply intelligence and tact

- Knowledge of a modern foreign language

- Computer literacy

If cross-cultural management is a form of knowledge work, then it needs to draw on people who are well-educated in a variety disciplines. They are needed to counterbalance those who may have received an education in management or business studies, who may have permitted themselves to be uncritically imbued with Anglo-American business concepts, and whose courses did not involve the learning of foreign languages and possible study in foreign countries.

People trained in fields like philosophy, classical languages, history and literature can be intellectually more rounded than people, who often, for career reasons rather natural academic inclination, choose management or business studies. A business education tends to produce people who think in the same way. Companies whose fate is linked to their competence as international concerns in the knowledge era need people from different academic backgrounds to stimulate high-grade creativity and find new paths to knowledge (and knowledge-sharing). Students of Latin and Greek may bring an unusual sharpness of mind, a clarity of thinking which was greatly appreciated in bygone eras and which should not be dismissed today.

IMPLICATIONS FOR MANAGEMENT RESEARCHERS AND EDUCATORS, CROSS-CULTURAL TRAINERS AND PRACTITIONERS

Back to culture and other things

This book began with a critique of the way in which culture has been handled in the field of international management studies. I have proposed an alternative way of looking at culture, focusing on the interactions of TNCs in the modern global economy. This view of culture is not universalistic. It is pragmatic, studying culture in terms of cross-cultural behaviour in organizational contexts. Positing culture and cross-cultural interactions as objects of organizational knowledge has provided a direction for investigation, description and analysis. The approach, for all its imperfections, challenges some long-established views and concepts.

There was a criticism of cataloguing culture by the method I likened to the periodic tables of chemistry. I have superseded the concept of communicative competence with the notion of participative competence, which has more explanatory power than the former, constructed as it is by linguists with dialogue, not multipolar communicative situations, in mind. I have proposed the notion of interactive translation (which is, I think, very similar to how social constructionists use the word 'negotiation'). No great claims is made for any of these concepts, but if people do not like them, find them unworkable or vague, let them improve them and invent more. But my plea is that researchers in the cross-cultural field break away from culture-as-essence and culture-as-difference. I can do no better here than quote the distinguished anthropologist Clifford Geertz (1993), who spoke of the necessity of 'cutting . . . the culture concept down to size, therefore actually insuring its continued importance rather than undermining it'. Unless this happens with respect to cross-cultural management studies, the field will simply stagnate intellectually and remove itself even further from practitioner concerns.

I have suggested that one challenge must be to understand culture and, in particular cross-cultural know-how, as an organizational resource. This means more study of internationally operating organizations and less imposition of culture's periodic tables on them, the intellectual equivalent of saddling a camel. The ever-expanding – and not infrequently imploding – universe of mergers and acquisitions is ripe for much more systematic study by researchers. The idea of seeing two organizations as coupling knowledge and experimenting with cross-cultural learning seems a particularly worthwhile field of study. The fact that 'the integration of an international merger is a process of many years rather than months' (Olie, 1995) presents an enormous challenge in terms not only of research design, but also of deployment of competent and committed researchers.

I concede that many things traditionally in books on cross-cultural management have received little or no treatment. Language in the sense of foreign language competence I have hardly touched upon; likewise negotiation in the conventional sense; likewise ethics, which is becoming fashionable in cross-cultural studies (see Carroll and Ganon, 1997; Deresky, 2000; Jackson, 2000). But I have not been governed by what a book on cross-cultural management should cover; I have been concerned to unearth what the study of four large corporations reveals when they are investigated from a cross-cultural perspective allied to knowledge management. For those who feel that I have made light of negotiation, then I refer them to Figure 12.6, which represents, as I noted, a translation process. Some will say that I have paid scant attention to the management of diversity. And yet, to a very large extent, the management of diversity is exactly what this book is about. It will been noticed too that I have hardly mentioned anything to do with cross-cultural management comparisons for reasons stated above: comparative management, which is descriptive in character, is co-terminous with, but not constitutive of, cross-cultural management, which is an interactive function.

As may have been evident to some readers, this book has evolved rather like a journey. It looks nothing like the concept offered to the publisher more than two years ago. When the journey started, I had no idea that I would be drawn into knowledge management. Nor did I expect to make such prominent use of Peters and Waterman's *In search of excellence* (1982). It was the re-examination of those authors' propositions about language (or 'language') that led me to an unexpected contribution to management studies: that the appeals for 'a new language' of business and management are a manifestation of the centuries-long quest for an unambiguous code of universal communication. It was satisfying to make this 'discovery', as management studies and management thinking are becoming severely disconnected from human history. Despite the refreshing contributions of Hampden-Turner and Trompenaars (1993) Lessem (1998) and Moore and Lewis (1999), it is a trend seemingly impossible to slow down, let alone reverse.

With the end of this book finally in sight, I conclude with comments for three classes of readers: management researchers, educators and students. The Epilogue that follows is, appropriately, one of history's footnotes on an innocuous, yet telling case of cross-cultural communication.

Management researchers, educators and students

I recall reading many years ago a book on lightning calculators, people with a formidable gift for mental arithmetic. One such genius was a French peasant boy who was very adept at the four basic arithmetical operations (addition, sub-traction multiplication and division). One day somebody introduced this boy, who was about four years old at the time, to the concept of square roots and powers. This opened up a completely new world of numbers to the youngster, who later became a professor of mathematics. It seems to me that the anthro-pologically derived concept of culture is rather like the four basic arithmetical operations in the field of management studies. So an aim of this book is to introduce, as it were, ideas about square roots and powers: in other words, a new way of handling the same fundamental material and identifying 'new' relation-ships within it. The analogy can of course not be pushed too far. Culture is, after all, not 'logical' like mathematics.

Thus, to management researchers and educators in the field of cross-cultural management (and intercultural management for those who wish to maintain a distinction), this book presents new challenges, not the least of which is the opportunity to break away from the essentialist grip of culture as well as the Hofstedian dominance. However, the intention of the book is not to supplant these influences, but to present culture and cross-cultural interactions more vigorously in organizational contexts of the modern business world. My treat-ment of culture as a knowledge resource, on the one hand, and the attempt to present cross-cultural management as a facilitator of participative competence and interactive translation, on the other, are embryonic ideas, but out of them may come new explanatory frameworks and improved methodological and conceptual tools.

It needs to be stressed that all these ideas about looking at cross-cultural management from new and rewarding perspectives have derived from empir-ical research. In this respect I can perhaps claim to have done three useful things, which have been singled out by Henry Mintzberg (1993) as urgently needed in international management research generally. First, I have been 'driven . . . by questions to be answered, not by hypotheses to be tested' (ibid.). Second, my research approach has not been influenced by 'half-baked ideas about the programming of human cognition' (ibid.). Third, I wanted to find out 'something about organizations themselves' without relying on 'concepts, at worst concepts rooted in the base disciplines of mathematics, economics, or psychology' (ibid.).

Generally, researchers in the field of cross-cultural management tend to avoid the treatment of the topic in organizational contexts. I hope that researchers may develop concepts that are organizationally oriented. In this respect, the Fink/ Mayrhofer model, which I modified, may also be found useful by others. Many hang on to Hofstede or stick to the safe and traditional concepts of culture. It is all in all not surprising that cross-cultural research has never lived up to its importance in the modern business world and why, as has already been noted, more and more management scholars are becoming frustrated with the dominant view of culture.

The case studies of Novo Nordisk and Sulzer Infra clearly demonstrate that companies are way ahead of 'the professors' in their pragmatic approach to culture, that is to say cultural diversity, as popularly received. It is corporations like these that provide new insights into the nature of cross-cultural interactions. Cross-cultural management can simply not be delineated by what are frankly outmoded and intellectually restrictive concepts of culture; its scope – for management is management – is ultimately as defined by corporations.

It is sometimes customary in books of this nature to indicate pointers for new research, often prioritizing areas for reasons of intellectual desirability or public policy. But I think that it is for people in the field of cross-cultural management research to do that for themselves, both individually and collectively. Of course, the six processes I referred to above – that is cross-cultural transfer of knowledge, experience and values, collaborative cross-cultural learning, cross-cultural networking, social translation, interactive negotiation and participative competence – throw open new fields of social scientific enquiry. Otherwise a desirable outcome would be if researchers would begin to apply the knowledge-based concept of cross-cultural management to investigations involving transitional economies, major regions like the Middle East or third world countries, which this book has all too consciously neglected.

As a subject area of management teaching, cross-cultural management has been based on a small number of textbooks such as Mead (1994), Schneider and Barsoux (1997) and Harris and Moran (1996), possibly supplemented by Adler (1991), Hoecklin (1995) and Tayeb (1996). Hofstede (1980) and Trompenaars (1993) of course feature to a greater or lesser extent in all these offerings. The knowledge management perspective presented in this book is a new departure and time will tell whether it will prove influential enough to inspire writers on cross-cultural management to focus on new topics which this book suggests. But it will be some years before there is a core of texts that can underpin the shift in cross-cultural management studies which Bartholomew and Adler (1996) advocated, namely 'a conceptual shift: from a hierarchical perspective of cultural influence, compromise and adaptation, to one of collaborative cross-cultural learning'. In these comments lies an implicit challenge to teachers of cross-cultural management: that they redesign these courses of instruction.

To conclude this section, I turn to researchers in the field of knowledge management. Like other management disciplines – HRM readily comes to mind – knowledge management is based, as it were, on 'domestic' theories for an activity which is becoming increasingly internationalized. Propounders of knowledge work have already been criticized for developing 'a form of analysis, and a platform for management action, which remains unconvincing' (Collins, 2000). This criticism, if justified, is a harsh one. The investigations into knowledge management in this book have exclusively concerned multicultural and international contexts. The notion of transfer of knowledge as a form of translation, even in 'narrow' domestic contexts, may give rise to alternate and better forms of analysis and platforms of management action.

Cross-cultural trainers

This profession, which embraces various kinds of consultant, cross-cultural educators, and teachers of languages for business purposes has been unkindly called 'the culture shock prevention industry' by the Swedish anthropologist Hannerz. My constant impression is that as a professional community it is somewhat out of touch with the operations of the very corporations it wishes to save from plunging into some kind of cross-cultural abyss. As the case studies show, and this is, incidentally, borne out by firms which are making massive investments in corporate universities (*Financial Times*, 2001; Meister, 1998), the 'mere' management of cultural differences is less and less important than creating environments, structures and procedures for facilitating cross-cultural learning and knowledge-sharing. And, as I have argued before, cross-cultural negotiation is taking on a new dimension for the TNC: it is no longer an adversarial head-butt involving at least one side as cross-culturally unwitting.

Negotiation can no longer be restrictively seen in terms of sales and contract negotiations, on the one hand, and a form of cross-cultural conflict resolution, on the other. Cross-cultural trainers (and writers) plainly *enjoy* approaching negotiation from these perspectives, where interactions can, as it were, be guaranteed to be snared on cultural clashes.[5] Thus negotiation has become a kind of special province of cross-cultural trainers, where all the wisdom from the periodic tables can be delivered to a benighted business world. But, as organizations become flatter, that is less hierarchically arranged, and in a world dominated more and more by business alliances, a new form of negotiating is emerging.

In shorthand, it can also be called 'interactive translation', which emphasizes 'dialogue, not deal making' (Spekman et al., 2000). In this scenario people create 'space' for people to negotiate their surroundings, whereby they gain, and *experiment* with, participative competence. The 'new' negotiators are members of multicultural project teams, who learn negotiation skills among themselves and then apply them competitively in the marketplace. In other words, the *company itself is the testing-ground for negotiations with stakeholders outside the company.*

Both Novo Nordisk and Sulzer Infra create this kind of space, but by using completely contrasting approaches. It is probably true to say that, as such forms of negotiation become an aspect of organizational life more clearly recognized for what it is, then firms will be interested in how to make this social negotiation productive. Since social negotiation is a demonstrably cross-cultural activity for TNCs, then they will be keen to know how to guide social negotiation to improve knowledge-sharing, learning and networking. This suggests to me a major market for trainers who can analyze such cross-cultural interactions within the context of specific organizations. Trainers who steadfastly cleave to Hofstede need to rethink what they are offering. Firms these days need what Moeran (1996) calls 'dialogue excellence': shared, crystal-clear, supportive mutual understanding for sustaining and animating inter-organizational exchanges on a worldwide basis. In order to meet this need, trainers must do the unthinkable: significantly unlearn what they cherish as sacred knowledge about culture in cross-cultural interactions. They must, in effect, create new maps, new models, new meanings.

Practitioners and knowledge officers

This book has not been explicitly written for practitioners, nor for one specialist community of those practitioners whom I will call knowledge officers. I have to concede that this text is not always an easy read and may not be replete enough with models and figures to attract this readership. Nevertheless it is possible that the book – especially the case studies – may contain insights that will be beneficial to practitioners, especially those in TNCs responsible for organizational development and the upgrading of a wide range of competencies for the new economy.

Knowledge officers have may the most to gain from this book. It is, as far as I know, the first book on the market which sees the international transfer of knowledge as a form of cross-cultural management *and* an activity which is analogous to translation. This and the treatment of the four informant companies from a knowledge management perspective may break a certain amount of new ground. On the other hand, the material considered merely reinforces the already obvious truth: that cultural facets are hard to capture and assimilate as useful knowledge. They are also hard to accommodate in the conventional schemes of knowledge transfer, such as those of Dixon (2000) and Davenport and Prusak (1998), which were featured in chapter 4.

Against that, it might be helpful for knowledge managers to see their organizations as composed of habitats of common knowledge, which e-mail, video-conferencing and other forms of virtual encounters can link people together provided that the all-important common language is in place or can be created. The distinctions between general common knowledge, specific common knowledge and cross-cultural know-how may prove more beneficial than using the 'dangerous' distinction between tacit and explicit knowledge. Problematical too, in the field of cross-cultural knowledge diffusion, is the distinction between physical space and virtual space. I suggested that Nonaka's (1991) notion of cognitive common ground may be more valuable, but mapping this territory against factors such as those that influence stickiness or absorptive capacity and forms of psychological, cultural and technological distance presents major challenges to knowledge officers. The challenges are even greater if those knowledge officers have very limited international experience. Global nerdism is not only no substitute; it represents a mindset that is unlikely to feel at ease with human quirkiness in myriad cross-cultural settings. Companies will have to rethink job profiles.

I also made the distinction between thin and thick knowledge, describing the former as the minimum amount of knowledge assumed by a knowledge user to be necessary for a specific objective, that is to support a decision. Knowledge, as it becomes thicker, needs more and more of the expertise of a domain specialist, whose real worth lies not just in interpreting it, but in making it convertible: that means appreciating its utility and relevance to users' existing knowledge domains. It seems logical that, as companies become more knowledge-based, they will increasingly need domain specialists. There is little doubt that when it comes to the cross-cultural transfer of knowledge the issue of convertibility is paramount. This is where real value gets added to knowledge, where knowledge gets its competitive edge, where cross-cultural management can come into its own.

NOTES

1. 'An alternative vocabulary' for management is urged by Collins (2000) on the grounds that 'the lexicon of management is . . . based upon a collection of terms which have been labelled as fads and buzzwords'.

2. For more than 20 years major Japanese corporations have understood the value of cross-cultural know-how as a core competence, but the significance of what the Japanese were, and are, doing has tended to be undervalued in the West. Western corporate management has never had to deal with a language barrier as intractable and complex as the one that separates Japan from the rest of the world (Miller, 1982; Neustupný, 1987; Wilkinson, 1991). Coping with foreign culture was, and is, a huge challenge and huge anxiety for many Japanese companies, as the Matsushita case suggests.

3. There already exists a framework, associated with Berry (1980), for examining these processes, which has been used to study the cultural dimensions of mergers and acquisitions (Gertsen et al., 1998):
- Acculturation: the transfer of cultural values and behaviour from one group to another
- Assimilation: the non-dominant group relinquishes its identity
- Integration: the non-dominant group maintains its cultural identity, but becomes at the same time an integral part of the same culture
- Rejection: the non-dominant group withdraws from the dominant culture
- Deculturation: the non-dominant group loses cultural and psychological contact with both its own original culture and the dominant culture

Based on: Deresky (2000) and Gertsen et al. (1998).

4. I have been influenced by Redding's (1993) perceptive writing on Chinese networks. I am indebted to him for the phrase 'collection of lineages'.

5. For a refreshing, pragmatic alternative approach, see Gesteland (1998).

REFERENCES

Adler, N. (1991). *International dimensions of organizational behavior.* Boston, MA: PWS-Kent Publishing Company.

Barham, K. and Heimer, C. (1998). *ABB: The dancing giant – Creating the globally connected corporation.* London: Financial Times Prentice Hall.

Barney, J. and Stewart, A. (2000). Organizational philosophy as moral philosophy: Competitive implications for diversified corporations. In Schultz, M., Hatch, M.-J. and Holten-Larsen. *The expressive organization.* Oxford: Oxford University Press.

Bartholomew, S. and Adler, N. (1996). Building networks and crossing borders: The dynamics of knowledge generation in a transnational world. In: Joynt, P. and Warner, M. *Managing across cultures: Issues and perspectives.* London: International Thompson, pp. 7–32.

Beer, S. (1966). *Decision and control: The meaning of operational research and management cybernetics.* Chichester: John Wiley & Sons.

Berry, J. W. (1980). Acculturation as vareties of adaptation. In: Padilla, A. M. (ed.). *Acculturation: Theory, models and some new findings.* Boulder, CO: Westview Press.

Bird, A., Taylor, S. and Beechler, S. (1999). Organizational learning in Japanese overseas affiliates. In: Beechler, S. and Bird, A. (eds). *Japanese multinationals abroad: Individual and organizational learning.* New York: Oxford University Press, pp. 235–59.

Bradshaw, D. (2000). Sea change in the market is gathering pace. *Financial Times.* Survey of business education.

Burton-Jones, A. (1999). *Knowledge capitalism: Business, work, and learning in the new economy.* Oxford: Oxford University Press.

Carroll, S. J. and Gannon, M. J. (1997). *Ethical dimensions of international management.* Thousand Oaks, CA: Sage Publications.

Collins, D. (2000). *Management fads and buzzwords.* London: Routledge.

Czarniawska, B. and Joerges, B. (1996). Travels of ideas. In: Czarniawska, B. and Sevón, G. (eds). *Translating organisational change.* Berlin: de Gruyter, pp. 13–48.

Davenport, T. H. and Prusak, L. (1998). *Working knowledge: How organizations manage what they know.* Boston, MA: Harvard Business School Press.

Deresky, H. (2000). *International management: Management across borders and cultures.* Upper Saddle River, NJ: Prentice Hall.

Dixon, N. M. (2000). *Common knowledge: How companies thrive by sharing what they know.* Boston, MA: Harvard Business School Press.

Fatehi, K. (1996). *International management: A cross-cultural and functional perspective.* Upper Saddle River, NJ: Prentice Hall.

Financial Times (2001). Survey on business education 26 March.

Fink, G. and Mayrhofer, W. (2001). Intercultural issues in management and business: The interdisciplinary challenge. In: Cooper, C. and Cartwright, S. (eds). *The international handbook of organisational culture and climate.* Chichester, UK: John Wiley & Sons, pp. 471–86.

Geertz, C. (1993). *The interpretation of cultures.* London: Fontana Press.

Gertsen, M. G., Søderberg, A.-M. and Torp, J. E. (1998). *Cultural dimensions of international mergers and acquisitions.* Berlin: de Gruyter.

Gesteland, R. (1998). *Cross-cultural business behaviour.* Copenhagen: Copenhagen Business School Press.

Griffiths, D. (1998). Core competences. In: Cooper, C. L. and Argyris, C. (eds). *The concise Blackwell encyclopedia of management.* Oxford: Blackwell.

Hampden-Turner, C. (1991). The boundaries of business: the cross-cultural quagmire. *Harvard Business Review* September–October: 94–6.

Hampden-Turner, C. and Trompenaars, F. (1993). *The seven cultures of capitalism: Value systems for creating wealth in the United States, Britain, Japan, Germany, France, Sweden and the Netherlands.* London: Judy Piatkus.

Harris, P. and Moran, R. (1996). *Managing cultural differences: Leadership strategies for a new world of business.* Houston, TX: Gulf Publishing.

Hatch, M. J. (1997). *Organization theory.* Oxford: Oxford University Press.

Hickson, D. and Pugh, D. (1995). *Management worldwide: The impact of societal culture on organizations across the globe.* London: Penguin Books.

Hoecklin, L. (1995). *Managing cultural differences: Strategies for competitive advantage.* London: Economist Intelligence Unit/Addison Wesley.

Hofstede, G. (1980). *Culture's consequences: International differences in work-related values.* Beverly Hills, CA: Sage Publications.

Holzmüller, H. (1997). Kulturstandards – ein operatives Konzept zur Entwicklung kultursensitiven Managemements. In: Engelhard, J. (ed.). *Interkulturelles Management: Theoretische Fundierung und funktionsbereichsspezifische Konzepte.* Wiesbaden: Verlag Dr Th. Gabler.

Jackson, T. (2000). Management ethics and corporate policy: A cross-cultural comparison. *Journal of Management Studies* 37(3): 349–69.

Jeannet, J.-P. (2000). *Managing with a global mindset.* London: Financial Times/Prentice Hall.

Kelley, J. (1990). Managing the new work force. *Machine design* 10 May. Cited in: Collins (2000), pp. 109–13.

Lessem, R. (1998). *Management development through cultural diversity.* London: Routledge.

Mead, R. (1994). *International management: Cross-cultural dimensions.* Oxford: Blackwell.

Meister, J. C. (1998). *Corporate universities: Lessons in building a world-class workforce.* New York: McGraw-Hill.

Miller, R. A. (1982). *Japan's modern myth: The language and beyond.* Tokyo: John Weatherhill.

Mintzberg, H. (1993). Globalization: Separating the fad from the fact. In: Wong-Rieger, D. and Rieger, F. (eds). *International management research: Looking to the future.* Berlin: de Gruyter, pp. 99–103.

Moeran, B. D. (1996). *A Japanese advertising agency: An anthropology of media and markets.* London: Curzon Press.

Moore, K. and Lewis, D. (1999): *Birth of the multinational: 2000 years of ancient business history – from Ashur to Augustus.* Copenhagen: Copenhagen Business School Press.

Neustupný, J. (1987). *Communicating with the Japanese.* Tokyo: Japan Times.

Nonaka, I. (1991). The knowledge-creating company. *Harvard Business Review.* November–December: 96–104.

Olie, R. (1995). Cultural exchange in mergers and acquisitions. In: Jackson, T. (ed.). *Cross-cultural management.* Oxford: Butterworth-Heinemann, pp. 308–25.

Peters, T. J. and Waterman, R. H. (1982). *In search of excellence: Lessons from America's best-run companies.* New York: Harper & Row.

Prahalad, C. K. and Hamel, G. (1990). The core competence of the corporation. *Harvard Business Review.* May–June: 79–91.

Redding, G. (1993). *The spirit of Chinese capitalism.* Berlin: de Gruyter.

Schneider, S. and Barsoux, J.-L. (1997). *Managing across cultures.* London: Prentice Hall.

Spekman, R., Isabella, L. A. and MacAvoy, T. C. (2000). *Alliance competence: Maximizing the value of your partnerships.* New York: John Wiley & Sons.

Sudarsanam, P. S. (1995). *The essence of mergers and acquisitions.* London: Financial Times Prentice Hall.

Tayeb, M. (1996). *The management of a multicultural workforce.* Chichester, UK: John Wiley.

Teece, D. J., Pisano, G. and Shuen, A. (1991). Dynamic capabilities and strategic management. Working paper. Center for Research in Management, University of California, Berkeley. Quoted in: Nonaka, I. and Takeuchi, H. (1995). *The knowledge-creating company.* New York: Oxford University Press.

Torrington, D. (1994). *International human resource management.* London: Prentice Hall. Cited in: Hickson and Pugh (1995).

Trompenaars, F. (1993). *Riding the waves of culture: Understanding cultural diversity in business.* London: Economist Books.

Weick, K. (1969). *The social psychology of organizing.* Reading, MA: Addison Wesley.

Wilkinson, E. (1991). *Japan versus the West: Image and reality.* London: Penguin Books.

Epilogue: a cautionary tale

This book has been a journey, an initial attempt to chart an area of management study and activity that is in urgent need of reformulation. It seems appropriate to conclude this book with an apocryphal story which reveals how deceptively easy it is to mistakenly encode knowledge from an unknown cultural environment and disseminate the error without anyone being the wiser.

The story concerns English navigator, Captain James Cook, who is most celebrated for his mapping of the Pacific and Southern Ocean. On one of his voyages he alighted with a small party of his men on the shores of Australia. Soon Captain Cook and his party encountered a group of aboriginal tribesmen. As the two sides attempted to parley, Captain Cook espied a breathtaking sight: a strange, bounding, furry animal propelling itself on its powerful back legs. 'What's that?', a startled Captain Cook asked the headman of the natives. 'Kanguru', replied the headman. Thus came the aboriginal word 'kanguru' into the English language, and countless other languages, to designate that remarkable creature. That, however, is not the point of the story. It turns out that in the tongue of the headman the word 'kanguru' means 'I do not understand you.' True or not, it is a nice story about wresting the 'wrong' knowledge from its cultural environment. Fortunately, as far as we know, in this case no serious damage was done.

Glossary

This glossary contains definitions of some of the key words and expressions for developing the 'new' cross-cultural management.

Atmosphere: A pervasive feeling, which is derived from experience and serves as a determinant of expectations concerning future cooperation in a business relationship or group activity such as collaborative learning or knowledge-sharing.

Business communication: The totality of procedures whereby a business enterprise seeks to initiate, influence and maintain relationships with its stakeholders and establish pathways to resources through networks. Under this concept relationships facilitate exchange processes between the business enterprise and its stakeholders, involving the transfer of money, products and services, and information, as well as values, experience and modes of behaviour. In these communication processes it is held that the function of language is not only to serve as a carrier of information, but also (ideally) to contribute to an atmosphere of collaborative goodwill between the business enterprise and its stakeholders.

Common knowledge: Knowledge which is available in one location in an internationally distributed organization and which through interactive translation can be diffused to other locations within the organizations in an appropriately intelligible form. Common knowledge is useful because there are different kinds of it, but it is dispersed messily both throughout organizations and the wider networks which encompass their stakeholders.

Common language: The language or code facilitating the transfer of knowledge, values and experience from one source of common knowledge to others; a source of symbols, with which it clothes company values and encodes attitudes and behaviour that the company wishes its employees to share; the language which supplies the content and context for interactive translation.

Convertibility of knowledge: This refers not only to the translatability of knowledge, but also its perceived utility and relevance to users' existing knowledge domains. It may also refer to the availability of domain experts (of whom one would be a translator) to reveal its import to the users.

Corporate knowledge history: A recorded version of events, experienced directly, indirectly or vicariously, by company actors ('narrators'), this version being an interpretation or elaboration of those events from a knowledge management perspective. Its purpose is not to provide *ex post facto* management wisdom, but to create a specific source of knowledge which, if judiciously analyzed, can provide insights into the tacit aspects of a corporation's behaviour. It is, above all else, a sense-making document.

Cross-cultural communication: Not to be seen in the naive way of 'effective communication' with people from different cultural, linguistic or ethnic background, but rather the key task of identifying and restricting the pernicious effects of noise, 'the ultimate limiter of communication', in a system composed of multiple cultures; networking behaviour for facilitating the cross-cultural transfer of organizational knowledge and experience.

Cross-cultural know-how: A facet of a firm's core competence, whereby its knowledge-sharing and organizational learning contribute to international competitive advantage. Cross-cultural know-how is a store of learning for cross-cultural knowledge-sharing throughout companies' entire webs of relationships, and is primarily internally created knowledge applied in cross-cultural interactions. It may be derived from two other kinds of cultural knowledge, but this kind of know-how is often subjective and experiential. This kind of know-how may also have a very high tacit content. It is knowledge that is passed from head to head. It facilitates interaction, informs participative competence and stimulates cross-cultural collaborative learning.

Cross-cultural management: A branch of international management whose task is to facilitate and direct synergistic interaction and learning at interfaces where knowledge, values and experience are transferred into multicultural domains of implementation. Cross-cultural management is also the study of the creation, evolution, and management of fusions of diversity in relation to organizations' policies, goals, strategies and achievements.

Cultural knowledge: This form of knowledge is considered to be composed of general cultural knowledge, specific cultural knowledge and cross-cultural know-how.

Culture: Varieties of common knowledge; infinitely overlapping and perpetually redistributable habitats of common knowledge and shared meanings.

Diversity management: Managing diversity is the art not just of harnessing the human potential specific to each form of diversity, but also of fusing the potential across internal organizational boundaries for the benefit of individuals and for the organization.

General cultural knowledge: General cultural knowledge refers to freely available knowledge about cultures. This kind of knowledge is explicit and is already available in online or printed reference sources such the world wide web, encyclopædias, country surveys in newspapers, and so forth. It can be formally classified.

Interactive translation: A form of cross-cultural work in which participants engage in (multicultural) groups in order to negotiate common meanings and common understandings in an international company whereby the participants also learn how to be able to work in those teams. Interactive translation calls for participative competence for facilitating and modulating the intra- and inter-organizational transfer of knowledge, values and experience.

Language of management: A set of linguistic symbols, manipulable in a given language (such as English, German, Japanese, Russian, etc.), and incorporating standardized terms and informal elements (such as oblique reference, humour, pretence, etc.) necessary for the conceptualization, description and execution of management tasks and sharing of management information; considered as comprising three modes in pragmatic space: as a descriptor of management tasks, as a network facilitator and as the repository of company wisdom, lore and vision.

Networking: The activity of creating pathways to resources, competences and capabilities needed by an organization to sustain its viability and to manage the resulting information channels. Effective networking requires business focus and is a significant cross-cultural learning experience.

Noise: Anything that distorts the intra- and inter-organizational transfer of knowledge and constrains the convertibility of knowledge.

Participative competence: An adeptness in cross-cultural communication for engaging in discussions productively in, say, a group project, even when using a second language; to contribute equitably to the common task under discussion and to be able to share knowledge, communicate experience, and stimulate group learning.

Specific cultural knowledge: That knowledge which is specific to a given source of common knowledge. It is subjective in the sense that it is selected for relevance to the firms' operations. Such knowledge can be tacit and explicit, according to the convention, but perhaps more crucial is the degree of relevant pre-existing knowledge on the part of those who gather it and interpret it.

Thick knowledge: Knowledge which is very rich, very wide-ranging and arcane, that is it requires specialist knowledge to be understood.

Thin knowledge: The minimum amount of knowledge assumed by a knowledge user to be necessary for a specific objective, that is to support a decision.

Index

ABB 5, 69
  global connectivity 44
  merger 6–7
  mini case 10–11
absorptive capacity 69–70, 246, 250–4
  definition 250
  language 252
  Matsushita 253
  Novo Nordisk 252–3
  Sulzer Infra 252
Alexander the Great 85
alternative methodology 14–15
  zebra analogy 14
ambiguity 265–6
  see also noise
Andersen, Hans Christian 181
anthropology 99, 293
  see also culture and anthropology
Aristotle 66
Association of British Retailers 159
atmosphere 175–7, 275–7, 285
  cross-cultural manager 300
  definition 315
  Japan 275
  Russia 275

Barnevik, Percy 7
  globalization 69
Beer, Stafford 232, 239
Billund 160, 162–3
Bloomfield, Leonard 236
Bochsler, Karl 195, 199, 202
Bonington, Chris 191
Bowen, Howard 156
British Institute of Management 80

British Petroleum (BP) 70
  Common Operating Environment 79–80
  Virtual Teamwork Business Networking
    Centres 80
Buddhism 66
bunka 23
business communication, definition 315
business focus 300

Canon 215
Cartesian Split 66
case studies 89
  characteristics 210–12
  cross-cultural management: interfaces/
    networks 208–9
  LEGO: transferring identity knowledge
    159–82
  Matsushita Electric: a learning history
    133–58
  Novo Nordisk: cross-cultural management
    as facilitation 103–32
  Sulzer Infra: creating *One Winning Team*
    183–203
  see also mini cases
Casson, Lionel 85
Catherine the Great 85
Cherry, Colin 230, 238, 265
Chevron 70
China 5, 11–14, 74–5
  participative competence 274
chishiki keiei 231
Christiansen, Godtfred Kirk 161, 165
Christiansen, Kjeld Kirk *see* Kristiansen
Christiansen, Ole Kirk 160–2, 164–6, 179–80
Churchill, Winston 98